PRAISE for B. K.

DAMAGES (nonfiction)

"Bazhe explores the full spectrum of his emotions. A revelatory, pained, unyielding ride. Hold on tight."　　　　　　　　*—Kirkus, NY*

"I enjoyed this story. The pain and longing of belonging, the joys and triumphs of love, the strength of family bonds, the agony of loss, the force of political events, and the power of letting go are woven together in this story that left me with a sense that something profound had been accomplished."　　*—The Family Journal, IL*

"Bazhe has led what Leo Tolstoy or George Eliot might have called an epic life."　　　　　　　　*—Lavender Magazine, MN*

"The author of Damages is an interesting writer. It held my interest until the last quarter. Bazhe is obviously very talented. Damages is enlightening as a history of the troubled Balkans and the dismemberment of Yugoslavia. It is an interesting book written by a bright young author with a gift for story telling."　　　　　　　　*—Rebecca's Reads, FL*

"Bazhe is a skilled narrator, and Damages never dips into being a dull read."　　　　　　　　*—Instinct Magazine, CA*

"Damages is much more than a mere memoir. In it's portrayal of one man's experiences with all its complexities … It is contrast in all its forms, it is a portrait with many perspectives, it is art, in a way, and it is life."　　*—Out in America, OH*

"Bazhe knew a world that turned to violent ethnic strife after years of civil unrest, echoed by his own inner turmoil. Damages is the story of his inner and outer wars."　　　　　　　　*—Recorder Newspapers, NJ*

"Vivid talent for powerhouse story telling. A remarkable, compelling read."　　　　　　　　*—White Crane Journal, NYC*

"Damages is Bazhe's memorial to the woman who raised him and loved him and who, in spite of it all, will always remain his one true mother. Though the author's stop-and-go use of flashbacks slows down the narrative somewhat, he never loses his focus, or the reader's interest. Bazhé's life story is uniquely his own, but at the same time it is a story that we can all relate to. That alone makes "Damages" a good book worth reading."
　　　　　　　　—The Weekly News, FL

"Very well written, fast-paced, occasionally shocking. *Damages* is one of the worthier novels I've read recently."　　　　　*—The Star Democrat, MD*

DAMAGES (nonfiction)

"It's a story you won't want to miss. With emeralds and lavish nightclubs to showcase his new persona, he finds some happiness and acceptance, and enjoys the theatrics of this life and the resulting love. But then, he is asked something unthinkable by his partner, and while he thinks about this unthinkable request, he finds out more. This is when he runs away, realizing that every happiness is a mirage. We can mirror traces of our life in Bazhe's search for meaning, and be supported by his strength and creativity, which get him through these incidents and a multitude more that you won't believe could happen to one person." **—*Idea Museum, Canada***

"If you're ready for a real-life story of a very difficult time in world history, as well as looking into some very happy and very sad windows into a rebel's life, by all means, this is an excellent book for you. You'll find it a tremendous surprise—A tremendously good surprise." **—*RLD Books, NM***

"This autobiography covers quite a bit of Balkans history. Damages gives an excellent look into the horrific world of the Balkans, and at the end readers are more than happy to escape with Bazhe to America." **—*The Raw Story, GA***

"Bazhe has a way of communicating with the reader that makes you feel like you are there talking face to face with him. It's a compelling read, and would make an excellent movie." **—*NZ Writers, New Zealand***

"Bazhe reveals horribly realistic experiences that had to be lived. No one could've made this up. A remarkable read." **—*Radical Faerie Digest, TN***

"Reminds me of Michael Ondaatje's The English Patient—love and history and tragedy that became a powerful Miramax film." **—*HPPUB Book Review, MN***

"Powerful read and certainly not one that one will forget in a hurry." **—*The Independent, FL***

"A book of amazing depth, emotion, and discovery. *Damages* is compelling, well written, and a book with which many will be able to relate." **—*Stone Wall Society, FL***

"Damages was a very difficult book...I have to challenge my denials and truths as accurately as possible." **—*Notes From Hollywood.com, CA***

"The values of this book are many. His memoir is not an easy read, but it is worthwhile and should be recommended for many who will identify with parts of his experience while varying with other parts." **—*Prairie Flame, IL***

"Bazhe has led fascinating life. The disintegration of Yugoslavia, with the rise of racial and religious strife, creates a fascinating backdrop for Bazhe's chronicle."
—Quatrefolio Library, MN

"The concept is delivered clearly and effectively. Damages is a personal exploration through life's trials and eventual tribulation—our soul purpose for survival. From an abusive upbringing, separation from his biological mother and death, the author struggles for identity and purpose to find the true meaning for carrying on. The author's tone and writing style is clear and direct. The author offers us an uncensored look into his personal life without holding anything back. I applaud the author for writing about things so close to heart. Most often these can be the hardest things to put down on paper."
—Editorial Review, NE

"Yugoslavia's disintegration creates a fascinating backdrop for Bazhe's narrative. The years of civil unrest, reverberates his own inner turmoil. The story is both erotic and historical, underlining love and tragedy in a young man's life."
—Art Circle, OH

"Such multifaceted talent ought to be applauded." **—Lambda Book Report, WDC**

"The story is told skillfully via a number of flashbacks, which constitute a retelling of his life story to his birth mother, once he successfully tracks her down with the aid of his former betrayer who is now a high ranking police officer himself. His story covers his early youth, life in police college, his travels in Turkey where a wealthy playboy puts him in touch with his feminine side, and his successful emigration in the United States, culminating in his return to his homeland to nurse his ailing adoptive mother. An enlightening read." **—Rainbow Network, UK**

"*Damages* is an important book … My hope is that it can work a similar magic on you." **—Chicago Pride, IL**

"The concept is delivered clearly and effectively. *Damages* is a personal exploration through life's trials and eventual tribulation—our soul purpose for survival. From an abusive upbringing, separation from his biological mother and death, the author struggles for identity and purpose to find the true meaning for carrying on. The author's tone and writing style is clear and direct. The author offers us an uncensored look into his personal life without holding anything back. I applaud the author for writing about things so close to heart. Most often these can be the hardest things to put down on paper."
—Amazon.com

IDENTITIES (poetry)

"Doors still remain open to those who dream."   **—Poetic Voices Magazine, AL**

"Bazhe's poetry is innovative writing, a provocative read."
—BarnesandNoble.com

"The poetry of *Identities* precisely captures Bazhe's particular viewpoints. Bazhe's work may, for the most part, lack iambic pentameter. That expected rhythm is found only rarely in this collection, as with *Where is Freedom, Dove?* which reads like the lyric for a 60s pop song. However, this prose poetry and the philosophical observations they impart aren't lacking in metaphors and imagery. He divides his work into eight sections. In Part I, *Whispering in Front of the Cosmic Altar*, he acquaints readers who haven't read *Damages* with the views of the world he's encountered during his early years. In *My Life is My Damn Question*, for example, his anger overflows, but he blames the quill of his pen. Bazhe often sees the world from the eyes of a poem's principal character, be it Vampire, Cat, Secret Lover or energy itself. *Identities* is a crowning achievement from the writer whose *Damages* has impacted so many of us."   **—White Crane Journal, NYC**

"Pure spirit-a beacon of Light, Wisdom, Hope, and Peace for all."
—Amazon.com

ART (paintings)

"Not only are his life and background interesting, but his work flows to many tastes and interests."   **—Art Circle, Out in New York**

ALSO by B. K. Bazhe

Identities (poetry)

Art (paintings)

Photography (pictures)

Videos (multimedia)

Posters (prints)

For More Information:
Reviews, Excerpts, Interviews,
Videos, News, Events,
Art, and Poetry

Visit **B. K. Bazhe's Website** at:
www.BAZHE.com

Watch **B. K. Bazhe's YouTube Videos** at:
www.YouTube.com/bazhe

Read **More of B. K. Bazhe's Work** at:
www.Amazon.com

Or **Google, Internet Search**
Key Words are:
BK Bazhe

To: Amy & John,

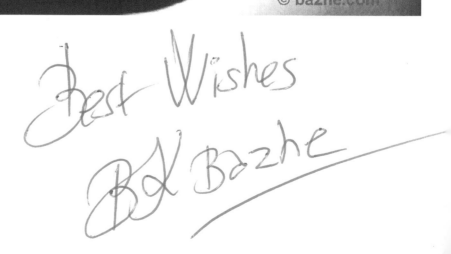

B.K. Bazhe
(author - poet - artist)
© bazhe.com

Best Wishes
BK Bazhe

DAMAGES

B. K. Bazhe

ISBN-13: 978-1469938332
ISBN-10:   1469938332

Library of Congress Control Number:
2012901695

This is a true story. To protect the privacy of the participants, the names of most of the characters have been changed, as have some details about them and the events recounted here.

Cover design by B. K. Bazhe

Cover Image from:
Identities (painting) by B. K. Bazhe,
(Oil & mix media on canvas, 36 x 24 inches.)

Author Photograph from:
Self-Portraits Collection by B. K. Bazhe
(Black, white, & green, 36 x 24 inches.)

Available wherever fine books are sold.
For more information regarding special discounts, or for bulk purchases, please contact
B. K. Bazhe at: **1-862-345-6170**
or **bazhe@bazhe.com**

Or Please Visit:
www.BAZHE.com

Printed in
the United States of America

In Memory of:
My Mother and Father

&

To My Beloved:
Fred, with Gratitude

"In this paradise from where we can see hell the best,
our short glassy lives are open glittering avenues.
But blurry and brittle without the honesty as the light,
and very damaging without the truth as the sun."
—B. K. Bazhe

"Not to expose your true feelings to an adult seems
to be instinctive from the age of seven or eight onwards.
In a time of universal deceit — telling the truth
is a revolutionary act."
—George Orwell

Three things cannot be long hidden: the sun, the moon,
and the truth. There are only two mistakes one can make along
the road to truth; not going all the way, and not starting.
—Buddha

"Anyone who doesn't take truth seriously in small matters
cannot be trusted in large ones either."
—Albert Einstein

If you tell the truth, you don't have to remember anything.
Truth is stranger than fiction, but it is because
fiction is obliged to stick to possibilities; Truth isn't.
Why shouldn't truth be stranger than fiction?
Fiction, after all, has to make sense.
—Mark Twain

Beyond a doubt truth bears the same relation
to falsehood as light to darkness.
The truth of things is the chief nutriment
of superior intellects.
—Leonardo da Vinci

Contents

1

Father

I was calling the cat from the back porch when the telephone rang. It was 7:10 A.M. *Another desperate salesman*, I thought, as I caught the receiver at the front of the third ring.

"Hello?"

"It's Mother. Your father just died. Ten minutes ago. At one o'clock. He was lying on the couch, asking me if lunch was ready. Then he was gone. Just like that. An easy death." She paused, then said in a sharp whisper, "Listen, the relatives and neighbors will insist that you fly here immediately. No need for it. Don't listen to them. You can't make it anyway. The funeral is tomorrow at two. If they suggest we put Father in the morgue, so you'll be able to attend the funeral, say you have something very important to do at work and your boss won't let you leave. Be persistent. Say you'll come for the forty days of mourning. I can't talk. They're all around me. And remember. We are free now. He is gone." Mother finished her statement emphatically, then fell silent.

Mother's silence was not the kind that moves you when someone close perishes. It was an ordinary silence, not one filled with grief, but an empty one. And I struggled not to break it, compressing my cry deep into my stomach, feeling I would betray her by any display of emotion for Father.

"Won't you need any help, Mamo?" I muttered softly, as if the relatives and neighbors might hear me. I still carried an intense phobia of them. They had never liked me, never tried to understand me.

"Don't worry, I'll be all right. You just stay where you are. Don't dwell on this. Do what you have to do. No need to fret over unplanned trips to morgues and funerals. He's dead. It's over. I can't talk. Here, they're coming to talk to you. Bye-bye, my gold."

"Bye-bye, Mother."

Condolences offered in familiar tones of phoniness emitted from the other side of the wire. I said exactly what Mother told me to the relatives and the neighbors, ever sensing the protectiveness of the woman who didn't bear me yet harbored a triumphal maternal instinct that put to shame that of most biological mothers I had known. And that definitely put to shame my father, who had never possessed such a force, never had the capability as a male, as a hunter.

That day, April 22, 1996, I felt like a bird without wings. My painting, my cat, my books, the TV, nothing was to my liking. *We are free now. He is gone.* The words stayed with me as I walked through the garden I was designing, a replica of the one I had known in Europe. The botanical product of my nostalgia took me back to my childhood and to Father, so I left and strolled towards the downtown area.

Morristown, New Jersey, is nothing like most bedroom communities, nests of alienated, busy people, and failures of human architecture and lifestyle. The fact that it had a center you could walk around appealed to me. More nostalgia. Morristown's resemblance to my hometown hit me, and I began to cry. With sorrow over Father's death? Or joy over my liberation? I'm the only master, I almost yelled. The conflict was so intense it was almost physical, as if the feelings could rake through my body like my cat's claws would through a kill. Was it a sin to feel joy when His authority was gone forever? I began to realize that Father's death was more important than anything that had happened to me—even my coming to America. On that day, everything began to change.

When your father is wasteful, drunk, stupid, poor, and ugly—simply a loser—it is easy to imagine that he might harm you one day. When your father is responsible, sober, smart, powerful, and handsome—simply a winner—it is harder to comprehend why he is hurting you. You realize that society's idea of a successful person can, in reality, be a failure. Then you question society's values, what really distinguishes a loser from a winner, and you realize that society can be wrong: that a father's love has nothing to do with peoples' perception of success or failure.

When Father died, I realized that my entire relationship with him was a revolving game of continuous attempts to win his heart, to love him in any way I could, to make him recognize my efforts, and to make him show his gratitude and love. But, like many fathers, he kept his love hidden in his heart. My father was a man who had a natural talent for ruling people. He was tall, dark, and classically handsome, like Tyrone Power, had the body of a football player, and his expression could freeze your blood. He was a militant and a Communist official who, like any official, loved the system that allowed him to wield his power, yet was manipulated by it and became its slave.

Father's mother was married twice and had thirteen children: seven from the first marriage, six from the second, and several stillborn. Only Father and four of his sisters reached adulthood. His father was a farmer and a candle maker on the side. Grandmother was mean, a workaholic, and a perfectionist. She was an excellent cook, but remained extremely picky and demanding, especially later to her daughter-in-law, my mother. Father respected her fanatically. Not a word could be uttered against her. I knew her only from the family portrait. She was frighteningly ugly, and I tried to avoid being around the wall where the picture hung.

Father and his siblings, some as young as five years old, were rousted out of bed every dawn to work in the fields. Often, he had to do hard labor on an empty stomach. As a small child, he would go to church and cry and pray to Jesus and the rest of the Holy Family for a piece of bread. When nothing changed for the better, he gave up on God and religion. It was long before he became a Communist when he realized that there were two major types of people: the exploiters and the exploited. He swore to himself that one day he'd fight against the privileged and build a new, more just system. His harsh upbringing and my grandfather's abuse, however, damaged his soul greatly and made him recalcitrant, someone who was hard to deal with.

When he was in his twenties, as a member of the proletariat, my Father got involved in illegal activities directed against the king of Yugoslavia. When World War II began, he joined the partisans' resistance against the Germans and their allies: the Bulgarians and the Italians, who shared Macedonia, helped by the Albanians and Greek fascists. He fought them fearlessly, and soon he was promoted to captain. After the war, he was elected president of our county and later nominated to be a minister in the state government. His mother did not want to move to the capital, Skopje, and therefore he turned down an opportunity to have lots of money, power, and a residence in an elite neighborhood. Several months later, grandmother died at the age of 94, and Mother was stuck in the province. She never forgave Father for that.

As the President of Prespa County, Father was the law. He ruled with an iron hand, demanding absolute submission from his subordinates. They despised him. Nonetheless, he was respected. He always helped the poor and the blue-collar workers, not forgetting his own roots. Father was the most honest man I ever knew. Like many others, I admired his modesty and dignity. He never took advantage of that power, turning himself into a greedy bureaucrat, like most of his fellow officials and politicians, who sank into the pervasive corruption that ended up destroying the concept of socialism in Yugoslavia. He never took a thing that wasn't his, which he hadn't earned. He strictly obeyed Marshal Tito's slogan: "What's alien, don't touch; what's yours, never give up." We could've had a private tutor, a mansion, a chauffeur, and many other privileges, but he refused them, he didn't even own a car. Mother constantly complained about his humble way of living and thinking. She fought hard with him whenever she purchased new things for the house but always managed to keep them, so she could show off and make our home more glamorous. Our manicured garden was the most beautiful in the county, signifying that we lived in the chief official's residence.

Father was handsome and powerful, yet he could not control his anger and his embarrassing, dominating temper. Mother was young and beautiful, yet she traded her happiness for status. And they had me: an adorable child, who possessed not even the slightest resemblance to them, yet always tried to be a part of their tense marriage. People were jealous of our "perfect" family, yet they had no idea what was going on inside that most splendid union.

2

Mother

A month later, I was flying over the Atlantic. It was an Austrian/Delta flight, a non-smoking one. This pissed off the Europeans, especially the Balkan passengers, who protested loudly. The absurd part was that the stewards provided us all this junk: desserts, alcohol, "brainwashing" movies and commercials, that was probably as harmful as smoking, in its own way. I heard cursing and the sound of someone throwing up. A woman veiled in a traditional Balkan Muslim blue scarf was bending into the aisle and vomiting into a black plastic bag. I closed my eyes. When I reopened them, the clouds had surrounded us. The passengers had stopped admiring the view. Some had closed the window shades and reclined their seats. A baby cried. A child complained. An older man cursed after that.

I stopped being annoyed as I stared at the endless field of white clouds, engrossed with the greatest of human enigmas: who we are; why we're here; why we're so imperfect and bothersome? The plane's trenchant wings sliced the clouds into pieces, which rejoined shortly afterward. Just as death divides human souls that join again in the afterlife, as religious people might say?!

"My ass," I mumbled. I took my notebook out of the pocket in the seat back in front of me. Opening it, I began to read a poem, written in my neat sixteen-year-old's longhand. I invented a melody, as I used to, and began to sing softly, so as not to annoy other passengers:

"Prince
To be in a dreamy boat from paper,
Is there anything more beautiful than to sail in the ocean of clouds,
And write, and sing, and paint on it,
And not give a damn if the people understand it?"

The stewards began serving meals. Once again, children cried and adults complained about the food. People moved about the plane restlessly. When I got up to use the bathroom, I got stuck in traffic, and instead of taking a leak, I got one from the careless teenager who bumped into me with his open can of Coke. I went back to my seat to soothe my nerves with a Hershey's almond milk chocolate.

I held my bladder until most of the passengers fell back asleep. The air in the cabin was stale and smelled like farts. When I finally made it to the toilet, the odor of my urine overwhelmed the smell of the previous occupant's, along with the stench from the plastic barf bag sitting atop the garbage can and looking like a breast implant, and the just-dumped tampons. In about nine and half-hours I arrived in Vienna and transferred to a small shabby airplane—one no American would ever consent to fly—to Skopje, and then took a taxi to my hometown of Resen.

As I rolled down the car window, I inhaled the aroma of the Balkans, my former homeland, its soil burned from wars and soaked in blood. I passed ancient ruins, where our Macedonian king, Alexander the Great, stood godlike on top of a tower. He was waving his truncheon ready for his epical conquest of Greece, Persia, and India.

The forts were nothing like the golden palaces of Versailles, or the Viennese marble castles, or the topiary gardens of Wales. I saw only rugged stone walls that seemed to have sprouted from the rocky landscape, forts that had been lashed by invaders for centuries. Then villages appeared, tucked among the hills. Peasants gathered in front of their red-tiled cozy houses. Among them, I could see a child clinging to his mother's dress, sobbing. In nearby meadows, cows grazed and playful sheep locked horns with each other. Goats dotted the hillsides, some of them chewing bark off the woody stems of plants. The breeze, perfumed with the rustic scent of scythed hay and compost, blew through my hair, and birds twittered in the trees. A tractor driver beeped his horn and waved to us.

The noises of the country were so soothing, so different from those of New Jersey. But the Western influence was all around me: Coca-Cola and McDonald's billboards, graffiti scrawled on some of the advertising for political parties and presidential candidates posted on the walls of the village buildings, many of which were built right at the side of the road. Some of the flashy advertising overshadowed the direction signs to our ancient cities and historic sites.

"Cultural disaster is coming," I mumbled. I couldn't swallow, so I cleared my throat, and spat the mucous through the open window onto one of the ads.

When the taxi reached the top of the mountain, I could see my county, Prespa—the southernmost county in Macedonia—in a basin girdled with bluish mountains. Its lake reflected the sun, and my county resembled a child's hand, cupping a mirror and catching the sun's rays from different angles.

With my binoculars, I scanned the lake where the frontiers of Macedonia, Greece and Albania meet. The churches and the mosques rose above the villages. My town was encircled by apple orchards that made a pattern on the Prespa Valley like a blue-green *kilim*, an exotic Turkish carpet. A prehistoric cemetery was on the west side of the lake. The village of Kurbinovo and its medieval church of Saint Gorge, adorned with the finest examples of Byzantine frescos, stood on a hillside above the lake on its east side.

I could clearly see the little island on the south side of the lake near Greece, called Big Town or Snake Island by the locals. I recalled seeing hundreds of water snakes around its stony coastline. The island was the residence of the first Macedonian-Slav Tsar, Samuel, who established a powerful kingdom in the 10th century. The Byzantine Emperor Basil II destroyed Samuel's kingdom after the battle of Mount Belasica, which took place in the year 1014 in southeast Macedonia. The cruel emperor, who captured most of Samuel's army, plucked out the eyes of the soldiers, leaving one eye in every hundred so they could guide the rest back to the Tsar's court. Samuel later died from sorrow and the Byzantine Empire annexed his kingdom shortly thereafter.

Legend says our lake was named Prespa, after Samuel's daughter, a great beauty, who drowned herself after being stuck in an unhappy relationship. There are rumors that Samuel's treasure is still buried on the island under the age-melted ruins and the crumbling church. In the spring, the island is adorned with old flowers that people say descend from Tsar Samuel's court. As a child I was frightened by the stories of Prespa Lake's mysterious whirlpools, which were said to catch unwary swimmers and small boats, sucking them into a watery grave. The lake would claim at least one victim per year. Each time it happened, my old aunt would say the lake was hungry again. My father would yell at her to stop her nonsense, explaining to me that Prespa Lake's water seeped through its limestone bottom into neighboring Ohrid Lake, which lies below, then drained into the Black Drim River, continuing through Albania and emptying into the Adriatic Sea.

The driver probably thought I was nuts, since I kept moving from one side of the car to the other, my eyes fervently trying to catch as much of the fascinating flora and fauna as possible. Pelicans flew above the lake, some diving for fish. For thousands of years, they had returned each summer to escape the cold Russian winters. Those white-winged gliders were subjects of an obsession as a child. I wished to be one of them and fly above the world. They were the ultimate metaphor for freedom.

My town had changed dramatically in the six years I had been in America. The quaint park at its center with the statue of the local World War II hero had been replaced with gray, tasteless concrete, and all that remained of the past were the children's whistles and laughter. I barely recognized my own street. It had become constricted and commercialized. There were more cars, bikes, trucks, even donkey carriages, and the houses were bigger. After the former Yugoslavia and its socialism collapsed, most of the locals immediately built stores in front of their houses. But they were not aware of one major law of capitalism: the big fish eat the small ones. Many businesses failed and, as a result, most of the stores ended up as empty brick buildings. The images of the "new Macedonia" and its chaotic form of capitalism were killing the old, nearly celluloid memories of my town and country. I tried to shut them out. I tried to come to grips with the fact that this place had nothing to do with the Yugoslavia I left in 1990. But the new images kept splashing my scared mind until I saw the dizzying garden in the front of my childhood home and Mother waiting for me.

She was dressed elegantly, as always, with one of her silky evening shawls wrapped quite loosely around her shoulders. But she had changed. Her medium-height body was stoop shouldered. Her soft face looked distressed. The yellowish tone of her skin and the light blue lines under her eyes shocked me. The driver was bemused when I hesitated, numbed by the sight, before hugging her. She had lost weight and it was easier than ever to wrap my arms around her. I noticed her limp had gotten worse since I left, but I veiled my worried expression with a smile, so my teary eyes would seem to shine with happiness.

She began kissing me crying: "Oh, my gold, if it was up to me, I would have never made you come here. He's gone. It's over. But it's our damned custom, you know. People would say that we raised you well, but that you don't care about us. 'Bazhe should have been here for the funeral, but now he doesn't even want to come for his father's mourning? Shame on him!' You know all the people do in this town is gossip."

Was Father ever born, ever existed for Mother? I questioned while nodding. I felt so safe in her embrace, as if I was half child, half adult. Mother whispered into my ear: "We'll never be ordered around again. Never carry out duties for him any longer. You can rule freely with me at your side, as always, without his opposition now. What he was, and what was his, is yours now. Forever."

Thankfully, Mother didn't announce my arrival to relatives and neighbors. Bisera, who I also called "Auntie," Mother's best friend and contemporary, was the only one there to welcome me. Mother, known for her hospitality, served the taxi driver a meal and, in exchange, he carried my luggage to the second floor, a significant break for me. I passed through the house before I unpacked. The house was overcrowded with furniture because of Mother's tendency to squeeze old stuff in among the new. I've never quite understood why she did that. Out of depression perhaps. I couldn't imagine how she had managed to hold Father's wake and funeral amid all that furniture. Now and then, my knees or elbows would hit the edges of chairs or sofas, and cold electricity would shoot through my body along with pain. I felt like throwing everything out the windows.

Instead, I pulled two boxes neatly wrapped with pink shiny paper and topped with red bows from my suitcase. As I walked downstairs, I could see Mother's soul in the flowers and plants displayed in every window—her small escapes from herself.

"I've got something for you," I announced, from the living room doorway. I kissed Mother, then Bisera, handing them the boxes. They weren't surprised. Every Friday for the last six years, I had called home and each month sent packages to my parents, and gifts for Bisera. The town people spoke of it with respect, and I wished AT&T or the US postal service would have given me free calls or stamps in appreciation for being such a good customer.

Mother opened The Lord &Taylor's box. She held the beige and bay dress up to herself, pressing it against her shoulders, right below her neck, "Thank you, my gold. It's beautiful. You have good taste." She kissed my cheek.

"Yes, he always had," Bisera said, admiring Mother's dress. She showed Mother her present, a dress similar in style and color, then thanked and kissed me. Bisera was like my mother's sister, like a part of the family. She and Mother enjoyed wearing clothes that looked alike, and I would always buy their gifts with that in mind.

I took pleasure, as always, in Mother's continuous joyful laughter, which drifted in from the other room as they tried on their dresses. Afterward, we had Turkish coffee with lemon, which, according to Mother, was supposed to prevent headaches. Bisera then excused herself, even though Mother insisted that she stay longer. She always did that with guests, and it was funny to listen to her then.

After Bisera left, Mother sat next to me at the table and began asking the usual questions every foreigner has about the endless opportunities in America, the Hollywood movies, and the big American cities—about the American dream. For my arrival, Mother served my favorite cake, which she had made with Le Petit Beurre cookies. Then she began to describe my father's funeral.

"When the captain asked me about displaying Father's medallions in the procession, I told him that you took them as a present from Father. He asked me for your phone number. I gave him the wrong number, and it was funny to see him dialing it and shaking in anger when he couldn't get through. It was a big funeral. After the Army guard salvo was fired in tribute, one of your father's fellow veterans read the speech. It was filled with nice things about the deceased, as usual. It was such an ideal portrait of your father, I thought I was burying a different man. Ha…" Suddenly, her laughter stopped and she moaned. She shifted her weight on to her right thigh.

"What's wrong?" I asked noticing the peculiar squinting movement of her eyes indicating discomfort.

"I've had this pain for a couple of months. The doctor says it's hemorrhoids. Nothing serious."

"Did he give you any medicine?"

"Yes, a cream."

"And?"

"And what?"

"Did it help?"

"No. I stopped using it. The pain is greater when I apply it."

"So what do you do then?"

"I use regular, over the counter, pain killers and the pain goes away."

"Then it comes back, doesn't it?"

"Yes. Then I take more aspirin."

"Show me the medication," I said. We got up and I followed her to the bathroom. After briefly reading the instructions, I said, "This cream is supposed to soothe your pain. At least temporarily. You should see the doctor again."

"Don't worry, it's nothing serious."

"No, we will go tomorrow," I insisted.

"You haven't been here a day yet. Tomorrow you have to visit Father's grave with flowers. People would ridicule if you don't."

"Sure," I said.

"Father loved you more than anyone. More than me," she stated, firmly. She pulled a blue envelope from her pocket and handed it to me. "This is the testament he left for you. Ten years ago, we went to court and he appointed you as executor, even before my death."

Father's old, unexpressed love for me was now a surprise in the form of paper in my hand. I took the envelope and stuffed it in my pocket. "Your check up must be done soon. Don't play with your health," I said, nudging Mother's shoulder.

She nodded. "Fine. After the mourning."

"Okay. After the mourning," I said cheerfully, content for the moment that she at least sounded sincere.

"Oh, God, we have to prepare so many things. The mourning has to be as grandiose as possible. Presents are ready to be given to all relatives and friends for the esteem of his soul. The restaurant will be great. The lunch will be rich. The tomb we're building will be in black and gray marble. The most expensive one. He was a big shot. We can't look humble or embarrassed. People would mock us if we didn't do it properly. Everything must be as extraordinarily as he was to people. He was, after all, an extraordinary man."

She spoke with passion. Public opinion mattered greatly to her. She was sinking into the provincial milieu, with its rules, customs, and plastic pompous emphasis on materialism and status.

"Yes, Mother. I've no doubts that you know what you're doing."

I shook my head and looked at Father's empty couch, still not discarded due to my mother's collecting mania. She had replaced the fabric, but I could still see the pit Father's body had made in it. It seemed as if he had only gone to the barber and would come back soon. It was hard to believe he was gone forever. I'd seen him laying on it almost all my life, watching TV, eating walnuts, cursing my mother if the food wasn't ready, sleeping on it: tied to it as if it was the only dugout left in the ocean. He loved that couch, probably more than the one in his bedroom. My gaze shifted to Father's picture above the couch. The medallions on his uniform reflected the camera flash, making them resemble remote stars. They were out of focus compared with the rest of the picture. As if it happened yesterday, I could see myself as a child, marching arrogantly in front of the mirror, pretending I was a general, saluting, and commanding to Mother, "Atten-Shun! Atten-Shun!"

"Oh, please put them back! Before he comes!" she would beg me.

"Mamo, please explain to me again their meaning?"

"Okay, but hurry up. This is the Medal of Freedom. This one, with the little man holding the big golden sword, is the Medal of The First World War II Combatant. It was given to your father for fighting on the front lines against the fascists. And this is the Medal for National Merit from Marshal Tito."

She would read the descriptions from little booklets in the fancy velvety boxes that held each medal. She spoke hurriedly and fearfully, aware that Father was so against me playing with them. He cherished them as if they were his eyes, his very pupils.

"Go to sleep, it's getting late." Mother's voice rang out, pulling me back from the past.

"Good night, Mamo." I kissed her cheek. Her eyes, which once shone like diamonds, were now unfocused, like my father's medals in the picture. She is happy to be free from him finally, I thought as I went upstairs, but something is wrong.

My bedroom smelled the same. Mother was still using lavender for the moths. Suspicious and a little scared, I opened the blue envelope, and began to read the testament. He cared for me. He loved me, yet in a strange suppressive way. I set it aside and curled up in my bed.

My mother was fourteen years younger than Father. Her mother was Greek and her father Macedonian. She had one sister and two brothers. She was the youngest, and the spoiled one. She was a pretty brunet, like Rita Hayworth early in her career, with kind chestnut eyes, a sculpted mouth, and a captivating smile that gradually dimmed after she married Father. Her family had been against their relationship because of my father's previous marriage to a blond "bombshell," a well-known beauty, with whom he was very much in love. But the marriage failed, as the government forbade it. They denounced her as *persona non grata* for being a Nazi collaborator during the war. Father believed the scandal was fabricated out of revenge from his enemies. But the government was his God and was always right, so he abandoned her. They had no children.

In the Balkans, a girl younger than legal age, who ran away from home to get married without her parent's permission, was known as an *escapee*. Mother was one. Getting a powerful man was, for her, the ultimate dream, and a chance to have status. But she was too young, too naive, and absolutely not ready to handle Father's complex personality. So she ended up being like a slave to him. I never heard them having sex. Big holidays were the only times I would see Father being affectionate to her. Even then, he would only give her a peck and a brief hug. I wished then I was a magician and could turn them to stone, so I could always see Mother's happy face and both of them in love. But when I looked into Father's eyes, his eyebrows furrowed and solemn, my happiness turned to fear of his reaction. He was very cold man. It was sickening to freeze next to him every single day. It really was.

3

Mourning

My father would have turned in his coffin if he knew that a cross had been stuck above his head.

In spite of my skepticism about all the pagan crap, which our Orthodox Christian faith had incorporated, I followed custom only to satisfy my paranoid mother. I took a small bottle filled with red wine from my bag and splashed it all over the freshly dug pile of soil, so that Father could have some. I took a bit from the bread and left the rest for him to eat. I placed his favorite pack of Kent cigarettes on top of the grave, for him to smoke. I lit the three candles I had bought for he and his parents. I plunged them between two mounds of earth so that the wind wouldn't blow them out too soon and their spirits would not go mad. And finally, I placed a vase with roses from our garden next to the cross, so he could smell them.

Balkan people believe that, until the fortieth day of mourning, the dead visit their homes each night and will do something bad if the family does not obey these rules. The light in the room where someone has died must be on during those forty days so the deceased can see how much we grieve for them. Mother was in a panic that Father was about to come and knock on our door because she felt no regret over his death. I didn't buy all that. Still, knowing my father's temper, I gave in a little to superstition, figuring that if he came to us, it would be because Mother stuck that damned cross over his head. It looked so incongruous. The severity of it all was too much, like an exaggerated macabre joke. It was ironic. I felt sorry for him knowing how much he hated the church. Suddenly, I began laughing like mad in the middle of the graveyard as I recalled the incident when Father had almost killed a priest.

"What the fuck are you looking for in a Communist's house, eh? A bullet?" Father screamed to the priest, who had showed up to sing Easter hymns. He was new in the parish and had no idea that he was entering the house of an atheist. Mother and I ran to the front door.

"I know your wife's religious, she's not an atheist! I know she lives with God. You're forcing her and that innocent child to follow Communism," the priest lamented.

I was too little to understand all that was happening, yet I enjoyed the scene: Father brandishing his German Walther pistol and chasing the priest through our garden, the poor fat, clumsy creature fleeing down the street, dropping the Bible, and yelling for help after Father fired twice into the air. Mother cradled me in her arms, crossing herself. Father joked with curious locals about humiliating the priest.

A raven perched itself on a pine branch above me, snapping me out of my reverie. I stopped laughing, transfixed, and looked around like a thief. *It would be a disaster if someone saw me laughing. The whole town would talk about it. Mother would be terribly ashamed, her image destroyed.* I cleaned up each side of the grave, straightening up the wreaths and the ikebana floral arrangements that people had brought for his funeral. Then I grabbed my bag and began to run towards the exit. A loud cawing echoed, and I turned around. Three ravens were squabbling over my offerings on my Father's solemn grave. I threw a rock at them and ran back. They had pecked apart the Kent package, assuming that it was food. I leaned towards the pile of soil that smelled of wine, candles, and death. My tears fell, penetrating the dirt, going to Father. I hugged the reddish-yellow earth and whispered "I wish we had understood one another, Father."

Mother and Bisera were calculating the cost of the mourning when I got home. Mother and I were idiots when it came to math. As a retired accountant, Bisera excelled at it. The TV was on and commercials were blaring from it, making me feel as if I were in America again. Commercials had been rare during the Socialist reign.

"You must have gone mad putting that cross on Father's grave, Mother. Everyone knows he was a Communist and hated religion." My voice overpowered those coming from the TV.

"The craftsmen are coming this week to build a marble tombstone. What was I supposed to do? Leave the grave without a sign? People would ridicule us," she replied, turning to gaze at Bisera's pen scratch across the paper as she totalled up our costs.

"You should have placed a temporary tombstone with a red star on it," I said firmly.

"So that people would break it into pieces?" she asked, raising her voice. "You don't know much. The communists are anathematized by everyone now. By the poor, because they gave up the good old system. By the nouveau rich, because they eliminated opportunities for them to be capitalists for forty years. Even dead communists can't rest in peace. People are destroying their graves. No. A red star is a bad idea. If I'd placed an epitaph without a symbol, it would've looked like a Muslim grave. Then I might as well have buried Father in their graveyard and embarrassed him even more." Her voice almost broke.

"She is right, dear," Bisera interjected softly, in an apparent effort to keep our conversation from becoming an argument. "Times have changed. You haven't been here long enough to experience the death of Yugoslavia, the uncertainty, the shaky birth of this new Macedonia and its fragile system. You should be happy for predicting it and avoiding it in time. Most of your generation is lost, with no future here."

My glance alternated between the two of them. Mother's gaze eluded me, as it always did when she disagreed with someone. I leaned over her and said, provocatively, "What a nice way to get revenge, Mother."

"Okay," she said bitterly. If you wanna think that way, fine. I won't stop you. I couldn't do this when he was alive, so I am doing it now. And I enjoy it. As much as he did, when he humiliated me my whole life. Yes. It is revenge. So what?!" Mother exploded in anger, without abashment. There was no need to hide it. Bisera and I knew everything. My father had been mistreated after his death. The burial site made a mockery of his strongly held beliefs, the beliefs of an idealist.

I growled and left the room. I didn't want to challenge Mother's anger or to shock her with the tears welling in my eyes. Climbing the stairs, I could picture how Father's body must have looked before he died: aged, tired, and weak. I could imagine him looking hesitant, clumsy, even pathetic, being unable to confront my mother any more. I could see Mother's face laughing at his tired mind, a mind that had once, as an official, had controlled everyone in the county. I could see him looking defeated, yet still doggedly arguing with visitors certain that he was always absolutely right. Poor Father. I walked into my bedroom, jumped on to the bed, and shoved my head into the down pillow that still seemed to smell as it had when I left. I had always done this when I had arguments with my parents. I was never right, never won one as a child. I shocked myself, crying for Father. No, I thought. I was crying for his loss of dignity. I was sure about it.

About fifty people showed up for the mourning. The new family tombstone was finished and stood glittering on the hill. Father's name was engraved in gold into the Impala Black marble on the left of the tombstone, with the right side left blank for Mother. A cross was already engraved above her reserved place.

First, drinks and hors d'oeuvres were offered, then dresses and boxes of chocolates were given to each woman, and shirts and a pair of socks to each man, as custom and Mother's status required. Everything was wrapped elegantly in dark shiny paper, and the whole affair seemed more like a celebration rather than a memorial. I hated it, but Mother had to be respected for her zeal to show off and follow the traditionally correct way. Anyone could have told you that she overdid it, and not for the sake of my father's soul, but for the sake of the family reputation. I knew people who stared into the sun at funerals and memorials so they would cry. I have done it, too. I suspect Mother did the same, to be politically correct. Her eyes were teary, but not from sorrow.

The restaurant was not far and the guests wanted to walk, rather than wait for a ride on that pleasant June morning. Mother's youngest brother drove us. The place wasn't to my liking, too glitzy, but even so it was clean and neat. My distant cousin from Father's side convinced Mother to have the commemorative lunch there—his best buddy owned it. He was as sneaky and untrustworthy as the owner, and in the end, they ripped my mother off.

The staff rushed with the servings as if we were contagious. Later, I found out they had to prepare for a wedding, which followed our boring gathering. Glasses were raised, toasting. People coughed and blew their noses. Now and then, someone would fart. The conversation was limited to television and newspapers and events—mundane, annoying, trivial, redundant, and in the end, all substanceless.

"What should I expect from these souls, whose lives have been spent in offices, who have traded in their integrity for more money and promotions even though they hate what they're doing? Talk about poetry? No one talks of poetry any more. It's too complicated. There are fewer intelligent discussions and a higher production of dummies in this commercial world," I whispered to myself, scrutinizing the guests.

After the appetizers and the aperitifs were gone, the main course was served. It contained a Macedonian salad mix of vegetables with Feta cheese, homemade chicken soup, and stuffed red peppers filled with mixture of ground beef, rice, and chopped parsley. More wine, beer, brandy, and juice was brought. I could imagine Americans' reactions, because drinks were never kept in the refrigerator or served with ice. Uncle Bogdan, Mother's brother-in-law, a widower, former womanizer, and current loner barked at me from the other side of the table: "Your father, what a courageous man he was."

I looked at him and nodded. Poor Uncle became estranged from his sons after my aunt died from a brain tumor. His life was a mess without my aunt, who, in addition to being a hard worker at the local textile factory, was an excellent housewife, an honest, humble woman, and one of the few I loved in the family. We will all pay for what we do to others, sooner or later, I thought. I pitied him even more when I noticed that he had gained substantial weight. A widower with an expanding belly is considered an unhappy one in our culture, although the reason he ate like a pig was because of his misery.

"When the Germans left town, after the capitulation in 1945," he continued, "they destroyed everything worthy, stealing priceless icons from our monasteries as usual. They set fire to the Saraj, the Ottoman palace that the Gestapo used as their headquarters for the region." Uncle paused to sip some strong homemade plum brandy, *Rakija*, then took a drag on his cigarette, and continued the story.

"I don't think you all know that the palace was constructed as a smaller replica of The Committee Building, the headquarters of French Revolutionists in Paris, by Adjutant-Major Ahmed Niyazi, an officer of suspect loyalty stationed in our town by the Turkish Sultan. He was a member of the Young Turk Revolutionary Movement at the beginning of the nineteenth century. He was also a visionary who wanted to turn our town into a 'little Paris.' Unfortunately, the Sultan's spies killed him towards the end of the Ottoman Empire."

"Yeah, Niyazi Bey." One of the other guests finally spoke, referring to the adjutant-major by his common name.

"Correct." Uncle nodded, and then looked straight on my eyes, as if he were my tutor. "Your father climbed from the balcony into the burning Saraj and put out the fire. He saved the building. The crowd below waited breathlessly for him to come out. He emerged clenching his fists in the air, as a sign of a victory, and leaped from the balcony into the arms of his admirers…Your father was a hero."

"Yes uncle, he was," I said, gazing into his drunken, red eyes.

Uncle gulped more brandy. "When the Partisans shortened his family name into Kargo, he liked it. The tone of it. The masculinity of it. And it suited him perfectly. In the fifties, when Vice President Kardelj, Tito's right-hand, drew up a new amendment reforming the local and state governments, your father rejected it!" Uncle almost yelled, apparently to make sure that everyone in the room heard him. "Then the people invented a slogan: 'Kardelj gives, Kargo refuses!' It caused an enormous scandal. To reject a proposal from the federal government in a communist country, you have to have big balls. And he did, and ruled the county according to his own authority, because people trusted him and loved him. He was the peoples' man. He wanted the county to thrive in prosperity. Drawing from his popular mandate, he dreamed of building a canal to connect our town with the lake, making a little Venice out of it. But the president of the state refused to lend him the money. He was jealous that our town Resen would look better than the one he was brought up in, the neighboring Ohrid Lake. That may seem strange, but many petty bureaucrats were like that."

Everyone listened attentively to the greatest storyteller in the family. He kept on telling stories of my father, tipsy from repeatedly pouring glasses of brandy and downing them in one shot. Mother's pride was increasingly obvious, as though she had won a Nobel Prize.

"*In vino veritas*," she pronounced in Latin, filling Uncle's glass. The comment made guests' eyebrows rise instantly. They stopped eating and looked at Mother. They knew she didn't love Father, but as always, she said good things about him in public. Poor Mother, she never realized how ridiculous she sounded, playing her game. Father rarely talked about his experiences in World War II. Many others did, though, especially his fellow veterans, and I didn't find it odd that only Uncle Bogdan would speak of them during the biggest ritual to be held in honor of his memory. To the family, Father was an intimidating and dominating ruler who was always absolutely right. They still hated and feared him, even though his absolutely right attitude was now rotting six feet under.

Like any small rural town, the citizens in my town of Resen talked about the weather, newborn babies, funerals, family affairs, apple prices, pesticides, and other peoples' business. Gossip was their way of compensating for their self-imposed sense of cultural inferiority. The whole county slumbered in cultural darkness, although a city person would have had found it quite entertaining, and a writer, inspiring. The intellectuals would never admit it, but I'm sure that dull provincial gossip was an effective anti-depressant. Mother would never go to neighbors' houses to gossip, except Bisera's, though she gladly encouraged the gossip society to visit her. She wanted to be updated on everything going on around her. Our garden was the usual meeting place, and I broke out in tears when I found it in such a bad shape, not even remotely close to what it used to be. Naturally, its splendor dimmed as my parents grew older, and Father couldn't control the gardener who had turned into a sluggard. He was a refugee from Albania, a Macedonian who came to our town as a migrant laborer. After the collapse of Communism, the country was doing worse than the rest of the Balkans because only the Albanian mafia and corrupt politicians were left to run the new system.

For the gardener, our garden was simply a place to make money. I felt far more attachment to it than he, even after all these years away from it. I spent half of my childhood in the garden, our status symbol. I remember running along its concrete paths, flanked with boxwood and privet hedges, getting stuck in the roses' prickles, being pierced when cutting them in the morning for my Mother's vases or for the neighbors, who decorated their cars with my bouquets. They would stick them under the windshield wipers, so they wouldn't fall when they went to funerals or weddings.

I began to care for the garden. The old routines reincarnated again. During free moments, I would dig the soil and even it up where it was bumpy. I cleared debris from around the plants and pulled weeds from between the concrete tiles. I also cut the dead rosebuds and bushes, watered them, and trimmed the hedges. In just a couple of days, the improvement was obvious, and the garden began to look more like I remembered it.

The boxwood squares appeared regal again with its manicured tower-like forms on each of its corners. The two tall evergreen trees caressed the house facade again. I began running around the boxwood mazes the way I did years before, and memories of my childhood came flooding back. I remembered the smell of Mother's meals and the sound of her voice calling me to eat before she went shopping. I stopped running and leaned against the fence to catch my breath. The neighborhood children were playing in the street. I remembered as a child watching them for hours with tears in my eyes. I longed for the sounds of their games and voices.

My mother's voice came closer, but I sneaked into the house and tricked her again. I spied on her through the hole I had made in my room's curtain. I hid until she left, then went back out to the garden, to one of my secret places. I was always alone, but I would fantasize about having many friends with me. I longed to start school, but Mother said I was too young.

My smile froze and my dimples shivered on my bloodless cheeks, when I heard my father calling for me. I tried to bury myself in the boxwood hedge, but he found me easily. Glaring down at me, his 6'4" frame resembling that of a dark evil knight, his always-angry eyebrows furrowed even more.

"You must finish your lunch!" he ordered.

I pushed myself further against the boxwood but it was too dense to go through. Quickly, I scrambled between his legs and tried to escape by hiding behind the cylinder bush. The dark knight's huge hands grabbed me, however, and propelled me through the garden and into the house. He sat me down at the kitchen table, thrust a plate of fatty meat before me, and yelled, "Eat!"

"I can't, Daddy. I don't want to. I'm not hungry." I began to cry, even though I had promised myself that I wouldn't. I'm a coward, I thought, wiping my cheeks.

"What?" He took the fatty meat from my plate and pushed it into my mouth. "Eat! Chew It!"

I hated meat. The fat disgusted me. Bile rose in my throat, and I threw up all over the table. Enraged, he pulled me from the chair and began to spank me, so hard that I flew out of his grip and on to the floor. I began screaming as blood ran from the corner of my mouth and my nose.

"Stop it, damn it! Stop, you bastard! I'll show you how to eat meat!" he yelled, pulling off my imported Italian sailor suit. Then he unzipped his fly, while he kept cursing louder and louder.

God, Father's *peenie* is so big compared to mine, I thought. He grabbed my hair and yanked my head back, then jammed his peenie in my mouth, suffocating me. He pushed his weight against me. My mouth began to hurt. One of his legs was bigger than my entire body. He blocked out all light, so everything around me was dark. The whole world was dark. Just as I thought my head was going to explode, he took his peenie out of my mouth and moved his hand over it.

"I'm begging you daddy, don't!" I grasped the first chance to speak.

"Eat! I'll teach you how to eat meat! I'll teach you good!"

Suddenly, white fluid was all over me. I was horrified. What is this? It was coming from my father's peenie. I was shaking in front of it, and hoped that Father's terrifying peenie would dry out. But it didn't. It kept dripping that disgusting glue-like stuff. It finally stopped, and Father smiled at me.

"Now, you've learned your lesson well," he said, caressing my golden hair and my cheeks, smearing them with the white liquid. "Come on. You have to take a shower. Don't cry! Your daddy just taught you how to eat meat!" He mumbled softly, then lifted me off the floor and carried me to the bathtub.

Did the white fluid get rid of his anger? I wondered. My left cheek and my chest hurt badly from the pressure of his thighs. I tasted blood. The bathtub's cold surface made me shiver more. He turned on the shower. Lathering up the soap, he began washing the sticky fluid off my hair, face, neck, and chest. He rinsed me, then picked me up with one arm, while he pulled down the toilet seat with his free hand, and sat me on it. He took an enormous blue towel off the rack and began to dry my body. When he finished he wrapped me in the towel and carried me to the living room sofa. I was still shivering, more from his presence and that disgusting smile on his face than from the cold.

"Put your clothes on!" he ordered, smoothing my wrinkled sailor suit before he handed it to me. "Faster, faster. Hurry up!" He took some ointment from the bathroom cabinet and spread it on my swollen face. Then he turned the TV on and said, "The Pink Panther will be on soon. Remember, today is our federal holiday. The Fourth of July. Day of Combatants. Be happy. We'll get you a nice present later. Let's wait for your mother now! Let me see your smile!"

"Yes, Father," I muttered, forcing a smile through my tears and praying for Mother to show up soon.

"Stop! Don't cry!" He picked me up like a pillow and shook me.

His smile had vanished. Better, I thought. His smile hurt. From that day on, I hated it. I'd rather have seen him angry forever than smiling at me like that, and playing with me, and beating me, and touching me like that.

"Don't cry, I said! Shut up!" He tossed me back on the sofa.

I must stop crying, I thought. I'm such a coward. It's dangerous to cry. When will Mother come home? My favorite cartoon seemed dreary to me, the images blurry. Father was recomposing his grandiose, scary bearing. I wiped at my tears, keeping my face turned away from him. When I looked at him again, he was settling into his armchair, getting ready to read the newspaper, as if nothing had happened. Finally, I heard the front door open and the welcome sound of Mother's voice calling for help. I ran out of the room, through the hallway, and right to my mother. Embracing her legs, I buried my face in her skirt. He was behind me. I was afraid that he would stop me. He didn't.

"They are so heavy. My arms hurt," Mother complained, dragging bags of groceries from the hallway to the kitchen. I stuck to her as if I were glued.

"You're so late! Where did you go?" he said.

"Ohhh, God and Golden Christ. Not again? Can't you see these bags? I was shopping! Why did I marry you? You have no respect for me. I'm too good for you. I wish I were like the bitch next door, careless and lazy and not giving a damn about her husband. Then you would've seen what women are like."

"Fuck you!" Father's roar was louder than thunder. "Without me, you'd have nothing! Absolutely nothing!"

"Better nothing than this life. Every day, the same thing. Can't you talk like a civilized human being? Oh, Golden Lord, what did I do to deserve this? Why you didn't stop me when I decided to marry him…?"

Mother looked up towards where God might be, pulling me towards her. Suddenly, Father tried to slap her. I grasped Mother's legs harder and pushed her backwards, beyond his reach. I was shocked. He had never tried to hurt her before, at least, not in front of me. His voice and facial expression became more dreadful than ever. For a moment, I felt frozen in place. But when he tried to hit Mother again, I jumped at him. It was the first time I would do that.

"Trying to protect your mother, eh!?" Father slapped me so hard that my head slammed into Mother's stomach.

Instantly, Mother sheltered me in her arms. He left us weeping, curled together on the hallway floor, the floor that Mother had recently washed and polished like a mirror. After a while, Mother's tears converted to rage.

"Idiot!" she yelled. "You damned tyrant! Why are you hitting him? Why? You disgusting tyrant!" Mother picked me up and ran out the door, still cursing him. Murmuring to herself, she took me to her secret place behind the big old pear tree in the backyard. We sat on a bench, where no one could see us from the street or neighboring houses.

"Did he hurt you a lot?" she asked, caressing my hair and showering my scalp with her warm tears.

"No, Mother. Don't worry, Mother." I lied, happy that she couldn't see that I looked different since Father's slap covered the previous terror on my face. She was too preoccupied with her own misery to notice, in any case. My face must have been very red. It was burning with pain again, and I prayed for Father's peenie to dry out forever.

I realized that, as I daydreamed, my fingers had been digging into the soil, so far down I could touch the roots of a nearby pine tree. I pulled my hands out and stared at them. They were covered with dirt, some of it jammed under my nails. The soil had supernatural powers. It calmed me. It was an antidote for my painful memories. The soil had always been my, and my mother's, therapist. That's why my mother and I loved our garden endlessly. Even though I knew, and I was sure my mother did not, that it was no longer the sanctuary it appeared.

4

Biopsy

I scheduled an appointment right after the mourning ceremony for Mother to have her hemorrhoids checked, this time in a real hospital in the city of Bitola, an hour away. Bisera came with us. When our taxi passed a little monastery on top of the forested hill, my mother began praying: "Golden Christ and Holy Mother, help me and protect me, please." She crossed herself, staring back at the monastery until it disappeared in the trees. Bisera and I hid our concern by making silly jokes.

The hospital was crowded, as I remembered it always had been, but didn't look as neat and sanitary as before. The country's new corrupt and chaotic economic system had affected it. We took the elevator to the second floor.

Dr. Vasil was the surgeon recommended by our neighbors as one of the best in the region. He was around fifty, quite arrogant, and overweight. His hair was mostly white, and he stunk of alcohol. Right after we met him he took Mother into the examining room, closing the door. Half hour later, it opened and he came back out, with my mother walking behind him. I jumped up from my seat. His face was deadpan.

"Is everything all right, Doctor?" My voice echoed in the hallway. Bisera said nothing, waiting anxiously for his reply.

"Yes. Come into my office and I'll give you the prescription for her hemorrhoids," he said, smiling at me, then at Mother and Bisera.

"Thank you, doctor," Mother said, appreciatively.

He glanced at her in apparent acknowledgement as he turned around. His shoes tapped on the blue tiled floor. Sunshine poured in from the terrace at the end of the hallway, illuminating all the busy nurses and shuffling patients in a glaring light. I hid from the glare behind the doctor's ample figure. People seemed surreal, tinged with an intense bluish light. When we set foot in his office, he immediately turned to me and asked, "Why didn't your mother come here earlier?"

I had expected him to offer me a seat first. This was a bad sign. Scrutinizing his expression, I said, "She went to the local doctor. When the pain intensified, they diagnosed—"

"Local doctors? Provincial peasants? What do they know? 'Here are the medications. You'll be all right. It's just hemorrhoidal. Next!' That's how they treat patients." He sat on the edge of his desk and lit a cigarette, then offered me one.

I took it, my fingers leaving damp spots where I touched it.

"I hope I'm not right, but I'm pretty sure your Mother has colon cancer. I hope it's local and hasn't spread yet. It appears to have been there for a while."

Silence. Petrified, I stared into his grayish eyes, unaware that the ash from my cigarette was dropping on the floor.

"We'll do a biopsy to confirm my diagnosis," he said. "Also, we'll scan her. I'll schedule it as soon as possible. You should've brought her here earlier."

"I live in America. I'm only here because my father just died. She took care of him for a long time. I didn't know. She never complained to me."

He shook his head. "Our mothers, so dedicated to looking after their husbands before themselves. So loyal to our dominating fathers. Women in America don't put up with that shit. Of course, their marriages don't last long. I did my specialization in Canada. Anywhere Queen Victoria stepped in, it is the same. Ha! Am I right or what?"

"Yes. You are." I was stunned at how casual his mood had suddenly become. He seemed to have a sense of humor. I could picture him with a wife, children, and a vacation house, a nice life. Finding cancer in yet another patient was, for him, routine. Another case. Easy come, easy go. At the same time, he seemed wise and serious about his job, even as he made light of other things. On the whole, I liked him.

"What could have caused her cancer, doctor?" I asked, still motionless.

"If we knew what causes cancer, we'd have cured it by now. Genes…stress." He began to scrawl on a thick blue prescription pad.

I was vaguely aware of someone coming in, picking up something from the corner, and quickly disappearing. Maybe a nurse. Nothing seemed real, except my agony. Mother would be scared to death if I let her know my true concerns, I thought. I struggled to concentrate on things other than cancer and death, but I couldn't.

"My father was a difficult man. Very hard on Mother. Her father, brother, and sister all died from cancer." I spoke to the doctor as if he were my conffesor, and, suddenly it felt easier to handle the shock.

"You answered your own question," he said, not looking up. He tore the scribbled note off the pad and quickly started scratching out another one. He did this several times. When he was done, he had a small pile of papers.

"All that hemorrhoid crap goes in the garbage! These are referrals for the biopsy and scanning. Here's a prescription for pain killers." He flipped through the prescriptions as he described them. "She should take them only when she has pain."

"Is it morphine?"

"Oh, no. No. Not yet. Not until the pain is unbearable." He handed me the papers.

The world was crumbling around me. "Maybe it's not cancer!" I said emphatically, as desperate as a beggar.

"Maybe," he said, unconvincingly. "Don't say anything to your mother yet. Be brave." He paused, then added, "This is part of life." He grabbed my hand, shook it, and walked me to the door.

"I'll see you next week," he said.

"Yes," I mumbled, pulling out the twenty dollars I had brought for him and sticking the bills into his jacket pocket, where the end of his stethoscope rested. I didn't hear what he said. Presumably, he thanked me. I walked down the hall, struggling to think of something funny before Mother saw me. I thought of the pathetic, hilarious American daytime TV soap operas. The talk show hosts, with their phony voices, consoling miserable people with weight problems, broken families, and cheating spouses. The TV evangelists, and other similar crooks, convincing hopeless folks to live, eat, sleep, and be sexually suppressed in obedience to God, while ripping them off in the name of that God. The satellite-delivered nuns, and other similar criminals, selling bibles for $19.99 and illustrated ones for children for $14.99. The scam advisors for platinum burial-care plans urging you to buy a grave through them, because the government won't pay when you or your loved ones die. So-called ministers hawking books on how to solve your financial problems with help of Jesus, and often with their God-driven investment schemes.

I began to grin at everything: at the nurses passing me by; at miserable-looking patients; at an dying plant in the corner; at the reproduction of Van Gogh's *Irises*; at Bisera; at my Mother. I must've looked like a lunatic.

"It's an infection. I mean, inflammation of the colon." I corrected myself quickly. "Nothing serious. He gave me prescriptions. Take the pills only when you are in pain. Next week, we have to come back for further treatments."

"No," Mother said, firmly. "Since he examined me, it hurts even more."

"It'll go away. It's irritated now, that's all," I explained. Mother looked down at her wrinkled skirt and tried to smooth it, pressing on it several times. My gaze met Bisera's. I could tell she was suspicious of my bogus smile. Mother wasn't. On the way back, I forced myself to talk with the driver, joking and laughing, hiding my devastation again.

That night, I took the cordless telephone from the library to my bedroom and called Bisera. She picked it up before the first ring finished.

"Hello," she said, in a tentative, shaky voice.

"Mother has cancer," I said, staring at my shadow on the wall.

I heard her howl. I waited. When she was able to talk again, she asked, "Are you sure?"

"I'm afraid the doctor is pretty confident about it."

Again, I heard loud weeping and heavy breathing, inhaling and exhaling. I waited some more until Bisera composed herself.

"I remember when she first started complaining about her leg," Bisera said, "about ten years ago. A year later, she began to limp. For months, she didn't go out, embarrassed by it. She refused to see a doctor. She just let it be. She could've prevented it. But her pride, as always, stopped her. When the pain in her leg intensified and she couldn't hide it any longer, she confessed it to me. This was last winter. We had to call the first aid squad a couple of times. She was injected with painkillers. Then the limp worsened and at about the same time she began to complain about her colon pain. I'm sure she'd had it for a long time. She's very secretive. She always has been. She finally went to the local doctor who diagnosed her with hemorrhoids. When she began losing weight, I got very scared, and very suspicious of—"

"I noticed it," I interjected. "I expected to find Mother contented after being freed from my father. But, she doesn't smile nearly as much as before, and when she does, her smile doesn't have that glittering quality, the way it used to. Her eyes don't shine like before." My voice wavered. "The doctor scheduled a biopsy and scanning for next week."

"Maybe it's not cancer. Maybe the doctor misdiagnosed her." Bisera tried to offer faint hope.

"Maybe," I said, vaguely. My tears fell on the pillow, forming wet circles.

"Good night," Bisera said, weeping. Abruptly, she hung up. She couldn't take it any longer. Neither could I. It was too much to bear. There were too many bad dreams ahead.

Bisera was the daughter of a successful leather merchant. He owned half of Prespa County's land, lots of real estate in town, a couple of stores around Macedonia, and one exchange office in Istanbul. When the Communists took over the kingdom of Yugoslavia after World War II, almost everything her family owned was confiscated or expropriated. Bisera's father and mother could never quite understand how the State could confiscate their properties, and they died shortly afterward. Bisera never got over it, constantly cursing the Communists about the injustice they had done to her family. Mother described Bisera as a rich girl who would cheerfully pee on the rare Persian kilims in a mansion, while most girls had to labor in the apple orchids to bring an extra Dinar to their households.

"Bisera was a princess with high manners. Yet she wasn't good-looking, nothing like me," Mother would say. Mother's looks were the only thing that made her feel superior to her rich girlfriend. Bisera became nearly destitute, but her former upper-class status in society wasn't easily forgotten. That was all Mother cared about. She often spoke publicly about it, abandoning many of her friends and bragging about having Bisera as her only true friend. Mother and Bisera's friendship was like a fusion of the old aristocracy and the new Socialist regime. That's how Mother saw it after marrying my father. And it worked well. They became very close. They loved one another. People were amazed how Bisera's upbringing showed in the way she dressed, even though she couldn't afford expensive clothes anymore. She exuded good breeding, despite losing her status and wealth.

Mother loved it. I did, too. When Mother offered Bisera some of her dresses, she would only select a few, claiming that the rest were too fancy and could only be worn by the first lady in the county, Mother. She was right. Mother was born with a sense of style that was reflected in every gesture. Mother would make heads turn anytime she took me to the promenade.

Bisera became a widow after a few years of marriage to a handsome womanizer, a local playboy, gambler, and alcoholic. He died very young from his extreme lifestyle and left her with two small children. His family in America offered Bisera help, but she refused to emigrate to live with them. She regretted that decision, later, through the rest of her life. Marked forever as a bourgeoisie's daughter by the Communists, she had a hard time surviving as a single mother in the new peoples' proletarian state, where classes no longer existed—in theory, at least. She was a strong woman, though, and she succeeded in raising her beautiful daughters, sending them to college, and marrying them off to rural-entrepreneurs who made an excellent living as apple producers. She worked hard to arrange these marriages, compromising her urban lineage to be mingled with the peasant's one, so her offspring would have the financial security that she once had. Mother was against it, but she wasn't in any position to criticize Bisera, since she had married for the same reason, security.

Mother took Bisera everywhere. They most enjoyed their annual vacations at the mineral spas or on the lake. On national holidays, Mother would practically drag Bisera to fancy government officials' parties, even though Bisera despised everything associated with the Communists. Mother had no clue what communism was. She just followed the one she married and played her role pompously. Ironically, she seemed more like a countess than a high-ranking official's wife. Father freaked out. Mother had fun. And I got stomachaches from laughing at all of it.

Ten days later, we were back at the hospital. I ran to Mother the minute I saw her leave the biopsy room. Her face and her slow body motions concerned me. I held her arm and walked her to a bench. She sat, putting all her weight on the right thigh.

"It hurts bad," she said, cringing. "Why did we come here? I don't need this."

"Yes, you do. And you know it's for your benefit," I said, taking a pill from her bag. I placed it on her outstretched shaking palm. "Here. I'll get you some water."

I walked to the fountain, took a cup from the dispenser, filled it up, and brought it back to her. Her lips were dry. She drank the water and asked for more.

"If you can't handle the scanning, the doctor said we can do it another day," I said.

"Oh, no. Let's get everything over with today. I don't want to come back here. I'll bet the hospitals in America are much more beautiful, aren't they?"

"Yes. Some of them are huge. Ten times bigger than this one. With well-maintained grounds around them." I spread my arms wide.

"Why am I asking?" Mother shook her head. "Who cares how nice they are? They are hospitals. Everyone hates them."

I also wondered why she would ask me that, in this place where the odor, a mix of alcohol, disinfectant and excrement, continually reminded you how horrible these dens of human suffering were. Maybe her subconscious was telling her she'd end up here.

We tried to walk downstairs, but after going only one floor, Mother said, "We have to take the lift." My left hand completely supported her body.

"No problem, Mother," I said, grasping her arm more firmly as we walked to the elevator. She is weak, I thought. Maybe only today, because of this biopsy thing.

We reached the elevator and I pressed the button. Shortly, the doors slid open. Inside were three interns, giggling in the corner. The worn-out machinery seemed scarier than any roller coaster at Virginia's Busch Gardens amusement park. An American would never have entered that elevator. My people, however, were used to it. They saw things, life, differently. Even in the face of danger and death, they enjoyed life more than the average American, who would complain for a week if the tiniest splinter stuck their little toe. *Did I envy my own people? Had I become spoiled, living on the other side of the Atlantic?* My face reddened. Mother and the interns noticed it, and I turned my face towards the elevator's quaking bottom.

"Ah, youth," Mother said, enviously. We all got off on the same floor, and she inhaled deeply as the interns ran like a horde of cheetahs through a door.

I guided Mother through a door marked "Radiology Clinic." Luckily, not many people were waiting. Most people preferred to use the scanner in the capital's oncology center, thinking it was better. Both scanners were given to Macedonia as part of the international charity and humanitarian efforts after Yugoslavia broke up. I took Mother into the waiting area and walked up to the check-in window.

The clerk was sitting at a desk behind a glass partition, drinking coffee and smoking. She didn't bother to look at me as she took my referral through the semicircular hole in the glass—the only possible contact with our bureaucracy. She was sluggish, making some people impatient. Most of them stayed calm, however, because provoking her would only make her bossy and they'd have to wait even longer. Mother was in pain, so I asked, as politely as possible, "How long will we have to wait for the screening, comrade?"

"The word 'comrade' is dead, mister," she said, sharing a mocking glance with the nurse who sat behind her, browsing a magazine and also sipping coffee.

"Sorry, madam, I'm not used to the new expressions. I've been living in America," I said, trying to be ingratiating.

"Oh, really. Thirty minutes wait. Next!" Her eyes closed halfway, into a mean expression. Her voice was cold and her manner was unapproachable, a product of her awareness that, even if she had the chance, she was too old to go to "The Promised Land." Many people had that attitude about someone visiting from America. They were disappointed in Macedonia's new system and jealous of those who had escaped it. It was sad.

"In America, you've got to work. Not like these people still waiting for the government to take care of them, like it used to be. Am I right, son?" An elderly, neatly dressed gentlemen spoke up behind me.

"Yes, you are, sir," I said, happy that I knew not to call him "comrade."

"We still long for Yugoslavia, don't we?" A short peasant spoke up, glancing around at everyone in the group. "What's wrong with being taken care of by the government? At least we feel like we're alive here. You don't have time to pee and shit comfortably over in America. Life goes like a light. Disappears quickly! Ba-bum!" He snapped his fingers, flicking his hand sideways and almost hitting the elderly gentleman's face. "I've lived there. It's not like in the movies. There is not a better place to be than here. Believe me. It's simpler and cleaner here."

At that moment I never felt more American. "The dollars you made in America has let you live like a king here," I said. "You probably have a big house and farm somewhere in your shitty village, and I'll bet you get either Social Security from the U.S. or a pension. Maybe both. So what's your problem with America? Relax. There's no single perfect place for everybody. Not yet."

"He must've been a ditch digger or left all his bones in some of those smoky factories over there! That's his problem." A fat man with thick dialect added.

Everyone laughed, except one young man who didn't seem to give a damn. Half of his face was brown. Skin cancer. I was terrified. I hoped Mother wouldn't notice him. Meanwhile, the peasant acted like he was going to kill the man who had embarrassed him. He shouted at him and spit in his face. The neatly dressed gentlemen, who seemed like he might be a teacher or librarian, tried to separate them, then started arguing with them and waving his finger in the air. Suddenly, everyone fell silent when an attractive, middle-aged nurse called the first patient in for his screening.

I walked over to Mother and took a seat next to her.

"You shouldn't provoke that man," she said. "He's probably sick and doesn't know what he is upset about. His suffering makes him talk like that." If she were feeling well, Mother definitely would never have let me argue in a public place. She reached over and clutched the radiator pipe, using it to help her stand up, then walked to the open window. She always loved feeling the summer wind against her face.

"Sorry, Mother, but he is wrong." I said.

"You love America, don't you, Bazhe? I don't blame you. A young man with ideals and dreams in a young country? A perfect combination." She kept her face towards the wind as she spoke. She seemed to be looking at something far away, beyond Europe and the Atlantic.

I stopped thinking about America and the peasant. Her posture looked so weak, I barely managed to hold my tears. The nurse called, "Kostadina!" We both turned and said, "Yes." Mother forced a smile.

The nurse smiled back. She was holding a Pepsi bottle filled with muddy fluid and a cup placed upside down on top of it. "Hi," she said in a friendly voice. "This is a contrast fluid. It has quite an unpleasant taste, but try not to think about it," she said, winking, and handed the bottle to Mother. "Every fifteen minutes, drink a whole cup. Four of them in an hour. Don't miss any doses, please." Her tone was pleasant, but firm. She smiled, somewhat affectedly, I thought.

"I won't," Mother said.

The nurse nodded. "Good. I'll call you in an hour." She turned and began talking to a passing colleague.

"The clerk said it would be a half hour wait. Now it's another hour more," I said, feeling irritable. I took the bottle from my mother's hand and poured the first cup, checking my watch. "Okay, start drinking."

Suddenly, Mother's face contorted in the most astonishing way: her eyebrows furrowed, lines formed on her forehead, and her eyelids drooped. She breathed heavily, her nostrils flaring and the skin on her cheeks and under her eyes wrinkling. At that moment, she looked older than ever.

"What's wrong?" I asked, alarmed.

"It hurts badly…since the biopsy. My stomach, too." She brought the cup to her quivering lips, drank from it, and made a face. "This is awful."

She had been suffering more than she showed. That's the way she was. She always hid the bad things, especially things about herself and the family, from everyone else. While we waited, she kept sipping the fluid between doses, lost in thought. Finally, the nurse called us. I helped Mother up, taking the nearly empty bottle from her and handing it to the nurse. Then we followed her to the scanning room.

A doctor sat in front of a computer, slowly moving the mouse around the pad. He nodded when we said hello, not taking his eyes off the screen. From time to time, he looked through a window into an adjoining chamber. The scanner, a strange looking machine, was in the center of the chamber.

On the doctor's signal, the nurse led us inside the chamber and told Mother to take her top off. She was unsteady and she put her hand on my shoulder, so as not to lose her balance. I helped her. When I took her bra off she became uncomfortable. I wasn't, but I got scared when I saw that her skin had a yellowish tint and her breasts were half the size of the perfectly shaped ones I remembered.

I hung her clothes up and put her handbag on the chair. When I turned back to her, Mother's eyes were searching for mine. She had one leg on the scanner's table and was struggling to pull the other up. I ran over, grabbed the ankle of her dangling left leg, brought it up to the table, and laid it next to the other leg. I centered the tiny pillow under her hair, which was wet with sweat. She crossed her hands on top of her abdomen, and I turned away. It reminded me of—Suddenly, the nurse gave me an okay sign with her head from the other side of the window and motioned for me to leave the chamber.

Once I was in the other room, the procedure began. I heard an electrical noise as the machine came to life. I stood behind the doctor, watching Mother's body disappear into the tunnel. Slices of her body appeared on the computer screen. The doctor changed them quickly, while murmuring to himself. Mother's body emerged from the tunnel. Then it went back in. A couple of times it did this, back and forth, until the scanner's noise finally stopped.

"You can help her dress." The doctor spoke to me for the first time.

"Is everything all right, Doctor?" I could scarcely wait for his reply.

"I can't tell anything until the results are ready," he said, quickly.

"Okay," I mumbled, feeling disappointed. I went into the chamber and walked over to Mother, who was struggling to sit up. She looked disoriented, slow, and shaky.

"How do you feel, Mother?" I asked, as I helped her to stand.

"Strange," she said. We started to walk, but she pulled my arm. "Wait, I have to sit for a moment." A few minutes later, she stood again, and I helped put her clothes on.

We said goodbye to the doctor. The nurse took the referral slip and accompanied us out, telling us that the results of the scan and the biopsy would be ready in a week. She flashed her contrived smile again, then called the next patient in the waiting room.

Mother asked me to escort her to the bathroom. I waited for her, and when she came out, she had teary eyes. I said nothing, pretending not to notice. Finally, she said, "Let's get out of here. Fast. It has been a terrible day." She began walking faster, but couldn't keep it up for long.

Slowly, we made our way to the ground level. Once outside, I called a taxi. My stomach was grumbling from hunger, as was Mother's, so I bought a bagel and yogurt drink. She took one bite and gave me the rest. The taxi arrived and, when we got in, she curled into the corner of the back seat, closed her eyes, and crossed her hands. She looked like she was asleep, but I didn't want to know what she was dreaming. I just kept chewing the bagel, sipping the yogurt, ignoring the awful singing of the taxi driver, and staring blankly into the endless woods ahead. I tried not to think. I had no desire to unveil future before its time.

5

Diagnosis

After we got back from the hospital, Mother took a painkiller and a tranquilizer, then went straight to bed. As usual, Bisera came over that afternoon. Mother had told me Bisera hadn't missed a visit with her for the last couple of years. She had helped Mother a great deal when my father was ill. She'd helped bathe him, bandage his persistent toe infection, and measure his blood pressure every day. She also calmed him down when he yelled at Mother for no reason. Bisera told me that, when Father got frail, Mother would yell back at him. Obediently, he would shut up, aware of his dependency on his much-younger wife. Too bad that Mother had the ability to confront him only for a short time, I thought, watching her dozing face moving in discomfort on the pillow.

Father loved Bisera. He constantly spoke of how essential she was to the family. Of the three of us, she actually helped me the most. Otherwise, I would have had to come back to help Mother with Father, who required intensive care in the two years before he died. He suffered from high blood pressure, kidney failure, thrombosis in his legs, a weakened heart, and, most of all, the psychological damage that came from his tough upbringing and his World War II experiences. As far as I know, Father had been bedridden since he received his first pension payment. The collapse of both: Tito's Yugoslavia and his idealism, for which Father had almost lost his life during the war, depressed him greatly. He refused to take care of himself and made a slave of my mother, forcing her to do the smallest things, even to bring glasses of water to his bed when he was perfectly able to get them himself.

After witnessing his behavior, I wondered if some people were born like that. If they had lived in America, Mother would have divorced Father a long time ago. But in my homeland, divorced women are labeled as unsuitable, have hard times to remarry, and are even compare to whores. In any case, Mother would have had nowhere to go, no job and no money. Her parents were dead, her siblings had their own families, and we lived in a tight economic market with no job opportunities. Like most of the wives in our society, she knew that she was stuck with her husband, and had to tolerate him. She also knew that marrying him had been her choice, that no one had chosen him for her. Her only consolation was that she would never have to worry about money. When Father died, she got his pension, which was one of the highest in the country.

I could see the pills start to work on Mother. Her fingers and her parted lips trembled. It's from the strain of the biopsy and the scanning, I concluded, as I watched her a little bit longer, then left Mother's bed and joined Bisera at the dining room table.

"She was in a lot of pain after the biopsy," I whispered to Bisera. "I had to help her with virtually everything. She was so weak."

"Seeing her every day, it was clear to me she was going downhill," Bisera said, also keeping her voice low. "She usually hides her weakness and suffering, but since last year, she hasn't been able to cook, walk, or garden. Not like she used to. I helped her to do these things. Of course, she never told you. She didn't want you to worry. She only wanted you to enjoy your life in America. In fact, she begged me not to tell you a word about her condition. I was not going to anyway. I wanted the same thing for you: to be happy, to explore your interests and enjoy your youth. You are young only once."

Bisera stopped whispering and looked at Mother, who was now resting calmly. "I so hoped that she would have a peaceful life after your father died and that she would finally be free of his pressure. She'd taken enough from him…you know that. But my hope is fading now, and that hurts me the most."

"Me, too. But her freedom came too late. He is a part why she is like this, a big part. The way he humiliated her. I hate him," I hissed.

"Don't talk against them. They did a lot for you, they rescued you from that terrible orphanage. They deserve your complete respect. Both of them." She avoided looking at me for a while, and then asked, "When are the results going to be ready?"

"Next week." I noticed a spider in the corner above my mother's head, spinning a web. Even though I have arachnophobia I didn't try to kill it, Mother believed spiders brought good luck, and I hoped she was right.

"I'll go now." Bisera stood and, as usual, I escorted her outside. We stopped at the front gate and she turned to me.

"I hope the doctor is wrong," she said.

"I hope so, too," I said, doubtfully.

"Good night," she said, hugging me. "If you need me, don't hesitate to call anytime. Understand?"

"Yes. Thank you, Auntie Bisera. Sleep well." Her hug was comforting, but her trembling betrayed the fear she felt.

As time went by, Mother's movements became slower and more painful. Some days, the pain was so intense that I gave her a double dose of painkillers

"We shouldn't have gone to that damned doctor," she said one day, as I read the label on her medicine.

"No. It's better to prevent than to cure, mother," I said, still trying to read the tiny print.

"What does it say?" she asked, sipping the tea I had made from the fresh mint we grew in our back yard.

"It says the pills are very safe." I pretended to read, recalling the times when Mother would tell me that positive lies were good, after lying to Father that her just-bought dresses, shoes, and cosmetics were old. Or when her oldest brother was dying from lung cancer and she would try to console him by saying that it was just a bad case of emphysema and he would be healthy soon. And at any time she would describe to strangers how wonderful her marriage to my father was.

"Besides soothing the pain, the doctor told me they help your digestion and the circulation in your leg." I made that up, too. The drug was a plain metha-done-based painkiller.

"Good." She smiled, delighted to hear that something would cure her limping leg and restore her self-confidence and vanity.

I was glad to use what she taught me: that positive lies can help in certain circumstances. It was the only way to make her take the drug, anyway. And it made her calm, even made her smile. Her method of positive lying made us happy. It worked well.

In the summer Macedonia often seems more like part of the Sahara than of Europe. That June 19, when I went to pick up the test results, people all around me were sweating. Most of them didn't use underarm deodorant, and I longed to be among Americans, who smelled so clean by comparison.

The doctor wasn't in his office. With some help from a janitor, an elderly gypsy woman who pointed me towards the end of the hall, I managed to find him in one of the rooms. The space was filled with beds, laid out close to one another, and it reeked of urine. I walked over to the doctor, who was talking with a nurse next to one young man's bed. She adjusted the infusion bottle on the hanger above the bed while the young man stared at her derriere. When the doctor noticed me, he whooped, "You're here. Good. Wait for me in the hall, please."

He acted so cheerful I thought maybe he had misdiagnosed Mother. Almost playfully, I said, "Okay. Thanks," and made my way between the beds back to the hall. Some of the patients whimpered loudly. They grimaced in pain, struggling to remain alive.

It's scary to see what disease and old age can do to people. I've always respected and helped sick and elderly people. I'm not getting any younger and may be weak and sick myself one day. I believe in karma. I've never understood why people celebrate their birthdays and other anniversaries. It just means you're one year closer to your frail and ailing days and your inevitable death. What's there to celebrate? People claim they are celebrating one more year of being alive, but that doesn't change the fact that they will eventually reach their feeble and unwell days. I tell people not to be in a rush to celebrate birthdays and anniversaries. I don't, and I always feel younger than I am. But people don't listen to me. I've stopped caring about this, having finally realized that humans are incredibly stubborn creatures. Listening to the patients' agonized cries, I was reminded how much the idea of aging terrified me.

Twenty minutes later, the doctor walked into the corridor, taking the stethoscope from his ears and hanging it around his neck. He carried a big tan envelope in his left hand. Pulling the X-ray from it, he held it up towards the fluorescent lights on the ceiling. He pointed at a small shadow on the charcoal-colored negative and said, "Your mother has *Adeno-carcinoma tu recti*, a colon cancer. It's located low, not far from the anus. The biopsy confirmed the cancer." He slid the X-ray back into the envelope and continued talking. "After the operation, we have to close the anus and attach a disposable bag, a colostomy bag, to her stomach so she can void her bowels. If the cancer had been on the upper part of the colon, the bag wouldn't have been necessary. We could have just removed the malignancy and rejoined the colon. Unfortunately, that's not the case here. The good news is that the scan shows that no other organs are cancerous. For now." He pulled a half letter-sized piece of paper from his pocket and held it out to me.

Swiftly, I plucked it from his hand. I suddenly hated him. I thought I'd been prepared for the truth; I wasn't.

"Son, the sooner you bring your mother in for the operation, the better. Many people live a long time after this surgery, if they act soon enough. We don't want the tumor to spread."

It took me a while to find my voice. "How am I going to tell her?" I asked, looking directly into his eyes. He gazed back at me in his detached, professional manner.

"Bring her here. I'll tell her. In America, doctors tell the true diagnosis directly to the patient. I prefer that."

"I do, too. I want to tell her. But what if she doesn't want the operation?" I asked, my voice quivering.

The doctor stood on his toes for a second, like many of my teachers did when students asked difficult questions. He moved closer, looking solemn, and said, "The cancer will clog the colon eventually. This will cause great pain, because her stomach will balloon, ready to rupture from the pressure. You don't want to hear about where she might defecate from in that case. It would be a nasty mess and require emergency surgery. I'm sure you don't want that for your mother. You, or someone else, must convince her to have the operation."

"Maybe it's better to take her to America?" I kept hoping there might be an alternative.

"There's no cure. They would do the same thing. They have better technology, but it would cost a fortune. She doesn't have American insurance. Here, the operation is still almost free. I always tell people there were some wonderful things about socialism, and we're all going to cry if we lose them, especially socialized medicine. So don't take her to America." He patted my shoulder. "It's hard, but you should take my advice."

"How long will she live?" My jaw shook as I asked.

"No one can say for sure."

I stared at him, still feeling his hand pat my shoulder in a perfunctory expression of compassion. He put his arm around me as we walked to the elevator. I shook his hand, speechless, before we parted. In America, the doctors could be friendly, but before they see you, they make sure you have insurance. They would diagnose me quickly, rushing to get to the next client, and definitely never embraced me to feel better. So why the hell was I upset? Here, I had a doctor who was helpful, honest, and ethical, and who never asked me for money or favors. The twenty bucks I'd given him was by my choice.

I wished my father were alive. It was odd. I'd never felt more insecure. Actually, I was afraid of being alone, without any family. I couldn't believe that I—an independent spirit—was longing for a family.

As soon as I got back in town, I went to Bisera's house. She could tell just by looking at me that the news was bad, and she hugged me before I could say a word.

Weeping on my shoulder, she asked, "What are we going to do?"

I thought I had no tears left, but they began again.

"I couldn't sleep last night," she said, making snuffling noises.

"Neither did I. Or Mother. What does it matter? After this?" I pulled away from her embrace and retrieved the doctor's report from my pocket, offering to let her look at it.

She studied it for a moment, then handed the paper back to me. I stuffed it in my pocket and began walking back and forth in the hall. Bisera began to cry.

"The doctor recommended an immediate operation, or she'll be in terrible pain," I said. "If I can convince her to have a colostomy, the doctor told me she could live a long life. Many people have."

Bisera's face dimmed with disappointment and anger. "An operation? A colostomy? Your mother's going to die if she hears this. A lady like your mother with plastic bags hanging on her? Oh, Jesus, my Lord, forgive me!"

"The doctor told me to tell her the truth. I think I should."

When I said that, her body quaked, as if an electric current had hit her. Her face blanched into a pale lemon-toned hue.

"Don't you dare!" she said. Her eyes flashed with anger I'd never seen before. Her voice was never so defiant. "Are you out of your mind? You and your doctor! What do you think this is? America? We don't tell people they have cancer. You'll kill her if you do!"

She paused, collecting herself, then said, "I understand, though. You've started thinking like an American. But the American way doesn't work here. Not at all. Doctors here aren't sued for not telling patients about their terminal illnesses. In America, you have too many greedy lawyers, looking for new ways to sue people. We don't have that mentality yet. Thank God. So don't worry. And, believe me, no one in the world wants to know that his or hers days are numbered. No one. Even in America, I'm sure."

I never would've guessed Bisera knew that much about America. I considered myself mature for my age, yet I felt like a child before this woman who had experienced so much turmoil in her life. She radiated confidence and what she said made sense. We faced each other for a while, saying nothing. Through an open window, I could hear cats hissing and crying somewhere out on the street. Bisera and I acted like cats meeting at the border between their territories, debating whether to part or fight.

"Okay," I said, breaking the silence. "I won't say a word to her. But you must help me convince her to get that operation as soon as possible. No one can do it better than you. Mother trusts you more than she trusts me."

Bisera embraced me, and I felt her devotion to my mother in the embrace. "Your poor mother," she whimpered. "I hope she'll handle it bravely. My aunt died from cancer. I know what cancer is about. It's Hell!"

Shaking my head, I left Bisera's house and trudged home. I didn't know what cancer was about. I had always envisioned cancer as a devil's whip flogging human souls, and I continuously questioned why God let it happen only to a certain number of us. Why hadn't he chosen Father, the hard-core heretic, instead of Mother, who believed in Him so piously? Sometimes, I caught my mother praying to Him and His Family to spare her from suffering, and it didn't make any sense. Shouldn't God love us all, according to the holy books and the religious institutions? Shouldn't he protect us all from evil diseases and treat us all equally?

My neighbors back in New Jersey, Nancy and Rhonda, told me that cancer is suffering we have to go through like Jesus did. If that was true, something was very wrong. Why would God want us to suffer like Jesus? Why would people believe in such an evil, selfish, bastard of a God? Were those "believers" insane, were they pretenders, did they believe in order to escape their bitter reality, or what? Bullshit! I thought. When I got home, I hugged my mother, who lay sleeping, and listened to her heartbeat. It sounded like the most beautiful clock in the world.

First, I tried to do it myself, then I used Mother's closest friends as my missionaries to convince her to submit to the surgery. Whenever she heard the word "hospital," she would say, "Okay, if I die, I die. But not there. Here, in my home. Ever since I saw that damned doctor, I've gotten worse. I should have never gone there. I made a huge mistake."

I wondered if she knew what was really going on, especially when I had to double the dosage of the painkillers and constantly lie that it was to soothe her colon inflammation. She would ask me when the pain would get better and I would conjure up more lies. Constant deception was a very exhausting job. It required professional acting ability. I was good at it. It was my childhood dream to be an actor.

After Bisera failed to persuade Mother, my last hope was Mother's youngest brother, who she loved dearly. When I called him, he said the doctor's diagnosis might be mistaken, and he would try to find a more effective anti-hemorrhoidal medicine for his sister. I told him over and over how important the surgery was, but he wouldn't believe me. After a long and exhausting conversation, he accepted my offer to send him the doctor's report. Two days later, after checking with his doctor friend, he called me back. He said he was shocked by the bad news and he couldn't stand the thought of his sister's unfortunate destiny. Uncle pleaded that he needed time to put himself together from the shock, that he was in such agony. I didn't believe him. All I heard was his fear of being next on the list. His father and his eldest brother and sister had died from cancer, and now his other sister had it. I said nothing. I needed him. I felt relieved when he said he'd come the following week to talk with Mother. But he didn't keep the promise. He scheduled another date, and again he didn't show up. Uncle finally came two months later, when he was in the area on business.

Mother trusted him and loved him more than anyone in the family. He spent a lot of time drinking our Turkish coffee, but he didn't bother to try to persuade Mother to get the operation. Uncle was simply a greedy son of a bitch. In disgust, I was accompanying him out the house when he asked me, "Why are you so concerned about your mother's health? Or are you more concerned about the inheritance?"

Anger built up inside of me, like lava in a volcano. For a moment, I thought I would explode. Instead, I took a deep breath and said, calmly, "Dear Uncle, I love my mother more than anyone in my life. My father left everything to me, according to a testament he created in Mother's presence, in court. Even if they hadn't created the testament, as you know, I don't have any brothers or sisters and by law the inheritance would go to me. I could've just stayed in America, abandoned Mother, even thrown her out of the house, and still gotten their property. So, what is your point?"

I had much more to say. I wanted to jump on him and tear his Adam's apple from his throat with my teeth. Was it worth it to end up in jail for this idiot and never see America again? I scrutinized him like a tiger eyeing its potential victim. The sarcastic smile Uncle gave me as he turned and walked away showed how "wounded" he was. I was still an angry tiger, ready to jump and claw at his back. What for, though? It was enough that I would get Mother's inheritance instead of him, that he would not profit from my family. My fingers grasped the white painted wire of the gate as I watched him slowly disappear from sight. The man was incapable of love and had no concern for Mother. Are we really the highest form of life on earth, I wondered? Could animals be this nasty?

Unfortunately, Uncle wasn't the only one in the family who wouldn't accept the idea that an adopted child could truly love its surrogate mother. Most people didn't. They would pretend they believed it for my benefit. But I could tell they thought differently: that an adopted child would never feel the strong connection that a child related by blood—the clone they thrived to create—would feel for his parents. People in my homeland were not proud to be foster parents. It was considered abnormal. I was constantly exposed to that kind of thinking and it hurt, but I fought against it by showing off my strong ties with my parents. My relationship with my parents was special, closer in many ways than that of many parents and their biological children. Therefore, I had a dual obligation to take care of them and always be there for them. First, I respected my adoptive parents as my saviors; second, I respected them as my nurturers who expected me to help them when they got old and weak. That's how I always felt, and I knew other adopted children who felt the same way.

6

Connection

Fall came, changing the landscape. I wished I could change Mother's mind about going to the hospital. I begged everyone who visited us to talk to Mother about the importance of the surgery, but she wouldn't give in. To Bisera and me, her behavior wasn't a surprise, but for the locals it was. They began to gossip about it, about her stubbornness.

Every morning, Mother and I would start the day in the garden, drinking Turkish coffee and watching people pass on the street in front of our home. In the past, we usually had a maid, but after she began taking the medication, Mother started doing the housekeeping herself. It made her feel healthy. I would help her clean and sometimes prepare lunch. She knew I had never liked to vacuum, even less to work in the kitchen. After lunch, we would watch her favorite shows for a while, then take a siesta. Before sunset, we would work in the garden, have a light dinner after the evening news, and watch the late cinema before going to bed. A couple of days a week, I would rent a car and take Mother to the lake. We would have dinner at one of the restaurants, sometimes even stay for shows so we could listen to the bands. Mother had always enjoyed going out. I tried to do this as much as possible, as often as she could handle it. Locals began to gossip about our unusual ideas of mother-son fun—unusual for the province, that is—and Mother and I would quietly giggle anytime we saw their grudging and jealous faces.

We had fun, and I was glad to see her happy and laughing again. As the days passed, however, her condition changed drastically. The cancer devoured her body, and after a while, she couldn't clean or spend a lot of time cooking. She stopped making intricate dishes and her appetite vanished. The pain worsened to the point I started giving her three analgesics a day, in the morning, afternoon, and at night. The cancer ruled her life and mine, tormenting me almost as much as her. Now and then, I had to disappear and seclude myself. But I would never leave Mother before making sure that she was in a good mood. It was usually when someone came to visit, when Mother would act as if nothing was happening to her, stubbornly hiding her misery. I would leave thinking I was escaping the horror, maybe go visit friends. In the middle of a conversation, Mother would pop up in my subconscious, at which point I would excuse myself and rush back to the house. The guilt from not being with her forced me to do that. That, and the fact that the countdown towards her death had begun. I was her only hope, and I couldn't be away from her for long.

Gypsy summer takes place in the Balkans in late autumn or early winter when the days are still mostly warm and sunny. I always loved that time of year. I took my old bike from the storage house, cleaned it, oiled its chain and pedals, and began to ride to the lake. The wind smelled like it had in the past, when as a child and later as a teenager, I would bike to the lake after the tourists were gone and the locals were busy with the apple harvest. The roads to the lake were abandoned then, and no one could see me riding alone. I didn't need to be embarrassed by my loneliness. After riding about seven miles I arrived at the shores of Prespa Lake. I leaned the bike against a willow tree, sat on the beach, and watched the lake's green water dance against the backdrop of the blue mountain ranges on the Greek and Albanian sides. It was a moment for meditation, reminding me again of the way things used to be.

I took my clothes off and walked into the lake. Welcoming its aroma into my pores and communing with nature always seemed like making love with some incredibly peaceful and beautiful stranger. An old feeling of loneliness haunted me, commingling with the new one, the helplessness that came from being unable to help Mother. I felt like a tiny lost particle in the vastness of space. I lay on the sand and looked at my naked body. I wasn't innocent any longer as I was the first time I went there and awakened my latent sexuality by touching my virginal body.

"No one will ever be as close to me as Mother," I yelled. "The hell with the future! I want seclusion! I have needs!" I got up and ran to the water, bending down to drink it, then stroked my neck and chest with one hand, reaching below my bellybutton with the other. My anxiety vanished. Still, the experience was nothing like the last time I was there, when I fervently took and enjoyed the new pleasures that my body offered me.

"I was a lonely virgin then. Now I am a suffering grown son," I said to my only audience, a pelican, whose eyes seemed oddly human as it watched me without condemnation.

I jumped into the water and the pelican followed. Again, I drank from the lake as I swam, going faster with each stroke. I recalled the day when, after swimming in that same water, I discovered that my body had changed, that I was growing up. As I lay on the beach, so long in the past, water droplets shone on my smooth skin, sparkling the strong Macedonian sun. Body consciousness, self-appreciation, I thought, observing my body parts, and I dove into the water again. Confused, hurt, and yet, ready to love and accept myself, I fought my loneliness then, just as I was fighting my anguish for Mother now.

I left the water, shivering. The chill gave me the creeps, and I started crying for Mother, which made it worse. I picked some wild herbs and fruit as I walked in the forest. I didn't dance, as I had years ago when I felt the rain wash the remains of my first orgasm from my body. But still I sang my poems to the trees, told them my stories, and said I didn't need friends as I used to. I kept talking to the lake, to forget my mother's approaching exodus from this world. On the beach, in the water, and in the woods, I could dance, sing, and run nude. I was far from people, my home, and the stupid rules and customs of my town. I felt pure. Naked, I felt free. In any season, I sought contact with my first and only legitimate teacher: nature. I wanted to stay away forever from that ugly swamp called society. I couldn't bear the thought of facing peoples' masks built of phony words, attitudes and actions. I didn't want to be part of them, of a society without true individuals, as well as collective, freedom and identity. I didn't want to survive just for the sake of survival. I was ashamed of the human race. I wanted to belong to another one—an honest and kind one.

Reluctantly, I dressed and mounted my bike to ride back to town. Lost in thought as I rode, I could feel the bike shake from time to time as I strayed off the asphalt and into the adjacent cornfields. In mulling over the past I was just trying to avoid the bitter reality waiting for me in the present. I wished I could escape from myself, but I knew I couldn't; I had tried too many times before and failed. I kept trying over and over anyway. I didn't give up then and I still don't now. If I give up, I might as well be dead.

"You have to go back to America. You're wasting your time here with me," Mother said, sipping coffee as we sat at the garden table and watched the passers-by on the main street. "Here, your generation is sinking in unemployment and poverty, regardless of education and skills."

"Finally, you're admitting I made the right decision leaving Yugoslavia before the civil war." It was something I had always yearned to say.

"Yes, Father and I were wrong to give you a hard time. We were selfish. We were afraid we wouldn't see you any more. We were scared to be left alone. You said you'd always be there, for us…for me. And you kept that promise. I remember when you also told us, 'Small country, small opportunities, and less freedom to explore.' You were right. That's what's happened to Macedonia and the other former Yugo-states. They're tiny and weak now. America must be an endless land."

Mother finished her coffee and took a deep breath, rotating her cup, then turning it upside down so the residue would flow from the bottom to the sides. She was ready for the neighbors to come and foresee her destiny by interpreting the patterns that the dried coffee mud made on the porcelain. It was a popular form of entertainment that the Balkan people inherited from the Turks, who reigned over the peninsula for five centuries. Mother enjoyed the ritual.

"How am I going to leave you alone, Mother?" I asked, trying to catch her attention, which was directed somewhere into the green of a nearby pine tree.

"I'll be alright. I can manage alone. I'll enjoy life without your father. Bisera is always there if I need a companion. We'll go to the mineral spas and on vacations again. Don't worry, and don't try to convince me to have the operation any longer. It's useless. Sorry, I cannot do it. Go back to America. If something goes wrong and I need your help, I'll call you. It only takes eight hours to get here."

Her stubbornness was good back when she fought with Father for hours, after he yelled at me about something. Now it was dangerous, and I wished she knew that. Maybe she did, but her fear of hospitals overshadowed her rational thinking. "Come to America with me," I said.

"Not like this, in this condition. I want to get healthy first. Then you can show me Fifth Avenue and take me to the big stores. You know that I'd love America; I could spend winters over there and summers here, as we always planned it. Oh, I wish I was alright."

"You will be, Mother."

"When?"

"Soon," I lied. I didn't pause, afraid that I would create suspicion with silence, but kept repeating words of false encouragement. It was so tiresome to say things I didn't mean, over and over, especially to my own mother. She had no clue what was really happening to her. Not yet.

A gaggle of women who lived on our street, the "gossip society" as I liked to call them, appeared at the front gate, and I jumped up to show them in. For once, I was glad to see them. Mother showed them the new doily she had knitted. They were amazed by its patterns, and as usual, began to fight over who would get the second ownership for it. Mother had created one of the biggest doily collections in town. Usually, a mother did this for her daughter, so she could add it to her dowry. Her girlfriends often commented that her efforts were useless, since she had a son. Mother would just smile proudly and say, "It's for my future daughter-in-law. I'll give it to her. Why not?" My face would blush then.

When nature finished painting its landscapes with dazzling shades of red and gold I flew back to America. Mother and Bisera escorted me to the airport in Skopje. Mother's sister-in-law, the wife of her elder brother who had died from lung cancer, drove us. She was a tough woman, with enough testosterone in her veins that she had to shave regularly to keep from growing a mustache. She had been a partisan during World War II, then a farmer. Even when my uncle was alive, she did most of the work around the apple orchards. She drove tractors, cursed like a hard-core truck driver, smoked cigarettes that hung from the corner of her mouth, and played cards with the men, always joking and ridiculing them. She was something. A real butch.

I could tell my departure was upsetting Mother. She tried to hide her face, but I would catch an occasional glimpse of her in the rear view mirror, forcibly laughing at my aunt's jokes. She didn't want me to feel uncomfortable. She managed to blink away some of her tears, but the rest slid down her cheeks.

At the airport, we waited in the bar. We didn't talk much, just listened to my aunt's jokes. When my flight was announced, they escorted me to the gate. After my butch aunt and Bisera hugged me goodbye, Mother gave me a long embrace.

"Don't worry, Bazhe. It's only natural for a mother to cry when her child is leaving. I can't control it. I'm happy that you are going where you belong and continuing your life. I'll be cured soon and come join you." She straightened up and her beautiful smile appeared, then slowly wilted. She took a small, fancy-looking box from her purse, and said, "This is for you."

I opened it quickly. In it was a gold bracelet and a chain. "Beautiful," I said and kissed her. I put the jewelry on and she helped me, forcing a smile. During my stay, she had tried to appear as healthy as possible. It broke my heart to see her pretend and I tried not to show her how upset I was. She noticed it, though, so I said, "It's only natural for a son to be sad when he is parting from his mother," as if that were the reason. I smiled, concealing the pessimism I felt about her making it to America. As I hugged her tightly, her kisses made me feel unworthy. I kissed her back. I heard the last call for passengers on my flight and gently pulled away from her embrace. Her touch had never felt so significant. I walked away slowly, turning to look back before entering the boarding corridor.

Her teary eyes shone like ambers under the bright halogen ceiling lights. I entered the corridor, and suddenly its blank white wall blocked Mother from my sight.

I began to wail, thinking about how I might never see her again. The security officer asked me if I was okay. People around me turned to look.

"No," I said, "Nothing is all right. You can't win against something that will send you to your grave, to rot."

Total silence fell around me. Some people looked sad, others confused, including the officer who may have thought I was freaking out or something.

After the officer checked my passport and ticket, I stepped into the passageway leading to the plane. It seemed like an underground channel, and I wondered if Mother's soul would travel in underground channels until it was liberated somewhere, somehow. I thought about that during the flight over the Atlantic. I also thought again about the age-old questions of who and what we are and what life was supposed to be about. I couldn't eat, read, or be at peace. It was the worst and longest flight in my life. Even the in-flight movie, a comedy, reminded me of death. Everything did. I couldn't wait to get back on the ground and disappear in the crowd at JFK. It would help me forget about life and death.

In autumn, Morris County resembles Prespa County in its landscape and climate. Fortunately for me, life is different in America; the quick pace of New Jersey kept me from dwelling on Mother. I would call her on Fridays, and she would tell me that everything was okay and that the pain wasn't bothering her much. She was lying, so as not to interfere with my life in America. She probably considered it a sin to create any inconvenience for me. Every Friday, our homilies flew back and forth through the wires between me and Mother, me and Bisera, me and the neighbors, or whoever else I would catch at our house. Lies, lies, lies, all because of cancer. All of us behaved like obsequious children afraid to upset their autocratic fathers. It was sickening, yet necessary.

Thanksgiving came, making me more depressed. We had people over for dinner and my lover Fred, made lots of food. Half of it was thrown out. None of our friends seemed to care that there were countless people around the world, dying of hunger. I kept envisioning children in third-world countries turning into living skeletons while I was scraping the plates, and I got so sick that I threw up. Fred and the guests were drinking in the living room, so no one noticed. I didn't drink. I rarely do. My only habit is smoking, my inheritance from the Balkans. I was glad to be done with Thanksgiving, even though I rarely eat more than I should. I cleaned up my mess. Cleaning was my contribution to our household, since I hated cooking. I devoured Fred's delicious dishes, though I wouldn't touch any made with meat. Most scientists are excellent cooks. If he would have been little less wasteful, I would've loved him much more.

It was good to be back at work at Lord & Taylor. I put in extra time, mainly to avoid the dark thoughts that kept tormenting me. The hour-long commute to and from New York City was the worst part. I just sat and stared at the monotonous suburban New Jersey landscape, while conflicting thoughts of the old times with Mother and the new reality flooded my mind. I became absent-minded, at work, at home, with friends, and with Fred. Sex with him became a duty. I got no pleasure from it at all. But I hid my feelings because I didn't believe in passing my misery on to others. I let my canvases and papers collect dust. All I could think about was cancer. Everything I painted and wrote was an ugly mess. The only thing that relaxed me, at least temporarily, was spending time with my cat, my most comforting companion.

On December 1, Bisera called me. I almost fainted when I heard her voice, thinking that Mother had died. I leaned against the kitchen counter for support.

"Bazhe, your mother gave in," Bisera said, sounding excited. "She'll have the operation. Her pain got much worse, so we saw the doctor. He told her about the tumor on her colon and that the only way to cure it was through surgery." She paused, and then said, more softly, "It was hard looking at the expression of horror on her face when the doctor explained that she would have a disposable bag attached to her stomach. Her only question for him was whether the thing could be removed one day. He lied to her and said 'Yes', to calm her down."

I could hear clicking and muted beeping on the line, over Bisera's breathing. I pictured Mother's reaction. I could hear her desperate questions to the doctor.

"The first aid squad came a couple of times," Bisera said. "They gave her injections. The old painkillers don't work any longer. The doctor replaced them with stronger morphine-based drops, called 'Heptanon.' He told me, confidentially, that it is a serious narcotic. You can't get it with a simple prescription; you need a special note, which he gave me. She has to have the operation soon, but there's a long waiting list. You have to think of someone, any connection that would help her, as soon as possible. We can't wait much longer. We've waited long enough."

I thought about how much easier that would have been if Father had still been alive, with all of his connections, but I didn't say anything.

Bisera continued to talk. "I'm calling from my home. Your mother doesn't know. She doesn't want to bother you with this. You know her. But you told me to call you when things got serious, so I am. I wish I didn't have to call you, but she needs you now. You're everything to her. I'm afraid you have to be here for the operation."

"Okay, Auntie Bisera, thank you for telling me. I'll pretend I don't know anything when I speak to her Friday. In the meantime, I'll try to think of a connection."

"Good, Bazhe. Goodbye now. Be brave."

"Goodbye, Auntie Bisera." Before I heard the receiver hang up at her end, I was putting together a mental checklist of people who might be helpful. It was amazing how quickly my mind could work when in desperation, putting my PC and Mac to shame. I dialed the Macedonian consulate in New York City and speak to the consul's secretary. Marina, was the daughter of a famous Macedonian painter who I had met through a friend. She immediately hooked me up with the son of a well-known surgical oncologist. Within a couple of days he had reserved a place in the hospital for Mother. Her surgery date was December 14. I called my travel agent and asked her to book me a flight. She told me no flights were available through the Austrian and Bulgarian airlines, the only ones that flew to Macedonia. She looked for connecting flights and other ways to get there and said that nothing was available before December 20. I began panicking, but she reassured me that seats usually became available, so I should calm down and wait. I had no other option, so I waited, hoping she was right.

The following Friday, Mother confessed about the operation. I told her that I would find a way for her to get in the hospital as soon as possible, and the next day, I called her back.

"Mother, our connection is Marjan, the son of an eminent doctor. He'll help you with everything you need regarding the admission and the surgery. He found the best doctors for your operation, which is scheduled for December 14. You should call him right away after we finish talking."

I gave her Marjan's number, listening to her breathing hard as she wrote it down. I could picture her fearful face reflected in the mirror beside the telephone stand, her pen scratching clumsily in the notebook that I had bought her at Bradlees.

"Bazhe, I'm very scared."

"Did you write down Marjan's number, Mother?"

"Yes, yes, I did. Thank you. I'm still not sure about the operation though."

"You must, Mother! Don't be a fool. You can't wait any longer!"

"The doctor told me I have a tumor. That's the same as cancer, isn't it?"

"No, it's not. What the hell are you talking about?" I shouted. "We all have tumors."

"He said that my tumor is bad," Mother murmured, fearfully.

"He wants you to be scared. You've got an inflammation of the colon, that's all."

"He said I'll wear a plastic bag on my stomach."

"So what? Do you know how many people wear those? Young and beautiful people, too. And after they are cured, they don't use the colostomy bag anymore. You won't either. Don't be a fool. Just do it. I'm coming as quickly as possible."

"Yes, please. I'm frightened. Sorry I'm telling you to come back."

"I was planning to come back, Mother. I hope I can get a ticket before the fourteenth. The travel agent's looking into it."

"I'm not as afraid now. I'll wait for you."

"Good, Mother. I'll see you soon, and after you are cured, we'll fly back to America together."

"I love you, son. Go now. You spend so much money calling me every Friday."

"It's okay, Mother, you are the only thing I care about."

Tearfully, she said, "I got you from the orphanage, a six-month-old, a few kilograms of flesh. I've nurtured you ever since with the greatest care. Indeed, if I had borne a hundred children, no one could have replaced you. You are the best. I love you more than anything in this world. More than myself."

I listened to the dial tone after she hung up, wondering if my biological mother could have loved me the way Mother did. Maybe. But no. No way! My birth mother gave me up. She abandoned me. Threw me away! How could I think such a thing? Even if I had hundreds of biological mothers, none of them could love me more than Mother. No one. Of this, I was certain.

7

Operation

On December 13, the day before Mother's surgery, the travel agent called to tell me that there was a last-minute opening on an Austrian flight. I was so delighted I could have jumped through the ceiling. My transfer to a Macedonian plane in Vienna was delayed, however, and I arrived in Skopje late afternoon, a couple of hours after Mother's operation. Marjan was waiting for me. The minute we met, I could see he was an easygoing guy, if a little spoiled by being a doctor's son. He was an economist, in his early thirties, married, with one child. Ten minutes passed without his mentioning Mother, so I said, "I hope my mother is doing well."

"She was doing great yesterday. She spoke only about you."

"Thank you for helping me. I hope I can return the favor someday."

"I didn't do this because I expect any favors from you. I want to help. My father taught me to be this way. It isn't just about money. He helps patients for the sake of his profession. He loves medicine."

"There are few people like him left," I said. I was truly pleased to have met him. I needed his kindness before seeing Mother. I was scared. I really didn't know what to expect.

On the way to the hospital, Marjan asked me about New York City, his favorite place. He was fascinated with what I told him. As we entered the hospital's parking lot, I stopped talking. I was filled with dread picturing the things that were done there.

"Your mother is over there." Marjan pointed towards the top of the gray highrise in the middle of the complex.

A large group of people stood in front of the building's entrance, where a doorman was posted. When he saw Marjan, the doorman smiled at him and yelled at the people to move aside for us. Marjan pulled a package of coffee from his pocket. He handed it off to the doorman, who stuffed it quickly inside his jacket and unlocked the door for us. To me, Marjan said, "Tip him!" I took all the singles from my wallet and handed them to the man. His eyes sparkled when he saw seven of them in his palm. His monthly salary was probably around a hundred dollars.

"Excellent," Marjan said, as we entered the elevator. "Always tip the doormen well if you want to get inside when patient visits are not permitted. Tipping with dollars can get you into the President's bedroom! Everyone is corrupt over here."

His laughter resounded through the white corridor as he guided me to the abdominal clinic, women's unit. There was no one at the reception desk. He stopped short, causing me to run into him.

"The next room," he gestured towards an open door ahead of us. "I'm not going in. You two should be alone." He grabbed my hand and shook it. When I thanked him again, he patted my shoulder and, turning, walked quickly back down the hallway.

The smells, mixtures of urine, perfume, pills, alcohol, antiseptic, fruits, and deteriorating flesh were traveling around. I couldn't stand them, yet I knew I had to get used to them. From behind me I heard a man sobbing. I knew it had to be Marjan, but I couldn't bear to turn and look at him. Maybe it's someone else, I thought, in denial.

I gulped an extra large breath before entering the room, slowly. To my left, I saw a line of beds. An elderly woman was sleeping in the first one. Her lips and hands quivered. The middle bed was empty. In the third, a heavy blond woman snored loudly. Her stained, unbuttoned nightdress was exposing half of her flesh. My eyes turned to the right, passed over an empty bed, and stopped at the middle one. Mother was lying peacefully on her back. Her eyes were closed. A transfusion bottle hung from a shiny metal pole above her head. Blood dripped from the bottle, down through a hose and into a needle that pierced a vein in her left arm, which rested on the edge of the bed. In the far bed, a woman sat, drinking from a white plastic cup. I said hello to her as I walked towards Mother. The woman looked distressed, like everyone else there.

"You're her son, aren't you?" the woman said.

"Yes, madam." I forced myself to smile. "Is she all right?"

"Yes. She was more disturbed about your delay then the operation. Since she showed up here, all she talks about is you."

I inspected Mother's body. Another plastic hose emerged from underneath the sheets and dangled into a metal urinal, half hidden under the bed. I leaned towards her and kissed her forehead. The woman abruptly turned towards the window. The twilight tinged her face and the tears on her cheeks with purple glare.

Mother's eyes opened. "Bazhe, you are here, my gold!" she murmured and spread her arms to hug me. Her left arm couldn't reach me because of the IV equipment, so with her right hand, she patted my hair. Her body looked bleached from the shortage of blood. She pulled my head towards her and began kissing my face.

"The operation was easy," she said. "I felt no pain at all. If I knew it, I would have done it a long time ago. I was so worried about you being late."

The bliss in her voice and her former beautiful smile returned, filling me with joy as I kissed her back. *She'd been in excruciating pain before the surgery.* I could tell that.

"The flight was delayed," I said. "I was supposed to be here before the operation. Sorry. This was the only connection I could find. All the other flights were booked."

"No need to apologize, son. Everything is all right now. Marjan told me that. He held my hand until the nurses took me in for the operation." She paused. I had felt exhausted from the trip, but her smile refreshed me and mitigated my guilt about not making it there before the operation.

Mother's look quickly changed to concern. "Marjan is a noble man. You should buy a gift for him and his family. He visited me every second day, and we've never even met before this. Make him a close friend."

"Sure," I said. "He is impressive."

"How did you find him?"

"Through Marina. A friend in New York. She's the daughter of a big artist."

"She must be nice, too. Send her many thanks from me."

"I will, Mother. I have to call her soon."

"I still can't believe you found a flight from America. That was a real surprise. Sorry I gave you all those headaches, refusing to come here to get the operation done. You are so good to me." Mother pulled me towards her trembling body and we exchanged kisses again.

Bending over her, I whispered, "We have to be good to each other, Mother. We only have one another."

"I love you so much, my gold." Mother smiled, though her eyes were wet.

It was hard to keep from crying, and I let my tears fall on Mother's shoulder. She won't suspect anything, I thought. She'll think these are my reunion tears. I must have hugged her for more than a half hour, when the on-duty nurse came in.

"You shouldn't be here, mister. The visiting time is between eleven and two." The nurse prepared a syringe and a needle, gesturing to the old woman to uncover her thigh.

"Please, nurse, let him stay for a while," Mother begged.

"What if the doctor sees him? I'll be in trouble," she said. She had an Eastern-Macedonian accent. She briskly stuck the old woman's thigh, evoking a groan. After giving the injection, the nurse moved to the foot of the old woman's bed, grabbed the chart hanging from the frame, and scribbled on it. She walked to the blond woman's bed and shook her awake, then injected her. As she was getting ready to leave, she turned towards me and said, "You have to go now."

"You mangy ghoul! He just arrived from America to see his mother, for Christ's sake!" the woman in the bed next to Mother's yelled. "You should be concerned about whether the patients need help. Once again, someone crapped in the bed across the hallway. Can't you smell the stench? Or are you paid to bother us? Get lost, bitch!"

The nurse threw her a mean look. "Tell them to pay me more, and I'll clean it. You aboriginal-hayseed cunt." She turned her back to us and left, laughing like a mule.

"Who do you think you are, slut? A townswoman? My ass. You stink more than any peasant in my village. All of you are here to fuck the doctors and get married! That's why you went to nursing school, to be a prostitute!" The woman hopped off her bed, glaring after the nurse for a few moments, then got back in. "She didn't inject me, damn it," she said, holding her head with both hands.

"Should I call her?" I asked.

"Hell, no. That needle won't make me healthier or more beautiful. Fuck it. That strumpet can go fuck herself!"

Everyone laughed aloud, except the old lady, who tried to subdue it. She acted like her whole body was in pain.

"She makes us laugh all the time," Mother said, looking at the woman, who was still mumbling curses. "This is my son, Bazhe. Bazhe, this is Lena."

I stood up and walked over to Lena, extending my hand. She grasped it firmly and shook it. Her fingers were rough from farm work. She was pretty, in a rough-edged way.

As we talked, I learned that her family owned a grape orchard in Central Macedonia and that she was a couple of years younger than Mother. Her curses sounded particularly nasty, spoken in her thick peasant's dialect.

"It seems as if they never operated on me," Mother said. "It's strange. No pain during the operation. Now and then it hurts, but nothing like before."

"What do you expect, woman. You were unconscious," Lena said. "Your surgery was a piece a cake. This is the third operation on my uterus. You're fine. You'll be out soon. I'll rot here."

"No, you won't. You're stronger than me," Mother replied, gazing at her with a look of sincerity. "And, again, thank you for cheering me up, Lena."

Mother turned to me. "She gave me such courage before the operation." To Lena, she said, "What would I have done without you?"

"Much better. You would've found a good-looking doctor to cheer you up instead." She chuckled. "You're a widow now, and entitled to a man. If I were an urban lady with a fine complexion like yours, I would've gotten any doctor in a second. Who wants to touch my sun-roasted skin? I can tell you've never worked in your life, have you?"

The women chortled, and the old woman complained, "Stop it, Lena, the laughter hurts me."

"C'mon, grandma. You're ninety and something and you still wanna live. What can we say? Who needs you any longer? It's time to recycle you!" Lena shouted flippantly towards the old lady's coiled frame.

The laughter was so loud it echoed out in the hallway. Lena became serious and looked at me.

"She doesn't have anybody to visit her," she said. "Her son and her daughter-in-law threw her in the stable after she got sick and wasn't able to help around the house. They hate her. She'd be better off dead, rather than putrefying with her cows and goats. Sad, isn't it? God only knows where her village is. Someplace where the turtles don't even fuck because they can't find one another?"

I tried to stop laughing. I was going to ask Lena if the old lady would get angry listening to her. She read my mind and started giggling. "She can't hear well. Only when I yell. So what if she hears me? I don't hate her. I'm only telling the truth."

After a while, everyone withdrew back into themselves, curled in their beds once again. I fed Mother some of the leftover soup sitting on her bedside table. I was wiping off her face and neck with a moist cloth when the nurse came to warn me that I should leave before the doctor's night visit. I kissed Mother.

"I'll see you tomorrow," I said.

She kissed me back and whispered in my ear, "Get friendly with the principal nurse. Throw a few dollars in her pocket. That'll do it."

"Sure, Mother. Marjan taught me that already."

I must keep every promise, even the smallest one, made to Mother. I had felt that way since I left home, and even more so since I found out she had cancer. After I left the hospital, I bought expensive presents for Marjan, his wife, and child, and went to their house, where Marjan was holding my luggage. They invited me to stay for dinner, and it was a real pleasure to eat a traditional Macedonian meal prepared by his wife. We had a healthy mixed Macedonian salad, delicious stew with fresh vegetables, kebab with the customary tasty paprika topping on the side, and crispy homemade whole-wheat bread.

After dinner, we sat in the living room, drank coffee, and talked. I realized then how much I missed Macedonian food and humor. When their son fell asleep on the sofa, I decided to go. They offered to let me sleep there, but I didn't want to disturb their happiness with my misery, so I told them that I would prefer to be alone.

I took a taxi to the Grand Hotel, located in the midst of the downtown district. It was my favorite hotel in town. I had many fond memories of the place from my student days. I stayed up watching satellite TV until late. It felt odd when I discovered the number of channels to choose from. I grew up having only one national station. Two more channels were added later. But living close to the border, we were able to pick up some others from Greece and Albania, as well.

I woke up as the dawn's light broke After a shower I went to the supermarket to buy Mother some oranges and a bottle of juice. The streets were filled with factory workers, walking, driving, or waiting at bus stops. It was too early to go to the hospital, so I went to a small café and had a strong double Turkish coffee. I killed some more time wandering around the city mall, and when my watch showed that it was almost 8 A.M., I walked to the hospital.

I looked for the surgeon who had operated on Mother. A frosty receptionist guided me to his office. When I tucked a couple dollars into her side pocket, she immediately became pleasant and told me to look for her if I had any trouble getting into the clinic. I waited while the doctor spoke with a couple that had arrived before me. After they were done, I went in. Interesting oil paintings hung on the walls of the doctor's office. It was clear that he appreciated avant-garde art. He was in his late thirties, balding, confident, quiet, and intelligent. As soon as I introduced myself, he offered me a seat and a cigarette. I pulled my American ones out and offered him one instead. He took it, lit mine first, then his, and bowed his head with gratitude. "You are Kostadina's son, aren't you?" he asked in a familiar way.

"Yes, doctor, I am." *Mother must have told the whole hospital about me.*

He inhaled hard on the cigarette and blew out smoke with a hissing sound. "Your mother had a tumor as big as a fist. It metastasized into the lymph glands of her pelvis. We took out as much as we could, then closed the wound, but we couldn't get it all. The tumor was only five centimeters above the anus, so we had to perform a colostomy and suture her rectum. But your mother is in bad condition. She will die."

He paused, took another forceful drag on his cigarette, and checked his open organizer. "I'm very sorry you came all the way from America to hear this. But I want you to know the truth. Do whatever it takes to help her go easier. That's all you can do." The surgeon avoided eye contact with me. The hopelessness in his voice made everything around me seem to turn gray, even the lively colors of his artwork.

"Can you predict how long she may live?"

"No one can answer that. Her heart is strong. She might live one year, maybe two…one thing is for sure, she won't get better. Gradually, the pain will increase and she will have to take stronger painkillers. When the pain is unbearable, she'll have to take morphine. She doesn't seem to know that she has cancer."

"I never told her."

"I thought so. She's not the type who could handle it. She was in a great panic before the surgery. Don't tell her I told you." He looked genuinely concerned. Someone opened the door, and the surgeon said, "I'm busy." The door closed again.

"Would it help to give her radiation or chemotherapy? Maybe I should take her to America?" I knew the answer, but I had to ask anyway. I kept searching for hope in his serious expression. "Are you sure she'll die? Maybe she has a chance?"

"Radiation and chemotherapy would prolong her life, but it would also weaken her body and her immune system. There are many unpleasant side effects, including hair and weight loss and nausea. She's a lady. She'd be devastated. You don't want that. In America, or wherever you take her, they can't do anything more than we would, that is give her painkillers and keep her clean and comfortable. *Summa summarum*, as we say, help her die in a dignified way."

There was nothing more to ask. I extended my hand and he shook it. I got up to leave but, before I opened the door, I turned and asked, "Can I visit you again for advice? Help? If I have any questions about Mother?"

"Oh, yes, feel free to do so," he replied, assuredly. He rose and walked towards me, pulling his wallet from his back pocket. "Here is my card. You are welcome to visit me at home. We'll have more time to talk there."

I thanked him for the invitation. As I opened the door, a man and a woman pushed me back in. A large, vociferous group had gathered in front of the office. I wove through the crowd and found myself in the middle of the busy hallway. A patient trudged down the hall, supporting herself with one hand on the white tiled wall. A relative was walking another patient, I assumed. A group of visitors poured out of one of the rooms. A couple of nurses ran by me. A medical technician pushed a hospital bed with squealing wheels out of an operating room. A young woman lay on it, still, and covered with bloody sheets. She looked dead. An elderly doctor followed them, saluting everyone. I ran to the bathroom. It smelled of puke, and I added my own. I washed my face and as I was drying it, glanced in the mirror. I looked like I had been crying, though I hadn't. I had suppressed the urge, but now tears were welling in my eyes. It was hard to hold them in. I practiced smiling a few times, until I was satisfied that I could do it. I had to be smiling when I entered Mother's room.

Mother was staring at the ceiling when I walked in. The blank white space was her silent companion. Sad, but true for anyone stuck in a hospital bed. She tried to smile when she saw me. I put the oranges and the juice on her side table and hugged her.

"This is the last bottle of blood I have to take. I can't wait to give you a big hug." She spoke cheerfully, looking at the blood dripping through the hose into her vein. "I guess I lost a lot of blood after the operation." Her sideways look at me was more serious.

"That's common, Mother," I said, and kissed her. Then I took the bedpan to the bathroom, to empty it.

"Would you please brush my teeth?" Mother asked, sounding both hopeless and embarrassed.

I found her brush and toothpaste in a drawer and poured a glass of water from the sink. After arranging everything on the side table, I started to lift Mother into a slightly more upright position. Surprisingly, she had the strength to lift herself. I took a basin from under her bed, squeezed paste on the brush, and began brushing her teeth, holding the basin under her chin with my other hand. When I was done brushing, I gave her the water and held the basin while Mother rinsed her mouth and spit. When she finished, she laid back, gradually. She said it was the first time she had sat up since the surgery. It had only lasted a short time, but she was glad she could do it. I put the basin back on the floor and moistened some gauze, using it to clean off the foam that remained around her lips, then to wipe her face and neck. I cleaned the basin and the toothbrush in the sink, cleaned the top of her side table, and sat back on her bed holding her hand.

"The surgeon told me I would be able to walk soon." She sounded thrilled. "Have you spoken to the surgeon yet?"

"Yes, Mother. He said everything is fine. Nice man. A good doctor."

"Not really. If he was good, the pain wouldn't be bothering me still."

Leila spoke up. "For God's sake, woman. You just got sliced. What're you expecting, a miracle? It takes time for the wounds to heal."

Mother shook her head. "I don't think my surgeon is experienced enough. He's young and has a long road ahead of him. Whenever I ask him about my illness, he nods his head, but never gives me specific answers. He just agrees with everything I say. It's like I'm talking to myself. The most he's ever said is, 'It takes time, madam. It takes time.' I don't think he knows much. But you should buy him a present of appreciation, anyway, Bazhe. We might need him in the future."

"Yes, Mother," I said. I wondered if she had the slightest clue that she has been manipulated by all of us. Not yet, I decided, when I saw the subdued sparkle of hope that gleamed in her eyes.

Shortly after the lunch and after the on-duty doctor's visit, a young woman wearing a neat white and blue uniform came to see my mother. She carried a brown leather suitcase. She cordially introduced herself and told us that she represented a company that made colostomy supplies. Mother was flustered when the woman asked to see her colostomy. She turned her head away from me as the woman rolled her nightdress up. She began crying, and her face turned scarlet.

"It's okay. It's fine," the lady-rep said, gently. She stroked Mother's hair.

It was shocking to see plastic hanging off Mother's body. It seemed surreal and inhuman. The woman took disposable gloves from her bag, put them on, and began checking the bag attached on the round base plate stuck to the lower left side of Mother's abdomen, right above her pelvis. I was curious about the orifice, but the base plate covered it completely and its color matched her complexion. The area around the base plate was inflamed. When the woman finished, Mother's eyes met mine. They were full of agony and despair for the woman she once was, a neat and glamorous lady. That woman was dead now, and it was damn hard to look at her eyes. But I grinned and, again, faked it.

"This neat device will help you recover faster, Mother."

"Definitely," the woman said, nodding and straining to smile. "It's a temporary thing." She showed Mother the manual, which had step by step instructions and drawings, and explained that the bag had to be replaced daily and the base once a week. During this recital, the woman continually bragged that her company made the easiest colostomy devices to use and install. She was a loud and fast talker. That was good, though, because it gave Mother no time to think about her misery.

I paid attention to every word the woman spoke. I tried to memorize as much as possible. The woman quickly reviewed the "do's and don't's" of colostomy equipment maintenance, then placed some promotional material, a manual, and her business card on the side table. She said she would be glad to visit us at home and train Mother to use the devices if she chose her company's brand. Then she shook our hands, smiling to everyone in the room before she left. She was a good sales rep; Western training could probably teach you how to sell your own family to someone. Under socialism you never saw sales reps from private firms selling products in a government hospital. The patients, who were still not used to the marketing that goes with capitalism, were stunned by her visit. They seemed fascinated by her sales speech. It was much more entertaining for them than staring at the boring white ceiling. Only I knew from living in America how annoying it could be dealing with sales reps and telemarketers.

That night I called Marina in New York City to thank her for providing Marjan's name. I told her that everything had gone smoothly, but when I mentioned Mother's diagnosis, she offered to let me stay at her parent's house. She said it was convenient to the hospital, so I could be close to Mother and save money. She was looking out for me. She had a big heart. A week later, I moved there. Her older sister, her younger brother, and her son-in-law welcomed me. Marina's mother was in New York City, visiting her. When I saw pictures of her, I could see why Marina's father, the artist, had married her. She was a real beauty.

The great artist seemed to be alive and present all over the house. His powerful work hung everywhere. The ambiance of his atelier was overwhelming. This highly artistic environment helped me deal with my mother's condition more easily. The artist's spirit visited me every night as I gazed at his oil paintings, adorned with real gold abstract shapes. They seemed like new Byzantine icons with a touch of Balkan folklore. I was taken to places of indescribable beauty and harmony of color, where illness and suffering couldn't win. The art healed my wounded soul. It infused me with the optimism and courage to face and fight the ugliness of my mother's cancer, even though it was clear we couldn't win the battle, and even clearer that we wouldn't win the war.

8

Colostomy

New Year's Eve 1997, I bought boxes of chocolate and flowers for everyone in Room 447. It would have been one of my saddest New Year's if not for Lena, whose brash humor turned the hushed, depressing place into a comedy club. In the morning, I expected Mother to be cheerful, but she lay staring at the ceiling and quietly crying instead.

"What's wrong, Mother?" I dropped the bag of lemons that I bought for her on the floor and made a beeline to her bed.

She embraced me tightly with both arms, now that her IV had been removed, but kept looking at the ceiling. I could feel her shaking.

"The New Year began with hell, my gold," she said.

I thought the sharp odor from her bed would suffocate me. Acid began climbing up to my throat and I gulped to stop it. I realized then that feces had stained parts of her sheet. I pulled slowly from her hug and uncovered her body. Another blast of the odor assaulted me. She kept staring straight at the ceiling, tears rolling down her crimson cheeks. Her sobbing became more intense when I rolled her nightdress up to her chest. The colostomy base was halfway unglued, and the bag was completely detached. I was furious.

"How long have you been like this, Mother?" I asked.

"Since dawn. I thought the nurse had fixed it well." She reddened more and started crying louder. "I rang them twice…You can't replace it. You haven't done it…You can't. Oh! Call the nurses, please."

"No time now."

"Call them. Please!" She covered her eyes and shook her head.

Mother sounded like one of those Puritan ladies back in America. Her conservative upbringing wouldn't let her tolerate this kind of intimacy with me, her son. *She'll get used to it. She'll get over it.* There is no time for a moral debate or preferences now, I thought.

"We can't rely on the nurses, anyway," I said. "Not after seeing this mess." As I checked the drawers in her side table, I added, "Besides, why am I here?"

She didn't say a word. She was in trouble and had to give in, just as she had on the surgery, after the pain increased. She continued to cover her eyes with embarrassment, cry, and shake her head. She wouldn't look at me.

I pulled out the promotional bags, the bases, and the manual that the sales rep had given us and spread them on the side table. I tried to recall every word she'd said. I flipped through the manual's illustrated instructions quickly. I took the scissors from Mother's cosmetic bag and began cutting the middle part of the base in a circle, to make it about as big as her artificial anus. I took one of the plastic grocery bags I had collected in the lower drawer, shook it open, removed the filthy colostomy bag, and threw it in it. I pulled the waste-soaked base off Mother's colostomy and dumped it in the plastic bag, too. Closing the bag tightly to hold in the stench, I flew out of the room to a waste receptacle at the end of the hallway. I must have looked like I was mad. When I got back, her roommates were pressing their noses into their pillows, discreetly watching me from the corners of their eyes. I pulled out another plastic bag and opened it wide on the floor, then gathered some gauze and a roll of toilet paper. Dragging the basin out from under the bed, I filled it with warm water. I picked up the biggest of the feces first with pieces of toilet paper and tossed them in the plastic bag. On the table was some homemade brandy that I had brought with me on a previous visit. Mother always used if for rubbing and disinfection. Using gauze moistened with the brandy, I cleaned excrement off the orifice, so the base would adhere to her skin well. Again, I closed the bag tightly and took it to the waste receptacle.

Throughout, Mother stared as if paralyzed at the ceiling. I retrieved another plastic bag to use for trash collection, then, after glancing at the manual's drawing, I began peeling the paper from the adhesive, textile-like material around the plastic ring of the base. Just before I finished, watery feces began gushing from her orifice. I panicked. I was out of gauze and there wasn't much toilet paper left. I placed the base upside down on the side table, so it wouldn't stick to the surface, scurried to Mother's locker, and pulled out all of the towels she'd brought. Squatting beside her bed, I gently covered the orifice with a towel to collect the discharge. When the fecal liquid soaked through one towel, I would dump it in the plastic bag and replace it with a new one. Mother's face was scarlet with embarrassment and shock. Her tears made damp spots on both sides of her pillow. Her mouth was tightly closed, quivering with a repressed howl. Her hands grasped each side of the bed frame, like dried ivy. My nose had adjusted so I didn't notice the smell of ordure anymore. But I smelled Mother's humiliation, agony, and longing to be the lady she once was. I smelled her terror of an undignified ending. I sensed the unknown space that, sooner or later, we will all visit and that we're all afraid of, regardless how much we lie to ourselves or others that we're not. My mother's agony was making everyone in the room aware of death.

The stoma stopped dispelling waste after the third towel was soaked. I cleaned traces of the feces from around it with dampened toilet paper and dried her off with a clean towel. Next, I wiped off some white translucent slime that had leaked from her sewn rectum. To make sure that her abdominal, vaginal, and rectal areas were completely clean and disinfected, I moistened the end of the towel with brandy and began rubbing it over them gently. Mother's body trembled.

"Does it hurt?" I asked her. She only shook her head, still not taking her eyes from the ceiling. She was lying, anxious to be finished with the hell she was going through. The artificial anus was an oval opening, a crater-like hole, surrounded with strange white pimples. The peripheral area was so red it looked scorched. I picked up the base, checked the manual again, and gently placed it on top of the orifice. I made sure the plastic ring was centered and pressed down on it, so it would adhere to her skin. Checking the instructions thoroughly, I picked up a new colostomy bag, carefully cut its opening, and placed it against the base's plastic ring. The bag's ring was slightly bigger than that of the base, and I pressed it on carefully. It worked like the snap-on lid to a plastic container. When I heard the last part of it click into place, I tugged at the bag gently, to make sure it was well attached. Finally, I exhaled. It is amazing how quickly you can learn a skill when you need to help someone you love. The ability to do the thing right comes directly from the need to act. Trouble is the perfect teacher, and, under stress, you can often do something for the first time instinctively, as if you've done it hundreds of times in the past. I cleaned up the trash I had created, washed the basin, and wiped everything with brandy. I used Mother's hospital gown, which she never wore, to clean the floor. I washed my hands and, from the locker, I took out new underwear, a nightdress, and socks.

"Mother, you have to stand up so I can change you."

She cast a sideways glance at me, her teary eyes glittering. I placed my hands under her armpits and tried to lift her, but she allowed herself to fall back down.

"Mother, please cooperate. You don't want them to see you looking dirty," I whispered in her ear, then glanced at her roommates, who pretended to sleep. I sensed that they pitied Mother and admired me, especially the old woman who had no one to visit her.

"Come on, Mother. You can do it." I kept encouraging her, until she finally helped me prop her up and move her to the edge of the bed.

"Let's try to walk to the bathroom," she said, staring at the door and gathering her strength. "We need much more water than this basin can hold. I've never been so disgusted with myself." She uttered the last thought with a sob as she stood up. Leaning on my arm, she took her first step. Then, slowly, her second. Her third. Step by step we went, out of the room and down the hall, until we made it to the bathroom.

No one was there, and I was relieved. That would have just complicated things. She couldn't stand and wait for very long. When Mother saw her face in the mirror, she began crying again.

"Can you wait just a minute like that, Mother?"

"Mm-hmm," she mumbled, grasping resolutely at the edge of the porcelain sink.

I rushed back to the room and took more gauze from her side table, along with the clothes that I had left on top of it. On the way back, I realized I'd forgotten clean towels and soap, so I rushed back for those. When I got to the bathroom, she was standing inertly. Her fingers gripped the edge of the sink like pliers. I undressed her completely, dampened and soaped up a gauze pad, and began washing her body with it, stopping now and then to add more soap to the pad. When the stains were gone and her skin started smelling clean, I washed and rinsed her once more, then I wrapped her with a towel. I gently patted her dry and began to put her clothes on. She started to whine.

"Stop crying!" I said.

"I look awful." She said, looking aghast at herself in the mirror. "God only knows if I'll get any better."

"What are you talking about!? You're already doing better. You began to walk before the doctor let you. Can't you see? You can walk."

"You call this walking?"

"What do you expect? To fly? Don't make me upset. You're doing fine. You just had an operation." I walked her back to her room. Patients in the hall said hello to us. I said hello back. Mother would only look down at the floor. When we got to the room, Mother was still crying, so I said, "Stop it!" and wiped her tears with my handkerchief before we went in.

I had Mother wait at the foot of her bed, supporting herself on the end rail, while I changed the bed with the sheets that Mother had brought from home. Then I guided her into bed and helped position her comfortably. I pulled a plastic bag from her drawer, and crammed the dirty sheets into it. I took another plastic bag and went to the bathroom to get her dirty clothes. When I came back, everyone's eyes were on me.

"I'll wash them at Marina's house," I said, stuffing the bags into my portmanteau that I had stored in her locker. I took the bottle of brandy and massaged her feet with it. When I finished, I put her socks on and pulled her sheet up to cover her. From the bottom compartment of my mother's side table, I took the comb and her cosmetic bag. I combed her hair and applied cream to her face, then handed her the Lancôme cosmetic bag, the one I'd sent her from America.

"Let's apply your make up now," I said.

Mother sat up a bit and opened the bag, seeming to lack confidence as never before. She began by putting on foundation. She powdered her face and neck, penciled her eyebrows, and applied mascara and cherry-colored lipstick. Her hands shook as she sprayed on her favorite rose perfume.

"You shine, Kostadina," Lena said to Mother with approval.

"Thank you. I wish I looked as good as before." Mother exhaled heavily.

"I'll never look like you. Like a townswoman and a real dame," Lena said enviously.

"Tell him how terrible it was this morning, when the colostomy bag came loose and I waited an hour for the on-duty nurse to come and fix it." Mother said.

"My ass, she fixed it. She just reattached the old bag. Sloppily!" Lena cast her baleful glance towards me. "She didn't clean your mother. She didn't change her either. Shortly afterward, the bag fell off again. If you hadn't come this morning, your mother would've been swimming in shit for who knows how long. Eventually, they would've changed her. But how? Like you? No. No. No. Swiftly, carelessly, and sloppily. Only because they have to."

Lena turned to Mother. "You're lucky he is here." Looking at me again, she said, "See who we have to deal with? Damned nurses! Sluts who are here to fuck the doctors and marry them for money. Forgive me, God, for these words." Lena made the sign of the cross, looking towards the ceiling, then back, deep into Mother's eyes. "I've never seen a son take care of his mother like yours did today. I'll pass on what I saw to my grandchildren, if I have a chance to see them. Don't you ever worry when he's here."

"Nothing scares me when my gold is next to me," Mother said, crying as she gazed at my blushing face.

"Mm-hmm!…Yeah!" The other women agreed, sounding fatigued from the combined effect of cancer and drugs.

After lunch and the on-duty doctor's visit, it was time for me to leave.

"Mother, I'll buy you fruit and peach juice for next time."

"And gauze, please" she said. "It's good to have extra, although the nurses would give more to me if I asked."

"I have the whole list of what we need in my head." I smiled and pulled her nightdress up to check the colostomy. "It's attached perfectly," I noted, proudly.

"I am so afraid," she whispered, as if the colostomy were her old foe.

I leaned over her and kissed her. "Don't worry, Mother. It won't happen again. You'll see. You are safe."

As soon as I left the room, I took out my pen and memo-book and wrote: 1-gauze; 2-small scissors; 3-trash bags; 4-adhesive medical tape; 5-small basin; 6-bottle of plum brandy.

I paused. I wished I had thought to bring the pine disinfectant from home; the one I bought in America. I continued scribbling while going through my mental checklist: 7-nightdresses; 8-rolls of toilet paper; 9-safety pins; 10-more towels. Then, straight from the hospital, I went shopping.

After the first colostomy horror, my main task in the morning was to check it completely. If the bag was more than two-thirds full I would replace it immediately. The bags tended to detach easily if they were too heavy. I would usually replace the base once a week and the bags every day, but sometimes the bags could last a second or third day, depending on her digestion and what she ate. Later, I found bags that she could clean herself, with an end that could open and close with a plastic clip. They lasted up to five days. Mother favored those because they made my work easier. The base itself usually lasted longer than a week, and sometimes up to three. Only the shower made it loosen faster.

Because I came to the hospital every day I would never let the nurses take care of my mother's colostomy. They were happy about that. Every day, I got better and better in installing and maintaining it, and even taught some of the medical staff how to do it. I would also help the patients in Mother's room, giving them water and tablets, placing a moist cloth on their foreheads when they had a fever, even emptying their bedpans. They loved me, especially the old woman who had no visitors. I also became popular in the abdominal clinic. The personnel were used to me and didn't bother me anymore when I would stay far longer than the regular visiting hours.

"You should always wear disposable gloves when you work around a colostomy." The remark came from a nurse who caught me tending to Mother one afternoon. She pulled a couple of tiny off-white rubber gloves from her pocket and placed them on the top of the side table.

"What are you talking about, you damned whore." Lena spoke up, before I had a chance to reply. "It's his mother. He is not disgusted, as you all are."

"Listen, you big mouthed bitch," the nurse said, in a rage. "It has nothing to do with love. It's a basic thing in hospitals, to prevent contamination."

While Lena argued with the nurse, ridiculing her and making everyone laugh again, Mother picked up the gloves and handed them to me. "Wear them. The nurse is correct," she said.

"Oh-kay, Mother," I put them on and continued to adjust the bag on the colostomy base.

Every afternoon, after lunch and on-duty doctor visit, I would take Mother out for exercise. I would walk her up and down the hallway. She was getting stronger, and her appetite was improving a great deal. Only her limping got worse, and I had to tell her repeatedly that she would walk normally soon. She listened to my words and believed me. My "positive lying" was the only force that kept her going. So I kept feeding Mother's hope, regardless that the cancer's image on her X-ray was shadowing my honesty every day more and more.

At the end of January Mother got her release document, and a few days before we left the hospital, I called the surgeon for advice and guidance. I was invited to his home, and I brought presents for him, a bottle of whisky and a tie. He repeated everything he had told me before: that radiation and chemotherapy would prolong her life, but wouldn't improve her condition. He warned me that the radiology clinic, with all those cancer patients around, was like an inferno, but added that if I wanted to do it for peace of mind I should. I agreed to it, and the next day I picked up the referral from his office. He scheduled the radiation treatments for March. He also told me that the supervisor of the radiology clinic was corrupt, but a necessary connection to enable Mother to skip the long waiting list. Along with the referral, he gave me a prescription for pain killers and a request for the free colostomy supply that Mother was entitled to receive as a pensioner.

The doctor hugged me before I left and told me to feel free to call him any time. I felt bad that Mother thought of him as a young, inexperienced jerk, but I also understood her blaming the doctors. The cancer was eating her alive, painfully and brutally.

Saying farewell to Mother's roommates was a very emotional thing. They all cried aloud and said they would miss us. They collected candy and chocolates they had saved and gave them to me, in appreciation for helping them. We kissed and hugged, and all of them walked us to the hospital door. As I looked at them from the taxi window, I had a disgusting thought: who's going first? I closed my eyes, but I could still see them, looking like a group of ghosts. I didn't want to think of Mother being in that group.

The moment we entered our garden, Mother's face brightened. She was glad to be back home. Bisera had cleaned the whole house in anticipation of her arrival. The daily routine at home was almost the same as the one at the hospital, except that the morning injection was replaced with twenty drops of morphine-based Heptanon. Some days, I had to double the dose or add a different pain-killer based on methadone. The temperature in the living room, where Mother stayed, was unbearably hot. I had to keep it very high because her weakened body was very sensitive to cold. Mother would tell all her visitors about Lena, her out-rageous attitude towards the nurses, her big mouth, and her sense of humor. She missed her. It was odd to see an urban lady, brought up all her life to put down the peasants, talk non-stop with admiration about one on them. Her illness had changed her. It had demolished the barriers of her ignorance and discrimination towards the class she never belonged to. But then, illness and death don't dis-criminate based on class or status. Anywhere.

9

Radiation

"Mother, I insist!" I yelled, over and over.

"God knows what I have. That's why you insist," she would answer over and over. I would drop the subject for a while, than try again to convince her.

"The radiation in March is a must," I said. "It will heal your colon faster." No matter how many times I said it, she kept being stubborn. I didn't really blame her. She'd had enough of boring white hospital ceilings. However, by March, the pain increased. Mother's walk got more erratic and she lost weight. She became alarmed, and finally, she gave in.

The radiology clinic was, truly, a scary and disorderly place. The surgeon had warned me about it. So, the day we went for Mother's radiation treatment, I left her in the waiting room and went looking for the supervising oncologist who was supposed to admit us. The nurses gathered by his office told me that he was visiting patients. I thanked them and continued my search. As I looked around I saw patients everywhere, jammed into crowded rooms. Most of them looked terrible. The scariest-looking ones had skin and mouth tumors.

"Mother would die if she saw this," I whispered to myself, as I continued peeking into different rooms. I couldn't find the doctor, so I asked one kind-looking nurse for help. She was helping one of the patients defecate. She promised to page the doctor and told me to wait in his office.

Fifteen minutes later, the supervisor arrived accompanied by a nurse and a technician. I introduced myself and handed him the referral. He shook my hand firmly, offered me a seat, and told the nurse to give me the admission papers to fill out. Before I put pen to them, I asked him if he had any less-crowded rooms, something with two beds or, even better, a room with a single bed. I told him I was willing to pay for it. For the first time, the oncologist looked at me for more than a second. His pupils turned into dollar signs, and his smile became inviting. He could probably tell from my accent that I was a Macedonian, but had been living in America for a while.

He grabbed my arm and guided me to the room next to his office. He pulled a set of keys from his pocket and unlocked the door. The room was clean and had two beds, a shower, and a terrace. I was delighted, staring at it as if I had never seen such a room. I asked him if there was a different way to get there from the waiting room so we could avoid passing the crowded rooms. He showed me a short cut through a hidden stairway and said, "Eventually, she'll see some of the patients in the hallway, coming to my office. She'll get used to it. Reality is tough, boy. You should always keep that in mind."

"I know. That's why I'm trying to shield her from this harsh reality as much as possible. Don't we always do it to ourselves, in many ways?"

"Certainly. All the time. Life is not easy. Get your mother now."

"Thank you," I said, and ran down the stairs.

The oncologist was about to retire. He had class, but he was a canny opportunist as well. Out-of-state patients, mostly Albanians from Kosovo, had to pay him under the counter to be treated in the overcrowded clinic, on top of a hospital expense, that in comparison to ours in America was ridiculously inexpensive. Macedonian residents who wanted to get in sooner had to pay him, too. Patients who couldn't pay, or were not referred by a connection, had to work on his property to get in the clinic. If they couldn't do that they had to go on the long waiting list. The emergency cases, the very poor, the elderly, and the disabled, he would squeeze in, regardless of their lack of referrals, money, or connections. That gesture helped make up for his despotic and corrupt way of running the clinic.

After Mother's admission I helped her settle comfortably in the room. The oncologist invited me into his office and, while serving me coffee, he said. "After the break up of socialism, the new system produced more uninsured cases as the work stopped being guaranteed by the government. As the new system brought more poverty, my salary shrank drastically. Doctors here don't make nearly as much as in America, so we have to override the system, charge the patients, and get money from outside."

"I wish the doctors and lawyers were as good as they are rich in America," I said, skeptically.

"That's a separate issue. One of the many problems that could ruin the United States," he replied.

The door opened and a young woman nonchalantly entered. It was his daughter. The doctor introduced us to each other. She had worked in the radiology clinic since finishing medical school and her father employed her there. Shortly after our acquaintance we began socializing regularly. She was bright, attractive, and just like her father. If she weren't as greedy as he, she'd probably have been a perfect doctor. My friendship with her cost me a lot though. She would invite me to family events, and I would end up spending a fortune on presents, expensive dinners, and all that. I couldn't turn her down, because I needed her father's help.

Mother was given the best treatment in the clinic, and that was all I cared about: her comfort. A week later, mother got a roommate. She was a young lady, gentle and fragile, who resembled Princess Diana of Wales. She often read and wrote in a blue hardcover notebook. I enjoyed our discussions on art and literature. Her poetry was moving. It was an ode to her impending death. It expressed her fear of the unknown but she had the courage to write about it, and it soothed her at the same time. She had a couple of tumors and had survived numerous surgeries. The oncologist told me that she would probably die before Mother. He explained that cancer metastasizes much faster in a younger body. He was right; she passed away six months before Mother.

Once a day, Mother and her roommate visited the radiation unit in the lowest level of the building, usually before breakfast. She would enter the chamber, lie down on her back or stomach, alternating position every other day, then expose herself for a couple of minutes to the radioactive rays. There was always a big waiting line for radiation. Now and then I would give packages of coffee, drinks, or dollars to the medical technicians to sneak her in sooner. On the days when Mother's roommate felt unwell from the chemotherapy, which she was getting along with the radiation, Mother would wait for me to escort her. She wasn't able to go by herself. The radiation weakened her body. Surprisingly, she handled it well, experiencing fewer side effects than her roommate. Ten days after she started treatment, Mother had her first check-up scan and the oncologist told me that her tumor had shrunk. I couldn't wait to give her the good news. I jumped like a child as I ran down the corridor to her room. It was one of those rare moments when she seemed as healthy as before. Happiness radiated from her face, and I wished it would stay there forever.

My chores around Mother were clear to me, and I become quite competent in doing them. I fell into a daily routine, much like I had when Mother was in the abdominal clinic, except I didn't live at Marina's house any more. It was too crowded. Marina asked her sister to give me a key to her vacant apartment, and I moved in there. I missed the artistic atmosphere in her home terribly. Nevertheless, I had much more privacy, a telephone, and one most important thing: a washing machine to clean Mother's clothes regularly. Again, most of the nurses had no training in taking care of Mother's colostomy, or at least they pretended they didn't. I taught them. I even helped them when they performed their sloppy skills on other patients. I became an expert in colostomy maintenance. The oncologist even offered me a job. He said that he would love to employ me in his clinic as a nurse if I decided to stay in Macedonia.

A Catholic nun, who occasionally visited the cancer victims, would bless me anytime she saw me help the patients. She was impressed with the immaculate care I gave my mother. I offered to teach her colostomy maintenance, but she avoided the subject and kept talking about how I would go straight to heaven and all that crap. I wished that she hadn't been so disgusted by the physical aspect of caring for patients. She could have been much more use cleaning the patients' colostomies than praying for them while they swam in their own feces. My younger uncle, Mother's favorite brother, finally brought a TV on one of his visits, after Mother begged him for two weeks for it. The older brother would visit her less and he kept his visits short, so he could rush back to his terminally ill wife, who had some kind of disease that was rotting her skin. She was a mean bitch. To both uncles' wives, I was a foreign element in the family, of different blood, an adopted orphan bastard. They despised me, especially when I said or did something to expose their phoniness in front of others. There was constant tension between us, all the time.

Every morning, I would wake up between 6 and 7 o'clock. I would take a shower, get dressed, and eat my breakfast in the bagel and pastry shop on the way to the hospital. It served a warm cheese, spinach, and meat pie called *Burek*, traditionally eaten with plain cold yogurt. It's one of most popular specialties in the Balkans. The Yugoslavs inherited the dish from the Turks during their rule.

After breakfast, and before going to the hospital, I would usually shop for the things that Mother needed in the stores across from it. On my arrival at the hospital I would immediately do maintenance on Mother's colostomy. I would take her to the radiation chamber, if her roommate wasn't going, then bring her back, help her with breakfast, and let her rest until after the doctor's morning visit. I would walk with her to exercise her weakened legs. We would walk up and down the fifty-foot long hallway, about ten times. From then until lunch, I would alternate between sitting with Mother, chatting and drinking coffee with the doctor, and strolling the hospital grounds. For lunch, I would grab something from one of the many nearby food shops and join Mother and her roommate in a meal on the small, shaky table that I never got fixed right. After the doctor's second visit, I would take Mother for another walk until she got tired and returned to bed for her nap. I would visit the oncologist for afternoon tea, or socialize with his daughter, who was obsessed with the West, in her office on the second floor below. Sometimes, I would talk about art and literature with Mother's roommate until Mother woke up, usually between 5 and 6 P.M. I would shower Mother, rubbing her emaciated body with homemade soap made from pig's fat, which she preferred to commercial brands. I would dry her, massage her body with home-made brandy, change her into fresh clothes, and then we would watch TV until dinner was served. When it was time to go I would check her colostomy and kiss her good night before leaving.

Exhausted, more mentally than physically, I rarely found peaceful moments for myself. My fears about Mother's future were everywhere. They splashed me through the water drops of the shower. They shone through my reflections on the mirror. They whistled through the winds as I walked the city streets. They yelled through the noises of the bars I visited. They visited me as I read before bedtime, and they haunted me in my dreams. I tried to shut out the thoughts, to no avail. As the cancer corroded Mother's body, it also corroded my soul. The cancer seemed like a violent ocean corroding an old ship—our ship of unconditional love that kept sailing, regardless. But, I knew, not forever.

10

Search

I had sought my biological parents for over a decade. Primarily, I tried to find my mother. The only information I had was her name from an adoption document that my father gave me after high school. I began to search intensively for her. I was angry at society and rebellious towards my parents, confident that they were always wrong and obsolete in comparison to me. I thought my progenitors would understand me better than my parents.

Before I immigrated to America, the drive to find my parents ebbed from lack of success. After I moved to the U.S. I nearly let the urge to find them become extinguished, since I was so far away from the resources that could lead me to them. Nevertheless, a tiny ember of that desire continued to burn in me. To dampen it, I did the only thing I could; I asked someone in Macedonia to keep looking for them.

I tried to reach an old friend from college, who I had heard was working as a state security inspector. Although we'd had a falling out, I hoped to enlist his help. But he never answered my letters, in which I begged and offered money for his help. When I called him he told me that he couldn't find any trace of either of them and that he hadn't written back because he didn't want to disappoint me.

He lied. I knew him well. He didn't want to deal with anything associated with me. He still held a grudge against me, although he was the one who betrayed our close friendship. I didn't hold grudges, but I had buried his friendship a long time ago. He was only a ghost from the past, but he was someone I could use to find my biological roots.

Naturally, the old urge to find my birth parents sprang to life after I returned to my native country. After a while, I realized that being close to the resources wasn't the only reason that the urge intensified. My mother's impending death was part of it. Maybe, subconsciously, I was looking for her replacement. The thought disturbed me. I felt as if I were betraying her. The urge was so strong, however, that I had to act. I counted the people who I could call on for help and realized that I only had one good connection, the old college friend who had turned me down. I found his number in my address book and called him. A woman answered. When I asked for him, she paused, then told me to wait a moment. I heard children screaming at the other end. At the woman's sharp voice they shut up. After a while, I heard the familiar, virile-sounding voice say, "Hello, Ivan speaking."

His gruff tone, once a pleasant baritone, made me nervous, but I didn't want to show it. With forced gaiety, I said, "It's me, Bazhe. How are you, Rambo?" I referred to him, as everyone used to, by his nickname.

"What a surprise. How are you? How are things in America?"

"Good. I'm here now. My mother is sick with cancer. I came to take care of her."

"I'm sorry to hear that."

"What's new with you?"

"Well, I got a promotion in the State Security department.

"Of course. I would've expected that from an ambitious person like you," I said, aware of his family's close connections with the police bureaucracy. "But you disappointed me. You never answered my letters. The last time we spoke, you wouldn't help me and you hung up on me. That wasn't nice."

"Listen, Bazhe, I told you I couldn't find your biological parents. You're my friend, for Christ's sake. It would've been unfair to give you hope. So I kept it short. I wanted you to forget them. I see you're still obsessed with them, and who that woman is. You shouldn't be. You're a grown man now. Who cares?"

A friend? I thought. I didn't trust him a bit. He was making excuses. I didn't let my anger show in my voice. I took a deep breath, then said softly, "You know that finding them means a lot to me. I don't intend to hurt them. It's just that all adopted children have the natural urge to find their biological parents, if for no other reason than to learn what genetic problems they may have inherited. Please, Rambo. I'll pay you as much as you want."

"Let me tell you something," he said. What I did to you back in college was wrong. I screwed up our good friendship. I always wanted to make it up to you. Always. Believe me. I still do…But understand, never for money."

While listening to his bullshit, I thought: *He must be stuck in deep shit. He has a good job and salary. It's pathetic to call a Post-Yugoslav Macedonian's earning a decent salary, though. Anyway, he's better off than most of my generation here, which barely survives on a tiny welfare check. He can talk to me from another galaxy and I'd know that he's in trouble, and lying. Time, wires, distance, could never falsify your knowledge of people you truly loved and trusted once. I used to analyze him like Freud had his patients.* When he finished talking, I cordially thanked him.

He suggested we meet the next day for lunch at a popular pizzeria near the State Security headquarters building and the hospital. The pizzeria was very trendy and pretentious. Rambo loved that type of establishment. I arrived on time. He was late, of course, since he knew I needed him. He still looked handsome, and he smiled as he approached me. It was the first time I'd seen him in a suit. It was perfectly tailored for his athletic build.

"Hi," he said. I stood up, and he embraced me and kissed my cheek in the traditional Balkan greeting among friends. "You look the same. What's your secret?"

"America, I guess." I inhaled the scent of Versace cologne on his freshly shaved skin as I kissed him back.

We got a table and I asked him what he was going to order, knowing that I had to pay for everything regardless of whether he helped me. Everyone at home expected it of me. People in my homeland act as if Americans are constantly showered with hundred-dollar bills from above. Hollywood movies and commercial propaganda create that impression.

Rambo ordered lasagna and a beer, and he recommended the ravioli, remembering that it was one of my favorite dishes. I ordered it along with apple juice. We didn't talk about the past, and that was good. It could have jeopardized my ability to get his help. Even though he apologized a couple of times about breaking up our friendship, I really wanted to choke him. The old anger began building in me, like a dormant volcano coming back to life, like my mother's rage towards my father, suppressed for years. Locals always said that concealed anger was like a poison and that it caused cancer. I think they may have been right.

I couldn't wait to dispense with pleasantries and get to the point of our meeting. My assumptions about his lifestyle, with his wife and two children, proved to be correct. His conjectures about my life were wrong, but he had never really known me, anyway. He figured I must be involved with a wealthy old American man living in the Hamptons or some other snobbish, upscale ghetto. He kept asking me about America, New York City, its nightlife, and the shows. My answers were short and fast.

Finally, he said, "This time I'll try harder to find them. I promise."

"I'd be so grateful. Thank you," I said, ecstatic. I pulled out a copy of the adoption agreement.

"This is all the information I have. It's about my birth mother only. It's a copy of the same document I sent you once." I handed it to him, adding, "On the back, I wrote some additional information, some things I found out after leaving the Army and before college. One or both of them had me transferred to an orphanage away from the capital to cover their traces completely. Later, I was returned to the capital, where my parents adopted me. My parents told me that they had heard that story. I don't know where I was born, but I hope this will help."

"Good," he said, and swiftly tucked the paper inside his fancy burgundy leather organizer.

I ordered a cappuccino for both of us after we finished lunch. He drank his quickly, stood up, and said, "I have to get moving. Where are you staying in the city?"

"A friend's apartment. Here's my number." I wrote it on the back of one of my own cards, which had my U.S. address and a picture of an American eagle on the front.

"I'll call you," he said, sounding assured. We shook hands and he walked away.

His physique had not changed a bit, but his sense of humor and vigorous temperament were gone. Maybe because of the suit? No. The police environment had killed them. It had made him older. His eyes didn't shine as they had ten years ago, in college. I watched him disappear into the crowd.

I lit a cigarette, opened my notebook, and wrote: "Life passes like a wind through the forest that shakes down all the dead leaves at autumn. Those are the leaves of your past and youth. And if you think that at spring you will replace them, like the forest does, you are wrong. Those moments are gone, dead, decomposed leaves in your memories. Life can control you, if you are not cautious. It can turn you into a fast-aging pathetic puppet. That is all life is; a sneaky game played on its players. You have to be keen and gain control of the game. You have to make your life your puppet instead. Then, you are the winner." I closed my notebook, finished the cappuccino, paid, and walked back to the hospital.

A week later, Rambo called me. We met at the same place, at the same time. Once again I ordered the drinks and lunch. He made me wait for whatever information he had, clearly enjoying it. An attitude typical of police, I thought. We were nearly finished with the appetizers when he pulled my adoption agreement from his pocket and unfolded it on the table.

"Some information is missing or incorrect. The date of her birth is wrong, for example. I have to investigate much further. I have to find out where you were transferred to from the Capital. I'm planning to go to the two remaining orphanages in the state and poke around in their archives. I'll have to pay people. Transportation. Food. You know what I mean, and—"

"No problem. How much?" I cut him off, excited.

"About five hundred deutsche marks."

I retrieved my wallet and began counting out the money. As I put the last bill on the table, he said, "One hundred more, just in case."

"Okay." I added more money to the pile.

He looked around and slid his organizer towards me.

"Put them in," he said. I did and he slid the organizer back beside his plate. The waiter came with our lunch.

"How is your mother doing?" he asked, his eyes still discreetly glancing around.

"Suffering."

"My wife knew someone who died of cancer. I know what you're going through. I wondered if it wouldn't be too much for your mother to handle if we found your biological mother?"

"Who said I would tell her? Are you crazy?"

"Good. And tell no one else. What I'm doing is illegal. My career would be fucked if someone found out."

"What do you think I am, a baby? I've been around. And I know that in this new country, people are just trying to survive. They don't give a fuck about other peoples' problems. Things have changed here."

"They have." He breathed a sigh of nostalgia for the old Yugoslavia. We all sighed for it, in one way or another. "I hope you'll invite me to the U.S. after I find her."

"Of course. That would be nice. Why not?"

"I don't care to go there myself as much as I want my children to see America. It would be exciting for them, wouldn't it?"

"Oh, yes. Fun. Lots of fun," I said.

"It's hard to get a visa, isn't it?"

"Not if you send your wife and children and you stay here. Or if you go and they stay. It's easier that way. But with a good guarantee letter, it's no problem for all of you to go." I took a bite of moussaka.

"I see. They need a guarantee that you'll come back."

"Mm-hmm." I nodded and sipped my lemonade.

Rambo ate quickly. He got up without finishing his meal or coffee.

"I have to run back to the office," he said.

"You act like an American," I said, hoping that I hadn't made an inappropriate remark.

"Capitalism, baby! Time is money. In money, we trust. The profit is God." He shook my hand, grinning. "I hope to have the information soon."

"Me, too,"

His hand was sweaty and, after he left, I smelled my palm. The familiar odor of his body was there. I ran to the bathroom and washed my hands, twice. But when I checked my palm later, traces of the old damage from him were still there.

11

Phobia

The radiation process lasted thirty-one days, excluding the weekends. We stayed at the hospital until mid-April, almost a month and a half. Rambo didn't call me. I decided to wait, and not to be pushy. Mother didn't want to take a taxi home. She didn't want to risk having a colostomy accident and being humiliated in front of a stranger during the approximately four-hour trip. She told me to ask her younger brother to drive us back. He didn't seem thrilled, but he pretended he was.

He came with his son in his old Volkswagen Golf, stuffed with cardboard boxes full of electrical devices and supplies he used for his business. Actually, he had scheduled a job in the county bordering ours, so our home was on his way. I regretted asking him for the favor. I only did it for Mother. I knew he didn't like me, but he was doing it for his sister, I thought, watching my mother's tired face as she leaned against a cardboard box. She slept for most of the trip, knocked out from the medications. Mother and I were mashed like canned sardines in the tiny, overloaded car.

Another, even bigger embarrassment, came when we arrived home. Again, Bisera had prepared the house for our arrival. I escorted Mother inside and returned to Uncle and his son, who were organizing the car's contents. Out of courtesy, I asked how much the trip had cost. They said the gas had cost 100 deutsche marks. I pulled a bill from my wallet and handed it to them. Shortly afterward, they came inside and joined us in the living room. Bisera served them cake that she had made to welcome Mother back. They ate fast and, as soon as they finished their coffee, they left. When I told Mother that Uncle had taken money for the favor, her face whitened with anger.

"I also asked them about that when you went to the bathroom," she said. "They said, 'Oh no! No money. What are you talking about?' I'm shocked they didn't charge us twice." Mother gazed up at the ceiling. The room was painted beige and the ceiling was decorated with imitation wood trimming that was once quite trendy in our province. At least our ceiling isn't as boring as the one in the hospital, I thought, nibbling on my cake.

"I thought, in case of a colostomy accident, I would deal with family, my brother," Mother said, looking back and forth between Bisera and me. "This is more embarrassing than any colostomy problem. I'm very sorry to have made you ask him for the favor, son. We could've taken one of those roomy Mercedes with the money they took from you and avoided being driven at his convenience, squeezed in among those boxes. He's no brother. He's a common crook. What a shame and a disgrace."

Bisera shook her head, repeating, "What a shame. What a shame."

"I'm glad you finally saw his true self," I said. "All these years, you've been in denial, dealing with a fake brother. If he didn't have self-interest, he wouldn't give a damn about anybody. If you and Father hadn't appointed me as executive inheritor, he would have been all over you, faking love for you from his greedy, rotten soul. Last summer, he said the reason I'm helping you is because of the inheritance. I never told you. I didn't want to upset you, Mother. I let you see his true colors on your own."

"Idiot." Mother shook her head. "I counted on him, as my family. Well, all I have is you and Bisera. And that's enough. More than enough." She opened her arms to us.

I squatted next to her bed. Bisera followed. Mother placed her shaky hands on us and kissed us. Bisera patted my head and said, looking at Mother, "But this golden son can replace all of us, hundreds of us. He is the one."

"I can't exist without him," Mother whimpered, shivering.

The next phase of cancer treatment was chemotherapy, which involved taking cytostatic drugs in an attempt to kill the remaining cancer cells, or at least keep them from dividing and multiplying. When I mentioned it, Mother said, abruptly, "I don't want to look like a skeleton. Like those men and women walking like ghosts, as if they've been held in a Nazi camp, with no hair left on their scalps and dealing every day with terrible side effects. Have you seen them? My roommate was infused with cytostatics. You saw how many times a day she would throw up and complain to the doctor that she was constantly dizzy. I've had enough of hospitals and doctors. I don't want to hear about it, even if I have to die tomorrow. Yes. There is something better then chemotherapy—death. I need peace."

The surgeon was against chemotherapy. The oncologist was for it, although he didn't promise any improvement afterward. I decided not to bother Mother any longer and to let her have her "peace." She didn't, though. The pain increased every day. We tripled the dosage of her painkillers. Some days, I had to call emergency services and the nurses would inject her with morphine. Mother would fall into a deep "peace" and, when she woke, she would ask me, "What's going on, Bazhe? You hide that I have 'that'. Do you?" Her eyes would freeze then. "That" referred to the cancer. She was afraid even to mention the word.

"No, Mother. You don't have it. You had a tiny piece of corrupt and dysfunctional flesh. It's something we all carry somewhere in us. Believe me."

Suddenly, Mother pushed me. "Move," she ordered. She strictly followed the old folklore beliefs that if you change position you will escape a curse. "I said move! I don't want you to carry that ever," she shouted.

"That won't help. I'm telling you, all of us have it in one place or another. Now that the little piece of bad flesh has been removed, there's nothing left but an inflamed colon. That's why you have the pain." I responded firmly.

We seemed to go through this sad little dance every time she awoke back in her bed. Mother was fanatically superstitious. She couldn't help it. She would push my body harder until I would move, at times even slip from the edge of her bed. She was content then, thinking that she had kept the curse from affecting me, but her smile didn't last. It turned into a sad expression that was becoming sadder every day. She looked as if she were counting the hours towards her final one. During those moments, I wished that I were blind. Not always, though, because I needed to see in order to help her.

During her hospitalization, Mother had about ten colostomy accidents. At home, they happened much more often because her appetite improved upon having homemade food everyday. Our neighbor, Frosa, the wife of my father's cousin, cooked for us. She also did our shopping. She volunteered to do this, not because she loved it, but out of self-interest.

When my father was alive, we always ate the best quality food. Mother was able to maintain that standard because she inherited my father's high pension. On top of that, we had my money. For Frosa, it was an opportunity. We knew she took money while shopping for us and lied about the cost of the items. Also, a part of whatever she made for us on any given day would end up on her table, even though her husband was a watchmaker with a reasonable income. Nevertheless, having a shopper and a cook, even one who stole, was okay with us. I didn't know how to cook. I had never needed to cook. Even if I had known how, I couldn't have, after Mother got sick.

When Mother gave Frosa a bonus at the end of each month, in appreciation for her help, she would say, "Oh, no, no, Kostadina. I'm doing this out of respect and love for you. Not for money." Her big face would subtly blush from the falsity of her words, and she would take the folded deutsche marks from Mother's hand and stuff them quickly into her pocket. Before she left our house, in the hallway, she would count them. I caught her a number of times, and I was sure she probably complained to her husband about how cheap we were. You can never satisfy greedy people. They're sick.

That night in May was pleasant, perfect for a good sleep, but I couldn't enter my bed until I killed the three big moths that circled like mad around the lamp. The exercise woke me up. I couldn't sleep, so I opened my notebook, and began to write.

Frosa was a daughter-in-law to my old Aunt Sandra, my father's first cousin and the surrogate for the grandmother I never knew. I loved Sandra. I called her Granny. She was widowed young, left with a son and three daughters to raise. Her husband died in a motorcycle accident, and the whole town talked about how perfect their marriage had been. She never remarried, convinced that she would never find someone who could match her husband's well-known kindness. She always cried when talking about him, and his death was a wound that never healed.

When her youngest daughter married a Turkish man she met at medical school, their inter-ethnic relationship was frowned upon by their classmates and the administration. Marriage between Christians and Muslims was forbidden by custom. To save their relationship, they moved from Macedonia to Kosovo. Granny did not talk to her for a long time, which was very hard for her because the youngest daughter was her favorite, and had her father's looks and personality.

Granny Sandra died when I started college. Every time I looked over our fence at her backyard, it seemed so empty without her there, hanging clothes on the line. Her rusting chair waited in the middle of her garden for her return, and so did I for a quite some time.

Frosa ran away from home and married Granny's son at eighteen. They lived one block from us, in Granny's old house, which once belonged to a Turkish aristocrat before the Ottoman Empire collapsed. Frosa was a real bitch. She was cruel to Granny Sandra. She closed the door to everyone who tried to visit Granny, with an ugly expression and a cold attitude. That hurt Granny a great deal, because gossip was a big part of her life, as it was to many others in my town. Their relationship turned ugly. Granny loved to make everyone laugh at the expense of her daughter-in-law, who she described as a hideous creature obsessed with washing her hair almost every day in an old metal bucket.

Once a week Frosa and her husband would bathe out of the same bucket. It was bizarre. They weren't poor, but they never installed a bathroom. Granny's son, Frosa's husband, acted child-like. Locals always made fun of him. Even Granny would sneer about how he stared at his wife like a dog for hours after she would call him her sweet angel.

One day, succumbing to temptation, he bought some fancy-looking clothes from the funeral shop, called, "Endless dream." Unfortunately, on the way home, rain began pouring and his flimsy clothes for the deceased fell apart. His toes poked out through the cardboard soles of his shiny burgundy shoes. He had to walk home barefoot. That was a big joke around town for a long time. I remember Frosa crying for days, embarrassed by her husband. Of course, Granny Sandra didn't comfort her. She accused her of not paying enough attention to her husband. They fought constantly, but in my presence the fights were usually short and the atmosphere was less tense because they would focus on me.

When my parents went to big government officials' parties or on vacation, they would leave me with Granny Sandra. I loved it. We would play with my toys, watch movies, and play cards. I giggled over her constant, hilarious gossip. She was like a radio station, broadcasting the news all over town. She would put Sally Jesse Raphael to shame. She particularly liked talking about the wars that often erupted between mothers and daughters-in-law because a son would traditionally bring his wife to live with him at his parents' home. Usually, the wives were faithful, committed to satisfying their husbands all the time, and were nice to their mothers-in-law. But sometimes serious disagreements arose and the combatants would almost kill each other. Nowadays, one can probably still find people living this way in small Balkan villages, but few other places.

Frosa was nice to me and I loved her. I knew how to make her feel important. One night, however, things changed forever. At the time, I was five years old. We finished dinner and Granny Sandra went out to use the privy. Frosa had huge fake butterflies hanging from all the curtains in the house. It was a provincial trend that she observed.

Frosa stood and removed the biggest one from one curtain. It was the size of a crow, with a big brown-black body, huge wings, long antennae, and skinny, spider-like legs. She began to make loud noises and swung it around my head in big circles. Back and forth, back and forth, coming closer to my face each time, until the butterfly's skinny legs touched my eyelashes and I closed my shivering eyelids tightly. I felt the big dark flapping wings brushing against my cheeks. I opened my eyes and gazed into the butterfly's ugly, lustful eyes. It seemed as if those twitching butterfly legs would grab me and hold me under the beast's gaping mouth, so it could drop sticky yellow liquid all over me, paralyzing my face, eyes, mouth, fingers, and legs before it killed me. I felt like a hopeless victim getting ready to be eaten, and that sick woman thought what she was doing was funny.

She began chasing me around the house. Weeping, I ran upstairs. Frosa chased me, laughing like an insane person, continuing to swing the monster butterfly towards me. Somehow, she trapped me in a corner of a room. I covered my eyes, crouched down, and began to scream for help. Finally, my Granny showed up, looking alarmed.

"What is happening?" she asked.

"Nothing, he's just a little scared." Frosa replied, flippantly. I was still crouched in the corner, defending myself from the winged gargoyle in her hand.

Granny picked me up, wiped the tears from my face, and carried me to another room. "Don't be scared. Butterflies are beautiful creatures! People hunt them and collect them to admire them. By the way, that butterfly is fake!"

Granny spoke kindly and convincingly. With my eyes closed, I could see big butterflies, led by Frosa, flying through the dark open fields. I opened them immediately. My tormentor stood before me, smiling, and I threw up on her. Frosa's anger radiated from her livid face, but she couldn't do anything. I was safe in my Granny Sandra's hands.

"Get me a towel, handkerchief, something! Don't stand staring at him like a lunatic!" Granny ordered, sneering.

Frosa ran downstairs. Shortly afterward, she came back with a bunch of handkerchiefs.

"God, what did you do to him?" Granny asked. She grabbed the handkerchiefs from Frosa's hand and began wiping the vomit from my mouth and chin.

"It was just a game," Frosa said, looking down with disgust at her vomit-covered blouse and skirt.

"You're really sick!" Granny shouted. "This child is scared to death, and you say it's just a game? I can't believe it! What do you have to say for yourself?!"

For a long while, neither of them spoke. They stared each other down like angry, feral cats. Then Granny clutched my shivering body again.

"Oh my God, what's wrong with you, my dear? Can you tell me please, what's wrong? What did this bitch do to you?" Granny looked at Frosa and whispered, emphatically, "Go to hell." Granny couldn't help being nasty. She loved me more than anyone.

"Why would you be so scared of my fake butterfly? It's a harmless ornament. It's just so exotic, it looks real," Frosa said.

I couldn't understand why she would ask me such a stupid question when a short time ago she was acting like a mad woman with that damned butterfly. From that moment on, I hated her more than anyone else. She was a witch. Her bushy black hair was a nest of butterflies. Her mouth was encrusted with butterflies, eager to attack me. Two pairs of skinny legs stuck out of her mouth, moving. One big wing dropped from her hair. She jumped, caught it, then she put it into her mouth and began chewing it, chortling at me. I vomited again at Frosa. Unfortunately, my puke didn't hit her. Again, Granny wiped the vomit dropping from my chin to my collar.

"Please take me home, Granny," I mumbled, sobbing.

Granny Sandra nodded, looking worried. She kissed me and lifted me in her arms. "Evil bitch," she muttered over my head at Frosa.

As we left the room, we ran into Granny's son who had just arrived from a poker game at his friend's house. He was a compulsive gambler. "What happened?" he asked, staring at my terrified face.

"Oh, get lost! Go back to your 'nice' wife! You pussy-whipped jerk! Damn the both of you together!" Granny shouted, then whispered towards the ceiling, "God forgive me."

He whirled around like a slapped little boy and ran to his angry wife's embrace. She tapped his shoulder, consolingly. The touch of Granny's hand felt as soothing as the summer night's wind that caressed my terrified face as we walked out. Through the opening in the bordering privet fence, we walked to our house. Granny Sandra made hot tea, and we curled on my bed, munching on cookies. She tried hard to cheer me up, gossiping about the primitivism of the newly emigrated peasants in town, now and then stroking my hair, and kissing my pale cheeks.

"Don't tell anyone what happened to you tonight, my dear. People would laugh at you. You have to keep it secret."

"Yes," I said, pushing myself closer to her.

"I don't understand, though. How could a stupid fake butterfly scare you so much?" Granny asked me, cautiously, raising her eyebrows.

I didn't answer. Neither I, nor anyone else, had a clue. Locals didn't understand that someone could be scared of butterflies, that a child could develop a fear of them. Entomophobia, in general, was an alien terminology for them. What's more, they didn't understand the damaging side of it. I clenched Granny's warm and soothing body while I fell asleep.

In my dreams, I saw Frosa's fat face and the queen-butterfly coming out of her mouth. It was flying above me, wiggling its antennae, and staring with its fluorescent eyes. I began running around like a chicken without a head. Frosa commanded the queen butterfly to reproduce. Thousands of offspring began flying after me, screeching in their high-pitched voices, I was afraid to look back. When I finally did, I saw Frosa and the queen-butterfly following their fearless posse. Some of the butterflies became blinded by the streetlights and fell to their death. Frosa plucked them from the ground and placed them in her hair and mouth. My legs ached. My feet were bleeding. My strength faded. My dread grew darker, as they surrounded me. I could see my end, as I heard the noise of their batting wings. It was midnight, and knocking on any of the passing doors would be useless. The town was asleep. Only the hotel was open, but the butterflies beat me to the door. I tried to stomp on them, kill as many as possible. I loved the cracking sound of their bodies being crushed. But more and more of them came. They attacked my face, flew into my ears, nose, and mouth. They blinded my eyes. Two strong ones landed on my eyelids and tried to pry them and drink the whites of my eyes. I shook my hands, legs, and head, to get them off. I wanted to scream, but I was afraid to open my mouth and let them fly in.

For the last time, I saw the frightening image of Frosa. Her eyes leaked smelly, sulfur-like yellow liquid, like the liquid that explodes from a smashed butterfly. The butterflies on her hair and face became more frantic as the king-butterfly emerged from her mouth. I slipped on the smelly liquid that was all over me and fell down. The butterflies started biting me, harder and harder. I felt pain all over my body. They worked their way from my forehead down to my lips, chewing around my eyes, nose, cheekbones, chin, and neck, and trying to enter my body through my ears, nostrils, and mouth. I couldn't see anything but their fluttering powdery wings, brown-black bodies, and spider-like legs as they crawled all over me. Faintly, I could see their devilish eyes and smiles as the sulfur-yellow liquid dried, gluing me to the street. The butterflies began eating my eyelids and sucking out my eyes. I awoke with a start, sweaty and shaky. That time, my Granny was there to hold and comfort me. Many worse dreams of butterflies were yet to come, however, and I had to deal with those on my own. They were horrifying.

The next morning, I was rinsing Mother's heavy, stained clothing with bleach before putting it in the washer when the telephone in the hallway rang. I ran, wiping my hands on my pants, and as soon as I picked it up Rambo's voice boomed through the receiver.

"I have big news, baby. I found her."

"You're kidding, aren't you?" After so many years of trying, I thought I was dreaming. I breathed deeply and looked at myself in the mirror. "Tell me, tell me more," I begged.

"I had a hell of a time tracking her. After hiring a lot of people and investigating in many places, I found out she no longer lives in Macedonia. It was very difficult to get access to the police departments of the former states of Yugoslavia, but I used some old connections and located her in the Croatian coastal region, Dalmatia, in the town of Split. Her name is Mila Bibulich. She's married to a Croatian-Italian man. She left Macedonia after your birth. She's a clerk in an architectural company. Get a paper and pen."

I ran upstairs to my room, grabbed a pen, opened the first book I saw, and picked up the cordless telephone from my desk. "I'm ready," I said, breathing hard.

After Rambo read me her address, and her work and home numbers, as well as those of her parents, brother, and sister, he said, "I have more good news. I think she'll visit Macedonia soon. Her brother's daughter is getting married. The wedding reception is scheduled for two weeks from now at the restaurant in the Hotel Panorama, in the town of Kavadarci. You can call to confirm this, but be very discreet. Unfortunately, I can't describe Mila Bibulich. I've heard that she was very beautiful when she bore you. I believe she still is. You have a young mother. Only she knows who your biological father is. If you're not comfortable going there to look for her, I would advise you to call her at work. It's safer."

I felt free of an old pressure and my heart raced with joy. I could feel my heartbeat even in the fingertips that held my pen.

"Finally," I sighed, when he had finished talking. "I am very grateful to you. Thank you. I'm so happy, I feel as if I could touch the sky."

"I can't talk longer. I'm calling from the office. Someone might hear this. You got everything you need. Let me know how things go. Okay?"

"I will. Thanks. Thank you very much again," I said, sincerely. After I put the cordless phone back in its recharger, my glow began to dim as I thought of Mother.

"She's probably whining in pain," I whispered to myself, and ran downstairs. Guilt halted me halfway. Am I writing off Mother while she's still alive? I cast aside my feelings of shame and continued down the steps as furtively as a burglar. I opened the living room door slowly. Mother was asleep. Good, I thought, afraid that if she weren't, she would have suspected that something was wrong from looking at my eyes. Mothers have the strong ability to sense things, and incredible intuition when it comes to their children's secrets.

What if she finds out? No, I can't allow that. She would die, thinking that I'm replacing her. Am I? My tears started falling, as I stood above her shrunken and motionless body. Her skin was tinted with the pale yellow color, and the fawn color of the spots on it indicated sickness and inevitable death. I went back to my bedroom and buried my head in my pillow, to muffle my loud crying.

12

Wedding

I continued to look after Mother's hygiene and the house, keeping both almost impeccable. But the stink of death was always there. I felt intense pressure, especially when I had to lie to Mother. My rage over her cancer, my guilt about lying to her, and the urge to find my biological mother turned my stomach into a pit of acid. I could feel the acid rise in my throat, burning my tonsils. I would struggle to suppress it. I felt like an asshole, deceiving my mother like that. But I had to find my roots and my identity. I had to manipulate my poor Mother.

I called the hotel to confirm that the reception was taking place there. That Saturday afternoon, I told Mother that I was going directly to the neighboring town's warehouse to pick up the colostomy supplies, since the delivery from the social service was late. I took a taxi to the town of Kavadarci, for centuries a famous producer of wine, located in central Macedonia. I wore plain white pants and a blue shirt, in an attempt to look inconspicuous and blend in with the locals. To disguise my appearance, I wore glasses.

The hotel was on a hill overlooking the town. Inside, at the restaurant's entrance, two children greeted the wedding guests and gave them ribbons to wear. I waited for more guests to arrive, then stepped in line behind a tall, heavy couple. While one of the girls pinned the ribbon to my shirt pocket, I glanced inside quickly. Two couples were greeting the guests and receiving the presents at the restaurant foyer. One of them was my biological uncle and his wife. I guessed that the medium-tall man with salt-and-pepper hair and green eyes was my uncle, because he resembled me.

Suddenly, I couldn't go any farther. I dropped some change into the girls' baskets and turned around as calmly as possible. The arriving guests stared at me, confused, as I walked away. I was sweating, frightened that someone would suspect I didn't belong there and say something to me. Nothing happened, and I kept walking towards the hotel's entrance. I entered, and cheered up when I realized that a glass wall separated the hotel lobby from the restaurant, and that there was a second entrance to it. By the way the place was decorated, I could tell that my uncle was a middle-class man. Suddenly, I walked out. A few moments later, I gathered my nerve and went back.

I waited until the restaurant was completely filled, then sneaked in, taking a seat at a corner table farthest from the one in the center, where the bride, the groom, and their families gathered. A typical provincial band began to play and drinks were served. I ordered a Coke.

The bride and the groom began to dance. She was my biological cousin, although she didn't look a bit like me. I started analyzing the features of everyone sitting at the head table and comparing theirs to mine. Unfortunately, they were pretty far away. I'd brought my glasses, but they didn't help much, being made for watching TV. I was afraid to take them off. *But who knows me here? You never know.* The world can be a small place. And my biological mother might know me. I had heard that could happen. I kept them on.

After I finished the Coke, I joined a circle of folk dancers, to get a closer look at the head table. My eyes were moist from straining to find the woman who helped created them. *She must be here. Her brother's daughter gets married. She has to be here.*

I began scrutinizing everyone sitting on the bride's side of the table. Right next to the bride was her father—the man I saw when I first arrived, and who resembled me. I was sure he was my biological uncle. Next to him, was his wife, followed by a young girl who looked like the bride—her sister. That's my other biological cousin, I thought. The couple next to her was older. My biological mother's older sister with her husband, I guessed. I kept looking for a woman in her mid-forties, fifteen years older than me, accompanied by a Croat-Italian man.

I became nervous when I noticed that people were staring at me, too. I stood out among the locals, who knew each other well. I stopped staring at the head table and concentrated on the dance. The joyous rhythm of our music helped me forget my fear, and I realized how much I'd missed it in America. More people got up to join the traditional circle dance, *Oro,* as the musicians segued from song to song. After a while, I moved to another spot in the circle, between two older women who were talking to each other and chuckling. I hoped to get some information before it was too late and they caught me. Steeling myself, I leaned towards the one to my left, who had that look typical of a provincial gossip and most likely knew the life story of everyone there.

"Hi. Nice wedding," I said. "But I don't see Mila around. Did she come from Croatia?" My Adam's apple jumped in my throat and my lips trembled as I spoke.

"Are you her relative? You look so much like her!" she exclaimed. Her smile revealed fake teeth, including one of gold that sparkled in the left corner of her mouth.

I was stunned and afraid, but also excited. "Oh, no. Just a friend of hers. I haven't seen her for ages. Are you related to her?" I leaned towards her ear as I spoke, almost kissing it, so no one would hear me. Of course, the music was loud and I practically had to yell to be heard. I glanced around, fearful that any minute I was going to be spotted as an outsider.

"No. I'm from the groom's side, but I know Mila. Last summer, she was here on vacation with her husband. Lovely couple. She's still beautiful, as always." The woman paused, and she began to look around the room.

I focused my unblinking gaze on her, as if I were a religious fanatic who thought she was the prophet. My ears became as alert as a German Shepherd's. I didn't want to miss a single word she said.

"I don't see her," she shouted into my ear. "Well, now Croatia is a foreign country. It's not as easy as it used to be flying here, particularly after all the problems in neighboring Bosnia. The connections are messed up. I have a cousin in Slovenia, and she had such trouble getting to Macedonia. There isn't one reliable direct line between the former Yugoslav counties yet. We're all angry at each other. And we still don't know what for."

"I see," I said, delighted that I didn't need to keep straining my eyes. But what if she suspected something? I could easily see this provincial hag advertising to anyone that a stranger was looking for Mila. I felt my Adam's apple leaping again. I danced a couple of more circles to calm myself down, then I returned to my table. As soon as I sat, the waiter approached me with a grim, investigative glare in his eye.

"By which side were you invited, mister?"

"The bride's side, sir," I said, feeling myself blush from my head to my toes. The glass in my hand began shaking.

He twitched his right eyebrow and quickly walked to the head table. As he spoke to the groom's father, he pointed at me. I had to do something before they came over to question me. Someone must have taken a head count of the guests before serving lunch, I thought, recalling a time when young guys would go to weddings uninvited and eat, dance, and have lots of fun without being bothered. Not in the new Balkan societies.

I watched the waiter leave the groom's father and enter the kitchen. *I'll go talk to the biological uncle. No, I can't do that.* I sat there, vacillating, nervously turning my glass, and puffing a cigarette. The musicians stopped playing and announced that lunch was served. Waiters came out of the kitchen, pushing serving carts. *I can't stay and eat. I'll wait until the uncle leaves the table. When he has to go to pee or something. He constantly moves anyway.*

My eyes focused on him intently. As the uncle took a couple of bites of his appetizer, a short man walked up to him and whispered something on his ear. Uncle stood up abruptly and walked towards the foyer. *Now,* I told myself. My urge defeated my hesitation, and I got up to follow him. Through the foyer's glass door, I saw a couple standing, waiting by the coat check. I sped up and caught Uncle before he pushed through the foyer's doors.

"Excuse me, sir. I have to talk with you." I said, firmly, from behind him.

He turned to face me, with a start, his expression one of surprise. He looked me over, appraisingly. "Yes?" he said, sounding uncertain.

Although I was pretty sure that the man was my biological uncle, I still had some doubts. I tried to stay focused, consoling myself with the thought that I might be seconds away from the end of my quest. "Are you Mr. Nelkov, sir?" I asked.

"Yes, I am."

"Well, I think your sister, Mila, is my biological mother."

"What?" His pupils widened. Quickly, he grasped my upper arm. "Let's get out of here," he said, keeping his voice down, and he opened the door for me. Smiling, he told the couple waiting for him in the foyer, "I'll be right back," and guided me out, through the crowd of guests smoking on the steps. He walked me to the middle of the parking lot, then stopped between the parked cars.

"You said my sister, Mila, is your mother? I had no idea she'd ever been pregnant before she married. Maybe this is a mistake. Are you sure?"

I pulled out the copy of the adoption agreement and handed it to him.

His hands shook as he read it. After he reached the bottom of the document, he looked at me and whispered, "God, there is her signature. If this had happened, there was no way I would've known. I was only five then. Jesus! She was only fifteen!" His forehead began to sweat. Tears welled in his eyes. Mine were already falling to the asphalt. He hugged me and murmured, "I have to go back and pretend nothing's happened. I have to be happy. It's my daughter's wedding. God, on this day! What's your name?" He pulled away from my hug and held my shoulders firmly.

"Bazhe," I answered, and extended my hand. "Congratulations," I said, smiling through my tears.

"Thank you." He shook my hand and embraced me again. "Stay for lunch, then come home for more of the festivities." He smiled and wiped his tears with his white handkerchief.

"I don't think I should. I'll bet many people have already asked you who I am."

"Everyone notices a stranger at these small town weddings. But don't worry; I'll say you are my friend's son from…?"

"America," I answered. "I used to live in Prespa County, Resen."

"Stay. I'll be glad if you do." He sounded insistent.

"Perhaps I'd better go. I don't want to ruin your celebration any further. I came to see her, but she is not here, is she?"

"How do you know that?" he asked, skeptically.

"I asked around, discreetly. Can I call you?"

"Sure, sure, here is my number." He reached into his suit pocket.

"I have all the information already. Thank you." I placed my hand on his, to stop him.

"How stupid of me. Of course you do," he said, blushing. "Call me Monday, after all this is finished." He looked over at the restaurant and asked, "Where are you staying now? At the hotel?"

"No, sir, at my parents' house. My mother is very ill. She has cancer. That's why I came from the U.S. To care of her."

"Oh, boy. Really bad news." He shook his head and embraced me again.

"Where were you? I've been looking for you everywhere!" The woman who accompanied him all the time and resembled the bride, strode towards us. She held her long violet dress up, so its back wouldn't trail.

"This is my wife, Donka," he said. "And this is my friend's son from America, Bazhe." He motioned at me, then looked cautiously back at her.

While we shook hands, I noticed that she was looking closely at my face.

"Congratulations," I said to her. "I have to go."

"Why now? The real wedding begins after lunch," she said.

"Thank you, ma'am. Sorry, but I'm afraid I can't stay."

"He has a sick mother back home," my uncle interjected.

"Oh, poor guy. I'm sorry to hear it," she said, her face colored with grief.

I congratulated them again and left, smiling. As I walked towards the telephone booth to call a taxi, I overheard the uncle saying to his wife, "I'll tell you everything later." She knew I wasn't her husband's friend's son from America. Women's intuition is usually superior to men's; it seems their DNA is composed entirely of "suspicion" genes.

From the moment that we first spoke, I could see that my biological uncle was a kind man. I paid him a visit the following week, and he introduced me to an older woman who knew all about my adoption. She was his and Mila's aunt, their father's sister, and my great-aunt. She was an invalid. Her left arm was missing. She was the one who sheltered Mila in her house in the capital while she carried me, an out-of-wedlock bastard, as the locals would say. She did everything to prevent Mila from being shamed before her family and the province. After the aunt browsed my adoption document, she said, "Yes, Mila is your real mother."

I intensely disliked the phrase "real mother," but I controlled my temper so as not to offend anyone. I had to keep things friendly, at least until I saw Mila. I lit a cigarette. Uncle lit one too. His wife came from the other room, carrying a dusty photo album. She opened it in front of me and pointed at a sepia picture of a young woman.

"This is your mother right before she bore you." She spoke reverently.

I scrutinized the picture closely. While comparing every part of her pretty face with mine, I felt any remaining uncertainty about our relationship vanish. I had no doubt that she was woman who bore me. I looked like her. The three of them cried as I studied the photo of the woman who had made me constantly search for my identity. I felt as if I were decoding ancient hieroglyphic scripts. I didn't want to miss the slightest detail.

"She has a husband and two sons. Your half brothers," the great-aunt said, plaintively.

Just like that. Now I have brothers, and God knows how many more siblings from the biological father's side, I thought. I felt the same as when, as a little boy, I found out I was adopted. Again, I felt like a puppet in the hands of adults that were creating and altering my destiny. I thought of all the puppets out there like me.

"When are you planning to call her?" the great-aunt asked me.

"Soon. Please don't tell her anything yet. I want to be the first." I raised my voice, as my eyes probed hers. I didn't trust her. I didn't like her, even though if she hadn't helped Mila, I probably wouldn't be alive now. Maybe that would have been better. No one knows why we are created. Some of us are destined to die as fetuses. Some are killed in the blossom of our youth. And some of us survive until an old age we don't deserve at all. If God is the one who really knows, he owes us an explanation. I didn't buy the usual explanation: that He wanted to send us to Heaven or Hell. Bullshit! What about the hurt He created for those of us suffering on earth? I was upset, and I kept looking into the great-aunt's eyes.

There was something evil in her. Nature, bad karma…? God, or whoever was in charge had punished her already, I decided, my gaze drifting momentarily to her missing limb. I looked back into her eyes, until she averted hers, towards my untouched glass of Coke.

"Please don't make any problems for her," she said, and whatever was left of her arm moved in her upper left sleeve like a cut wing.

"If I had any such intention, I would have done it already," I said. "I have complete information on all your family. I'll call her at work, not at home."

No one said a word. The three of them looked as abashed as convicts, their heads down, staring into their laps. I guess they sensed my desire to find her. They didn't seem thrilled about what Mila had done, nor did they seem terribly ashamed. I couldn't put my finger on it, but I got strange vibes from them and sensed a lot of family dysfunction in their midst.

They asked me to stay for lunch. I didn't. I had so much to think about. I needed to be alone. Uncle was silent as he drove me to the taxi stand. Out of the blue, he remarked, "I thought I knew my sister well. It turns out that I don't know her at all." He lit a cigarette and sped up. When we arrived, as he opened the taxi's door, he said, "Feel free to call me anytime, if you want to talk."

I shook his hand and slid into the back of the cab, speechless. I was touched by the closeness he felt towards me. I thought the events of that day would fade from my mind when, two hours later, I was beside my mother's bed. I was wrong, though. As I added painkiller drops to the water in her favorite Romanian crystal glass, the image of Mila crossed my mind. I began comparing her to Mother. Not Mother as she was at that moment, but as I remembered her, when she had the aura of a classic Hollywood movie star and attracted people everywhere we went. I looked in the mirror and confirmed my suspicion that I looked more like the woman I grew up with than the one in the picture. It was amazing how many of Mother's features I had.

"No wonder people say that, after a while, you start to look like the parents who raised you, not the ones that made you," I whispered, content with my discovery.

The next day, after I had seen to Mother's needs, I dialed Mila's work number. In Serbo-Croatian, I asked the operator for Mrs. Bibulich. I still spoke it very well. After waiting a couple of minutes, a gentle voice came over the line. "Hello, Mila Bibulich speaking."

"Hello." I paused to take a breath. "This is your son. My name is Bazhe. I'm calling from Macedonia."

Dead silence for a couple of seconds, then a loud cry that seemed to last for fifteen minutes.

"Oh, God," she said. "I knew this would happen. I knew you would find me one day. I tried many times, but I couldn't find you. I'd almost lost hope of ever seeing you. More than thirty years later, and here you are. It's like a dream. It feels so unreal. Is it really you?"

I waited for her sobbing to subside, then said, "I was adopted in Resen. My father died last year and my mother is ill with cancer now. I live in America. I came back to take care of her."

"Oh, I am very sorry about your mother. It's noble what you are doing for her. You are a good son." She began to cry louder.

"I didn't want to call you at home. I know you have a husband and two sons. I didn't want to cause any problems. You haven't told them, have you?"

"No," she said, softly.

"I met your brother, his wife, and the aunt who helped you when you were pregnant with me. They told me—"

"Believe me, I didn't want to give you up. I had to. I was fifteen then." She cut me off, her voice filled with guilt and the long-remembered suffering of an adolescent girl forced to give up her child.

I said nothing, waiting for her to talk again.

"How did you find me?" she asked, weeping. I heard voices in the background at the other end. "Wait a minute, please," she said. She spoke to somebody, then said, "Yes. I'm back." Her voice was sounded more composed.

"Can you talk? I'll call you another time if you can't," I said.

"Oh, no, no! It's all right. Tell me. How did you find me?"

"It's a long story. I'll explain it when we see each other."

"When?" she asked, quickly.

"It's up to you. I have to stay near Mother."

"I understand. I'll try to fly there as soon as possible"

"When you have a definite plan, call me. I'm at home all day. If I don't answer, I'm busy with Mother or in the garden or showering. Just leave a message."

"No one checks it?"

"There's no one here except Mother and me. She hasn't gone upstairs since her tumor operation. No problem. Good day."

"Wait. Watch your mother. She is our angel. She has done everything I was supposed to do for you. Kiss her for me. Say it's a greeting from your old friend. Please." Her sobs became louder again.

"Thank you," I said, and hung up.

Mila had wanted to talk more, but I figured we'd had enough for a start. I went downstairs, trying to look happy. Mother was lying on her side, watching a children's educational program, the one I used to watch instead of doing my boring math homework. I hugged her.

"Ready for a little walk, Mother?"

"Yes, my gold." She tried to lift her body. I encircled my arms around her chest, to help pull her up. Her limbs were getting weaker. They began struggling to handle her weight, even though with every new day she was getting lighter. As usual, Mother put all her weight on my lower arm, wrapping her hand around it as firmly as she could. Slowly, I guided her outside, to the garden.

"My roses are lonely. I wish I could take care of them again." She touched their fragile new stems and buds as we walked along the concrete path. "You look disturbed. Is everything all right, son?" Her tired, melancholy voice consoled me, even as it broke my heart.

It took all my strength not to scream. "Everything is fine, Mother," I lied.

"Good, Bazhe. You're young. Everything ought to be all right." She lifted her face towards the sky. "It's such a beautiful day, isn't it? One day closer to my end. I should enjoy every second of it, though, because soon I'll have no more sense of time, dates, and seasons. But it's better that way. It's going to be easier for me, going towards death. Unfortunately, it'll be harder for you." She caressed the roses with her dried yellow fingers.

"Mother, you're freaking me out now, talking this bullshit. You'll see. By the end of this summer, you'll be flying over the Atlantic with me."

"You mean flying with the angels? I doubt I'll make it to next May. Your month, my gold."

"What the hell's wrong with you today? You're making me feel worthless. Is that how you show your gratitude? By underestimating my abilities? Eh?"

"Never," she replied, earnestly. Her face turned serious, and she kissed my cheek adding, "I'll be all right next to you. I will."

Making her feel that her words were against me was the only way to make her stop talking about death. It always worked. Yet, she talked more often about it. Much more often than before. And it was harder listening to her, denying to her, and arguing with her, while wondering if she knew the truth.

13

Mila

Mila Bibulich called me every couple of days. Our conversations were brief, because she was at work and I was always occupied around Mother. Slowly, we began to discover one another, often describing how we looked. We spoke about our families; we compared life in Macedonia, Croatia, and America; we talked about Mother's cancer. When I brought up the adoption, she wouldn't say much, only general things that I already knew. She insisted on waiting until we met to discuss the details. She had wanted to visit me around my birthday in May, but couldn't get leave from work. The next month, her boss gave her a week off and she booked a flight for June 20.

That day, I told Mother, I had to go to the capital to meet an American friend who was passing through Macedonia on his way to Greece and Turkey. The airport was crowded, mostly with Albanian families and their hordes of children, carrying enormous luggage that made them look like they were in an exodus. Most of them were probably going to Switzerland or America. Macedonian nouveau-capitalists paced the halls, speaking loudly into their cellular phones, showing off. In one corner, a nervous group of Bosnian refugees cursed the delay of their flight to Sarajevo. Police officers drank, smoked, and laughed at the bar. Noisy taxi drivers, mostly illegal, circled like sharks around the exit, aggressively hawking their services to passers-by. UN soldiers and foreign officials complained about the check-in clerks' slowness. In many respects, it was like a microcosm of Macedonian society. I drank my coffee and waited for Mila's plane to arrive at noon.

Her flight was delayed an hour. It was to be expected because the plane belonged to one of the two newly formed airlines that served Macedonia. When it finally arrived I walked to the gate. Out of the crowd, I picked out a woman in red with a striped black shoulder bag, carrying a black suitcase and a blue book in her right hand. I was holding a blue book, also.

The minute our eyes met, we were instinctively drawn together. We stood for a moment, just looking at each other. She was crying; I was smiling. She dropped the suitcase and leapt to embrace me. As I hugged her, I could feel her body tremble.

"Oh, son," she said. Her gray-green eyes gazed into mine, and then she began kissing me, her hold becoming tighter. She lay her head on my left shoulder, sobbing. I kissed her back.

"Finally," I whispered to myself, delighted.

I have two mothers now, I thought. Still, it was the mother who raised me, not the one who made me, that counted. I couldn't call Mila Bibulich "Mother."

A woman crying and a younger man smiling in the middle of the airport. People turned and stared at us, confused. I was more annoyed than Mila about all the attention. I wished we could have met on a desert island.

I'd solved half of the mystery of my identity. The other half, my father, was less important, but she'd tell me about him. She'll help me. She has to. She owes me that.

"Son, son," she said, repeatedly, lamenting her lost motherhood. I couldn't think of her as my mother, though. Mother was in bed, fighting the devil that continued to consume her, still hoping to defeat it and join me in America one day. I missed her, even though I had longed for this moment for more than thirty years. Again, I felt guilty.

When Mila calmed down, I picked up her suitcase, placed my arm around her shaking shoulders, and guided her to a taxi. As we rode, she cried more loudly, reaching for my hand and pulling it towards her. She kissed my palm. It felt odd. To try to lighten the mood, I asked, "Did you imagine me as you see me now?"

"Close," she replied, and smiled slightly through her tears.

"Me, too. You haven't changed much from the picture I saw when you were fifteen," I said, smiling back.

"Thank you." She blushed, enveloping my hand with both of hers.

Out of courtesy, I let her hold my hand during the whole ride to the city, listening to her sob and to the driver complain about his standard of living and the system while playing his ex-Yugoslavian folk tapes that brought back memories of peaceful and secure times.

"Soon the lies will be corrected. Questions about my past will be answered," I said to myself, looking at Mila's reflection in the car window.

In the city, I told the driver to pull over in front of the Grand Hotel. I paid him, took her suitcase, and said, "The restaurant here is quiet in the afternoon. We can chat and have a drink before going home. What do you think?"

She nodded, embracing my arm.

"Are you hungry?" I asked, as I led her in.

"No, thank you. But you should eat, if you are."

"Later," I said. We found a table, and I pulled out a chair for her.

A few customers sat at the bar, drinking and joking. The sluggish waiter finally dragged himself to our table. We ordered cappuccinos. I took a pack of cigarettes from my pocket and offered her one. She said she didn't smoke, but thought she'd have one anyway. I guess she needed it before her confession. Her gaze penetrated deep into mine; I waited eagerly for her to say something. After taking a couple of puffs, she placed her cigarette in the ashtray and began.

"I was fifteen, at the end of my first year in high school, when we went on an excursion to Belgrade. We stayed in a famous downtown hotel, called Salvia. Groups of eminent people were staying there: company directors, politicians, and big shots. We saw them going to meetings and seminars and eating dinner in the hotel's restaurant—a very popular place. That night, most of us were in the lobby watching TV with the teachers. We were exhausted after taking a long tour of the capital's historic sites and having a late dinner. As I walked to the bathroom, I noticed a tall, well-dressed man in the foyer. He was drinking and talking with a couple of other men. He caught me looking at him and smiled. He was so handsome. I blushed and smiled back. It was quite a boost to my teenage ego. I went into the ladies room and began to fix my hair and makeup in front of the mirror. I was so into my damned looks. You know how girls are at that age." She raised her eyebrows, regretfully, and stubbed out her cigarette.

I nodded, engrossed, waiting for her to say more. She took a deep breath, then continued.

"No one was in the toilet. The door opened and closed quickly. I looked, but no one was there. When I turned back to the mirror, the door opened again. This time, I saw the man in the foyer. He smiled as he walked towards me. When he was about a meter away, I managed to say, 'Comrade, this is a ladies' bathroom.'

"He said, 'Do you consider yourself a lady? Then show me.' He spoke perfect Serbo-Croatian. His grin made my blood freeze. I took a step backwards, and he jumped on me and began kissing my face and neck. I started pushing him away, but he was too strong. Then he said, 'You don't want your teachers and schoolmates to see you all messed up, do you? The whole village, town, wherever you're coming from, will talk about the teenaged girl who did dirty things on her trip to the big city. No one will believe that you didn't want this.' He hissed his words at me, smirking, pressing me against the cold tiled wall. 'You have everything a hot, sexy lady should have. Do you know that?' He bit my earlobe, then my neck, unbuttoning my shirt and grabbing my breasts, legs, and rear. He started growling like an animal.

"His threats paralyzed me. I stopped resisting, realizing that if anyone found out, I would be humiliated before my family, my school, the whole province. I pictured myself returning to my small town, marked with shame for the rest of my life; my mates, teachers, and locals, all spitting at me and calling me a whore; no one willing to marry me, because I was no longer a virgin; my family disowning me. I could see myself ending up in a mental institution, without help from anyone. It was the Sixties, and that sort of fate was a distinct possibility in the Balkans, as in many other places. I thought I had to give in. If I had only known what bigger horror lay ahead, I would've screamed, scratched his eyeballs out of his sockets, and never let him rape me. I was only a fifteen-year-old provincial girl, in the big city for the first time and in the clutches of an experienced molester."

Mila stopped. She asked for another cigarette. I took one out and lit it for her. She began to smoke again, looking out the window. Her hands and body shook as she began crying again, and she bit her lip.

"He unzipped his pants. He ripped my skirt, then my underwear. My little purse fell to the floor. I kept looking at the door, terrified that someone would come in and catch us. He bit the top of my nose, then he said, 'Don't worry, angel. One of my guys is making sure no one will disturb us.' His voice was low, but sharp. I kept thinking, God, I hope this won't be a gang rape. God help me, please. I closed my eyes and prayed. Nothing is more frightening than being helpless, in the hands of a rapist. It was painful, and he shut my mouth after my first scream. Thank God it didn't last long. A couple of minutes or so. He left me shivering against that cold wall, and before he closed the door, he yelled, 'Straighten yourself up and get the hell out of here. Now!'

"I picked up my skirt, underwear, and purse, and ducked into one of the stalls. I heard men's laughter coming from the corridor. He was bragging about his successful conquest to his security guy. I wiped his disgusting traces off myself with my ripped underwear, threw them into the toilet, and kept flushing it until they disappeared. I wrapped the skirt around my waist and fastened it with my hairpin, so I could make it to my room. I ran to the mirror and quickly touched up my make-up. My teeth were clenched; I was a wreck.

"I stepped outside, hesitantly. Two girls from the other class were down the corridor, walking towards the bathroom. I looked down as I passed them, figuring they would guess everything if they saw my face. I was overreacting, but I loosened up a bit as I got in the elevator and pressed the button to my floor.

When I got to the room, I grabbed my nightshirt and locked myself in the toilet. My roommate was still downstairs watching TV. The smell of that beast on my torn clothing made me sick. My pale body was covered with red spots, from his malicious bites and kisses. There was no blood when I inspected my private area, still in great pain. I panicked, aware that I was supposed to bleed, being a virgin. I showered, stuffed my clothing into a plastic bag, and threw it into the tall, lidded garbage can at the end the corridor. I didn't want to take a chance with my roommate, who loved to poke around. I crawled into bed and tried to sleep. I had been so sheltered. I felt so hopeless. Also I—"

The waiter interrupted her as he brought us the cappuccino. She took a sip from her cup, then wiped her tears with a pink handkerchief and caressed my face, as if I were a little boy. It felt peculiar. Actually, I hated it. Yet, I didn't react. I figured she needed to do it.

"I changed that day," Mila said, with a sigh. "I withdrew, as any rape victim would. My schoolmates and teachers noticed it. My family noticed more than anyone. My body began to change, but I hid that from everyone. It was you, of course, growing in me. After a while, when I couldn't hide it any longer, I told my parents what had happened. They were furious. They didn't believe I was raped. They threatened to kill me and disown me. I would've stopped him. I would've screamed and gouged his eyeballs out. I would have done anything to stop him, if I had only known he would impregnate me...that he was sending me to a worse fate than being called a teenage whore...and that was to give you up. I remember, while he was raping me, I thought, I'll let him do it to avoid the scandal, then I'll hide the secret and marry a guy from the city who won't care if I'm a virgin or not. But luck wasn't on my side. Not at all.

"To avoid the shame that would come if people found out I was carrying a bastard, my father immediately sent me to the capital to stay with his sister, the aunt you met. He told everyone that he transferred me to a better high school. My parents didn't want me to have an abortion. They were afraid that I would never be able to have children again, and it was against their religious beliefs. But they made it clear that I had to give you up and go back to school. I didn't want an abortion either. I was hoping maybe, after you were born, they would soften and let me keep you, or that villain would show up and ask me to marry him. I prayed for some miracle to happen that would let me keep you."

Mila paused, wringing her hands. Her tears were falling again, making spots on the tablecloth. She picked up the napkin and wiped them away, fiercely. Shaking her head, she continued in a quivering, bitter voice, "The hardest thing in my life was when the nurse took you from my hands and I thought I'd never see you again. I fainted. I had no choice, believe me! To cover more traces, my aunt and parents decided for me to give birth out of the capital, in the town of Kumanovo. Later, you were transferred to the orphanage back to Skopje, from where you were adopted. You must believe me. I had no choice."

Her voice had grown louder, and a man at the bar turned to look at us. Her face was filled with guilt. I kept calm, simply listening and watching, taking in her pain, and suppressing the rage and confusion that had built in me over the years.

"I couldn't keep you," Mila said. She bowed her head. I started to drink my cappuccino, but she placed her hand on mine before I could raise my cup. "Fifteen years old. No place to go. No education. No money. No support from anyone. With an illegitimate child, I couldn't have survived, even as a whore. Prostitution was a criminal act in Yugoslavia. I wish it hadn't been. I would've done anything to keep you. Believe me, I would have!"

She was shouting now, her red eyes begging for my understanding, her hand clutching mine.

"How about your aunt? She didn't want to help you?" I spoke for the first time since she'd begun her story. I was probing, testing whether she had really wanted me. I wanted to know what might have been, if she'd had other options. She squeezed my hand reassuringly.

"My aunt agreed to take care of me until I bore you. She never agreed for me to keep you. In everyone's eyes, I was just a whore with a bastard. I wish I could kill them all."

She opened her handbag and pulled out a dry, yellowish piece of paper.

"This is the report from the hospital, after you were born. It says that the doctor had to cut my hymen in order for you to be delivered. I was, medically, a virgin." She pointed to where the report said that. "When that animal raped me, I didn't lose my virginity. The doctor told me it was one of those rare cases—a virgin birth."

"Ah, how biblical," I said. "Like the Immaculate Conception." I took the document from her and browsed it. Sure enough, what she said was true. I turned my face to the ceiling, and said, "Hi! *Jesy Christy*. I was born from a virgin, too."

I expected she would laugh at my impudence, but she didn't. Instead, her expression turned weightier. "I want you to know that I wasn't a whore. I was an inexperienced and naive adolescent, without any luck."

I folded the paper and gave it back to her. "Even if you were a whore, that's irrelevant to me. I'm not judgmental. I don't care. All I ever wanted, and still want, is the truth! I wanted to meet both of you. That's all…So what happened to him? Who is he? Where is he now?"

"I didn't want to leave the city until you were adopted," Mila said. "Six months later, I received confirmation from the orphanage that you were given to a family. It was hard, but I was happy you were safe in the hands of a nice and prosperous couple, as they assured me. Ten days later, around the time I was getting ready to go back to my parent's house, I was shopping in the local grocery for my aunt, when there he was. He about scared me to death. I almost fell to the floor.

"He approached me, calling me by my full name. I wouldn't shake his hand. He insisted that we talk. I turned to leave, but stopped when I saw two men standing near a black Mercedes outside the store, watching us. He ordered me to walk with him, and I followed him through a nearby park to a quay on the river. We sat on the bench, and he introduced himself as Dusan. A Serbian name, yet who knew if it was his real one? He said, 'I hold an important position in the federal government. I'm a married man with two kids. I know when and where you bore the child. I know you were pressured by your family and left it in the orphanage. Take him back. I want to take care of you and our son. I can help.'

"I cut him off cold. You're too late,' I said. 'Your son was already adopted. Ten days ago.'

"He jumped from the bench and began to pace back and forth. His eyes were teary. After he calmed down a bit, he said, 'I'm offering you help, if you need it.'

"'My baby was the only reason for me to accept help from you and be a mistress to a man I despise so much that I would've killed him if I could have. So, please, get the hell away from me and stay away.'

"'Good luck.' Those were his last words. He couldn't even look at me. He walked towards the Mercedes, waiting for him outside the park. I didn't move from the bench till the sun had set. I cursed my destiny and talked to the river about you. I remembered the feeling of your fragile, delicate body in my arms before the nurse took you away. It seemed as if it was floating near me, on the river surface. I ran to the water and touched it. You weren't there."

Mila took another cigarette. Her tears were pouring like the river she once talked to. She grasped my hand and kissed it as if I were a saint. It wasn't easy for me to understand her suffering, and I pulled my hand from her grasp. Her eyes widened with sadness. I think she knew that I was anxious for her to continue the story. She probably knew that was all I really cared about.

"When I returned home, my parents thought I looked dirty and that locals would suspect something," Mila said. "They were afraid I'd get close to some guy, and the town would find out I was not a virgin. They had no trust in me at all. They didn't want me around. As soon as possible, they arranged for me to continue my schooling in Croatia, where my mother came from, and stay with her sister in the capital, Zagreb. A year later, I met my Croat-Italian husband, Ganny, and I married him right after he proposed to me. When I moved to his house in Split, I was so content to have left Macedonia, thinking that I'd forget about you. I was wrong. I never did. The hardest times were on your birthdays."

"So I'm one-quarter Macedonian, one-quarter Croat. What about the other half?" I asked.

"As far as I know, he was Serb. I'm not sure if his parents were mixed or not. You know how in the former Yugoslavia we all mixed before the nationalist nonsense began."

"Well, I'm a real product of Yugoslavian unity. A real South Slav," I said, happy with the thought. "Maybe that explains why I love to speak Serbo-Croatian. Along with English, I think it's one of the most soothing languages around. Anyway, mixed blood is healthier, isn't it?"

She nodded. Reaching into her handbag again, she pulled out an envelope. She took a couple of pictures from the envelope and spread them out on the table.

"These are your two half brothers. When they were infants, any time I held them, I thought of you. It took me a long time to realize that they were not you. This is my husband." Mila pointed to them with her shaking forefinger.

The two handsome young men looked so much like their father. "I look more like you then your two other sons, don't I?" I said.

Crying louder, Mila patted my head. She recalled then that I wasn't comfortable with her touching me, so she pulled her hands away and crossed them in her lap.

"Yes, you do," she said.

"Do I look like him?"

"Yes. A little bit."

"Was he handsome?" I asked, intrigued.

"Yes, but a damned rapist," she said, shaking her head.

"How can I find him? I want to meet him." I nudged her shoulder.

"Believe me, I have no idea. I've told you everything I know about him," she said, assuredly. She was glad that I touched her.

"I'll go order a taxi," I said, getting up.

She nodded, continuing to weep and squeezing her soaked napkin.

I didn't trust her, but I didn't want to show it. I've waited so long, I thought, walking towards the desk. I'll wait a little bit more. I'll make her tell me who he is. He might still be an important person. Maybe that's why she's hiding him. *If she's hiding him.* Or maybe there is another story?

"Whatever," I said to myself, with determination. "She has to tell me. She owes me that."

14

Party

Mila didn't eat at all when I took her to dinner at one of the authentic national restaurants near the Turkish Bazaar. We stayed in the city until sunset, so I could sneak her into my house in the dark, safe from the curious eyes of the neighbors. We didn't talk much during the trip home, except when she asked me the names of the towns on the way. I had the driver drop us off on the road behind my house. I took Mila in, through the stairs that led to the second-floor entrance to my room, and then I went downstairs. Bisera and Mother sat at the table. Bisera was peeling apples for Mother and herself, while they watched TV.

"Oh, you're back. We didn't hear you. Damned old age," Bisera said, and Mother nodded.

"No problem with the colostomy?" I asked.

"No." Both shook their heads, simultaneously.

I pulled up Mother's skirt to check. "It's pretty full, but it can stay on 'til tomorrow."

"Are you sure," Mother asked, hesitantly.

"I'm a colostomy expert by now, aren't I?"

"No doubt, my gold, but you know how unpredictable that thing can be. I don't want to wake you up in the middle of the night. You've already had enough of me."

I hugged and kissed Mother, then Bisera, before joining them at the table.

"Don't worry, Mother. If you insist, I'll change it before you go to sleep. Did you take the analgesic after dinner?"

"Yes, I did," Mother replied, and took an apple from the crystal plate. "This is the best-looking one and it's for you," she said, and slowly began to peel it, forgetting that I liked to eat them with the skin. I didn't say a word, aware that peeling the apple meant a lot to her. She always tried to find small ways to show her gratitude.

"How did the meeting go with the American?" she asked.

"It was fun. He enjoyed the trip through the Balkans."

Bisera gave me a suspicious look.

"You should've invited him over. It would've been better if I were healthy. I could've helped you show him how well we treat foreigners here. You could've entertained him for a few days, rented a car, and driven him around. I'll bet he would've liked the historical sites along the lakes," Mother said.

"That sounds nice, Mother, but he didn't have much free time in his vacation schedule. He had to continue to Greece and Turkey."

"You sound very American now." She smiled, briefly, and it seemed she would injure her hands with the knife at any moment. Her moves were sloppy. She cut the peeled apple into four pieces and placed them on a small plate in front of me. I thanked her and began to eat. I knew Mother was dying to cook the best Macedonian dishes and serve them to me, to clean the house and tend the garden, and to show her grand hospitality to my made-up American friend. Disappointment was written on her face, though she tried to camouflage it with a forced smile. She stroked my face and pinched my cheek, as she always did, and it was comforting. Her touches were nothing like Mila's in the restaurant, which felt lifeless. Mother's touches were spontaneous and natural. Or at least I was accustomed to think of them as such.

A half-hour later, Bisera left. I stayed with Mother until 10 P.M., her regular bedtime. To comfort her, I changed the old colostomy bag, gave her a sedative, tucked her into bed, and kissed her good night. When I went up to my room, I found Mila curled in the beige armchair across from my desk, crying quietly.

"Sorry for the smell," I said. "I usually change her colostomy bags early in the morning and air out the rooms before anyone comes over. She insisted I do it tonight. If she knew we had a guest, I'd bet she wouldn't have let me do it."

"No problem. How is she doing?" Mila asked, worriedly.

"Okay. Her best friend, Auntie Bisera, was watching her. When I leave Mother in her hands, it's as if she is in mine. Let me show you where you'll sleep."

I picked up her suitcase and walked to a door across the room, gesturing for her to follow. Opening the door, I said, "This is my parents' old bedroom. My mother sleeps downstairs now. She hasn't been on the second floor since the surgery. You can lock the door, if you prefer. The bathroom is on the first floor. Do you want to take a bath?"

"It's late for a bath. A shower would be fine. But your mother will hear it, won't she?"

"Don't worry. She sleeps very soundly because of the drugs. Even if she woke up, she'd think it was me. She uses a bedpan overnight. It's too much of a hassle for her to go to the bathroom. She feels cold afterwards."

I opened the armoire across the bed, pulled out a towel, and handed it to Mila. She took a cosmetic bag and nightgown from her suitcase and followed me to the bathroom. While turning the water on, I said, "Only a host knows how to adjust his own shower quickly. Am I right?"

"It's true. I had never thought about it. Thank you."

"Sleep well," I said, as I opened the door to leave.

"Likewise," she said, and her body moved slightly forward. She wanted to kiss me good night. I turned away and left.

I set the alarm clock for the usual time, 6 A.M., and curled up in bed. "I should've let her kiss me good night," I said to the lamp, as I turned it off. "This is so odd, so surreal, isn't it?" I still couldn't believe the event that I had longed for all my life was happening.

I slept little. When I got up, after I washed my face, I checked Mother's colostomy bag, then served her breakfast, with a cup of mint tea with painkiller drops, one multi-vitamin pill, and one aspirin. From the drawers of the chestnut cabinet, I took out my prepared set of her clean clothing. I undressed her and helped her to take a shower.

As I soaped her body, she complained, "A shower can never clean you as well as a bath."

It was impossible for her to take a bath; her colostomy attachment would have gotten soaked and come off. There was nothing I could do to change that, so I just said, "I keep you clean, Mother, don't I? Now you are very American, showering every day."

She smiled and kissed my cheek, and I began to rinse the shampoo from her thinned hair. I changed her and helped her lay comfortably on the bed, covering her with an extra blanket. I opened the window to air the living room and began to vacuum. I peeled her an apple, brought it to her, then took my bath. When I went upstairs to my bedroom to change, my parents' bedroom door was open. I caught Mila nude, poking in her suitcase.

"I'm sorry," I said, when her eyes met mine. I blushed.

"It's okay. There's nothing wrong with seeing your mother's body nude. It's a very natural thing. You came out of it." She stated it forthrightly.

It felt peculiar to hear that. I was never allowed to see my mother nude, until she got sick and needed my help. I turned and walked into my bedroom, amazed at how elegantly shaped Mila's body was. Her legs were long. Her buttocks were round, and her breasts firm. They were not hanging low. She didn't seem to need a bra.

I got dressed. When I came out, I almost bumped into her. She was waiting for me outside my bedroom, wearing a royal blue silk robe. She was holding the towel and the cosmetic bag in her hands. She looked like a Greek goddess.

"What do you eat for breakfast?" I asked, stunned. I felt glad to have been born from such a beautiful creature.

"I don't eat breakfast, thank you. I just need to use the bathroom."

I waited by the bathroom until Mila had finished.

"I'll be back upstairs shortly," I said.

"Take care of your mother. Take your time," she insisted, and ascended the stairs.

Our cook and shopper, Frosa, came to pick up the money and the grocery list. She updated Mother on the local news, as usual, and left. I accompanied Mother during her morning walk in the garden. When I brought her back to bed, she said, "You didn't deodorize the room, Bazhe."

"I'll do it right now, Mother." I sprayed her favorite vanilla deodorizer, which I had bought from Bradlees on sale. Every morning, when I would forget to do it, Mother would remind me. She knew that her deteriorating body smelled stronger as time went on. She wasn't embarrassed anymore to ask me to deodorize her room and freshen the potpourris around the house.

"You have no idea how much I hate this…that I have to make you put up with all of this smell, the colostomy…how hard it is for me that the one I love most is the closest shareholder of my misery." Mother waved her hand in disgust.

"Stop this nonsense, Mother," I called back to her, continuing to spray the hallway.

She waited until I was done, then said, "Sorry, but I have no choice."

"Nor I," I said, hugging her.

I was delighted that our bond was becoming stronger then ever. It was growing faster than the cancer that pushed her mercilessly towards death. I left the deodorant container on top of her bedside table. She preferred it there, so she could reach it. I organized her colostomy supplies and disinfected the scissors I used for cutting them to fit her artificial orifice. I wrote a memo to Frosa, asking her to buy extra gauze and Band-Aids, then talked to Mother until she fell asleep. She always took a nap in the morning.

I went to the kitchen. I took an orange juice, two glasses, and a box of cookies, placed them on the silver tray that I left on top of the refrigerator, and took it upstairs. Mila was surveying my toy collection, displayed in a glassed-in section of the wall-to-wall library cabinet. She was wearing an attractive beige blouse, black trousers, and beige patent-leather sandals.

"Are these all yours?" she asked, her eyes shining with tears.

"Yes, I was good at saving my toys."

"Which one was your favorite?"

"This one." I pointed to the pale orange rubber cat.

She pulled the glass door open, took the cat out, and sat in the armchair.

Putting the tray on my desk, I poured both of us some orange juice and opened the box of cookies.

"Please help yourself," I said.

"Thank you. Later. Would you show me photographs of you and your family? Tell me what your life was like here. Tell me about your parents."

I pulled open one of the lower desk drawers and took out a couple of photo albums. I squatted next to her and opened the first one. "This is me as a baby. Here, I'm three years old. In this one, I'm six," I said, pointing at the black-and-white photographs.

"You were a beautiful child. You had blond hair then…and awesome eyes. You look like a girl. Like a Hollywood child star." Enraptured, she quivered with emotion as she looked at the photos. She reached out and patted my hair.

"Thanks to my mother, who took meticulous care of me." I pointed out Mother; she was holding my hand in front of her rose garden. "There were many girls in the neighborhood that fought to take me on a promenade in my stroller. I almost got killed once, when the stroller slipped from one girl's hands and rolled down the hill. I suffered only a few scratches. Fortunately, I was strapped in."

"Your mother is beautiful, too. That must be your father?" she asked, pointing towards the photo of a tall man in uniform.

"Yes. He was a First Combatant and First Class Captain in Tito's partisan army. A government official later."

"Handsome man…gorgeous couple."

"Yeah, they were. Mother left home at age sixteen and married him without her parents' approval. She was fourteen years younger than he was. He was a difficult man, hard on her. He was demanding and domineering. A soldier. An arrogant womanizer. She wasn't happy, yet he provided everything for her. She never had to work or worry about anything material."

I rose and walked to the rocking chair opposite her, to keep her from patting my hair. She began patting my old cat toy in her lap. For a while, we said nothing. Finally, I broke the silence.

"I had everything: my own playroom, my own bedroom, a spectacular toy collection, expensive imported clothes, and attention from everybody. I also had a nanny. Later, she stole some of my mother's jewelry and escaped to America. The rumors were that she was a beautiful young lady and Father's mistress. Anyway, my parents treated me like a possession, not a human. They took me to many parties held in luxury hotels by top people in the government. Mother constantly smiled. She exuded elegance. She was always ready to show off and play the role of the arrogant governor's wife perfectly. She hid the misery of being with my father, underneath all that. And oh, my god—my appearance! Mother treated me like a pretty little girl, dressing me flamboyantly, while Father treated me like a little soldier, waking me every morning promptly at 7 o'clock. For both of them, I was their little prince, a trophy child. Mother would spend hours and hours adoring me. 'You are the brightest and the best looking of all the children in town.' She would whisper that to me, continually, while she combed my long golden curls in front of the mirror. Then she would put her mascara on my lashes, dust on a little bit of powder, and apply her favorite rose lipstick. 'Gorgeous,' she would sigh afterwards, and I would run excitedly to my room, slam the door, and dance in front of the mirror to the rhythm of American music.

"Before leaving for one of those New-Year's-Eve parties, my father was screaming at Mother for keeping him waiting. I bolted down the stairs, rushed outside, and ran straight into my father's legs.

"'Oh, you look wonderful, stunning,' he said. 'Where is she? Bitch! Always late! Do you remember your list of presidents for the speech?'

"'Yes Father!' I said, standing straight as a soldier.

"'Don't make a mistake! Remember to speak fluently, like a river! Recite your poem clearly. Don't rush and trip during your speech. Be eloquent. Understand!'

"'Yes, Father,' I told him.

"I started biting my nails and he slapped my hand down. He said, 'You are going to be in front of many important people! Don't even think about doing that! Understand!'

"'Yes, Father!' Again, I straightened up my posture, the way he always told me to.

"My mother came downstairs, walking like a glamorous movie star. She complained to Father, 'Don't yell at him! Don't touch him again, you tyrant. There's no doubt that he'll impress them. Isn't that right, my dear?'

"'Yes, Mamo,' I said. I remember taking her hand and how silky it felt.

"On the way to the hotel, I kept trying not to bite the rest of my nails. My mother looked amazing. Her designer black gown and antique gold jewelry went together perfectly. She had an oblong, delicately spun antique gold silk shawl draped around her bare back, with each end of it wrapped loosely around her lower arms. The shimmering tassels of the shawl's ends hung below her elbows, and they swayed lavishly with her slightest motion. Mother had a collection of shawls for any occasion, and even for every part of the day. She loved them. They were her trademarks.

"My parents' friends, who drove us to the party, were a quiet and humble couple, as different from Mother and Father as day from night. A half-hour later, we arrived at the hotel "Villa Yugoslavia," located near the cliff overlooking Prespa Lake. The politicians and the company directors with their wives gathered around. While the host escorted us to our table, people were noticing my mother's classy and elegant appearance. Father, as always, looked so proud of his trophy wife. The local band started playing an easy waltz. Father gave the first toast at our table. The party began. The Communist elite was ready to have fun, and couples walked to the dance floor. Mother loved to dance, but Father seldom invited her, although he was known as a dance leader, always at the center of attention. He was my idol at those parties. I admired his dancing style. I used to practice in front of the mirror for days, so I could be the center of attention some day, like my father. And I succeeded. Later, I became an expert dancer among my peers, especially Yugoslavian folk and American club dancing. I created my own style, and many students copied me. Poor Mother. She usually sat alone, while Father danced with other women. Many men would have loved to dance with her, but she was very conservative and couldn't imagine dancing with someone other than her husband. She told me later that Father often publicly humiliated her: He'd get drunk, dance with singers, force them to strip on the table, and make a big show for his friends. She had to attend and watch smiling and pretending it didn't bother her, even though her heart was breaking and she was ashamed of his comportment. She couldn't avoid it. He considered it Mother's duty as his wife to put up with all that.

"The countdown to midnight began, and when the clock chimed, everybody in the ballroom hugged and kissed each other, wishing each other a Happy New Year and raising their glasses in toast. Shortly afterward, my father went to the microphone and announced that I was going to recite two poems, *Mother,* and *Tito*, and play the heavy accordion afterwards.

"'Go, and show them how intelligent you are,' my mother encouraged me, and I strode to the stage. The musician adjusted the microphone to my height and left the accordion next to my feet. I bowed and began. The first poem went smoothly, followed by applause. But, in the middle of the second, I put my finger in my mouth and stopped reciting as my eyes met my father's. Quickly, I clasped my hands together, and I managed to finish the poem *Tito*. Biting my nails was such an old habit. I was shaking. I felt trapped, pinned down by my father's choleric expression. When everybody applauded, I loosened up and picked up the accordion with some help from a musician who also brought me a chair. The instrument was heavy, bigger than mine at home. In fact, it was bigger than I was. Father had to carry my accordion to school for me for a while. He bought it right before I started first grade. My parents forced me to practice for hours every day on that noisy thing, like it or not. When I finished playing a few Revolutionary songs, a long applause followed. Father smiled, and I exhaled happily, feeling like a star.

"Father's best friend, the director of a textile company, climbed on-stage, took the accordion off me, and proudly announced, 'Now, my dear guests, this little angel can tell you the names of any president in the world. Ask! Just ask!' Questions flew from everywhere. 'Who is the president of the Soviet Union? Of France, Columbia, the USA, India, Morocco, Syria, Japan.' I replied to all of them, quickly and correctly. The crowd cheered me, impressed. Then someone yelled, 'You should know the world's rivers and mountains, rather than the presidents, who change all the time!' Everyone in the ballroom laughed, and I turned to stone in the chair, blushing. The director shouted, 'Oh, stop it. You are just jealous. Your children must be dumb, comrade. Let's award our little performer, shall we?' Again, people grinned, applauding and hollering, 'Yeah! Yeah!' Then he shouted, 'Oh-kay, folks. Let's make a bet!' He jumped from the stage among the tables. "Is it a boy or a girl? Boy or a girl? Eh? Who wants to put their money down?' He pointed at the tables, yelling, 'Throw your money in the patterned plates if you think that it's a girl! Or into the plain ones if you think it's a boy! The ones from town and anyone else who knows this smart little angel, shut up, please! You'll get some of the profit. Some of the less heavy plates, at least. I promise. Big bills only!' he said, making everyone giggle.

"Everyone got excited. The men were screaming, 'It's a girl! It's a boy! It's a girl!' and frantically throwing money into the plates. Their women laughed. The director grabbed me from the stage and propelled me to the central table. He placed me on top of it. I stood there numb and frightened by all the noise. It reminded me of a local market place. The director waited until all the plates at all the tables were filled. Then he took the waiter's cart, collected them, and placed the plates on either side of my trembling legs. The patterned ones were fuller. For a minute, there was absolute silence as he pulled down my Italian sailor's shorts. I was the center of their attention, barely six years old, standing frozen in the middle of the ballroom. I was surrounded by monsters that began cheering, clapping hands, more than half of them drunk. The director grabbed my blouse, which was cut like a skirt, covering me down to my knees, and pulled it up, hollering, 'I hope you see it well down there.' Blushing, shy, confused, but at the same time feeling like a little idol, I stared at that blatant crowd, giggling and screaming like mad. The director took two of the patterned plates and handed it to me, triumphantly. 'Well, the rest of the plates should go to our great band and waiters. They deserve it, don't they?' he said. The audience's inebriated yes's boomed around. Then he lifted me up in his arms and carried me back to my parents' table. The social game was over at four am.

"'You were excellent,' my mother said. She buttoned up my outfit and caressed my head. My drunken Father hugged me and began stuffing the money I was given from the plates into his pockets. I was content that he was satisfied. But not for long. On the way home, Father screamed at me because I had bit my nails while I recited the poem, *Tito*. I felt so hurt, after trying so hard to make him proud of me. I felt like a powerless little vampire, like a creature from another space, sitting in the back seat, watching the sun come up from behind the mountains. Mother began to chat with her girlfriend about an old flame she had met at the party. He was a company director who was once madly in love with her, but she had rejected him because he wasn't a man of power at that time. For the rest of her life, she blamed herself for that. Father was snoring in the front seat, thank God; otherwise, he would have thrown her out of the car window. The party and the game may have been over, but I was still confused and disturbed. And I would stay that way for a while. Later, I was the subject of another social game. And another. After a while, I kind of got used to it. That first night, I took the toy you are holding now, and I covered myself with the blankets in my little bed. My little brain was trying to analyze it all. It couldn't. The world of adults seemed even stranger, more confusing after that New Year's Eve."

Mila's tears fell on my photo album. She continued to pet my cat toy, as if it were alive. I lit a cigarette. She reached out, and I gave it to her.

"I'll go downstairs and check Mother," I said, as I stood up from the rocking chair.

"Okay," she mumbled, with her head down, staring at the images of my childhood.

15

Childhood

Since she had been diagnosed with cancer, my mother's eyelids moved much more frequently while she slept. I wondered what she was dreaming about. I hoped it was not about her cancer. A discharging noise from her stoma stopped me as I turned to go back upstairs. I waited until it was gone. The bag was new. I had changed it that morning. Nothing to worry about, I thought, and slowly left the living room.

Going upstairs was like traveling from one dimension, where I felt like I was dying along with Mother, to a new one, in which I was getting to know Mila. The stairs were a bridge between the two women. It never felt so wearying to walk up them as then. I must have looked very somber. When I walked into my room, Mila jumped from the armchair, leaving the photo album on the desk. She still held my toy in one hand.

"Is something wrong with your mother?" she asked.

"No. She's sleeping. She usually wakes up around one in the afternoon and asks for lunch."

I opened the box of cookies and offered her one. She shook her head as she thanked me. I bit into the cookie and sat in my rocking chair. As I rocked, the voices of Father and Mother came back to me. Their young voices, long dead in me, echoed in my head. Mila wanted them to be alive again, much more than I did. I could tell by the eager look of her eyes, and the short movements of her mouth and fingers.

"My parents constantly told me, 'You cannot play with the children on the street. They are from blue-collar and peasants' families. You are a most intelligent, most well mannered, and most beautiful town's boy. They don't deserve your company. Don't ever think to invite them over. Those savages will break and steal your toys!'"

I explained this to Mila, thinking that things could have been so different if she hadn't put me up for adoption. I could tell from her eyes that she could sense that I blamed her.

"Because of Father and Mother, the neighborhood kids thought I was a selfish, mean bastard who didn't want to share his toys. I had so many. I would take them and sneak out to play with the other kids, who acted as if I were an alien. They avoided me constantly. If my parents caught me, their punishment was to make me read a book from the library. When I complained that I couldn't understand them, they would shout, 'Comic books and that dumb Walt Disney junk are for hooligans like the neighborhood kids. They'll never know Dostoyevsky, Hugo, or Dreiser. They can't even pronounce the word "alphabet," and you can read well. You are above them. Way above them! Build your wisdom, and remember you are a superior child!'

"My parents' domineering voices would ring out as I obediently pulled another heavy book with a fancy cover from the shelf and tried to comprehend it. I was losing my innocence while reading about the complex adult world. But as soon as Mother and Father left the room, I would run to the window and watch the kids playing. I would imitate them and imagine myself with them, playing a warrior, or a king, or a queen. I'd add scenes from a movie I had memorized, where the queen fell madly in love with the prince. I created my own special playground. And when the story was over, I would go back to the window, watching them play and crying for hours.

"It was a warm March day when I saw an opportunity to have a friend. Some people were going to throw a kitten into the river. I rescued it and hid him in the storage house at the corner of our property. I knew it would take an ocean of tears to convince my parents to adopt him. When they gave in and I brought him into our house, it was one of the happiest days of my childhood.

"He loved to play hide and seek and to climb with me on the old pear tree. My cat and I both found sanctuary there, he from his enemies, and me from my parents. Eventually, my parents would order me to go to my room and read books instead of playing with the cat. My cat would sneak into my room later and curl in my lap, and for hours I would question him on why I couldn't play with the kids and have a playmate like everybody else.

"Gradually, my parents came to accept the cat. His extreme cleanliness and friendliness won their hearts. The touch of the wild he always kept, his great hunting skills, the way he licked his fur until I couldn't stare at it for the shine, and his superior instincts for surviving and adapting, fascinated me. More than anything, I wanted to possess his independent and uncontrollable nature."

"What was his name?" Mila asked.

"In my province, we didn't name cats. That was considered coo-coo. Insane. Only mad Westerners did that, and locals would comment if someone tried it. But my cat got a name when my first cousin, the son of Mother's oldest brother, and his wife from America visited us during their vacation. It was the first time I'd met him. When his wife saw my tabby cat, she immediately called him Tiger. That was the first word I learned in English. I was fascinated by it. My cousin and his wife also fascinated me. They weren't like anyone else I knew at the time. My Mother's family called my cousin a loser, but Mother and Father said he was kind. They thought his Jewish wife was from outer space. Of course, they were wrong. They were too primitive to understand my liberated cousin and his wife, who were so much fun and intelligent, sort of like hippies. I wanted them never to leave our house.

"My dreams of America intensified after meeting them. I wanted to beg them to take me with them, but I was scared to place my trust in strangers. The complex my parents had inflicted on me took away my ability to ask anyone for help. Father was always around, and his frightening presence also inhibited me. I was afraid if I said something, they would tell my father and I'd be punished for it. I prayed for them to suggest it first, even hint at the idea of my going to America with them. It never happened. There was no one to blame, though. My first cousin and his wife had no clue I was in misery: stuck in a cage with expensive toys, books, clothes, and straight A's at school." I paused, stood up, and said, "Come. I'll show you something."

Mila sprang from the armchair and followed me like an obedient servant to the window in my bedroom. I pulled open the curtain and said, "That is the old pear tree, and under it, Tiger rests. His nine lives expired when I was in high school. He was poisoned for a second time because our careless neighbors had thrown lots of rodent poison in their storage houses. I tried to do what Father had done to save Tiger's life the first time. I was so grateful to him for doing that. I filled a syringe with a mixture of sugar and milk and spritzed the fluid into his mouth. I repeated this a couple of times. Sometimes he couldn't swallow the milk and it made the fur around his mouth sticky. I watched him all day. I couldn't sleep. The following afternoon, as usual, Tiger was by the door, waiting for me when I came home from school. But he wasn't standing. He was lying down, barely able to move. I picked him up gently. He took a deep breath and died in my arms.

"I wonder if all animals, like humans, wait for their loved ones to come and embrace them, so they can die calmly?" Mila asked, walking back to my room.

"If they have loved ones, I guess."

I opened the cocktail cabinet, and took a Coke from it. When I offered one to Mila, she shook her head. I poured a glass for myself. I lit a cigarette and sipped on a Coke—my favorite combination of habits. When Mila was seated in the armchair again, I continued recalling my childhood.

"One other break from my loneliness was my old Aunt Sandra, Father's first cousin and a neighbor. She watched me when my parents went to parties or on trips. One night, she saved me from her daughter-in-law, who terrified me with her fake butterflies. Since then, I've had a phobia of them. I called Sandra "Granny," because I never had one. I felt secure next to her; she was full of love, kindness, and understanding. I'll never forget the warmth of her expression. Whenever I had problems, I would run to her. I felt so sad that she would get lonely because the neighbors refused to have her over. My father despised her passion for gossip and daily visits. After Father had a falling out with her son and daughter-in-law, he forbade them, including Granny, from visiting us. I was angry about it. So was Mother, since she wasn't able to call her when she had fights with Father, or when she was sick, knowing that Granny would come right away to help her. But I didn't give up. I would often sneak over to see her. Her face was like an icon. I worshiped her, and I could feel her love for me. She was like an ointment for my bruises of loneliness. She died when I started college. That was devastating.

"However, neither Tiger, nor Granny Sandra could be a complete substitute for a friend of my own age. So I tried hard to get closer to Abdul, a Turkish boy and my contemporary, who lived a block from my house. I would occasionally play with him. He was a harmless child. My parents knew that, but they never liked him. He was Turkish, and on top of that, his family were farmers. I loved bringing him to my room and sharing my huge toy collection. Any time my parents were away, I would sneak him into the house. I cherished those rare moments. I treated Abdul like the imaginary brother I had always wanted. Mostly, we played at his house with his wooden cowboys, Indians, animals, and houses. We pretended to fight the Germans as partisans. I had meals at his home, served in the old-fashioned Muslim way: sitting on the floor in the lotus position before a monogrammed copper table, drinking sherbet from a tall pitcher, *Ibrik*, and eating yogurt and other delicious homemade food from their elaborately engraved plates. I enjoyed learning the Turkish culture at an early age, but my parents were very disturbed when they found out I ate there.

"'No Christian eats in a Turkish house! How could you?' my father demanded. 'The Muslims stink! I don't want you to go to his house anymore. Am I clear?'

"I said, 'Abdul is my friend. His family is very kind to me. They don't smell. They're very clean people.'

"My father would roar, 'Shut up! You will not eat in Abdul's house anymore. Period! Go to your room now!'

"Abdul's grandmother had the soul of a deer. For the major Muslim holidays, like *Ramadan*, *Seker* and *Kurban Bayrami*, she made the best baklava and gave it to all our neighbors. One time, she brought some to our house, and my father threw the pieces in the garbage right in front of her, even though he knew you could have eaten off her floor. The animosity between Balkan Christians and Muslims was so damaging, a few of them had friends of the other religion. I couldn't understand why. But, no matter how forbidden Abdul was, I kept playing with him. I kept sneaking him into my house and visiting his. I was hungry for the love and warmth his family showed me. I even attended part of Abdul's *Sünnet* celebration when he was circumcised. There was a three-day party, and lots of food and dancing. Then Abdul enrolled in a Turkish elementary school, and I went to the Macedonian one. My parents were finally happy."

Mila shook her head. She took out a cigarette and lit it. I drew deeply on mine, sipped the Coke, and continued.

"Usually parents would send their children to school at the age of seven. I started first grade at six. I couldn't wait, ecstatic that I would have hundreds of mates to play with. I was the smallest kid in the class. Father had to help me carry my bag, which was bigger than me. Actually, the main reason I was enrolled in school early was Bogoja, the boy that lived across the street from us. He was even old enough to attend second grade. My parents saw that as an opportunity for me to have a convenient school companion who would look after me. They were convinced I would benefit from it.

"To my surprise, they suddenly didn't care that Bogoja's father was a truck driver, and his mother a nurse and a very sly peasant woman. Except for a few of us, almost all the families in the county, in order to have decent lives, had to do extra work in their apple orchards along with their regular jobs. People were very jealous of my family. But Bogoja's family was especially jealous of us. My parents didn't quite get it. They were determined to follow their plan, and made the teacher seat us at the same desk, even though we were as different as cats and dogs. Bogoja and I hated it. Soon everything between us became a competition.

Bogoja's parents used their son's abilities as a weapon against my privileged family. He was the better in math and science; I was in liberal arts.

"Oh, god, I tried so hard to be his friend, but he would constantly ignore me and play with others. He would rip my school uniform and ruin my special school slip-on shoes. He would incite the other boys to pick on me and beat me up. One day, while defending myself, I stuck my ruler down a boy's throat. There was blood all over the place. My schoolmate looked like a little Dracula, with spurts of blood coming out of his mouth. They took him to the hospital immediately. After that, nobody had the courage to bother me except Bogoja. Almost every day on the way to school, he would knock my bag to the ground, leaving me alone in the middle of the street to pick up my notebooks and pens. He destroyed a lot of the expensive, imported toys given to me by my father's rich friends, especially by my godfather. Bogoja despised my status, my nice clothes, and my looks. In comparison, he was overweight, awkwardly dressed, and plain. When I complained to my parents that he was hurting me every day, they didn't listen. They would say, 'You must have a schoolmate. He's the closest to you, a good student, and that's all that matters!' The only one who understood my suffering was Granny Sandra. She called him *Besh*. She explained it was Turkish idiom in our language that meant ugly and evil. I enjoyed joking about him with her—it was my only retaliation.

"One day, he broke my nose. When I got home, bleeding, Father got very upset and wanted to complain to his parents. Of course, Mother stopped him, advising him that if he argued with Bogoja's blue-color father and peasant mother, he would ruin our upper-class image. As time went by, he continued hurting me. When my parents asked why I was crying, I would lie and tell them I had injured myself, even though I felt like killing them. I had no more energy to explain how miserable Bogoja was making me. How lonely I was. How much I needed to have a good friend. I gave up and withdrew. They didn't listen. They didn't want to see it. It seemed as if they were punishing me. Finally, I finished elementary school and we were separated. I was enrolled in the old middle school my parents considered urban and classy. Bogoja was sent to the new school, which was mostly for peasants. I've often dreamed of him as a ghoul in the form of a butterfly, with a disgusting smile, shark-like mouth, and red wings, ready to drain my blood. After somehow surviving those dreadful four years with him, I was convinced that some children are born evil."

"Absolutely," Mila interjected. She looked towards the library, as if she were going to retrieve words from the books using some supernatural method. "Since ancient times, it's been said that the root of hell is in all of us. Some of us let it grow into a tree. Those who can't cut the tree are predestined to be evil."

"Interesting," I said. I realized I had been staring through the window at Bogoja's house, clenching my teeth. I turned away and tried to relax, as I continued telling the story.

"At the end of every August, the village of Jankovec, which nearly touches my town, celebrated The Holy Mother of Jesus, *Sveta Bogorodica*. The religious festival was a big deal, a happy occasion for everyone in the county. It marked the end of the tourist season and the beginning of apple season. People would go to the monastery in the old forest above the village, where there was a flea market. There was dancing, eating, and drinking, and people would gather around the monastery courtyard for two days. My parents insisted that I attend it and socialize. I wanted that more than they did, but I had no one to go with. Every year, I went and hid deep in the woods, so I wouldn't be seen alone. I spent the whole time watching the celebration from my hiding place. It felt odd.

"When I came home, Mother and Father would ask, 'Who did you go with? How was it?' I would lie and tell them that I'd met my schoolmates there and had fun. I couldn't understand why they bothered asking me such nonsense when they had created my desolation and made me live like a vampire in a dark solitary world. They were in denial. I kept fighting to have a friend, though. As I entered fifth grade, I felt more confident. I was growing. Still, none of my new schoolmates were good enough for me, according to Mother and Father, so naturally I looked for options around where I lived. My persistence paid off and I became comrades with Nikola, a Macedonian boy who lived next door. His father once worked in America. His mother and a sister were very nice. His grandmother was scary, constantly singing and talking to herself. She was a widow who resembled an old witch, forever dressed in black.

"Nikola became like a big brother to me. He was a sophomore in high school. I was barely ten years old. He loved the performing arts. We would re-enact theater plays or American movies in his attic. As the director, he insisted that we play the big love tragedies like *Anthony and Cleopatra*, *Romeo and Juliet*, or *Anna Karenina* and *Count Vronsky*. He had a reason for doing that. While teaching me the roles, he would touch and kiss me. The day he almost raped me was the first time I'd seen semen and was aware of what it was. I had to wash my pants before I went home. Nikola would end all the plays with sexual themes, and I would suffer pain from his body weight, pain in my buttocks. His kisses were bites, his touches rough, and his intercourse forceful. Yet I didn't resist enjoying his closeness and scent on my clothes. I was so desperate to have a friend. I didn't know or care what I was doing.

"We were playing *Caesar and Cleopatra* when I raised my voice to him for the first time. I was confused. I said, 'Caesar got murdered and Cleopatra went right into Anthony's arms. You can't be Anthony now. You're dead.'

"'Can you see anyone else around who can play Anthony?' Nikola replied, irritated by my rebellion.

"'No,' I said trembling.

"'Then I'm everything. Caesar, Anthony, warrior, king, director. Everything! And you!' Nikola pointed at me imperiously. 'You can only be Queen Cleopatra! And you should be proud to play her. Part of her blood was Macedonian.' He dragged me to the mirror and, gazing at my reflection, he sang: 'Mirror, mirror, on the wall, whose eyes are the most beautiful and green?' Then he jumped behind the mirror and said, 'Don't worry, my lord. The most beautiful eyes are those of your darling, her majesty, the queen.' And, as he began to chortle insanely, he jumped on me. When I felt his sperm in me, I ran to the corner of the attic and curled in a ball. I told him that I was afraid my stomach would grow huge and explode. I threw up from the very idea. Nikola hugged me. Comforted by his warm body, I fell asleep in his arms. Two years later, he went to college, and we'd barely exchange a word when we'd meet, frightened by the forbidden friendship we once had and the secret we buried between us forever."

"When you are afraid you are going to be lonely again, you do everything you can to avoid it," Mila said. "Loneliness is a killer; it's the biggest human fear. I think bearing it is harder than keeping any secret."

She pulled a cigarette from my pack. "Jesus," she said. She began coughing, and her body rocked back and forth. In between coughs, she gasped, "How about the summer and winter breaks? Were they also lonely?"

I handed her a glass of juice. She nodded thank you.

"During summer breaks," I said, "my schoolmates would go to the lake with friends. I wasn't allowed. Even if I had been, I had no one to go with anyway. Occasionally, my mother and I would go to the beach by bus. I was proud of how she looked in her fashionable swimsuits. She'd always had more style than any woman in town. Thanks to my father, she could spend countless hours in front of the mirror, indulging her vanity, while most of the local women would pass their days working in the apple orchards, getting sunburned.

"On the beach, there was always a parasol between Mother's milky skin and the sun. 'Look at these people, lying out on the sand like cows in the middle of the day,' Mother would say with a chuckle. She told me that tanned skin was low class and very dangerous for one's health. The strong Macedonian sun was malignant, no doubt about it. Father rarely joined us, claiming that his heart had become too weak since the war. He was self-conscious about his health and would come only if friends drove us there. He would sit in the shade almost all day, swimming now and then. Thanks to him, I became a good swimmer at an early age. Mother never learned to swim. She would walk back and forth in the water, pretending to do a frog-stroke with her arms.

"I loved when Father was with us. Otherwise, Mother and I looked so sad and alone. Most of the other people were with their families or with big parties, barbecuing and socializing. The two of us would quietly eat our sandwiches or talk to each other, looking as forlorn as a couple of refugees."

Mila laughed. It seemed like the room brightened and each object in it smiled with her. She had a contagious smile, like Mother's before the cancer.

"Almost every winter break, Mother and I visited her youngest brother in the capital. I used to play with my uncle's two sons and their collection of miniature cars until we were exhausted," I said. "Uncle worked overtime, uncommon in the old socialism, as a private stereo repairman. He made good-enough money to take us on a skiing vacation at a popular resort called Popova Shapka, an hour away from his home. I didn't care much about skiing. I remember being fascinated by the famous local shepherd dog, the Sharplaninec. It was a real gladiator, big and courageous enough to ward off the occasional wolf or bear. I loved animals and nature. But I loved the city most of all. Anytime Uncle drove us through it, I would jump from the excitement and stare at the tall buildings. Then his wife would kill my pleasure. She'd say, 'Don't act crazy, like you've never seen a building before.' She was a mean woman, and never liked me. She always saw me as the bastard of the family."

Mila's face reddened with anger. She picked up a cookie and took a bite of it. She chewed furiously, squeezing the toy she continued to hold in her lap. "Bitch," she shouted. She sounded protective, like a mother. But yet, not like Mother in so many ways.

16

Schooling

Was Mila's reaction real and instinctive? Or was it made up, so she could get closer to me? I wondered if we would ever be of one mind, like my mother and I had been, so many times and on so many issues. I stood and began to walk around my rocking chair.

"I know you don't like the word 'bastard.' You can't deny it. But I am one. Don't ever think that I'm special, like my parents did. Constantly telling me that no one deserved to get close to me, that I was above my schoolmates in intelligence and looks, and that my isolation was an opportunity for me to grow into a superb individual by concentrating in school and reading as many books as possible!"

With each word, I spewed spittle. Mila sank deeper into the armchair, as if the saliva were guilt and she could hide from it. She was scared of me.

"My schoolmates studied with their buddies! They had sleepovers, even though many of them didn't have their own rooms. I had two rooms for myself, but was cursed with desolation!"

I realized I was shouting. I took a moment to calm down, sitting down again in the rocker. Mila stopped sobbing. She looked at me, uncertainly, waiting, her posture stiff with anxiety. Then she relaxed visibly when I lit a cigarette and proceeded in a more normal tone.

"I constantly cursed Mother and Father for their cruelty. I decided to rebel against them. I decided to befriend the peasants, whom they despised the most. Few of them came to my preppy school. One day, I got up the nerve to bring one home with me after school. Father and Mother were visiting relatives. I remember he was so intimidated by our home. Signs of Father's power and reputation, like his World War II pictures, were everywhere. I tried to make everything as simple and natural as possible. I showed him my room and played tapes for him on my stereo, one of the first in town. He got even more excited when I showed him my toy collection. He was amazed with my porcelain musketeers, imported from France.

"'Would you like to play with them?' I asked.

"'Yeah,' he replied, shyly. The room fell silent as he cautiously picked one up, gazing at it for a while. He grabbed two more and spoke to them. We began to play with them on the table and he was having a great time until he dropped one, shattering it to pieces. He was motionless, stunned, in pieces, like the musketeer. I grabbed another figurine from his grasp and smashed it to the floor, laughing. I couldn't quite believe my lack of concern about destroying part of my totally untouchable world.

"Our fun, our liberation, made us feel as if we were far from the world, enclosed in our own spaceship, until Father's voice brought us back to reality. They were home. That's what I wanted. Anxious, but happy, I could hear them coming upstairs. Father opened the door. My schoolmate froze as Father fixed his angry gaze on him. The boy gasped for breath and rushed from my room. I followed him, yelling, 'See you tomorrow!' He didn't answer. I clutched at the front gate, watching him run away and trying to hold on to the happiness I had been feeling just moments ago. I wondered if he would ever speak to me again. From behind me, Father yelled, 'You invited that stupid peasant in our house? How dare you!'

"'So what!' I yelled. 'He is my school friend and a nice boy!' For the first time, I talked back to Father. He was ready to explode. Mother, standing behind him, raised her eyebrows in surprise. I ran into the house and up to my room, locking the door quickly. Shortly afterward, Father was banging on it and yelling for me to open up. I laughed like mad.

"I tried to recall where I had put some small pieces of bare wire I had brought home from my physics class. I kept cracking up, so forcibly that it hurt. I finally found the wires in a toolbox in one of my drawers. I ran to the power outlet and stuck them in the holes, holding them tightly. The electricity shook my body, and the distorted faces of my parents, my schoolmates, and my cat, flashed before me as I was thrown into the corner. Damn me, I'm not strong enough, I thought.

"Everything seemed indefinite and gloomy. Father's shouting and banging became background noise, like the raindrops that began pattering on my window. I lay on the floor for a while, then crawled over to my desk. From a drawer, I took a hidden cigarette. I lit it, choking as I inhaled. It was my third one in my life. Resting my arm on a windowpane, I groaned and thunder seemed to rumble in sympathy.

"'God, Jesus, Mohammed, Buddha…whoever is up there. I've never hurt anyone. Why do I hurt so badly?' I whispered towards the gray depressing clouds that moved heedlessly above."

Mila wasn't aware that my toy had slipped from her hands on her lap, and her knees were shaking. I had taken her back to the time when my solitude was reaching its culmination. Her eyes, glinting with tears, looked past me through the window and into the blue sky. They scanned the white, slow-moving summer clouds. She seemed as if she wanted to talk to Him, to *whoever* was up there, and ask why both of us had been punished with bitter destinies. She picked up a clean napkin, wiped some of her tears, and gave me a look that went through me. Covering her mouth, she breathed into her cupped hands, "That must've been terrible." The words echoed in her hands and she sat completely inert.

"I kept fighting my solitude, and my mind kept giving birth to new ideas," I said. "Being unable to develop a friendship with my male schoolmates, I turned to the girls. They became a substitute for the male friends I was supposed to have. I was tricking myself, really. Girls are not boys, but they helped to ease my solitude, at least. It was a lot of fun hanging out with them.

"After a while, I was always in their company, and the only place I couldn't go with them was the ladies' bathroom. I became very popular among the upperclassmen. Many boys tried to befriend me. Getting the girls was their greatest challenge, and through me, it was a piece of cake. I enjoyed their company, but I wasn't their friend. I was only their matchmaker. When the girls talked about the boys, they were quite graphic in describing their first kisses, touches, and crushes. I liked it, but I felt uncomfortable. Something had irrevocably changed in me then, but I kept suppressing it. I couldn't explain it. There was no one to ask about it. During long nights, my thoughts turned into poems:

"Some day
Some day, one day, I'll reach the stars above,
I'll touch the fingers of happiness, and hear its voice.
Some day, one day, I'll have my little smile back,
I'll meet luck, I'll see my dreams, and kill my fears.
Some day, one day, my little human being will be free,
From sadness, desolation, and I'll be whoever I want to be.

"My only skill on the football field was as a goalie, but I excelled at doing gymnastics with the girls. The whole school began calling me sissy. My parents almost died with embarrassment. They ordered me to stay away from the girls, and once again, I withdrew into my dark, deserted world of misery."

I paused and walked to the window. I looked back at Mila, then out the window, then at Mila again, waiting for a reaction. Her eyes were wide and unblinking, and she looked at me with infinite despair. She remained glued to the armchair, once again holding my old toy. Tears slid down her cheeks, some dropping into her cleavage, others dampening her blouse. I handed her a fresh napkin. She nodded in thanks.

I sat in the rocking chair again. "I didn't give up on girls completely, though." I said flippantly. "Aishah was one of the most beautiful girls I'd ever seen. She was a blonde Turkish beauty. Her family worked in Denmark and almost every summer they would come to town. We were neighbors and contemporaries, but it was the summer before I started high school that I really noticed her. Many times, I would follow her, and I got chills when our eyes would meet. She had the most elegant walk.

"Raised in a strict Muslim family, she went shopping with her mother on a regular basis. One day, to my surprise, I happened to see her coming home from the store alone, so I greeted her. She looked at me as I were a rapist or something, and she called me a disparaging name that I didn't understand. Then she ran home, struggling with her heavy grocery bags.

"I was curious to see how she lived, among other things, so that night I decided to spy on her. First, I peeped through her living room window. Her parents were watching TV, and her little brother was playing on the floor. She sat on the other side of the room, turned in profile. Then she stood up and left the room. I saw the light in the bathroom come on, so I climbed a tree and watched her through the window. I saw her pee, take a shower, and rub her body with lotion in front of the mirror. It was like watching a Hollywood movie. Her perfect, delicate, snow-white figure captivated me. It aroused me. Then she turned the light off and the show was over.

"At the end of the year, I found out that her parents had sold her to some rich peasant. It was sad, but it wasn't a shock. Prearranged marriages among Turks, Albanians, and other Muslims, as well as some rural Christians, were a reality. They could be profitable for the bride's family, if she was a beauty. A few years later, I saw Aishah walking down the street with her husband, who looked like nothing. Her beauty was veiled by sadness. She smiled faintly at me. We never could have been anything other than a modern, Macedonian, Romeo and Juliet. Our families would've massacred each other if we had ever gotten involved. …And religion is supposed to make you love and respect others?" I sneered, shaking my head.

"Anyway, there was one relationship from which I got great satisfaction: my godfather. I adored him. He was a wise man, a history professor and politician. As my first mentor, he exposed me to our rich Balkan culture by showing me the monasteries and ruins, teaching me their value and importance. Every time he visited us he would bring me expensive imported toys. When I got older, he brought books. He was the only one who encouraged me to write poems and to paint. He was very artistic, and my first role model. But he would only stay with us for a couple weeks during the summer, and I was dying to see him more often. We had so much fun together. Father loved to go hunting with friends, but I only wanted to go with him when Godfather went along.

"I'll never forget the summer vacations I spent with him. We usually went to the national park in the Pelister Mountain. Its breathtaking blue ranges rose above Prespa Lake. We slept in little wooden cabins near the peak. Surrounded by Father's comrade politicians, I learned a lot about Balkan politics at an early age. My fondest memories, though, were of being with Godfather. I loved to ride horses with him and listen to his speeches about nature and world history. I used to help him fish in the clear springs. On those fishing trips, we would eat wild strawberries. Back at the cabin, we'd make herbal tea, while Father and his comrades played cards under the stars, cursed, and told jokes until dawn by the bonfire. At night, I was scared by the sounds of animals, echoing in the woods, but I would fall asleep next to Godfather, feeling protected and secure."

I took a deep breath and jumped from my chair. "The damage was done!" I shouted, making Mila start. I could see she was hurt and that listening to my story was hell for her. "Too bad," I mumbled selfishly. "My hell is greater."

I took out a new cigarette and *shwaitzed* it, lit it from the smoldering remains of the old one. I took a couple of puffs and proceeded with my story.

"During the four years of high school, in the local *Gymnasia*, I was a complete loner, incapable of making friends after all those years of isolation. My peers had fun; they went to parties and on vacations. Even if I'd had friends, I wasn't allowed to go on vacation without my parents, who kept acting as if I were in first grade. It was agonizing, and pitifully, I was rather used to it. Then I got my first bicycle.

Convincing my overly protective parents to let me have one was more difficult than cutting my first tooth. They thought I would kill myself. Instead, I nearly killed someone else. I ended up crashing into an old woman returning from the market. Her bags flew into the air, as my tires rolled up her crotch, over her stomach and chest, and finally stopped on her mouth, splitting it open. It broke her jaw. Blood was everywhere. It seemed as if her cracked, bloody mouth was going to devour me, while she lay there, writhing in pain. I was frozen with fear; I just stood there until a passerby pushed my bike away from her. A neighbor called an ambulance. Everything happened quickly. I could hear her saying, 'You little bastard! Go to hell!' Blood was flowing from her deformed mouth. People stared at me, as if I were a little Lucifer. I thought Mother and Father would punish me and I would never be able to touch my bike again. Instead, they said, "She'll be fine. She's just a tough apple-knocker."

Mila's laughter had brightened the room like a lustrous rainbow. Now, she smiled, looking more like me than ever. Blood is thicker than water, I thought. Nibbling on another cookie, I continued.

"I was delighted to be allowed to ride my bike and anxious to reach distant places: to be alone with nature, to feel free and uninhibited, and to talk and, dance and sing, in the middle of the forest, in the fields, or by the lake. I did that all during my high school years, and my bike was my loyal friend. I loved it like a brother. But it was not a substitute for a live companion. I still wanted a friend, and no one got closer to me than one particular girl, who followed me home from school almost every day. I was in senior high. She was in sixth grade. She was wild and sensuous, with catlike eyes: a mixture of green and yellow that would drive anyone crazy. Her dark hair contrasted beautifully with her porcelain skin. She was a virgin, like most of the local girls who were saving themselves for marriage. We made a cute couple. At least, that was what almost everyone told us. However, my parents didn't think so, so I couldn't invite her over. One afternoon, we were strolling by the little church near the big aluminum factory when it began to pour. We went inside.

"'You never have me over your house. Your parents don't like me, do they?' she asked, as we began to light candles. Her feline eyes glowed as the matches flared.

"'I'm not allowed to invite anyone to my house. It's hard to explain.'

"'Is it because my parents are villagers or because my father is a simple police officer?' she said, angrily.

"'Who cares what they think? They are sick anyway. The important thing is that I like you a lot.'

"'Show me,' she said, in a teasing manner, then scampered away. We began to chase each other around the candle posts arranged symmetrically in the middle of the church. The flames shimmered, projecting our dancing shadows on the walls and on the grayish cement floor. We entered the altar and sat on the Bishop's chair. We were allowed; we were still clean. Soon, we were almost nude, ignoring the saints' expressions that were like those of judges condemning the guilty. We kissed. We weren't virgins anymore. That's what our parents had taught us. As our final virginal breaths mingled with the candle smoke, I thought Saint George was going to throw his spear at us instead of the dragon. Little devils were flying around, dragging us into their house of pleasures. Trembling, we stared at Maria's compassionate face, as she held baby Jesus, who smiled with forgiveness.

"Suddenly, the door opened wide. 'Get the hell out of here, you heretics!' A man stormed towards us. He was the priest who once came to bless my Granny Sandra's house. He sang the liturgy like a donkey. After he finished it, I was supposed to kiss his hand. Instead, I grabbed his crotch and kissed him on the mouth. Three old ladies, Granny's friends, hollered, "Nooo!" The priest turned as red as a cooked lobster. Granny chased me out, calling me every name that Lucifer was ever known by, and waving her handbag. I climbed the first tree I saw and didn't come down for five hours. That was the only time Granny raised a hand to me. She was a religious zealot. She didn't know I had been waiting for such a moment, since I lived in a communist house and had no opportunity to get near a clergyman. Grabbing a priest's balls was something my schoolmates aspired to. When I told Father and my schoolmates, they called me a hero, and I felt so important.

"The priest was old. He couldn't chase us for long. When he stopped to catch his breath, we laughed at him, mocking his angry face in comparison to the sweet expressions on Mary and her baby Jesus. I yelled, 'Who the fuck are you to call us sinners when the Holy Mother and her Child don't even mind! Take a close look at their kind faces!' He just stood there, stunned and getting angrier as we rushed out, chuckling. The gentle raindrops began washing away our sin. Green and reckless, we always had a good time together. Nevertheless, the pressure from my parents to dump the police officer's daughter was enormous, and I left her one month later."

"God, they didn't even let you be in love," Mila broke in, angrily.

"Of course. No one deserved me." I answered.

"Didn't your parents ever invite their friends over? Have parties?" she asked, sounding curious and skeptical.

"National holidays were the only occasions my father really cherished and the only times he would invite family and friends over. Religious holidays were not observed in our home. They conflicted with his position and communistic ideology. When Father got older, however, there were two exceptions to that rule. First, out of his egoism, Father allowed celebrations of his patron name, Saint Cyril. He was proud of Cyril, who with his brother Methodius, were Byzantine missionaries, spreading the word of Orthodox Christianity. In the ninth century, they also developed an alphabet for the Slavs, later called Cyrillic alphabet. Cyril and Methodius were later canonized Saints.

"Second, out of love for me, he let us celebrate my patron name, Saint Blagovest. His name means bearer of good news, and he was the one who first told the people of Jesus' resurrection. Granny Sandra told me that. I got my name from Father's youngest brother who died in World War II. Boys were customarily given the names of their grandfathers, but sometimes they came from other relatives. It depended upon who your Father loved most dearly. My father loved his younger brother. He always talked about how extraordinarily courageous he was. Mother's patron name saint, like any woman's, was not celebrated. Another male chauvinist practice.

"The relatives thought Father was a terrible host. His authoritarian and domineering behavior pissed them off. His friends were used to it. Even outside his office, he always had to be in control. He had the last word in all discussions. He acted like a supreme judge, claiming he was always right. They couldn't stand it, but they loved Mother's glamorous hospitality. She always made fancy food and put up lavish decorations, particularly for my birthdays. For my eighteenth birthday, she threw the biggest party ever. The house was absolutely posh. Fine drinks and hors d'oeuvres were served, while relatives and friends chatted about family matters. Soon, the men got drunk and began their awful singing, accompanied by their wives' jokes and gossip. Everyone celebrated the party but me. The only guest who came for me was a Turkish fellow I occasionally exchanged tapes with during class breaks. He brought me a tape. Like me, he loved to record world music. My parents treated him as if he were invisible. Poor guy. He stayed fifteen minutes, hardly tasting the cake. After I walked him to the door, my parents asked me, 'Who the hell is he? Where are your schoolmates?'

"I said nothing. I wanted to reach out and choke the two reasons that I had no friends. I turned around and lurked grimly by the door, waiting for a miracle to happen: for the friend I never had to visit me. I cursed everyone in the house celebrating my fancy birthday, crying and asking myself, 'What's so good about a damn birthday when all I feel is older, uglier, and lonelier?'

"I hated my eighteenth birthday. The high school prom a few weeks later was even worse. We celebrated it in the hotel by the lake. The custom was to go with a date. My parents chose my partner, my third cousin. She'd had a sweetheart since the seventh grade who she married after high school. Her parents were against it, but she got pregnant, so they had no choice. We were one of the best-looking couples, but as soon as we arrived at the hotel, she left me and spent the evening with her boyfriend. Everyone knew that would happen. Even her parents. I wasn't offended, knowing how crazy they were for each other. The irony was that I was one of the best-looking, best-dressed students. I had to be. My parents wouldn't have it any other way. Students loved to look at me, and I think many of them wanted to be close with me. But the person my parents created was unreachable—a wise and well-off preppie, weird and arrogant, and so damn special. They had no idea how unhappy and damaged I was. I was dying to be one of them and have partners and go to high school parties. No one had a clue how good a dancer I was, either. If one of the girls who had a big crush on me hadn't invited me onto the floor, the prom would've been just another long, lonely night.

"The end of high school was marked with the final excursion. It was the longest one. For three weeks, we toured all six Yugoslavian states. I had the biggest embarrassment of my entire school career. I had to wait like a beggar while my literature teacher tried to find another student to share a hotel room with me. No one volunteered. Usually on these trips, some introverted type would agree to share, but on this one even the shyest boy had a roommate. When everyone picked up their keys from the desk, my teacher turned to me and said, 'You can share a room with me if you want?' Honored by her offer, I nodded immediately and almost didn't feel the pain of my schoolmates' collective rejection.

"I was uneasy for a while, but as we began to discuss literature, I relaxed. Everyone thought that she was a very tough teacher. I didn't. I was her best student. She loved my poetry. She constantly pushed me to write more. When later we watched the movie she propped her head on her hand and asked me, 'Why don't you have friends?'

"'I don't know.' I said defensively.

"'Maybe your parents know. I should talk to them!'

"'Oh, no! No way! It's too late now, anyway. I'll make friends soon…In the Army. Then in college.' I jumped from the chair, agitated.

"She caught me in a hug and stroked my face, as if I were in first grade. 'You're a nice guy. You'll make lots of friends. You have one now,' she whispered, smiling warmly and assuredly.

"The teacher kept me near her during the whole excursion. Anytime she showed us the sights of the big cities, explaining their histories, I swore to myself that one day I would live in a city. Their layouts, the freedom exuding from them, the different people who lived in them, seduced me completely.

"I suddenly realized that no matter how big a fish my father was there, Resen was a little, little pond. And for the first time in my life, I had seen not just a lake, but the ocean."

17

Adoption

The telephone rang. Our neighbor, Frosa, called to say that lunch was ready. I excused myself and went to pick it up. Frosa stood on her side of the fence and handed me the main dish in a pot. I brought it into the kitchen and went back for the salad. Mother wasn't awake yet. I arranged grape leaves with lamb, the main course, on three plates, then put one of the plates on a tray, with two slices of bread, a bowl of salad, and a glass of water, and went upstairs.

"Lunch is homemade. Delicious." I slid the tray along the desk towards Mila.

"Thank you," she said. "How's your mother doing?"

"I have to wake her up for lunch. See you in a while."

"Yes." She nodded, and, as I closed the door behind me, kept nodding and staring blankly in front of her.

I stepped gingerly down the stairs, as if to ease my transition from Mila's dimension to Mother's. The simple act of descending the stairs seemed to be fraught with meaning, a meaning that weighed heavily in my mind. I tried to imagine the situation being reversed, if I'd been born of Mother and raised by Mila. It felt weird. I couldn't even begin to imagine replacing my father with the one about whom I knew so little.

I entered the living room and announced, "Mother, time for lunch." I gently prodded her hand, which lay, palm up, on her pillow. Both her hand and her lips trembled slightly.

Her eyes flew open. "What? What time is it?" she asked, instinctively.

"Almost two," I said.

"I thought it was morning," she mumbled sadly, aware that her time orientation was worsening. I helped her to the kitchen table, and when she saw the plate, she complained, "That's a lot of food. I can't eat it."

I put some back in the pot, upset that she was eating less each day.

"What you're doing isn't good," I said. "You must eat more. How will you be cured if you don't?"

Her smile was ambiguous. "To make more trouble for you with this bag," she said, pressing through her robe on the colostomy bag, the plastic making a dreadful crinkling noise as she did. "To live longer…is that what you want for me?"

"Yes," I said, firmly. "To live longer and to be healthy again."

"I hope so," she sighed, and started to eat.

I didn't say anything, to avoid an argument and more stress. I wasn't able to tell my lies as well as before. She had become bolder and more skeptical. Did she know about her cancer?

The question continued to haunt me as I watched her eat slowly. She only ate half of what was on her plate. I ate all of my lunch, washed the dishes, checked her colostomy, took her to the toilet, and gave her the medicine. We watched TV until Bisera came over at four, the usual time for Mother's walk around the neighborhood. As soon as they left, I climbed upstairs, quickly this time, to avoid heavy thoughts.

Mila was looking out the window, leaning on the sill. "I'm trying to see your mother's face," she said.

I noticed that Mila hadn't touched her lunch. The glass of water was one-quarter empty.

"You're not going to eat?" I asked.

"I'm not hungry," she said, walking back to the armchair and putting my rubber cat in her lap as she sat. "When did you find out you were adopted? How?"

Mila tucked her legs beneath her. I looked at my reflection in the glass of the cabinet and began to talk.

"The physical differences between me and my parents were obvious. I had been suspicious about my heritage since I was very little. Nevertheless, I was afraid to broach the subject for a long time. I feared my parents' reaction. The urge to find my biological roots was like a cloud heavy with rain, just before a downpour. My urge became unbearable as I grew older and learned more that confirmed my suspicions. When I finished high school and became more confident, I decided to ask them. I waited for the most opportune moment, which turned out to be one hot July night after dinner and the main news at 8 o'clock, when my parents usually seemed most relaxed.

"'I've longed to ask you something since I was child,' I said. Their sedate expressions suddenly became colorless. They looked at me with apprehension, waiting for my next words.

"I took a deep breath. 'Who were my biological parents?'

"'Oh, no! No!' Mother jumped up and ran to me, hugging me, practically crushing me in her arms.

"'You are my real parents. I love you. I only want to know where I came from. I'm curious. That's all. Just to see them…her. Nothing else.'

"Tensely, Father took out a cigarette, lit it, and offered me one. For the first time, I saw him unable to control his tears. Mother pulled me closer to her trembling body. Father stared at me with a hopeless expression. Mother asked in a choking voice, 'Are you going to leave us now?'

"'Are you crazy? Of course not. Where the hell would I go? You are my family. I just need the truth. And I want to hear it from you.'

"A half-hour later, they were still in shock. Mother clung to me. Father kept smoking cigarette after cigarette. He stared down at the kilim and sobbed quietly. I went over and sat next to him. Mother followed me. I felt strangely comforted when he put his arm around me. I tried to remember the last time he had hugged me like that. I was speechless, waiting for them to calm down and talk.

"'Your mother wanted to adopt because she couldn't give birth,' Father broke the silence. 'I didn't want to at first.' He glanced at Mother and something unspoken passed between them. 'Your godfather was Minister of Culture at that time, well connected, so we told him about our decision. He was delighted to hear it and, soon afterward, he found a baby boy for us. Your mother had wanted a girl. She decided to go with him to the orphanage anyway, to see you. I didn't go. I felt embarrassed, not being able to have my own child.'

"His cigarette hand shook and the ash fell on the couch. Neither Mother nor I moved to clean it; we sat eagerly waiting for him to go on, as if he were preaching the Holy Gospel.

"'We didn't know who your parents were. All that mattered to us was that you were from good Christian Yugoslavian blood, not a gypsy or Muslim. Your godfather assured us of that and arranged for the adoption.'

"'You were the most neglected-looking child in the room, yet the only one who didn't cry,' Mother interjected. 'You smiled with your beautiful eyes and won my heart immediately. Even if you hadn't been recommended, I would've picked you for sure. You took my breath away.'

What a slut I was as a baby, I thought, *to have sold myself so successfully.*

"'The only thing we heard later,' Father continued, 'was that your father was a big shot in the federal government and had an affair with a high school student. We understood. It was the sixties. She had to give you up. Even now, it's frowned upon. Also there were rumors that your mother was extremely beautiful. That's all we heard from your godfather, who was the only one who knew the whole truth. Too bad he's dead.'

"'What about my godmother?' I urged.

"'I don't think she knows anything,' Father replied, resolutely.

"'How about documents? Do you have any?'

"They went mute.

"'Father,' I said. 'I remember when I was in second grade, one afternoon you got a blue envelope in the mail. When you saw me in the hallway, you quickly stuffed it in a jacket hanging on the coat hanger. I knew something was strange, so later, I went back and read it. It was an agreement from her permitting you to change my given name…something like that.'

"'I knew those awful, jealous idiots would tell you everything,' Mother said, standing at the window and gazing out at passers-by. 'We have so many enemies. They want to destroy our family. Otherwise, you'd never know. You'd never find out—never.' She paused, then whispered sharply, 'We would *never* have told you!'

"The first one to give me a clue was our neighbor, Menka. She used to curse me. She'd say, 'Little bastard! You should never have been taken from that damned orphanage!' as I fought with her granddaughter on the playground.

"'That peasant, wicked witch!' Mother reacted with rage.

"'Not only her,' I added. 'Other people: playmates, neighbors, relatives, students, would throw words at me sometimes, like: Bastard! Orphan! You mistake! However, most of the truth I found out myself. I was afraid to ask you, afraid I would be punished. I wasn't a stupid child, Mother. Over and over, you've told me that. You would always redden when people said: Oh, what a beautiful boy. Your grandchild? Then you would panic and quickly change the subject. I could tell from their expressions that these people were doubtful. Is it any surprise that all I need now is a mirror to see the difference between us?'

"Mother began to whine. Father stood up.

"'He's right,' he told Mother. Turning to me, he said, 'I'll bring you the document.'

"Mother's eyes flashed with anger. To her, that paper was my ticket for a trip down a road she thought I would never be able to take. In her eyes, I was her possession and searching for own my identity would change that. She avoided looking into my eyes, and when Father came back and handed me the familiar blue envelope, she closed hers tightly. The envelope was brittle, bleached from age.

"'This is the adoption agreement, the same that one you saw as a boy. That day, I had showed it to a close friend, a judge. There had been some changes in the adoption law. I was afraid it would affect us. I needed advice.' Father said. 'You can invite her here if you find her. No problem.'

"His attitude didn't surprise me. He had always been more realistic, compared to my emotional Mother.

"Father sat on the couch again. 'On two occasions,' he said, 'I saw a woman, loitering on the street in front of our house. You were about six then, and the woman was watching you play in the garden. The second time, when you were about 10, a car stopped out front, and a woman and a man inside were observing our house. I couldn't tell if she was the same one. There are many cases when biological parents want their children back. We became very concerned after that.'

"I wasn't the woman," Mila interrupted. "I wish I had been. I didn't know where you were. I was only told that a nice family had adopted you. Do you believe me?" She posed the question as if begging for my compassion.

"Yes, I do," I lied. "Maybe my father was looking for me?"

"I have no idea. Maybe," Mila said.

I didn't believe her. All I knew for sure about her was that she bore me and left me in an orphanage. How could I trust her? I began rocking the chair, took another cookie, nibbled it nervously, and continued my story.

"'We were in constant fear that she would make problems for us if she found you,' Mother said. 'Also, the Center for Social Affairs and the orphanage advised us never to tell you that you were adopted. Everything was confidential. It was the law.'

"'What kind of law is that? Forcing you to lie and hide the truth?' I asked.

"'We had to,' Mother said, raising her voice. Father nodded in approval. 'Maybe in big cities and other countries, people don't need to. But in towns like ours, where everyone knows everyone, we had to hide it.'

"'So you agreed that it was better for me to hear those awful words from the locals, too young to understand, yet old enough to be hurt! You didn't think that the truth would come out, sooner or later?' I shouted.

"They gazed at each other speechless. Waiting for their answer, I tried to calm down, wondering: *Why am I getting upset? They didn't, and still don't, know any better. It's too late, anyway.*

"Father finally spoke, 'She gave you the male version of her name. We assume she loved you. I guess she had to give you up.'

"'Jesus Christ, The Holy Mother, and all The Apostles. You assume. I don't!' Mother glared at Father, as if he had raped her whole family.

"'A mother who gives up her own child is no mother!' I said. 'There is no excuse! Only in death or by force. I'm sure of that.' The look of alarm left their faces and they relaxed after I said that."

Mila lowered her head. Her legs curled tighter into the left side of the armchair. Her tears began coming faster. Tough shit, I thought. The truth hurts, but lies can kill. She'll handle it. I sipped from my glass and continued.

"That night, none of us got much sleep; too many cards had been laid on the table. Every morning, Mother would come downstairs first, so she took advantage of that time to talk to me alone.

"'I could have given birth,' she whispered, as she joined me at the kitchen table. 'The doctors told me I was just fine. It was your father's fault. I tried to persuade him to get checked, but he refused. You know, male pride. Especially from a top official like him. Can you imagine him admitting his sterility? So I've covered up his problem all this time.'

"She sipped her coffee, wiping her tears. 'He experienced all that poverty, hunger, World War II, torture. No doubt his sperm weakened. He's been through a lot of trauma.'

"The truth was emerging. She told me about the trip. The day she took my six-month-old self from the orphanage. As she spoke, I recalled a buried memory from long ago. I don't know how. I still can't explain it, but I remembered a trip as an infant, and being held by another woman next to Mother. I told Mother, and we were both stunned when she confirmed that the wife of one of Father's best friends had accompanied her. It was unbelievable how closely my memory and my mothers' story matched. Mystical, even. How could I have remembered all of it, any of it, at that age?"

I paused, gazing at the ceiling for a while, then I said, "My parents pretended that they didn't mind that I was going to investigate my past. We were passing by one another, without looking at each other, as if we were in a library or a museum. We couldn't look at each other, perplexed for our own reasons. Soon, I began my search for you. I went to the street in the center of the capital, next to Universal Hall, and looked for the address you had provided. None of the neighbors could recall anyone who lived there under your name." I stopped there expecting Mila's explanation.

"I made up an address. I'm sorry," she said.

Sorry my ass. It's the easiest word to say when you screw someone. "Sorry" is like a final insult being thrown at you after you've been damaged. People shouldn't say anything after they've fucked you up. They should just sink in shame and regret.

I wanted to scream that, but I didn't want to be a jerk, so I set aside those thoughts.

"My parents assumed the biological father's supposedly high-ranking position was the reason why things in your letter were falsified."

Silence. Mila seemed like a whipped, vulnerable prisoner whenever my biological father was mentioned. I wanted her to drop her defenses and say something about him. She began sobbing instead. Noises came from downstairs. Bisera and Mother were back.

"I'm going to see what's going on," I murmured, instinctively.

Mila nodded and pulled a cigarette from my pack of Marlboros.

I ran downstairs and hugged Mother in the hallway. "How was the walk?"

She twitched her eyebrows and waved her hand in a habitual, hopeless gesture. Bisera shook her head in a way that told me not to ask more questions. After Bisera left at the usual time, 7 P.M., Mother remarked, "You are spending more time in your room these days."

"I'm studying American English. I need to concentrate."

"It must be a joy to read American literature in its native form."

"Yeah, much better than the translations I used to read."

"Read, learn languages. I wish I could do it."

"You will, Mother. Soon."

She gazed at me with an indifferent expression. I kept changing the TV channels. I didn't want to look her in the eye for a while, until I had succeeded in transforming my face into a happy mask. We ate dinner, and I tried to make light conversation with Mother. She didn't talk much, and I couldn't wait for her to retire, hoping to escape the strange ambiance that had descended upon us. I had grown accustomed to Mother's mood swings since she had gotten ill, but that night the tone of her voice seemed to say: "You lie. You don't study; you hide someone upstairs! I'm dying, but I'm not stupid."

No, Mother, I thought. *You're not stupid. But for both of us, just this once, try to be a little less smart.*

18

Army

That night, the pain kept Mother awake longer. She asked me for more medicine, and I put ten more drops of methadone in a cup of chamomile tea. Around midnight, she closed her eyes and I tucked her blanket securely around her, after making sure that the colostomy bag was in place. I prepared a dinner plate for Mila and climbed to my room. I wished the stairs weren't there, but I couldn't avoid them.

When I got to my room, I moved the photo albums aside to make room for the tray. My old rubber cat was on top of them. I figured she must have browsed through the albums several times by now.

"Thank you, but I'm not hungry," Mila said.

"If you don't like homemade food, I'll buy something else."

"Don't bother. I'm fine. I need to use the bathroom."

When Mila came back, she retrieved the rubber cat and began fondling it in her lap again. She picked up a cookie and sipped cherry juice. She looked as if she had not left the armchair. For almost two days, she'd consumed nothing but liquids and a few cookies. Her eyes focused on my lips. She sought out my words, like a jogger would seek water from a faucet. She was prepared to drink deeply, despite the bitter taste.

"After high school, in September 1983, I enlisted in the Army," I said. "It was a celebration month, and parents were giving big farewell parties for their sons. Mine was humble. Some relatives showed up. The day I left, I was surrounded by young recruits with crumpled faces and their crying parents. I wasn't sad, though.

"As I set my foot on the train, Mother embraced me and whispered in my ear, 'I've always protected you from everyone who has tried to take advantage of you. Who's going to protect you now? I'll miss you terribly. Yet I feel happy and envious that you'll be away from Father.'

"I didn't comment. I kissed her and entered the car. At the window, I waved briefly at my father's proud figure. I was content to be leaving all the local people.

I felt grown up, leaving Mother's protection behind, seeing the last traces of it in her teary expression. I was generally scared of institutions, but I was certain that the army would be better than my home. I felt an orgasmic thrill when everyone disappeared from my sight as the locomotive pulled us into the forest.

"The army base was big and well-equipped. It was in the small town of Koprivnica, near the Hungarian border in Croatia. The first couple of months were tough. Intense classroom training and arms and bomb practice sessions took most of the day. I was trained as a communications specialist, taught Morse code. For me, army life wasn't as difficult as it was for many soldiers. I got used to the discipline, having already been trained to wake up early, to be on time, to be fast, and to obey Father's rules. Unlike many, I favored the idea of requiring everyone to serve one year in the Army, to build strength and discipline.

"The winter games of 1984 were to be held in Sarajevo. Our division was ordered to do special training nearby, for national security reasons. The Bosnian mountains, oh, God, they were cold jungles. Forty of us slept, packed like canned sardines, on moist straw mats, in tents without heat or showers, without enough water or food. We stunk like pigs, unable to change clothes for a month. After a while, my socks stuck like rubber to my skin. I had to cut them off. The skin underneath was so tender, it bled. My whole body ached. During guard duty, I froze in the knee-deep snow. I was allowed to sleep four hours before I did the two hours of guard duty. Twenty days in a row, I did that. Then someone stole my gloves, and I couldn't use my machine gun. I was taken to the hospital for frostbitten fingers. Since then, my hands and feet have developed poor circulation. I never understood the purpose of being so humiliated in training. It's for developing endurance, the officers would say.

"For the second half of my army service, I was transferred to my favorite town, Varazdin. The Baroque architecture from the Austro-Hungarian monarchy and its famous cemetery, laid out in the style of the gardens of Versailles, made the town beautiful. The western influence there was overwhelming in comparison to my hometown in Macedonia, where Balkan values dominated. My desire to see the West began to skyrocket then.

"The new base was small, very disorganized, and located deep in the heart of town. It was liberating to see soldiers in civilian clothing jumping the fence almost every afternoon; walking around town as if they were long-time residents. One night, a fellow soldier stole a bicycle from the street and brought it into our bedroom. Another was caught playing his Walkman and dancing on guard duty, completely boozed up. It was a wacky place. A mess. The complete opposite of my first base.

"Mother wanted to see me, but Father didn't want to be without her for a minute, naturally. She was like his slave, serving him twenty-four hours a day as if he were a king. Finally, she convinced him to let her visit me when she found traveling companions. It was a Turkish couple, whose son was a soldier on my base. They couldn't afford airfare. So Mother took the train and commuted for a day and a half with them.

"My Slovenian captain was a real asshole. He hated southerners. He considered Serbs and Macedonians to be Gypsies. He wouldn't let me stay overnight with Mother, not even half a day. Mother cursed him every fifteen minutes. It was strange to see someone like her, who discriminated against Turks, associating with them. She overfed me with my favorite chocolates and cookies. She hugged me non-stop for a half-hour before parting, whispering how lonely Father and she felt without me. For a few minutes, I felt sorry, but I stopped when I remembered that I had barely six months before I would have to return home. I wasn't rushing to go back.

"The economic crisis hit much harder in the south then the industrialized north. Now and then, I would send products back home, and my parents would brag to everyone about what an attentive son I was. I hadn't seen so much attention being given to the President's speech since Tito's death in 1980. Everyone was concerned about the economic crisis, but more so the political one that came with it. Albanian separatism, irredentism, and Islamic fundamentalism exploded in Kosovo, especially after our Marshal's death."

Mila's eyes widened. "I can clearly picture those scary times. Albanians were screaming their slogan, 'Kosovo Republic,' and demanding independence from the federation and Serbia. No Yugoslav could imagine Albanians annexing any of their country to create 'Great Albania.' Albanian fanatic nationalism was a cancer to the Yugoslav Federation, supported by powerful Albanians, drug and prostitution dealers from around the world, not to mention Western Europe and the US. Serbs were not thrilled to give up their minerals or part of their heritage to the Albanians. Serbs considered Kosovo and Metohia as their Holy Land, as Jews do Jerusalem."

"That's for sure. A state of emergency was declared. My base was in full readiness. The Army had to intervene along with the police to stop the violence, rape, and murder, and to bring back Serb families who were leaving the province in fear of the Albanians. The Albanian soldiers constantly kept to themselves on the base. People of other nationalities and ethnic groups mixed easily. It was annoying and alarming to listen to the Albanians talking loudly in groups and not to understand a word, because they refused to speak the official Serbo-Croatian language. The officers were pissed. They couldn't stand it. The Albanians, like any of Yugoslavia's minorities, were taught Serbo-Croatian in schools. They were privileged to be educated where their native language was used, too. They enjoyed the same rights as everyone else. Unlike other minorities, however, they loved to take advantage of it and abuse it.

"The Serbs, the Montenegrins, and the Macedonians hated the Albanians the most, since most Albanians lived in their states. The Croats, Slovenians, and the Bosnians didn't care as much. The Albanians declared that Macedonia was part of Albania, that it shouldn't be a separate state. Demonstrations were organized in already Albanized West Macedonia. The Yugoslavian public was sick and tired of the Albanian separatism, irredentism, and fanatic Islam. As tensions grew, the Yugoslav army and police concentrated more troops in the province, trying to stabilize the situation. Kosovo looked like a war zone, the soldiers who were sent from my base told us later. The tragedy was that innocent people were raped, humiliated, and killed, while extremist groups and politicians were only focused on achieving their goals.

"Because of the high Albanian natality, Yugoslavs were afraid they would reproduce to the point where they would demand their own constitution and republic. Many predicted that if they continued multiplying at the same pace, they would soon be the biggest ethnic group, not only in Yugoslavia, but in Europe. I had heard from the officers that, other than the Chinese, they were the fastest-reproducing people on earth. I had also heard that phenomena was called "Identity War"—the consciously-planned, rapid reproduction of one ethnic group, race, or nationality, in order to become a dominating force in a multiethnic society to achieve their ultimate goal: developing their own state, constitution, religion, and government.

"Mind-blowing news came one night in the TV room. An anchorman announced that at one of the southern army bases, an Albanian fundamentalist soldier slaughtered innocent Christian soldiers with his machine gun while they were sleeping. My fellow non-Albanian soldiers were devastated. It felt bizarre watching events unfold next to the Albanian soldiers. The tension and the anger in any Christians' eyes were obvious. Fights and accidents took place in our barracks that night. I had an Albanian buddy, but it was clear that he could no longer be my friend if I wanted to stay alive.

"On the way back to the bedrooms, I stepped into water that was coming from the bathrooms. There were broken bottles all over the corridor and a few still rolling on the floor.

"'So many damn bottles for their asses and they still reek,' a Serbian soldier blurted out.

"'Maybe we should introduce douche bags with perfumed ass cleansers for them. Ha, ha!' his Croat friend said, smirking. 'They use the same shitty bottles in each stall. Can you imagine how many germs they transmit? Fuckin' water poloists!'

"'Water poloists' was a derogatory term Christian Yugoslavs used to describe Albanians, who wore traditional skullcaps, cone-shaped hats that resembled those worn by water polo players. Christian soldiers often smashed the bottles of water that Muslim Albanians, Bosnians, Turks, and Gypsies used to wash after defecating. Thus, they would anxiously search from stall to stall for unbroken bottles. The Muslims couldn't complain. The officers were mostly Serbs and Croats. Their only recourse was to use paper instead, which was against Islamic custom.

"The next day, it was odd to be in the dinning room, listening to the soldiers, and seeing a plaque on the wall with a slogan: 'Brotherhood and Unity!' Tito's dream for the Yugoslav nation seemed surreal.

"'I love it,' the Serbian said. 'Look at them.' He elbowed his fellow soldier and pointed to a group of Muslims. 'They're not eating! They're leaving! Everything's made with pork tonight. Oh man, I love it! Fuck them. Let them starve! Who needs them! I love this institution! I love when they get officially fucked!'

"'Tomorrow, after the training, you'll see how they lick pork flesh. They won't give a damn about the fuckin' Koran when their stomachs start singing. They'll even eat pig shit! Ha, ha, ha.'

"Everyone grinned at the Croat's mockery. Someone in the group asked, 'What's the Koran?'

"'A porno magazine!' the Slovenian said, sarcastically. 'You dumb ass!'

"'The Koran is fuckin' Islam's Holy Book, which prohibits Muslims from eating pork!' a Macedonian explained.

"'That's why they all smell like pigs!' A Montenegrin piped up, and everyone chuckled again. I didn't. It was sad watching my country being torn apart by hatred, nationalism, and discrimination. It was a bad sign."

I paused and lit a cigarette. Mila asked for one. I doubted that she had ever smoked that much in her entire life.

"Times were tense, weren't they?" She sighed. "In Croatia, the Albanians who usually ran confectionery shops or restaurant businesses were exiled from the Republic as quickly as possible. Croats weren't delighted to see them settle and breed like mice in their yards. I never thought about their excessive birthrate as strategy. Identity war. Interesting."

I yawned, a couple of times in a row.

"You should go to sleep. It's getting late," she said.

"Oh-kay, let's sleep," I stubbed out my cigarette.

"I'll stay up for a while."

"Good night, then."

"Sleep well," she whispered.

She didn't lean forward like the night before, to kiss me. Her eyes revealed nothing, but she seemed to be waiting for me to do it first, spontaneously and desirously. She's still a stranger, I thought. I could feel her eyes on me, as if she were using her gaze like a flashlight beam to search for something. I left the room and closed the door behind me.

I couldn't sleep, thinking of all the things I had not told her, things about myself developing and changing rapidly. About my 5'11" well-proportioned frame becoming better defined and stronger after intense daily exercises. About being proud of my dynamite virgin body, making sure to stand up straight, with my butt and chest stuck out, as I reacted swiftly to officers' commands. About being anxious when soldiers looked at me, acting like a living example of an ancient lover boy. About my almost hairless, light-olive complexion, which contrasted well with my jet-black hair and green eyes.

I hadn't told her about the shower room, either. I couldn't take a shower in peace. In that sweaty, scalding place, the guys would trail behind me, poking my butt, grabbing my springy waist zealously, lustily simulating sex, rubbing themselves on me, and screaming, joking, literally reeking with animal passion. My body would turn red, start throbbing, and I would slyly long for more of their touches. At one point, I complained to the sergeant, but he treated the matter like a joke and just said, eyes twinkling, "Don't drop the soap in the bathroom anymore." I would break the rule when a handsome Yugoslav soldier would shower next to me. I was a real teaser, with ancient blood streaming in my veins. The blood of my ancestors and of great lovers, of Alexander the Great's people, the Macedonians. I enjoyed being called a fuckable boy. That's how the soldiers would describe me. Fuckable.

As I lay there with my eyes shut, trying to fall asleep, I recalled one incident. Corporal Sinan Dedich emerged from somewhere in the darkness. It was a lonely late Sunday afternoon. Most of the soldiers were in town on furlough. I was in the bathroom, washing my face. He was in his thirties, a construction worker from Sarajevo. A Bosnian Muslim who was born for the military, he was promoted faster then anyone in our division to corporal, but he wasn't a careerist.

When he quickly stepped out, then back in the room, I assumed something was up. The next thing I knew, he had grabbed me from behind and begun rubbing himself against me. He turned me around to face him, grasping my arms and pinning them against the wall.

Through his bright, even teeth, he muttered, "Nobody's gonna see us. Stay quiet. I checked the area. I just wanna smell you, feel your smooth skin. Wanna taste your lips. Swim into your eyes…Badly."

I couldn't move, pressed against the wall by his well-built tall frame. He was panting like a dog, totally out of control. The epitome of Balkan manhood was staring at me, his pupils wide with desire. I could feel my face blanch as the blood drained from it and paleness spread through the rest of my body. He kissed me. I panicked when he ripped open my army shirt, and all the copper buttons scattered noisily on the cement. He pulled his pants down, and I felt his firm thighs and penis. I thought someone was going to catch us, and I tried to break away. I couldn't. Maybe I could have if I had tried harder. But I loved the harshness of his touches and being overwhelmed by his manliness. He pushed me hard against the wall, and I could feel his corded arm muscles through my shirt as he embraced my torso. He began rubbing his penis harder against my tense stomach. When he was done, he put his pants back on quickly and disappeared.

I pulled out my handkerchief and cleaned his traces off the sink and the floor, shivering. Then I ran into one of the bathroom stalls to clean the rest of it from my pants, shirt, and stomach. I straightened myself up and I went to bed. Nobody had seen it. The soldier on duty was talking to himself at the end of the hallway. Suddenly, I felt frustrated. As I recalled the details of what happened, I found myself wishing it had lasted a little longer. I daydreamed of his strong grasps, his heavy breaths, and his kisses that marked my neck. I couldn't wait to see him at dinner.

As I walked into the dining room barracks, I couldn't miss the slogan posted on the wall, "Brotherhood and Unity!" Yeah, that's how I felt about my big Bosnian brother. Marshall Tito was right. It was a great slogan; anyway you looked at it. I hated myself for having been so inhibited. It was natural, though. It was the first time I had been kissed as an adult, by a man.

I wanted to tell my mother this, but couldn't. Now I had another option, Mila Bibulich. But I was still timid. What if she accused me of acting against my nature? What if she judged and rejected me? I feared all those possibilities, simultaneously longing for a mother's approval of what I felt. I was craving a mother's acceptance of who I was. Like any child. But which mother? Could either of them accept me as I was and not as they wanted me to be?

19

College

Mila's tears woke me. She was sitting next to my pillow, patting my hair. I jumped from the bed. Some of her tears slid from my cheeks and dropped to the floor.

"I am not a baby. I am a grown man," I shouted, backing away from the bed.

"Sorry. I couldn't help it," she said, lowering her head.

She looked as if she hadn't slept all night. Her face was puffy and she had rings around her eyes. It was 8 o'clock. I had overslept. I left her sitting at the edge of my bed and ran downstairs.

Mother was up, drinking her coffee. She stood up slowly and offered to make one for me. She seemed happy to do it. It was the last thing she could still make in the kitchen.

"Did you sleep all right?" she asked, watching the coffee as it heated up, to make sure it wouldn't boil over.

"Not really. I had bad dreams."

"Anything about me?" she said. She was superstitious and believed dreams could predict someone's future.

"No. I can't remember…Is everything in order this morning?"

"Yes. Change my bag and go back to sleep. I'll be fine. I'm not that hungry. I'll make something later if I need to."

If only she could have, I thought, as I walked to the bathroom to wash my face. I can never get back to sleep after I get up, so I began making breakfast. The telephone rang. It was for Mila. I ran upstairs and told her to pick it up. She was crying, curled in the armchair. Her pink nightdress was the only thing about her that didn't seem to be in disarray.

After I had finished taking care of Mother and she had gone to sleep, I made breakfast for Mila: scrambled eggs, bread with margarine, an apple, and a glass of milk, and took it upstairs.

"Is everything okay?" I asked her placing the tray on the desk.

"Yes. My family called. My brother says hello to you. My mother, father, and sister can't wait to meet you. They wish I were with them, but they know how important it is for me to be with you during these few days. My husband has called twice. Each time, they told him I went shopping."

"Feel free to call him."

"He's fine. He knows I'm always happy to see my family and go shopping with my sister. He doesn't suspect anything. I might call him later. Thanks."

"I forgot to ask, how many days is your leave?"

"A week," she answered, sounding despondent.

I sat in the rocking chair, as usual, expecting her to eat. She didn't. She looked like a refugee, except that she was perfectly neat and clean.

"You must eat something," I said. "You can't live on water, juice, and a few cookies."

"Don't worry about me. I'm fine."

"I have to take you out then. I'll arrange it with Auntie Bisera."

"Don't bother. You have to be around your mother. Besides, I don't feel hungry. Not at all. Believe me," she said, emphatically.

"What if something happens to you? I can't take care of two mothers. That's way too much for me to handle."

A look of intense happiness crossed her face when I finished the sentence. A second later, I realized I had called her "mother." I blushed.

After I sneaked Mila downstairs to take a shower, I took one myself. As I was coming back to my room, I could hear her Dalmatian-accented voice, speaking Serbo-Croatian. I put my ear to the door. She was talking to her husband and my half brothers. *Who knew how many more there were from my biological father's side? Maybe half sisters, too.*

It was weird thinking about having siblings while the memories of my loneliness in the house where I grew up were still fresh in my mind. Why do people have so many children? I wondered. Was it because of their insane instinct for reproduction? Their sick desire to clone themselves? Demanding religions? Whatever. People produce and hurt too many children. They control and make miserable too many innocent souls. All because they've been controlled and miserable. What a vicious circle. Didn't they see that they should plan how and when to have children? Instead, they reproduced without thought, like mad rats.

As I eavesdropped on Mila lying to her husband and children, I felt controlled and miserable. Lies, lies, lies. I waited for a break in the conversation and walked in. Mila was dressed in a golden robe, holding an almost empty glass of milk in one hand and the phone receiver in the other, nodding. She resembled Mother in the old days.

"Excuse me," I whispered, and stepped backwards out of the room. At least she had eaten something. I was happy to see that. I waited in the hall. A few minutes later, she stuck her head out the door and said, "You could've stayed. I have no secrets, except you."

She was lying. She had a secret—my biological father. Sweat began gushing out of my pores. I didn't go there, though. I stemmed my anger, hoping that after I had finished my story, she'd tell me who he was.

Once more, Mila became attentive as I sat down. I lit a cigarette. I couldn't sit across from her for long without talking. It felt peculiar. I was avoiding something. Maybe I was trying to avoid feeling something. I didn't know. I knew that it bothered me to be face-to-face in silence with the woman who bore me. In some ways I think I was afraid of her.

I tapped the cigarette ash into an ashtray and began talking, "After a year in the Yugoslav Army, my parents enrolled me in the College for National Security and Social Self-Defense. It was October of 1984. The college was in the suburbs of the capital, Skopje. One hundred students were accepted each year. It was a four-year school, so there were less than 400 students, excluding the dropouts. Most of the students were from Macedonia, some from Serbia and Montenegro, a few from Bosnia and Croatia, and none from Slovenia.

"The school was prestigious and trendy, one of the highest-ranked in the country. Only officials, war veterans, and high-profile army officers could send their children there; it guaranteed employment in state and public security, the police, or the legal system. Besides social status, acceptance was based upon having the highest grades in high school and passing a written and physical test. My parents didn't ask me what I wanted to study. They chose for me. They were creating my future. When I told them once that I wanted to study something related to art, they screamed that those professions were for losers and that I should be grateful to them for making sure I got a degree that would allow me to have an eminent place in our society: to become an official like my father, a state security inspector, a judge, or a lawyer.

"When I first arrived, the place intimidated me. Iron fences surrounded the college. The watchtowers of the state prison rose nearby. The special police forces, the police high school, the college, and their dormitories were together in one complex. Students called it 'The Center.'

"I showed my identification and permit to the police officers at the reception cabin by the entrance, and they opened the iron gate. The grounds were well maintained, with lots of trees, zigzagging concrete paths, and peacocks wandering around. The freshmen were waiting in front of the main college dormitory building. The atmosphere was part private school, part military academy, although private schools technically didn't exist under socialism. The students were prep pie-looking. Two-thirds were civilians and the rest wealthy peasants. About twenty percent were girls, and they looked strong enough to send two of the men across The Center with one punch. Most of them were closet lesbians who were good at acting 'straight.'

"The police officer in charge welcomed us, grinning. He checked off our names on his list, then gave us a tour. Afterward, he assigned us rooms, three of us per room. I shared a room on the third floor with a local from Skopje and a West-Macedonian peasant.

"Every morning, we had to get up before 8 o'clock and assemble in front of the building for roll call before our first class. Since I was exceptionally communicative and friendly, I became very close with our supervisor and he appointed me to do the roll calls. Only proof of sickness or family trouble could be an excuse to skip classes.

"New Year's passed quietly, and as the deadlines for our first exams came closer, everyone got excited. I stayed up, night after night, studying Marxism and Sociology. I passed those classes with high scores. My parents were delighted. I wasn't. I felt like a black sheep among the herd of conventional students, sickly conservative and closed-minded. My repressed free spirit decayed as the days passed.

"Now and then, I would go with my roommates to the city to see a movie. We couldn't stay late, to go dancing or partying, because the last bus came through before midnight. Once a month, I would visit my parents, and of course that was anything but fun.

"At a student assembly, I suggested once that a large empty hall be converted into a discotheque.

"'Maybe you would like us to teach ballet as well,' the college administrator blurted out sarcastically, making everyone snicker. 'This is the college for National Security and Social Self-Defense, not for a national dance!'

"I think most of students felt like I did, but they kept quiet, staring at their laps like cowards. That was the first sign that I was going to be a lone soldier in many battles to come."

I paused, then got up and walked to the window. An old, thin, gaunt man on the street was leading a crippled donkey that was pulling a small, shabby wagon. A dirty dog with one eye followed. I laughed, then immediately stopped. I recalled how awful it was to be ridiculed by everyone in The Center when I wore my tight leopard pants held up with a wide military belt; my short see-through sleeveless shirt; my high boots; and all the jewelry and accessories I made in high school, long before Madonna made them fashionable. You don't laugh at people in misery. You don't laugh at people like me, trying to stay confident and fight against an entire system. I turned towards Mila. I asked myself: *Should I tell her who I am? This is my chance to have a mother to whom I can talk to freely, who can take the heavy burden of my secrets off my chest. This would be the task for Mila to earn her motherhood back. To know the real me. And if she doesn't accept me, who cares? If I lose her, I already have a mother downstairs that I will never lose. I can go back to America and it will be as if none of this happened.* I began to pace back and forth, Mila's eyes following me as if I were her prey. No more lies, I thought. No more manipulations. I resumed my story and my words flew like cards on a table.

"When students and special police officers from similar institutions all over Yugoslavia came for the annual spring competition, there was extra security at The Center. The police officers walked around arrogantly, parading their masculinity and hiding their inferiority complexes. It was funny to watch them. That year, our college was the best for running and soccer, and on the final day we had a big party. The lunch hall was turned into a dance club. I was dancing with my roommates when I noticed a pair of familiar eyes watching me intently. They belonged to an athlete. His nickname was Rambo. He had been extremely friendly to me since we had met at the beginning of school. As he watched me, I didn't know how to react. My body began trembling. My heart was beating hard. I felt so uneasy; I scurried out and went to my room. I decided to change into the 'new wave'-style Italian outfit I had bought in Croatia, in one of the Zagreb's chick boutiques, on the way home from the Army. It made me look completely different than my communist colleagues.

"I returned to the dance and, as I strolled back onto the floor, the crowd began murmuring. Miami Sound Machine's hit, 'Dr. Beat' began to play, and I got into it. The students formed a circle around me and started clapping. But only *his* black, shining eyes gave me the élan to dance better and faster. The song ended, but the crowd kept clapping, encouraging me to go on. I was thirsty, so I went to the bar for a glass of water. As I turned to see what was happening on the dance floor, a fleet kiss brushed my lips.

"'Good job!' Rambo said, and he disappeared. I panicked, afraid that someone might have seen. Apparently, no one did. The crowd was too involved with the party. Most of them were drunk, including the two policemen who were supposed to be on duty. Kissed by a man in public, and in the heart of The Center? I couldn't believe it. It felt as if I were daydreaming.

"A few days later, during judo classes, Rambo maneuvered to become my partner. Each time he threw me on the floor, he would pump up his chest and arms seductively. His build went perfectly with his deep, penetrating expression that I tried to avoid, not to be snared by it. His dark hair, eyes, thick eyebrows, and eyelashes gave him an ancestral appeal, true to his half-Macedonian, half-Greek origin. When class was over, I quickly ran away from him. I was afraid of something, but I didn't know what it was. During the next class, in the amphitheater, he sat three levels up and to my right. Now and then, our eyes would meet. After the General Public Defense crap was over, we drew towards each other like magnets. We took a stroll around the complex, not saying anything for a long time. Finally, I broke the silence.

"'Rambo. Is that a waggish nickname?'

"'I got it in high school where I broke many noses.'

"'Are you still violent?'

"'No. I try to be sly now. That's all you need in this profession.'

"'Oh Yeah,' I said, adding, 'Also keen, sneaky, and fake.'

"He smiled, and when we went back to the amphitheater, he sat next to me. After that, we attended class together, studied together, and ate in the mess hall together. Within two weeks, Rambo made my peasant roommate switch rooms with him.

"The corridors of the buildings were empty one early summer night. The students were rushing to the TV hall, eager to see the soccer final. I didn't care about it. I stayed in my room, listening to news about the incidents with the Albanian nationalists and fundamentalists that were demonstrating all over Kosovo and West Macedonia. A cadre of politicians explained how good it was for our people to keep living and prospering in the unity that had benefited all of us for forty years. They said that separating would make us weak and that the united Yugoslavia had the fastest-growing economy of any socialist country in Europe. Without Marshal Tito, though, I knew it was the beginning of the end of Yugoslavia."

"I felt the same," Mila interjected. Her views were shared by all Yugoslavs who lived in Tito's era.

I smiled, nodding. She smiled back. For a moment, we silently commemorated the good old days in the Balkans when Tito led Yugoslavia. Then I returned to my story.

"I was drinking water by the sink, when Rambo suddenly appeared behind me. For two or three minutes, we watched one another in the broken mirror. Our cat-and-mouse game ended when he grabbed my waist with one arm and pulled me to him, unzipping his pants."

I stopped there and walked to the window. I wasn't comfortable describing my intimacy while looking into Mila's eyes. Not yet. From the distance, it was easier.

"'Hey, are you crazy? Do you know where we are?' I tried to move away from him and reached out to lock the door.

"'Don't! The danger's exciting.' He smiled and grabbed my hand before I could get to the lock. 'C'mon, loosen up. I know you love it.'

"'No, I don't!' I responded, louder.

"'Oooh…You dooo!'

"'You are craz—'

"He covered my mouth with his hand. 'Yes, I'm crazy. And I want to do it.'

"I was bathed in sweat, shaking, afraid that our roommate or someone would catch us. Rambo wasn't. I turned quickly and somehow I broke his chain-like hold, yelling, 'Get the hell away from me!'

"He pushed me against the wall and left, zipping his pants up and slamming the door. That night, he didn't sleep in our room. In the morning, when he came over to prepare for class, he said, in a jesting manner, 'I know you would love to do it. Don't you regret it now, eh?…I do.'

"'Is that the reason you moved into my room?' I asked, infuriated.

"'You are smart and popular here. I like you. But I'm not what you think I am. I'm not gay!' As he spoke, he stroked his crotch, inhaled deeply, and puffed out his body like a peacock before a mating ritual. He looked stupid.

"The following Friday, our roommate went home for the weekend. Rambo didn't. Tired from a long day of classes, I went to take a shower in the communal bath at the end of the floor. Shortly afterward, Rambo showed up. He handed me a washcloth and asked me to wash his back, as usual. Even though we had showered together many times, his presence felt disturbing. I was afraid he would cause trouble. Everything went smoothly until I opened the door to our room. Our beds had been moved next to each other. I looked at him, waiting for an explanation.

"'Your bed makes a shadow. I can't read,' he said, nonchalantly. He dressed up, sprayed cologne on himself, and then splashed some on me.

"'Now we smell like one body,' he said. As he walked out, he smiled and added, 'I'm going to watch the soccer game. Good night.'

"'Uh-huh,' I mumbled, feeling suspicious. I began to study. I must have fallen asleep. I thought I was dreaming. I could feel something heavy on me. I opened my sleepy eyes. The right side of his face was highlighted. His sparkling black eyes reflected the flames of two candles set on top of the chest of drawers. He snatched at my torso and whispered, 'If I fuck you in the middle of The Center, in the middle of the police, wouldn't that be exciting, eh?'

"As I tried to push him off me, he grabbed my wrists firmly, pinning them above my pillow. The mattress shook. I stopped resisting when the bed began to squeak loudly. I was terrified that someone would hear. Anyway, he was stronger. His intentions were clear. In general, I hated the smell of alcohol, but on his breath it was different. It was inviting, like some kind of an aphrodisiac. I totally gave in, physically and mentally.

"I said, 'I wrote many poems when classes were boring, thinking of you. I couldn't give them to you. I know that we can't be what we want to be here. I want to be free of this punishing, strangling society. I want to be free. I feel I'm caught in a web, and I know other webs are out there. Many more, everywhere I go. But there are options, also. Freedom is hardest to earn when a man loves another man. That's why I'm sheltering my love for you, rather than letting it be destroyed in this airless place. I want something more than sex…Please don't start if you don't understand what I'm saying. I don't want to look for you when this is over and for you not to be there. I don't want to reach for your shirt thrown on the edge of your bed every night to inhale your aroma, just so I can fall asleep. My vision of love is not an experiment. It's much more than getting laid.'

"'You don't need to look for me, baby. I'm here. On top of you. Ready to make love to you.' He smiled and with his touches, he began to conquer my virgin body, slowly making me surrender, completely.

"'You have beautiful eyes,' he whispered, kissing them. He nuzzled the tip of my nose. I lifted my head and, for the first time, I was French-kissed by a man.

"'So do you. I love to look at them,' I said, touching the delicate surface of his half-closed eyelids with my trembling fingertips. He turned me over and began to bite my back and rear gently. I reached his head from behind me. My fingers raked his thick hair, and passed over his stony neck and arms. His washboard stomach on top of my calves slid gradually up along my spine.

"'You're not a virgin anymore,' he said, sinking his teeth into the back of my neck like a hungry vampire, stifling his moans, stifling my scream by pressing his hand to my mouth, as I clutched the sheets of our improvised king-size bed. Then, he flipped me over, grabbed my ankles, and put my legs on his shoulders. He began thrusting in me harder. 'Wrap your legs around me tight!' he commanded, then lifted me and carried me around the room. This position gave him great pleasure. He smiled. His animalistic masculinity, pride, and control were reflected in each of his movements. Is this what every woman experiences, or is it only when a man makes love to a man that one can truly feel and understand the male power, I wondered? The next thing I knew, my back was bouncing against the wall, and his fingers were laced through my hair, protecting my head. The pain was gone by the time we moved to the chair. His gold bracelet dug into my skin, and my fingers into his. He began thrusting in me faster. As we lost our balance and fell to the floor, bringing the chair down with us, he issued a final blaring moan. I locked his lips with mine.

"We lay together intertwined for a while, staring at the broken chair. Then he lifted me in his arms, checked the hallway, and carried me to the shower. As the water washed away the last traces of our lovemaking, his deep kisses liberated me from the fear that had overwhelmed me for so long.

"Back in the room, we fell back onto the bed together. From a drawer, I took out a box of my favorite chocolates, *Griottes*, filled with morello cherries and liqueur. I took one and tried to feed it to him. Before I reached his mouth, he lifted his head and lunged like a cobra for it, biting my fingers slightly in the effort. He leaned over the box, plucked up another one with his lips, and guided it above my mouth. He squashed it onto my lips, then got aroused again as he watched the liqueur drip into my mouth. He licked off the drops that slid on my chin and neck.

"'Mmmh,' he groaned. 'It tastes much better when I lick it off your skin.'

"'You're unbelievable,' I said.

"He stood up, looking quite pleased with himself. He lit a cigarette, poured me a glass of cola, and said, 'With eyes like yours, we're gonna have the most awesome baby.'

"'And with lips like yours,' I said, laughing.

"'With legs like yours,' he shot back.

"'With arms like yours,' I added.

"'But, definitely, with a face like yours.' He smiled and caressed my cheek, wrapping his body around mine on the messy bed.

"'And sexy, like you are,' I whispered, kissing him.

"It was as if we were exploring the universe, discovering unknown places. We were like young lions playing in a forbidden field, in a country where such things were illegal, but done behind the scenes with great pleasure and curiosity.

"'My atoms, molecules, cells, my whole existence has a new meaning, Rambo.' I clasped his hand, my fingers laced through his, and gripped it like pliers. 'You're the aerial gazebo in my poetry garden, where I cultivate secret words only for you. I even wrote that I will be with you until the end of this world.'

"'Really? Let me see it,' he said, anxiously.

"I pulled my red notebook out from under my pillow, found the page, and handed it to him. He grabbed it eagerly and began to read."

I wanted Mila to know exactly what the words were. I rose from the chair, went over to the bookshelf, and pulled out the same notebook. Opening it to the same page I had shown Rambo, I began to read:

"*Corridors*

(To my secret loved one,
in the college for National Security and Social Self-defense.
Spring of 1984.)

1. The first corridor—A kiss that ignored faces and fears.

Two sounds, human sounds, are transforming our fingers into fires. Your attempts are bold. My thoughts are modest. I only want to be romantic and watch the river through the window with you. We can never kiss in this college. This space, where love is prohibited, can never be our nest. But you kissed me when I finished my dance. It was a miracle, and the hunters were around us. I fear these people and crave to escape with you to an unapproachable place where the steam of our collective thoughts can clean our bodies in absolute freedom. Will that ever happen to us?

2. The second corridor—The law is fake, so don't leave me.

Were we ancient lovers once? I wondered. Your eyes hunted mine, as each day we came closer to capturing one another. Your eyes, my eyes, diminish the law that prohibits a man from looking at another man in love. This is the temple of Almighty Law bragging that declares freedom for all. You must run like a bull across the river before they catch you. But you have to take me with you. If you don't, I'll be buried fresco in the middle of this evil system. I'll pray endlessly to the only God that exists, The Sun. I'll beg him to light above your shadow, fire it, but not to leave it behind you, to torture my memory forever.

3. The third corridor—We're vampires, and no one can beat us.

With red cat eyes, which music am I listening to now? Whose breath am I inhaling now? Above this black satin, we are ready to pounce one another. I'm setting free my green lasers to see better, to touch you better, and bite you properly. David's skin I smell, your familiar scent. I'm taking an internal bath in your tasty, sweaty drops that glow red like the finest wine. Because our teeth have punctured each other's bodies, for who knows how many times again, freely and lecherously. And now, I can be with you until the end of this world. No one can kill us in love. Together, we are immortal."

Mila sat motionless, looking as if she weren't breathing. Her gaze moved from my notebook, trembling in my hands, towards the sunlight. She was ready to say something, but before she could speak, I said, "As with many people out there, he never cared about poetry. But a broad smile appeared on his face. He loved it. My words fed and inflated his ego unselfishly. Rambo's being was filled with absolute haughtiness."

I glanced at Mila. Unlike Rambo, there was no haughtiness in *her* bearing. I could tell that she was trying to incorporate this latest revelation into the mental picture of me she had been constructing over the last few days.

20

Diary

For the first time, Mila saw me weak, as tears began to fill my eyes. I got a cigarette, then offered one to her. She took it with trembling fingers and, as I extended her a light, she enveloped my hand gently in hers. Steadying my hand seemed like an improvised excuse to touch me.

"Very romantic," she said. "Beautiful."

My tears changed from those of grief over the past to celebration of her acceptance. Were her words a trick to win my heart? Again, I doubted her and the happiness that warmed my body ceased. My thoughts returned to Rambo, and I continued.

"Regardless of gender combination, there are not many people who make a good-looking couple. Even fewer who make an extraordinary-looking one. Rambo and I were extraordinary. People would stare at us; some with envy, some with joy. We were like an inseparable pair of swans. We were among the best students. We always studied, exercised, and practiced martial arts together. We went to movies, dancing, and dinner together. We made love during weekends that our roommate spent at home. I was introduced to his friends and his family, who made me feel like one of them. We were happy…

"I've always dressed fashionably, but now I began to dress more flamboyantly, as my old desires began to emerge. My need to show people that we all come in different shapes, sizes, and attitudes was overpowering. I was the only bird in the history of The Center who ever attempted to fly free. Rambo supported me. He enjoyed my rebellion. He encouraged me to express my emancipated spirit and my eccentric behavior through my feathers. It was very risky to be close to me, and he knew that. But he didn't care about people's reactions and gossip, which soon became the main entertainment at The Center. I guess I was what Rambo wanted to be; I had the courage he wanted to possess.

"One morning, he said, 'Tell me about all those guys you've had. What did you do? How many have you had?'

162

"'None. I had no one before you. There were some attempts in the Army, but you're the first one.' I said.

"'You must have had someone before me.'

"'You're the first, I swear.'

"I figured he would love hearing that, being a Balkan man. He hated it. He wished I had lied, so he could absolve himself of any guilt. His face took on a fussy expression as he said, 'I had permission from God to do it.'

"I would never have guessed he was religious. Confounded, I said, 'Listen, Rambo. God has nothing to do with this. Keep him out of it. Keep him where he belongs, in a museum, along with the people who created him. People who don't have a clue what nature intended for this planet and us. People who think they're absolving themselves of their sins by studying homemade fairy tales; so-called Holy Books, written and rewritten a million times by weird, inhibited, and insecure psychos. People who need Him to escape this harsh reality. Come on, baby. The twenty-first century's knocking at the door and you still want to join my grandmother's church club? How pathetic.'

"He laughed. Then he said, 'I'm straight. You know that. And what we're doing is just a game.' He repeated that several times.

"'Life is a game, my dear. Let's not be late for class,' I replied, and walked out the door. He followed me silently. At the end of the hallway, before the stairs, he snatched my arm and pulled me back to our room. He pressed himself against me, hard. I could hear the strong beat of his heart. I embraced him back. I shared his fear. That was the burden we carried in a restrictive society. We shared a long hug. Then he stepped back, closed the window shade, lit the candle on the night table, and walked back towards me looking as stealthy as a tiger. He took my hand, guided me to bed, and curled up next to me like a child.

"'What's your biggest dream?' he asked.

"I lit a cigarette, patted his hair, and said, 'To go somewhere far from here. Some place where I can be free to love and live.'

"'Somewhere with me?' he asked, emphatically.

"I nodded. 'Yes. I would love to.'

"'Maybe Mauritius, Hawaii, Tibet, or San Trope?'

"'Sounds good, but we have to go somewhere much, much farther away. Evil would catch us there.'

"'And where's that,' he asked me, squeezing my hand gently.

"'One day, we'll find that place,' I said. "Or we'll create it," I added.

"'How?' he asked, taking my cigarette from between my lips and inhaling on it.

"I smiled. 'Loving each other.'

"He smiled back and reached for my lips in that turquoise-dyed morning that seemed too perfect to be real while we were clutching its seconds selfishly. We tried to read each other's thoughts; his were floating in his penetrating black-eyed gaze, and my green eyes grabbed them, lustfully. We had never missed a class before. That morning, we had to."

I took my poetry notebook from my lap and put it back on the shelf. Mila lit a cigarette. She seemed like a panicky animal, one that could feel an earthquake coming. I sat back in the rocking chair, took a deep breath, and said, "Things drastically changed in the fall of 1985, as I entered my second year. The gossip about my looks, my behavior, and our friendship escalated. Rambo became scared. So did I. There was no turning back for me, though. I was already entrenched in battle, fighting against an army of closed-minded creatures to whom I was some kind of mad public enigma. I decided to endure the heat, to handle the reality of my situation, even if I had to die. I decided to be true to myself. Certainly, no man at The Center had ever come out before me. I was the pioneer in that bloody process. Definitely, I was one of the first guys to walk on Macedonian soil wearing an earring and make-up. My college mates completely avoided me. Rambo gradually shifted his attention towards our roommate, making him his new buddy. Then he found a girlfriend, and I was left with no friends again.

"Rambo's girlfriend was one of the prettiest and most feminine girls there. The daughter of an important bureaucrat. A real spoiled brat. They were together, night and day. I barely saw him after that. Rambo didn't choose her for her looks or personality. Every student's dream was to work for the state, instead of public security. For that, you needed important connections. Her father was a big shot in the federal headquarters for state security in Belgrade, and that explained it all. She didn't care about his intentions. To her, Rambo was just another hot-looking addition to her list of conquests; another man to satisfy her nymphomania.

"One evening after dinner, a loud voices came from my room. When I got there, it was crowded with students. Rambo was lying on the floor, and his girlfriend was kneeling next to him. I ran towards him, pushing the students aside. His eyes were red. His face was pale and disturbed. I asked him what happened, and he said that he wanted to kill himself.

"He shouted, jumped up suddenly, and ran towards the window, tossing aside books and other things in his way to reach it. I tried to stop him. He opened the window, roaring like a wounded animal that he wanted to die. I begged him to tell me what was going on, while pulling him back inside. I was terrified. He pushed me hard, and I was thrown to the floor. I had never seen such a disgusted expression on his face. Half his body was out the window by the time I was able to grab his waist. I shouted for his girlfriend and our roommate to help me. They didn't react. No one in the room did. Suddenly, I felt ridiculous. I let go of Rambo's waist and told him to jump and kill himself, that I didn't care. Rambo gibbered. I stood still in the middle of the room, feeling humiliated and stupid. I should've known how good an actor Rambo could be. But, he was supposed to be afraid to show something had gone on between us. Even if he did it to feed his ego, or to show people that I was mad for him and make a joke of my feelings, it still didn't make sense. If there was no logical explanation, maybe there was a pathological one that I never understood.

"When everyone left the room, I fell to the floor, crying. I felt so desolated, while listening to students joking about me in the hall. Rambo's smell, once so aromatic, felt putrid. It was terribly hard to be apart from him. I had to hide it, though. I had no choice.

"One day, his girlfriend invited me over to her apartment for a drink. I gladly accepted it, hoping I would find something out about Rambo that I didn't know. She was provocative and sleazy, and she took off her clothes, leading me to the bedroom. We kissed, and when I said that I had to run, she smiled knowingly. It was obvious that someone from The Center had put her up to it. It was her job to find out what everybody suspected about me. I didn't care. I laughed in her face and left. Rambo was the only thing that mattered to me. After that, I noticed I was being followed.

"I thought Rambo had gone to his parent's house one weekend. To my surprise, he walked into our room. I quickly closed my diary and stuffed it into my school bag. He hugged me. I just stood, rigid, with my arms hanging at my sides. He let go of me and locked the door.

"'You must desperately need some part of me to be complete,' I said. 'Is that why you're here?'

"'Shut up! I'm not a faggot!' he yelled, pushing me away. My back hit the wall. He grabbed his bag from the closet and ran out. I slid down the wall until I was sitting on the floor. My eyes felt irritated, as if they were filled with salt. I heard footsteps. He appeared in the doorway.

"'Don't even imagine saying something about us,' he hissed. "I swear, I'll kill you!'

"'You are afraid, aren't you?' I whispered back.

"'What!' He came inside and shut the door. He dropped the bag and punched the wall. Its plaster cracked. 'If anyone's a pussy, it's you! And you love it! If you don't want your pretty face to be smashed, you better remember I'm not a faggot. I'm a man!' He spit in my face as he yelled. We were so close, we almost touched noses.

"'These tears are falling, not because I'm scared of you, but to wipe you for good from my heart. You don't deserve a single one.' I stared into his face, burning like a lumpy ember of a huge extinguished bonfire.

"'Gooood. Good for you. You just fuckin' remember. I'm not a faggot. I'm a man!' He picked up his bag and left, slamming the door.

"Every night, I would take my notebook out from under my pillow and write to keep the old image of him alive, to keep my sanity. It was no use, though. I no longer studied with the same intensity. I was already skeptical of courses that taught the dream of communist unity and social equality. Most professors and officials owned a few villas: one for skiing, another for swimming, a third in a foreign country. They had chauffeurs for their late-model Mercedes, plus servants and housekeepers. What kind of fuckin' communism is that? I thought. How can the average Yugoslavs trust them?

"Thinking about it made me more aggravated everyday. Eventually, I went a little crazy and my main priority became to get laid as much as possible. I always tried to look chic and trendy. I kept in perfect shape. I stuck my ass and chest out, as I paraded around. Honestly, in comparison to the women at The Center, who looked like greedy, competitive bitches who had forgotten their femininity, I looked like Elizabeth Taylor from Tennessee Williams' *Cat on a Hot Tin Roof.*

"I began to sleep with professors and their friends in the government: police officers bored with their wives, students tired of their girlfriends, who nagged them to get married. I would take advantage of anyone who expressed any desire or curiosity. I engaged in orgies, S&M, fetish, but never intercourse. I considered that special, something I did with the only one I loved, Rambo. I made a list of lovers in the back of my diary, assigning them pseudonyms, including little descriptions of them in brackets, and evaluating their performances with stars. I became more popular at The Center than anyone in its history. People talked more about me than God, Tito, and all the World War II heroes together. The police officers that I slept with, naturally, didn't turn me in, but their fellows always had an eye on me. My sexual encounters were well planned, however. They were always outside The Center, usually out of town, in private villas and country houses. The police never caught me."

Mila stopped crying as I paused to help myself to a cookie. As I looked at her alarmed expression I wondered if she had ever imagined this about me. She had probably expected me to be a proper citizen with glasses, a big stomach, a couple of children, and a wife who complains 'til kingdom come. She looked at me as if I were a Martian. I resumed my story.

"One warm January afternoon, Rambo was being unusually friendly. He leaned against me while I was reading criminology and closed my book, saying, 'I want to talk to you.'

"'What's there to talk about?' I opened my book. He put his hand on my shoulder and I punched his arm away.

"'You have slept with some people at The Center. Haven't you?'

"'Don't tell me you've become jealous.' I laughed.

"His face took on a serious look and he left the room quickly. He didn't give up, however. To get what he wanted, he used the most effective technique he knew. He became close to me. He invited me to the movies, his home, and to dinners. Like the old days. I let my suspicions of his sudden change go, deluded by his kindness and affection. For several weeks, I enjoyed it. Then, one snowy twilight, after dinner at the Panorama restaurant overlooking the city, Rambo suggested we go for a cup of coffee with one of his best friends. He said I would enjoy meeting him, that he was a cool state security inspector who worked at the police station near the Turkish Bazaar.

"As soon as we opened the office door, a tall, slim man writing something at his desk welcomed us. From his dialect and rough handshake I was certain he was a peasant. He didn't seem intelligent. Rambo introduced us, and we sat on a leather sofa across from his desk. He chatted with Rambo for a while, then he casually asked me how I liked The Center. I told him that it was interesting to learn how our security and defense system works. He smiled and offered me a drink. Rambo abruptly rose and went to the buffet table. Then he locked the office door and handed me a glass of Coke. A fiery wave passed through me. I broke into a cold sweat, but it stopped as the inspector pulled a chair across from me and straddled it, arrogantly. He leaned against the chair's back and began swaying back and forth. His gaze was piercing, as if he wanted to hypnotize me. Rambo handed him a glass of brandy, then poured one for himself. The inspector clicked his glass to mine.

"'To life and health.' He clicked Rambo's, and asked me, 'You have fun learning how our national security system works, ah?'

"'What do you mean, comrade inspector?' I rotated the glass in my hand.

"'You know well.' His eyes narrowed. 'We know all about it. The list in your diary.' He rose from his chair and walked in front of it.

"Cautiously, I looked at Rambo. He stepped in front of me and said, 'I read the list in your old diary. You used pseudonyms. You just started the new diary. I assume you left the old one at home. Did you?'

"I stood, took a cigarette from my pocket, and started walking around the office.

"'What the fuck is this about?' I said. 'I don't need to tell you anything about my private life. I have the right to be with whomever I want. That's my business!' I alternated looking at the two of them.

"'Professors, government workers, and Albanian nationalists are definitely our business. Whether you did it out of pleasure, satyriasis, or something else, we don't care. All we want are their names,' the inspector explained calmly, bending forward and smiling.

"'I'm not going to discuss my emotions. That's absolutely personal,' I said to the inspector's face, which was turning wrathful. 'Ruining the lives of my lovers won't help you prevent this country from collapsing. What you really need to do is hunt for corrupt bureaucrats, nationalists, and fuckin' religious fundamentalists.'

"'Shut up! Don't tell me what I need to do,' he screamed, glaring at me through half-closed eyes in a typically bureaucratic manner.

Rambo took in every word. He observed the inspector's every gesture. When he opened his mouth, he sounded like his idol.

"'Here it is.' Triumphantly, he pulled my new diary from the inside of his jacket. He was exultant at achieving his first task; it was probably his visa to becoming a part of our depraved police system that cared only about screwing the lives of others. I was disgusted.

"'Useless.' I smirked at him. 'I won't tell you who they are. I enjoyed what we did. So did they. I'm certain about it.'

"'You're not leaving until you identify who these people are! I can throw you in jail!' The inspector strode towards me.

"'So what? I'll have fun there!' I forced a smile back at him.

He turned to the right and, as he turned back, he slapped me. Blood began running from the left corner of my mouth. When he punched me, I tried to defend myself. He kept punching my head and face, until I fell to the floor, almost unconscious. He grabbed my collar and pulled me up. Blood from my nose stained his sleeves.

"'Where's the list! The old diary!' He showered me with his saliva.

"'It's in my house,' I mumbled, thinking of a young police officer that had supposedly drowned himself on duty at the man-made lake a week before. The officials said he was depressed. They killed him, I thought. They were capable of doing it. I caught a glimpse of Rambo, who acted as if nothing were going on, and nodded. "I'll tell you everything you want to know."

"'I knew you could be a good boy!' The inspector pinched my chin in a fatherly way, smirking. Then he threw me in the chair and turned to Rambo. 'Job well done! Give him napkins to clean his mess!'

"Rambo was beaming. He grabbed a pile of napkins from a cabinet drawer and handed them to me. He looked as if he was a crowned heir.

"'Comrade Inspector, can I be alone with you for a second, please?' I asked, wiping my face and swallowing the blood in my mouth, while holding my head up so my nose would stop running. Rambo's face discolored. His arrogant, treacherous eyes shrank. His crown of victory was falling off. When the inspector gestured for him to leave, he did it slowly, closing the door hesitantly. I could picture him, ear glued to the door, trying to hear what I was going to say.

"'Comrade Inspector, the first man I slept with, and the most often, was him.' I whispered, motioning my head towards the door.

"'I assumed that. But thanks for telling me.' He grinned.

"'You're welcome. Now I feel you should know everything. From A to Z.' I made myself smile, thinking: You dumb fuck; you'll know only what I want you to know; I'll screw you, before you both ever fuck with me; the ball's in my court.

"'I like you this way. You're getting the idea,' the inspector said, showing his bulging horse teeth.

"I began throwing out names of the most important people at The Center and some government officials. I slowed down after a while, to keep my lies from getting out of hand. My head was still pounding with pain. I didn't want to be suspicious at all.

"'Hold on! Wait!' He cut me off. 'Talk is cheap. We'll sit with your list in front of us, and you'll reveal them name by name. One by one.'

"'Deal.' I gave him a winning smile, as if I were going to get laid by my all-time favorite actor, young Marlon Brando.

"'Super.' He grinned back, looking content, and called Rambo.

"Rambo walked in. He glanced at me first, then stopped by the door. He stuffed his shaking hands in his pockets. He was still colorless, but striving not to freeze completely. He looked at the inspector.

"'He is in your hands, ready to cooperate.' The inspector smiled at Rambo, then at me. 'Follow Rambo's instructions. Be good. So long, guys.' He bid us farewell as if he were leaving a neighbors' afternoon coffee chat.

"What a hick. He never thanked me, I thought, as I followed Rambo. I felt so undignified. The few clerks and officers who passed us stared at me as if I were a serial killer. Just before the exit, Rambo gestured towards a small passage and guided me to the bathroom. I couldn't recognize myself in the mirror. My face was swollen with crusted blood all over it. I had no idea it was that bad. Even a gentle splash of water hurt me.

"Rambo couldn't wait for us to be alone in the car, so he could ask me what I told the inspector. I said that I begged the inspector to promise me that he wouldn't tell my father about my list, to protect us from the scandal. Rambo's fearful face relaxed for a second, then his eyebrows curved in thought.

"'Don't even think of saying something about us,' he said.

"'Of course not. You know I'll never do that to you.' I smiled, laboring to change my expression to the one I had when I would have died for him.

"'I read your diaries. There is hardly anything in the new one. I browsed through the old one. I wasn't there. How about in the list? Was I noted? What was my pseudonym? I couldn't figure it out.' Rambo sounded anxious.

"'You're not in the list. I started that after you left me,' I said.

"We didn't speak any further until later that night, when we drove to my hometown. He wanted the evidence right away. I sneaked into my house through the bathroom window. My parents were sleeping. I took the diary and tore the pages that had more obvious descriptions of my lovers' identities.

"On the way back, when Rambo noticed the missing pages, he clutched my neck with his hands and shouted, 'What have you done now!'

"'I tore off the pages where you and everything about us was revealed,' I said, gasping for air.

"'You lie! Jesus fucking Christ! I went through it! Nothing was mentioned!' He squeezed my neck further. 'What the fuck did you do? What are you coming up with now? Who's the special one you're protecting?'

"'I see you haven't read it attentively. Nothing was written obviously about you and me. However, it was implied in many parts of the diary. So, I destroyed those sections for your absolute security and safety.' I was gaping, struggling for breath, like a fish out of the ocean. 'You know I still love you.'

"I used my old standby—the alluring, charismatic, childlike tone and facial cast that had saved my ass for as long as I could remember. People, especially men, adored that precious look on my face and the sound of my voice. It was a chaste quality and, most of all, convincing and vulnerable. It made everyone feel as if I were an obedient follower of their wishes, as if they could control me, use me, abuse me, and possess me, as much as they wanted. To them, it must have seemed like nectar, feeding their insecure damaged egos. In reality, it was like a contagious disease poisoning their minds. My enemies never understood the true essence of it—that it was then, when I didn't give a damn about them, that I used my perfected skill as a self-defense tool. They were deceived and, at the same time, enraptured by my apparent naivety. The Devil comes in different forms to teach us to trick others. Unfortunately, I learned God does the same. I'm convinced of it. However, I feel blessed to possess my skill, thanks to both of my mothers."

Mila's eyes unfroze. She seemed ready to say something, but she didn't.

"Rambo's hands loosened around my neck. He smiled as I breathed deeply. He embraced me and kissed my battered, tender face, muttering, 'I'm sorry. Thank you for looking after my welfare.'

"'You're welcome…As always,' I whispered, through my angelic smile. I hated his kiss more than ever."

21

Artist

I compared the intimacies that Mila and I were sharing with the ones I had confessed to Mother. The new intimacies seemed to come more easily, and may even have been deeper, than the ones I told Mother.

"Nothing hurts more than when the one you love unconditionally betrays you," Mila said, setting aside her damp napkin and picking up a new one. "You were really in trouble."

Knowing that Mila understood who I was made me feel as majestic and powerful as the falcon, gliding on the early morning updrafts into the rosy sky. I was a happy falcon. But was Mila honest? I still doubted her.

"Yes, I was in trouble. But that was nothing." I shook my head. "Soon after the inspector got hold of my diary, the dean called me into his office.

"'This is neither a fashion academy nor a sex club,' he preached. 'People are outraged by your appearance and the rumors that you've had sexual encounters here. I also hear that you've criticized our system. You're jeopardizing your position. You're embarrassing yourself. All of us. Your family. I honestly respect your father and support what he has done for this country, so I'm warning you. I hope what I'm saying is crystal clear to you. Do we see eye to eye?'

"'I'm a very free creature, comrade Dean, and whatever I do is self-expression. No one can stop me. You teach us about freedom...Well, I'm simply enjoying it. Now you're denying it? Did I kill, rob, or hurt someone? Have I done anything to deserve being humiliated and labeled, as you're all doing to me? Of course not! And no matter what happens to me, I'll be myself and nobody else! I've made up my mind!'

"I paused, took a deep breath, and shouted, 'And tell that jackass inspector and his marionette, sleazebag rat, that I'll gladly decode my list of lovers and recite the whole diary, if they want me to. It would be my pleasure! I'm ready to do it publicly.'

"'I was very upset when I found out what those morons did. Stupid,' he confessed. 'Do you want the diary back?'

"'No. You should frame it and hang it to remind everyone here that there is not one place on earth that is immune to homosexuality. There is no such place.'

"'Fine! Let's just forget about it. Like it never happened...I'm trying to help you. But you also have to try to get back on track. If you don't, you might be expelled. And I might not be able to prevent it.'

"His remark tempered my anger. I realized then that he was on my side.

"'Thank you, comrade Dean. It feels wonderful to know there is someone here who cares about me.' I grinned, then shook his hand. He was a member of my godfather's family, and my main connection for getting into the college."

"The dean was right to worry. People couldn't stand my freedom. A psychiatrist would have had a good time analyzing the people at The Center and their reactions to me. It would have presented a scientific challenge, no doubt about it. The other students didn't have the guts to even look at me. They were scared to be associated with me in any manner. They looked so vulnerable, so unintelligent when I was around. I couldn't believe people that insecure would attend such an institution.

"I wasn't surprised when Rambo transferred out of my room. He ran away from me like I had cholera, yet *he* was the disease that completely crippled me after our final break-up. I lost interest in studies. I began failing exams and telling my parents I had passed them. I attended classes and performed my duties, but habitually, like a robot. I needed a replacement for Rambo, someone to keep me from consigning myself to a dungeon of solitude and depression. It definitely wasn't going to be one of my sexual partners, those outwardly proper men locked up tight in their well-defended closets. They were only interested in sharing one thing with me, getting off. I stopped seeing anyone. Still recovering from Rambo, sex seemed odious and was the farthest thing from my mind."

"You needed the gay community," Mila interjected.

"Exactly. I longed for my own kind of people. I needed support to survive through my crisis. I knew they were in the underground there, as in any society, despite Article 104 of the Criminal Code, which I well knew prohibited homosexuality or "Lewd Acts Between Two Males." I had no idea how to find other gays. Ironically, the information came from a source I never would've expected, the police students.

"During dinner one evening, I overheard a group of them making fun of Stefan, a successful Montenegrin entrepreneur and the owner of a bar that was popular among intellectuals and students. It was amazing to see how easily straights could be fooled into thinking that Stefan wasn't gay because he had a wife and children. That didn't fool me a bit. Near rumors, the truth always rests. I believe in that maxim, so one afternoon, I decided to go over and see for myself.

"The place was done entirely in mahogany, and interesting art decorated the walls. Stefan was in his fifties: slim, tall, and queeny. I spotted him at once. He moved around constantly, giving orders to his good-looking, all-male employees. It was hard to get close to him, so I sat at the bar. A group of guys between sixteen and twenty were hanging out there. Those were his 'chickens,' the guys that he paid well for sex. When I told the bartender why I was there, he disappeared briefly, then returned and told me to wait. A few minutes later, Stefan came out. The bartender pointed my way, and he walked over.

"'Oh, look at this cutie pie,' he said, pinching my cheek. His delicate fingers had long, manicured nails. He turned towards the guys. 'Isn't he a doll?'

"'Oh yeah,' the boys uttered in unison like a chorus, giggling.

"I introduced myself, and said, blushing, 'I've heard of you. It's taken me a while to get up the guts to meet you.'

"'You're too pretty for me, darling.' He surveyed his boys. 'But I know someone who would be perfect for you. His name is Gebul. He's a famous artist, a sculptor.'

"Stefan struck me as one who had been around for a while and had played matchmaker for many people. He scrawled the address and number on a piece of paper and handed it to me.

"'The best time to visit Gebul is in the morning. Announce yourself before you visit him. For the moment, you can have fun with my boys. I've got rooms upstairs.' He caressed my chin and, turning to them, he ordered, facetiously, 'Entertain this doll, boys.'

"He bent towards me and whispered in my ear, 'You like the Serbian stud, don't you? He likes you, too. Be free.' Smiling, he announced, 'Excuse me, kittens. I've got to run to the bank. Let me know how it goes over there, honey.' Stefan threw me one last glance and, before I could thank him, his hyperactive figure was out the door.

"The guys seemed eager to talk with me. The Serbian was anxious to get me laid. They were immature, and the 'blah-blah' quality of their chat bored me quickly. I left consumed with excitement at the thought of meeting the famous sculptor whose monumental work was all over the country. I could hardly sleep that night, imagining what the artist would look like, romanticizing our acquaintance, and even planning a future with him.

"I awoke the second sunlight struck my face, anxious to prepare myself for him. I practiced what I would say and how I would act, while giving myself a facial, putting yolks in my hair to make it shine, showering, filing my nails, and pedicuring my feet.

"'Artists are never regular and tedious people. There's a hope for me.' I kept repeating that as I ran from The Center to catch the bus. I didn't call him, as I was supposed to. My narcissism. I wanted to be a special surprise. My heart was pounding, as if I were going to meet God."

Mila leaned forward. "Artists are true Gods. They sacrifice for beauty, idealism, and truth. Your great grandfather was one. My father's father."

I felt elated when she said that. I had an artist's DNA. It was a pleasant surprise. I felt as if I were going to sing instead of speak.

"Gebul's house was huge," I said. "It had a manicured garden adorned with his marble sculptures. I rang the bell, and an old Gypsy maid answered. When I asked for Gebul, she told me to wait. A young woman in an exotic, toga-like outfit showed up next. She inspected me from head to toe first, then told me he'd be down in a moment. She walked off, looking less than thrilled.

"When Gebul showed up, he looked very serious. He extended his hand and introduced himself, sounding confused and nervous. I gave him my name and said that Stefan had referred him to me. I reddened, and my lips quivered. With a movement of his grayish eyes, he signaled for me to follow him.

"I entered the high-ceilinged foyer filled with paintings, sculptures, and icons. The ambiance seemed unearthly. Even the Gypsy maid looked artistic. The wide staircase led to his roomy atelier on the second floor. A huge marble head in progress was in the middle. To the left of it was a kiln, to the right, an oriental sofa with a coffee table. A shiny black piano stood by the windows. He gestured towards the sofa, and I sat at one end. He sat near me, on a walnut chair. He was in his fifties. He had an aristocratic, upright posture, an angular nose, and full lips. His hands were covered with chalky looking marble dust. He discreetly inspected me, looking slightly puzzled. I looked him over as well. Finally, I said, 'Grandiose art.'

"'Thank you. Why were you looking for Stefan?' he asked.

"'To meet my people, gay people. To find a lover. He told me I'm too pretty for him. He gave me your address and number and said to visit you in the morning.'

"'Lover? Just like that?' He tapped his hands on his thighs. Standing up, he began stalking around the studio like a hesitant commander.

"'I should've called. My mistake…I like unpredictable things. Don't you?'

"He didn't answer. He just kept staring through me.

"'Okay, okay! If I'm upsetting you and you don't like me, I'll go.' I declared. My knees shook as I began to rise.

"He rushed to me and placed his hand on my shoulder. I flopped back into the seat, pleased with his action and the feeling of being wanted.

"'You don't upset me,' he said. 'I'm shocked. You've come like a bird on my window ledge to tell me you're looking for a lover, when my lover just left me. I haven't had an hour of peace since. I'm happy Stefan sent you here. I wonder if this is a coincidence, destiny, or if you are a *fata morgana* for my deserted soul that deludes me in the early spring light?'

"There was a long silence after he said that. Rubbing his forehead, he offered me coffee. I thanked him, nodding. He called the maid and, shortly afterward, she brought traditional cherries in sweet syrup, a glass of water, and Turkish coffee.

"'So where is your ex-lover now?' I asked, as I began with the cherries.

"'He is in London. He left eight months ago. He's a fashion designer and went to work for someone I knew. A wealthy client. I referred him.'

"'Why did you do that?'

"'I loved him,' he replied, hastily. His voice had a wistful resonance. The painful fruits of love, I concluded. Gebul walked to the bar and poured himself a brandy. We exchanged a significant look. He began asking me about the usual things: what I was doing, where I was from, my family. When I mentioned The Center, he grimaced.

"'How can a gentle guy like you study at such an ugly institution?'

"'Why not? There are gentle guys everywhere, even in prisons. It was my parents' choice. But I do write poetry, and I paint,' I said, jubilantly.

"'Very good. Stefan can effortlessly sniff out artistic souls. He knows my taste.'

"'Has he sent you lots of artistic souls?' I asked, feeling suddenly jealous and skeptical.

"'Twice. Between relationships. Didn't work. The physical part is very important to me. It inspires me.' He sipped his brandy, then a broad smile crossed his face. 'What about you? What kind of man do you want?'

"'Intellectuals, nonconformists, and creative men. The ones who know what they want. Looks have always been a minor factor for me.'

"'Very mature for your age,' he said, delighted.

"We discussed art for a while, and after having another coffee, I decided to leave.

"'You are very cute,' he said, as we shook hands.

"'I know that. But thank you,' I said, tittering.

"'How arrogant.' He laughed back and added, 'Phone me.'

"As I left his house, he leaned against the door frame and watched me. It felt great. I called him the next day, and he invited me for dinner. He looked poetic in his dark Italian suit and scarlet ascot. He led me to the dining room and introduced me to his wife and daughter. The conversation progressed slowly, and it was nothing like I was used to. I didn't understand much of it, but it was very challenging for someone as young and anxious as me.

"Gebul's wife was in her late forties, a Bulgarian, though she looked Egyptian. She had finished architectural school in Paris and met Gebul while he was a professor at the art academy in Skopje. Gebul adored her. He would constantly speak of how wise she was. I didn't doubt it. She was a special woman. She was remarkably modern and, at the same time, she seemed as if she had emerged from ancient Greece or Rome. She completely understood her husband's needs. They lived separate lives but stayed under the same roof, dependent on each other's presence, knowledge, and artistic skills. That kind of family was hard to imagine, even in the most liberal countries. I haven't seen another one since.

"The daughter resembled her mother. She was a fashion designer, and growing up in such a family allowed her to be secure with her creativity and nonconformity. That self-assurance threatened men, so she was not successful with them. She had no problem with my relationship with her father, except when he gave me gifts. She got very grumpy and jealous then and wouldn't speak to me for months. I recall that she got sick when she saw me wearing a sparkling sapphire family ring he gave me. I don't think she ever got over it.

"Within days after we met, my relationship with Gebul became very intense. Anywhere we went: the opera, a concert, restaurants, the park, he would hold me, hug me, and kiss me. He acted like any straight person would towards his lover. Most gay men in Macedonia couldn't imagine being out of the closet, since homosexuality was illegal, but Gebul didn't care. I felt confident, proud, and lucky to be next to him. My happiness was obvious, and people at The Center noticed it. One midnight, Rambo sneaked into my room, for the first and last time since he had moved out.

"'How's it going?' he asked, turning on the light next to his former bed.

"The light blinded me. I felt like I was caught in a web, and he, the spider, was coming to hunt me.

"'I wanna sleep,' I mumbled, turning my back on him and pulling the covers up. I knew without looking that he was boiling mad. Ignoring him was the worst thing I could do.

"'Everybody says you look so happy lately,' he said, gently.

"'I guess everybody would rather see me die. Is that your wish as well?'

"He didn't reply for some time. I heard him come closer. He sat on my bed and put his hand on my shoulder.

"'Do you really think I want that?' he said.

"'No, I don't think you want that,' I whispered, lying, and buried my head further into the pillow. My anger towards him grew, but I decided not to start a fight. Rambo wasn't my concern any longer. I loved him, but he had hurt me badly. He was out of my pictures and poems. He was dead, one of the living dead. I had buried the memories of us deep in my mind, and his visit only served to dig them out.

"'So would you tell me why you're so happy?' he asked.

"'Why are you so curious about it?' I rolled over to face him.

"'Well, I care about you.'

"'There's no other diary, baby.'

"'The diary was a job that had to be done. If you were clever, you could've taken advantage of being our informer and enjoyed the privileges that State Security would've granted you. Your life would've been a joy, and your achievements monumental.'

"'You trust them? Poor dreamer. Of course, you care more about your career and the reputation of this institution. I care about my feelings and other people. That's the biggest difference between you and me.'

"'Opposites attract.' He tried to smile.

"'But they can be poisonous. Like our relationship. The old cliché doesn't always work.'

"'I know what makes you happy,' Rambo said.

"'Now you know me so well. Too late. Let me sleep.'

"'Who is he?' Rambo grabbed my hand.

"I stared at him a moment, wondering whether he was worth an answer. Then, 'He's not from The Center. He's neither a student nor from the police. He's an ordinary man. Don't worry. Sleep well. You've got the names of everyone from this institution who fucked me. This is something outside your sphere of influence. Let me enjoy. We had a chance. Go have your girlfriend and be happy. We walk on different paths.'

"I turned over and closed my eyes. The air was reeking with his insecurity and melancholy. His belief that he possessed absolute power over me, and that I would never be able to turn my back on him completely, was proven wrong. The relationship with his girlfriend was an opportunity and a refuge. He was frightened of himself. His slow footsteps towards the door proved his attraction to me. He was unable to express it because of society and his career. He was at war with himself. I knew I loved him because I hated him so much. He never hated me, so he couldn't have really loved me. Was that what love was all about, I wondered, briefly. I was hurt first, and Rambo was left hurting. Maybe he had loved me, but I couldn't be sure, since all that remained of what we had shared was his lust for success. It was over.

"Anyway, I seldom slept at The Center any longer. Gebul began taking me on trips, and I began to skip classes. On one of my favorite vacations, he rented a room in a little mountain cottage with a potbellied stove, no electricity, and a small stable next to it. The woodsman was a crippled old guy with great knowledge of horses. He was a loner who had fought in both world wars, had his own garden, made his own bread and honey, drank goat's milk, and smoked homegrown tobacco. He considered stress the killer of the modern world, and his marriage with nature was the key to his excellent health. He was something: a Balkan guru. The woodsman inspired us. Gebul made a sculpture of him, and I wrote a poem about him. Although the woodsman modeled for hours for Gebul, he refused to take money, believing that it was evil. He enjoyed conversations with us. Unfortunately, we were among the few who paid any mind to that interesting man.

"Every day began with art. Gebul would take his clay or small blocks of marble to sculpt, and I would paint or write poetry at the clearing. We would bathe in the cool spring water scented with pines and herbs, a combination that could never be bottled and sold. Tasting traces of it on our skin while making love like mountain gods was intensely erotic. After we ate, we would nap and awaken to the sound of the woodsman saddling horses for us to ride. We would usually gallop nude up to the rocky peak, where we would sit together until the ember color of sunset would envelope us. Then back we'd go to the cottage, to listen to the old woodsman's stories by the bonfire and eat homemade soup for dinner, and wild fruits before bedtime.

"Women have periods, and men have middle-aged craziness. Revolting adolescents like me have something more destructive. My rebellious anger turned me into a miserable, callous, and neurotic sex maniac. I began cheating on Gebul with his friends, making a list of names in my diary again, and feeling proud of my self-destructive talent of getting laid easily. Late at night, when I came back to Gebul's, my dinner and bed would be ready. I called him old and gross. I pushed him away when he would try to hug me, then go sleep in a different bedroom. I exhausted him, but he wouldn't give up. He told me that no matter what I did, to come back to him always. His voice became rueful, slow, and drunken. I'd never seen him in such a state before. Once when I woke up and caught him kissing my forehead in the middle of the night, I screamed at him like a lunatic: 'Stay away from me.' I'll bet he tried to connect with me every night and, instead of going to bed, he would work in his atelier, turning the hurt into beauty. My words, attitude, and actions were loathsome. I wish he had listened to his wife, who had always advised him not to engage in relationships with young guys.

"One afternoon at the end of the summer I called him from college to ask if my book order had arrived. The maid told me that Gebul had been taken to the hospital. I hopped into a taxi and went straight to the emergency room. The nurses directed me to the mortuary. His body was covered with a light blue blanket. I lifted it and backed off the minute I saw him. I ran outside the building, stumbled to a nearby bench, and sat down. The world was spinning. I grasped the edge of the seat, then fainted.

"I felt so guilty. When I watched the sunset, I would see Gebul's face or hear his words and remember his tenderness and kindness. Why did I act so evil when Gebul was like an elixir for my life? Is it always like that? I wondered. When your lover is an angel, you can be nothing but a demon? Did I turn myself into a demon? Did I stop his heart? Was it nature alone? Or were we both responsible? Why was this happening now, when his career was reaching its peak after his Paris exhibition? Why now, when I needed him most? I went crazy thinking about it. I was young and reckless, hurt by society and my parents. I transformed my anger into a sexual madness and, sadly, directed a great deal of it at Gebul. Unhappy people inflict their misery on those they are close to. It's an unfortunate human tendency that eventually comes back to haunt us.

"I couldn't bring myself to attend his funeral and face his wife, his daughter, and his friends. I felt they would despise me. On the day after, I went to his gravesite, taking with me the first piece of art Gebul had given me. It was a bronze medallion of our greatest king. 'Alexander III of Macedon (356–323 BC.)' was engraved on the back, along with: 'To my greatest love, Bazhe.' I hugged his headstone, kissed the golden letters of Gebul's name, and left a poem that I had written for him:

"*White horses and I*

"The White Horses and You are arriving in gallop,

In the stable is desolation, and in My room the same,
The lawn, with dense pallid Loneliness, it is all that is left,
Because you didn't stop. You just passed by, and ran away."

Mila's eyes shone. She whispered, "You must have loved him greatly. The poem says it."

"Yes, but I didn't fully realize it until after his death. I went home and lived the rest of the summer like a hermit. I didn't talk to anyone. I stared at his sculpture for hours. Meanwhile, the dean left The Center. He was offered a powerful position in state security. One of the professors took his place. He was a bigot who despised me. He would give me a disgusted look whenever I walked by him. Things were not going well. I was being punished for my treatment of Gebul. Karma, I believe in it.

"In the fall, when I returned to The Center, the officers at the gate said I couldn't come in, that I had been dismissed from the school by order of the new dean. They smiled like the small fish in the tank do when they get to exercise their authority. They shoved me away as if I had the plague and closed the gates in my face without warning. When I asked if I could get my belongings, they got three plastic bags from the guardhouse and tossed them in front of me as if they were garbage. Once again, I read the slogans posted above the main gate: 'The force of the individual is the force of society!' 'Everything that is ours is yours, everything that is yours is ours!' 'Free individuals, free society!' It was ludicrous. The officers wouldn't let me use the phone to call a taxi. They had a good time smirking at me. Finally, I left my things and walked to the village to call a cab.

"What am I crying for? I wondered. For this institution surrounded by iron fences? For this dungeon swarming with brainwashed officers, guarded minds eager to control, and government slaves? I stopped weeping and I promised myself I would open that gate again, if only to show them that the loss of one battle doesn't decide the war. When the taxi arrived and I went back to pick up my refugee-like belongings, students and officers were there to ridicule me, and more came to see my humiliation. I didn't care; I was too busy trying to figure out how to tell my parents. I feared their reaction. I decided to tell them when I got home.

"I went to the city bus terminal and bought a ticket. I was going from one inferno to another. When I got home and told my parents what had happened, they freaked out. I couldn't express my feelings, wishes, or plans. They didn't want to hear that I was unhappy and that I hated being there. They blamed me for my expulsion. They wanted me to stay at The Center, to avoid embarrassment. Immediately, they called the old dean for help. He promised them he'd do everything he could to help me get back in. Two days later, he called back. He explained that the new dean and the college board had decided to expel me and they would have me back on one condition: that I undergo psychotherapy and cure my unwelcome and inappropriate behavior. He also said that I would have to enroll as a part-time, non-resident student until I got on the right track and passed the exams I had skipped. If I did that by next fall, I could start my third year then.

"My parents agreed to this without asking me what I wanted. They were enraged that I lost a year, but delighted that I would be staying at The Center once again and even happier that I was going to get psychotherapy and become 'normal.' I knew nothing was wrong with me, but I agreed to do it only to escape the damnation of being with my parents, who continued to tell me how awful I was.

"The sessions took place at the same building where I'd had my physical exam before entering the college, at their clinic in the capital. I was assigned my own room at The Center during the course of my treatment. I stayed completely to myself, since I couldn't trust anyone there. The students and staff were shocked to see me; my comeback was like a slap in their faces. I was fighting back, and they hated it. More than anyone else, the new dean couldn't stand the fact that he hadn't succeeded in kicking me out. It was quite a blow to his authoritarian ego.

"I had two psychiatrists: a young woman, at first, then a man in his late forties. The lady psychiatrist's room was decorated with big, ugly reproductions of masters' paintings and of her framed degree, which glittered above her desk. She looked like an owl and she questioned me as if I were interviewing for a job. She was one of those phony, cold fishes who didn't give a damn about her work as long as she got paid well for her time. During the first two sessions, she told me to draw whatever I felt like and left me alone for a couple of hours. Then she came back and told me to leave. At the third session, browsing my drawings, she said, 'The things that you most love and are most important to you are...?' She stopped talking. It took me a while to figure out that she was asking a question. The hell with her, I thought. I won't explain what I drew. She should. That's her job. I walked out. At the first phone I saw, I called my parents and complained. They contacted the ex-dean, and the following week, I had a new psychiatrist.

"Doctor Ognevski was an interesting man. He didn't seem like he belonged at the institution. He was well mannered and a good listener. During the first three sessions, he told me to talk about my life in general. At the fourth, after he served me coffee, opened my file and said, 'I have consulted my colleague and don't agree with her diagnosis that you are manic-depressive.'

"I began to laugh, then apologized. He grinned and went on to state that my drawings showed a fear of butterflies. No one had ever detected my phobia. I shook my head, impressed. He opened a cabinet and pulled out a book entitled *My Peace*, which he handed to me.

"'It was hard to make it as a poet,' he said. 'so I became a psychiatrist. You are perfectly fine. You don't need therapy. They're trying to cure you. From what? You need to get out of The Center. What will you prove to them or to yourself by staying here? Nothing! You'll suffer further at the hands of this narrow-minded bunch.'

"He lowered his voice. 'You've been studying law here. Don't waste any more time. Transfer to law school. They'll accept all of your credits.'

"'I can't. My parents want...' I sounded like a frightened child.

"'I know,' he said. 'It doesn't matter. You've got to do it regardless of their wishes. Fight them! You're not dumb! The therapy is over. I'll send them the report tomorrow.'

"He shook my hand and, as he walked me to the door, he added, 'Don't waste your time. Take my advice. And good luck.'

"'Yes...Thanks.' I trudged into the corridor, grasping his book tighter. I didn't want to leave the man who had filled every cell in my body with confidence. Buoyant from his encouragement, despite the gray autumn light, I felt as if I had been released from an old gloomy dungeon into an open field. I must move on, I thought. He's right. But how to convince my parents?

"If only I'd been able to have more sessions I could have talked to him forever. No one had ever given me such strength and positive energy. I read his poems over and over, imagining I was talking to him. I missed him as if he were my father. I wished that he had been. I called home and told my parents what the doctor said. They loved the diagnosis, but hated his suggestion about transferring to law school. Once again, I was trapped and tortured in their web of misunderstanding. A week later, we heard from my godfather that the new dean was beside himself after hearing from the psychiatrist that I was one hundred percent healthy. He had no way to get rid of me anymore. I won that war, but a bigger one sat ahead for me: to persuade my parents to let me leave The Center."

22

Gossip

As I gazed around the room, Mila's gaze followed mine, and then focused on the wallpaper pattern behind me. In the light from the window, she resembled one of my schoolboy drawings of Mother. Was it real or was my mind playing tricks? I leaned forward to see her better. She was the woman who bore me and had nothing to do with Mother. I leaned back into my rocking chair.

"Your development has been like a sea constantly hit by hurricanes." Mila sounded like she was reciting the sentence. She shut her eyes.

My intense stare was making Mila uncomfortable. I thought about her childhood. To me, it's the most important period of our lives. We experience traumas and joys that will impact us until we die; basically, our characters are built. Maybe soon she'll tell me why she abandoned me, I thought.

"How about *your* childhood?" I asked.

She opened her eyes and said, "It was happy and careless. My development was ordinary. It flowed like a peaceful river, until the day that cad raped me. I lived like any girl next door. Then my stomach began to grow and everything changed. I lost all the battles and the war. You were taken away from me. I'm very happy to hear you were a better fighter then I was. I'm glad you showed people your strength and managed to stay at The Center. I know how it feels when everyone says you're insane, but you're actually just different, a perfectly fine misfit. Those ignorant bigots are everywhere. I know that very well."

As she reached for a new napkin to wipe away her tears, Mila's hand quickly brushed against mine, which lay on the edge of the desk. That brief contact spoke clearer than her voice. It felt like an electric spark passed between us, transmitting the agony from her failed fight against her parents and society to keep me. She was happy I was a fighter. But I was even happier that she approved of who I was, though I continued to harbor doubts about her sincerity.

I continued with my story. "The whole situation was funny and mournful at the same time. I became the subject of the main gossip in town. When I went

184

out, the locals would smirk at me. It was like having a dull knife plunged in my chest. They spread rumors that I was expelled from college because I'd been a male prostitute and had been infected with that strange new Western disease called AIDS. They also made me out to be a junkie and an alcoholic, although I never drank or used drugs, except tobacco. Even the people I knew from high school wouldn't talk to me. They'd turn away as I approached, afraid they would be labeled as I was.

"Locals enjoyed trashing my family, many out of jealousy of our easy life. Mostly, people hated my free spirit. Many secretly envied it, but also feared it. They were willing to destroy something they couldn't have. I was persona non grata along with the provincial sluts, who were equally despised, and I'll bet I was the subject of many closeted men's wet dreams. I was declared one of the living dead, even though I never did anything to hurt anyone. I could have, but as I told you, I strongly believed in Karma.

"Like a vampire, I slept during the day, waking up at odd hours, writing poems, reading, painting, talking, and praying to my favorite authors for help. Hess, Baudelaire, Hemingway, Pasolini, Dostoyevsky, Rimbaud, Shakespeare, Lorca, I imagined them present in my room, answering my questions through their writings. I was dying for a companion, feeling like I was handicapped. I knew that I was suffering the consequences of my upbringing. Over and over, I asked myself what I had done to deserve such a hard punishment.

"People claimed I was a devil. The town was preoccupied with me, its anti-hero. I was the worst influence on teens, a fashion eccentric, and a fugitive who had crossed the line and brought public condemnation on myself. Locals thought I was insane, spoiled, and wild. They were so uptight, it was as if they had umbrellas up their asses, ready to open any minute. It felt like there was a conspiracy to kill me. My parents freaked out.

"I hated any change to my growing body, interpreting it as yet another sign of my difference from others. I slept lightly and had frequent nightmares. I dreamt uniformed priests in black and red marched into my bedroom, nailed me to a rusted cross, and dumped me into our cold lake. The lake's surface would ice over, and I would drown forever. I feared I was really losing it. I would spend hours just staring at the phosphorescent star glowing on the ceiling, the one godfather bought me for my seventh birthday."

I looked up at it. Mila's tears sparkled as she raised her head. The room looked so much as it did in those days. I wanted to burn it down that moment. I closed my eyes and whispered, "All I had was this room. This coffin. Sometimes I hid in the apple orchard out back, but only during sunsets, so no one could see me. The neighbors thought I'd gone nuts when they saw me once, loitering around like a vampire's shadow.

"The town was usually dead after 8 o'clock in the evening. It was a cultural desert. There was no good cinema or theater. The circular promenade *Korso* was no longer in the town center. Everything was destroyed by the rise in peasant immigration that escalated during the seventies. The townspeople were bored, which partially explained the declining entertainment value of gossip.

"One beautiful winter night, snow was falling and making our sleepy town look dreamier than it really was. I couldn't resist taking a stroll. As I crossed the main street, I noticed a group of teenagers drinking and joking by the seniors' club. When they saw me, they began calling me names. They followed me and, shortly after, I was attacked. I got pretty badly beaten, but when I leapt up and broke one guy's jaw with a loose paving stone, the rest of them ran away. Rivulets of blood streamed from the motionless guy's head, resembling a dead octopus. I screamed to his mates, who were still running away, 'Pick up your friend, you motherfuckers, before he freezes!' I rushed back home.

"That was my first bashing. It was an alarming sign that I wasn't safe in my town any longer. My parents made the matters even worse, though. They never understood my suffering, even after I was beaten like a punching bag. They didn't want to hear about me transferring to another college and leaving town. They just said I had to study hard and catch up as fast as possible, so I could go back to The Center as a full time student."

"How could you study under such terrible circumstances?" Mila interjected.

"I couldn't," I replied. "My misery usually inspired me to write or paint, but this time it was so overwhelming that it completely blocked me. I could only read literature. New Year's of 1987 came and went like any other day. I watched TV for a couple of hours and went straight to bed. None of the shows cheered me up, even though New Year's programming was usually pretty funny."

"As a part-time, non-resident student, the work was sent to me from The Center. In February, I had to go to there to take exams and I needed a place to stay. My parents insisted I stay with relatives, so someone could look after me. They didn't want to pay for a hotel. They didn't trust me at all. My mother had two brothers. She was closer with the younger one, so arrangements were made for me to stay with him.

"When I showed up at his apartment, his wife opened the door as if it were a bank vault. My uncle was working late, as usual. Their children were not there. My aunt offered me neither dinner nor attention. I watched TV on the sofa, and when my stomach began to growl from hunger, I went out for a burger. I wasn't in a rush to get back. I wandered around until midnight. By the time I returned, I could hear Uncle snoring in the bedroom. I asked my aunt about my two cousins. She said, curtly, that they were staying over at a friend's house. I expected to sleep in the spare bedroom, as I usually did when I visited with Mother. Instead, she threw a tiny blanket at me and said, 'The sofa is large enough.' Of course, it wasn't. I ended up sleeping on the floor, but only for a few hours because she rousted me at 4 o'clock that damned morning.

"'You must go,' she said. 'Your uncle and I have to get ready for work. We won't be comfortable leaving you alone. What if something happened to you? How could we face your parents?'

"I said nothing. Her expression seemed fake, as did that of my uncle, who passed through the hall like a specter. They were probably afraid I would give my 'sickness' to their children if they came near me, or that in their absence I'd bring a man over and turn their apartment into a bordello. I didn't need to change since I'd slept in my clothes. I rushed into the bathroom and splashed water in my face quickly. My aunt was waiting for me at the door. She pointed to the kitchen and offered me breakfast. A piece of bread, margarine, and a cup of hot water with a pathetic-looking leaf floating in it were waiting for me at the table. I left without touching it. I took buses from one end of the city to the other to kill time until my exam at 10. It was a brutal winter, and it was too cold to be outside so early.

"My parents didn't believe me when I told them what happened. They thought I was exaggerating. For my next exam, however, I persuaded Mother to arrange for me to stay at her older brother's. When I got there, I rang his doorbell twice. Nothing. I rang again. Nothing again. I thought maybe they were shopping, so I went out for a smoke. When I returned, I heard a noise in the apartment. I glued my ear to the door. When I heard voices, I knew where I stood. But I wasn't upset. I was accustomed to the hurt. My parents were to blame. It was getting late, and again I hopped on the city bus to nowhere in particular. I stayed on it until 2 o'clock in the morning, when it went out of service.

"It was a stormy night. The icy wind blew snow mixed with sleet into my face as I walked the streets. I had no friends to call, no place to stay at The Center, and no money for a hotel. After I tried unsuccessfully to enter a number of buildings, I found one that wasn't locked. It was tall and pretty rundown. I sought refuge in its old elevator. I got in, pressed the button for the seventeenth floor, and squatted in one corner, huddling under my coat. It was my first homeless night.

"It wasn't even dawn when the elevator started slowly going down. I hastily stood up and straightened myself. A blue-collar worker and his wife got on at the ninth floor. I had to leave, but nothing was open at that hour, so I went to the Grand Hotel and lingered around the foyer to keep warm. I felt even dirtier than I was as I walked in, passing neat businessmen who were leaving the hotel for their appointments. I bought a cup of coffee at the restaurant and took it to the foyer's sitting area. Two long-legged, trendily dressed prostitutes came over and sat on the huge, cushioned chairs.

"'Common partisans,' a handsome man who looked like a body builder called to them, as he came downstairs.

"The receptionist jeered, 'Uh-huh, look at those pieces of ass. I'll bet your partisans could serve as front-line nurses better then any of their counterparts in World War II, pimp. I can tell they're highly skilled.'

"The bodybuilder rushed to the desk and punched the receptionist so hard that he flew against the wall, bleeding. I had to go back out in the cold before the police came. I couldn't afford to be held and questioned. I didn't need more trouble. I had no luck. The hotel's foyer was such a comfortable place.

"My parents were furious when the results of my exams came back: Failed. Since the psychiatrist had diagnosed me as normal, Mother figured I must be cursed. She insisted we go to the monastery of Saint Nikola, a humble cottage built on the top of an old oak forest. I did it out of desperation, although I had given up on the Holy Family a long time ago. I had always loved the little temple's natural setting. Mother used to take me there as a child. As in the old days, she made sure no one was there to see us and tell Father about her secret ritual. Next, she had me fill the candles lamps with sunflower oil, then kneel with her and pray for me and for our family's health and prosperity.

"I was a high school freshman the last time I went there to beg God, Jesus, the Holy Mother, their families, and the Saints for help. I spoke to their beautiful Byzantine portraits until a violent lightning storm began. Saint Nikola's scary voice echoed, 'Sadness has a hundred legs, but it takes ages for it to bury a single human soul.'

"'Jerk! What kind of hope is that?' I shouted at his kindhearted face. 'Preaching to me about the strength of the human soul? I don't want to endure more loneliness and sadness! Enough! Just shut up if you can't help!'

"Abruptly, I left. The rain splattered my face hard as I ran through the woods. People always told me how kind the Holy Family was, that I should worship them and truly believe in them. But I realized that no one wanted to help me, not even the Ones who were supposed to be up there watching over us. I ignored their tumultuous voices, shouting through the lighting. My loneliness and sadness were like giant centipedes crawling through me, taking bite after bite out of my abandoned heart and soul. After a while, all I could hear was my own voice, cursing the two people who had created me. I hated all women because of the one who left me. I wished I had been aborted and had never existed."

The doorbell rang. There were five rings total, and evenly spaced.

"It's our neighbor delivering lunch. She rings five times. It's our sign," I explained.

Mila seemed to be far away. Probably she was envisioning me as a child, in the Army, or in college, trying to build the whole picture of me.

"When Auntie Bisera arrives, we'll go out. I'm sure she'll enjoy that. Be ready soon, so we won't waste time!" I said.

Mila nodded, so much like my mother. Her face was so similar to the one I was going to see within minutes. They were both suffering. Meanwhile, I was happy to reveal, bit by bit, my accumulated load of secrets to the "savior" for whom I had searched for so long; who I had cursed at constantly out of desperation; who I had questioned in a frenzy, wondering why she ever bore me.

Now I realized that she couldn't have saved me. No one could have. It had to be that way. Something or someone created life to be that way. I was predestined to walk the road I was on, to have my share of luck and misery. The damages were done, but with each passing moment, they felt more bearable. By sharing my story, I was ridding myself of the pain. In contrast, Mila's old guilt was building and Mother's struggle with the cancer was emerging as we drew closer to saying farewell.

I wondered what would happen next. Maybe nothing. Maybe we would go our separate ways as if nothing happened, carrying the aching memories with us. Hopefully, we would heal one day. Except Mother, who would not carry them much longer. She was going someplace where you didn't have to carry aching memories, going to an "unknown next." It pleased me to picture Mother ending up better off than us. She deserved that. I surprised Mila when my weighty stare turned into a broad smile.

"I'll be back as soon as possible," I said.

I left Mila crying and let our neighbor Frosa in. The inviting smell from the pot she carried permeated the hallway. We found Mother crying. She was staring at the ceiling, her trembling hands crossed atop her pale forehead.

"What's wrong, Mother?" I ran to her bed.

"She's a little bit disturbed," Frosa said, twitching her eyebrows pessimistically. "After she tastes my lunch, she'll be fine." She took the pot into the kitchen.

"Oh, I wish food tasted the same as before Frosa. Nothing is like it was." Mother wept louder.

I sat on the edge of her bed. "Let's eat. No need to stress yourself. You'll be fine. You'll see. You have me. I'm here to make you strong again. I will."

I kissed her. Mother placed her trembling hands around my neck, putting all her energy into embracing me as tightly as possible. Her colostomy bag made a noise, and her face fell, as did Frosa's. By that time, however, I knew all the noises her colostomy bag made and could easily tell when they actually represented a problem.

"Everything is alright," I whispered to Mother.

"I'll go now. The lunch is in the oven to keep it warm," Frosa said. She left through the kitchen, looking away from us to hide her tears. I went with her to lock the door after her.

"What was that?" Frosa asked me.

"What was what?"

"The noise coming from her stomach that terrified your mother."

"She has to defecate from somewhere. Am I right? Actually, it's easier than doing it from our asses. No constipation to worry about, ever. No paper. No killing trees. Once the bag is filled, you throw it out. Simple as that. I wonder why Mother Nature didn't make us all shit so easily?"

"Oh, my Lord and Holy Mother of Jesus," Frosa mumbled and ran away.

"Too bad people can't face harsh reality," I sighed, as I locked the door. I double-checked it. I never had to do that before Mother's illness. Mila's presence was another reason to make sure the door was locked. In my home country, neighbors and friends would simply enter your home uninvited. The lifestyle was completely different than in New Jersey. Sometimes I wished my neighbors in America could socialize so easily and not always be busy and alienated, with that "don't give a damn about anyone" attitude.

After lunch, I changed Mother's colostomy bag and offered to walk her in the garden. She refused. She also skipped watching TV with me, as she had on other afternoons. She said she felt fatigued and soon fell asleep. I organized her medicine drawers and her clothes, and I watered her plants. I watched TV until Bisera arrived.

"I need a favor, Auntie Bisera. I want to go out. Can you stay with Mother until I come back?" I asked.

"It's about time you had some fun," she scolded. "You need to get out more. How many times have I told you that? You're like a prisoner, stuck in this house.

You need fresh air, badly. Go now, and don't rush to come back early. I'll be here."

"Mother felt weaker today. Right after lunch, she went to sleep."

"Don't worry. Just go and enjoy this gorgeous day." Bisera tapped my shoulders. She was prepared to do anything to make it easier for me. She was the only one who truly cared about me, besides Mother. I hugged and kissed her, then climbed the stairs, the bridge between Mother's and Mila's worlds, moving quickly to dispel the weighty significance they seemed to have.

Mila was dressed up and waiting for me, glued to her favorite spot, the armchair. I changed and told the taxi to park on the back street, to avoid our neighbors' curious eyes. Mila's graceful walk enhanced her already striking appearance in red. I took her to the historic town of Ohrid on the east bank of a nearby lake, a half-hour drive from home. The lake was very popular and more commercialized than our own Prespa Lake. The town and the villages along its shore featured lots of cafes, restaurants, and entertainment.

I took Mila to a restaurant in town overlooking the water. I started off ordering salad and fish soup for both of us, suggesting the famous Ohrid's trout for her and ordering fried calamari for myself. She seemed to be forcing herself to eat.

"Finally, you ate something," I said happily, after half of her meal was gone.

"Thank you." She smiled, then her face became solemn. "I wish I could have been there when everyone turned their backs on you."

"You were my last hope; my unfulfilled, endless desire. I was convinced that finding you would stop my suffering and change everything."

"It would have," she declared sharply. Her eyes shone and she sat up straighter. She appeared eager to touch me, hug me, or kiss me, but reluctant to do so after my cold reaction to her previous overtures. Her entire being communicated approval of who I was, making me like her more. She probably knew that I liked men from the moment she first saw me at the airport. She never asked me if I had a girlfriend. Women's intuition, especially in an intelligent person like her and one related by blood, tends to be strong. I put my fork and knife down and lit a cigarette. She helped herself to one, also.

"I began thinking hard about where to go and who to ask for help in finding you." I spoke to the quiescent, turquoise lake that was such a contrast to the choppy emotions I'd felt since Mila arrived. "I became obsessed. I considered all my possible connections. First on the list were the influential men I had slept with. They promised me plenty, but did nothing. They were afraid to break the law. Second, I tried bribing some guys from The Center, who were already working for the police, but they couldn't find anything useful. Then I went to the Social Center directly. The staff acted indifferent when I told them I was looking for my biological parents. They told me that it was illegal to give me any information. Again, I had to face Big Brother's games and manipulations. Again, I had to deal with a stupid law that prohibited me from having essential information about myself: knowledge of my biological roots and identity. Again, I felt completely betrayed. Failure was killing me, and after getting nowhere with the social workers, I felt compelled to try the orphanage.

"The main entrance opened into a hall crowded with children who were playing and running, crying and laughing. I had never seen so many beautiful, little creatures in one place. For some reason, orphans usually turn out to be exceptionally good-looking. A group of women were instructing them. They looked like nurses. At once, I found myself at the center of the children's attention. They immediately surrounded me and began embracing me. 'Are you my father?' they asked, in high-pitched, innocent voices. 'Have you come for me?' I was trapped in the midst of all those precious, rejected souls.

"I looked down at one little boy who was the loudest. His little arms encircled my legs. I noticed a lonesome little girl in the corner, staring at me with the most forlorn expression I have ever seen on a child. Somehow I managed to disengage from all those little arms, those weak, human chains around me. I managed not to hear those little voices. I stepped towards the girl but she ran off. She knew I was only a visiting stranger who wouldn't take her away. 'Take me home, please,' another boy shouted, rolling towards me in a wheelchair. He had a breathtaking smile. 'God, what the hell did they do to deserve this?' I asked the most popular Guy up there, trying to hold back my tears, so as not to add still more sadness to the place. I noticed the boys were more aggressive than the girls. I heard a baby's cry from the end of the hallway, where they seemed to keep the infants. An elderly woman came over and greeted me warmly.

"'May I help you with something, comrade?' she asked.

"'No, thank you. Frankly, I wanted to see the place where my life began.'

"'Adopted folks always come back to their first home.'

"Two little boys appeared, begging me to take them away. They shook my legs the way I used to shake my neighbor's plum tree to steal the fruit.

"'How come all these gorgeous children are not adopted yet?' I asked.

"'Some are sick. Others are disabled or gypsies. The rest simply have no luck,' she explained, her angelic expression full of sorrow and compassion.

"'Life's a game. A cruel and unfair game for those who are manipulated by others, like these innocent souls.' I sighed. 'I have a home and parents.'

"'You are lucky. Very lucky,' she whispered.

"'I wish I could adopt them all,' I murmured, impulsively grabbing her warm hand.

"'Goodbye, comrade. I wish I could, too.' She took my hand in both of hers, then tapped it three times—the number thought by many Macedonians to ward off curses.

"To reach the door, I had to plow once again through the dense crowd of innocent, damaged souls. They ran after me. They kept trying to stop me, pulling me and hugging me. I tried to move faster, to free myself from the heavy burden of their misfortune. Looking at their tiny, fragile bodies, feeling their needy touches, and hearing their desperate, tiny voices was hell. The whole thing was like a sad movie. Some of them tried to follow me, but their instructors' firm commands and grasps stopped them. When I opened the door, they peered out into the world of those who created them and betrayed them. I lingered at the door, and it felt as if I were committing a crime when I closed it. The door was heavy, and I felt useless and feeble. I couldn't look back. Each step away from the orphanage was as hard as the thought of going back again.

"I spent the rest of the day pondering my life with my parents, guessing how things would've been growing up with you, who abandoned me, trying to picture life without any of you, contemplating alternative realities. My experience at the orphanage motivated me to search harder for you. I went to the main police station in Skopje and applied for a duplicate of your birth certificate, pretending I was a relative. Nothing on file was under the name I had for you. I called hundreds of people with your last name, in towns and villages around the country. It was embarrassing, degrading, constantly calling the wrong places, ending up in wrong households and disturbing innocent people. I cursed you, my parents, my destiny, God, everyone who could've designed such a hellish world for me.

"The possibilities were endless, and they all weighed against me. You could have gotten married or just changed your name. You could have been dead or out of the country. You could have provided a false name, which my parents thought was the case. I was like a confused junkie with a desperate craving. I didn't want to hurt my parents, but there was no way to avoid it. We fought all the time. I accused them of knowing where to find you but hiding it. I was hard on them and myself. Deep inside, no matter how destructive my behavior was, I sensed that it served a purpose. Now I'm sure that if I hadn't felt mad and destructive, I wouldn't have achieved my independence. I wouldn't have gone to America, and I wouldn't have found you.

"My failure to find you made me question the value of the search. Why was I doing it? To find my identity? To understand myself better? To achieve my freedom? I wondered what I would do if my biological family didn't want to meet me or refused to help me. Maybe it was better not to have an identity, not to know what nationality I was, not to be part of the nationalistic furor which continued to grow stronger each day. I consoled myself with the thought that I was immune to being classified and numbered. Even though I felt more liberated without an identity, the lies I'd been told all those years hurt me deeply. Why can't people handle the truth? Were all those manipulations really necessary?"

"Manipulations are Big Brother's lifeblood. That's how the system is kept alive," Mila broke in. I could tell when she was preparing to change the subject, when her lips began moving silently. She'd had enough of the manipulations that damaged me, her, and, one way or another, all of us. Wiping away her tears, she said, "Then Rambo helped you find me."

"Yes, he did. For money, although he said he wanted to make up for what he'd done to me. And to be my friend again. My ass."

"Has he changed?"

"The wolf changes its fur, but never its character. He's still a handsome opportunist."

"Don't you still feel something for him?"

"No. Only leftover anger towards that asshole. Ironically, he keeps calling to ask for my help now. He's ten thousand dollars in debt. Jerk."

"Important jerk, though! He connected us."

"Important to you, maybe. Not to me. Anyhow, he owed it to me."

"You're very angry. You still love him, don't you?"

"No, I love an American now. Fred. A Virginian."

"Great. Is he nice to you?"

"We've been together almost six years, since I moved to the US."

"Then marry him."

"The U.S. may be an economic and military power, but it's not the freest place on earth. It's not Holland yet, but eventually it will be. There's hope for the MTV and Internet generation. They're growing liberated. They don't give a damn about the thickheaded crones and old bigots, who are all dying anyway. Soon we'll all be able to love whoever we want. It will happen. Same-sex marriage is only important for getting benefits. Papers cannot guaranty you'll love someone, make your partner happy, or your children, if you have them, loved. The institution of marriage has changed. We live in a different era."

"Correct," Mila said, nodding. Her tears had stopped. "Success comes from your relationship with loved ones. Precisely, how much you work to connect, to communicate, and to get involved with them."

"Unfortunately, in this busy, greed-driven world, many people can't do it," I said. "Yet they keep getting involved in relationships, making children, and spreading their misery, just for the sake of it. People are usually pushed into relationships and birthing by religions that crave more believers. The religions are afraid of dying out, because they can see that with each new generation, more people reject the faith. I wish people could see that and learn to be alone and keep their misery to themselves and get involved with others only when they're prepared, when they're truly in love." I puffed morosely on my cigarette, then added, "The bright side is that more companies are beginning to recognize alternative lifestyles."

"Good. That must drive the bigots crazy," Mila said.

"MTV began digging their graves and the Internet will execute them completely. Soon. Trust me on this. Those are two of America's greatest achievements."

Engrossed in our own thoughts, we gazed at the turquoise, serene water of the lake, quietly sipping our cappuccinos. This open discussion with the woman who bore me was the realization of an old dream. It was interesting and kind of fun. It was what I missed with Mother all those years. As I looked at Mila, who was caressed by the breeze and squinting from the sun reflecting off the water, she seemed more tranquil than the lake. Was she? Or was it guilt that made her seem that way? Or the open conversation that was bringing us closer? Or that the time would soon come for us to part?

Suddenly, the restaurant's terrace felt like a neutral ground; there was no reason to continue my confession. I felt no pressure, being out of the house. I didn't want to reopen old wounds, and I could tell she didn't want me to. She enjoyed celebrating our closeness. Neither of us wanted to revive the painful past. I suggested we stroll along the lake's paved quay. She smiled approvingly, and a half-hour later we were sitting on a bench, watching gulls swooping over the harbor, the fishermen tying up their boats, and tourists taking pictures and admiring the town's old architecture. Mila's body moved in an almost effortless way. I thought she would ask a question when she placed her hand on mine, on the edge of the bench. I let her hand touch mine longer than ever. Abruptly, I stood and suggested that we climb to the old fortress overlooking the town. When I took her hand back, she glowed with happiness. We reached the top of the highest tower, where we could view the whole lake and the blue-green mountains surrounding it like a garland. The wind was stronger up there, and it tousled Mila's shiny hair and made her collar fly up and down like that of a happy little red finch.

Still, my mind was adrift in speculation. *Did I trust my biological mother? Did I really trust her?*

23

Istanbul

Mila asked me for a cigarette. Again, she took it with shaking fingers and thanked me, nodding. Again, she waited for me to light it, so she could steady my hand with hers. Again, she was going to use that as an excuse to touch me.

"Two more days together," she said in a quiet voice, looking at her unlit cigarette. I lit it and, as I had expected, she touched my hand. "Friday, I stay with my parents, and Saturday, I'll fly back to Croatia." She sounded melancholy.

I didn't say anything, struggling to hide my feelings. I hailed a taxi and opened the back door for her. She got in, and I sat in front, debating: *do I want her to stay longer or leave so I can be around Mother more?* I realized I was growing attached to Mila and that confused and scared me. I kept telling myself I couldn't betray Mother, but my feelings for the woman sitting behind me were intensifying. My pulse was racing, and it seemed she knew that, as she would give me a concerned look now and then. That was okay. I was more worried that Mother would figure out something was wrong. I couldn't let Mother detect my mental betrayal of her.

I tried to think something other than my two mothers as we drew closer to home. The moment we arrived, Mila strode upstairs, quickly. I took a deep breath in an attempt to look relaxed, and entered the living room. Bisera was giving Mother painkiller drops.

"You came home early. You could've stayed out longer," she said, stirring the drops into Mother's water. "Did you have fun?"

"Yes, thank you. I hung around with some friends," I answered hastily.

Mother gave me a suspicious glance. Her face contorted with repugnance from the bitter taste of the drops as she sipped from the glass. As she left, Bisera told me that Mother had acted very strangely, that her body shook in quick intervals throughout the day, and that she got up only for dinner. I had to do something to make Mother feel better.

After making sure her colostomy bag was on right, I rubbed her body with plum brandy. I tried to keep Mother at the table, watching TV with me. I talked to her during the shows, trying to choose interesting topics, but eventually she laid her head on the table. It was hard watching her fight the evil of cancer, and even harder to witness her attempts to stay out of bed. Her eyes closed, and I gently shook her forearm to wake her up. Immediately, she grasped my shoulders and let me help her into bed. She kissed me, and shortly afterward, she began to sleep. Her eyelids, lips, fingers, and shoulders all twitched spasmodically. The cancer wasn't giving her a minute's peace.

I hastened upstairs. Mila looked refreshed. I was glad that the lunch and fresh air had helped her.

"How's your mother doing?" she asked, patting my old cat toy in her lap.

"Weaker today," I replied nervously.

"Sorry to hear it. It's going to get worse every day. You have to be prepared for that. The good thing is that you're very strong. No doubt about it. Not after everything you've been through. She's lucky to have you," Mila said with envy, shaking her head in genuine concern.

"I would rather see her without me and without this damned cancer, than with me and helpless as she is. She doesn't deserve this…No one does."

"I wish I could change that. I wish I could help you."

"No one can. Not even that famous God, Mary, and Jesus, the whole damned crew Mother trusted and worshipped so obediently all her life!" I shouted. "In English, 'God' spelled backwards is 'dog.' That explains his character perfectly."

Mila's eyes widened. She wasn't thrilled to hear my insults to the Holy Family, but she nodded without realizing it, agreeing subconsciously. She wasn't very religious, less so than Mother. She cared for Them at a normal level. She didn't try to argue for and protect Them. She knew I had a point. She also doubted Them, like many of us who will never admit it. She was joining my club, like Mother, who belatedly realized as her misery progressed, that God had betrayed her, like so many of His loyal followers.

"Woe is us. Too bad it takes cancer, AIDS, a real catastrophe, for us meek, manipulated people to finally understand that all that fancy business about how good He is didn't, doesn't, and never will, make any sense. That He will never protect us from harm. That He and His damned family are a horde of merciless, human-made assholes, no better than the people who created Them!" I yelled, pacing around the room.

Mila jumped from her seat and hugged me. "You love Mother," she whispered in my ear. "That's good. That's very good." She sat down again in the armchair.

"Tell me what happened? Did you leave The Center? Speak. Tell me all you've been through. Get everything off your chest. Forget religion. Forget ideologies. I want to know everything about you."

She was right. It didn't do any good to get upset over the imaginary gods other people created to fill the emptiness in their lives. It was a useless waste of energy and time. I sat down again in the rocking chair, sipped my Coke, and returned to my therapeutic divulgence.

"I couldn't study. I hated the pressure of exams. I needed a break. I needed to escape my isolation, those evil locals, and the fights with my parents. I decided to do something else, rather than just continue to hate everyone, pity myself, and wonder about the purpose of my existence on this planet. Unable to find any trace of you and worn out from the search, I was ready for something new. I wanted to set aside my confusion and become a happier person. Finding the truth always has been and will be my ultimate goal, but for the first time I was tired of it. In fact, my search for the truth was hurting me. I was ready to be free of the old me. Instead of looking upon my destiny as poison, I wanted to think of it as wine. I knew I couldn't escape from myself, but I needed a new environment. I needed an adventure.

"As summer approached, I began preparing for that journey. I needed a visa and connections to travel to the West. Istanbul was the closest big city, and Turkey was the only neighboring capitalist country that didn't require a visa if you came from the former Yugoslavia. Actually, my desire to go there didn't just pop up out of the blue. Turkey has always intrigued me, since it divides Western from Eastern culture, Christian from Muslim, yet also mixes them in a mysterious way. After I gathered all the information for my trip, I lied to my parents that my college friends were going there on a very inexpensive vacation for a week. Desperately dependent on their money, I tried to persuade them that a vacation was just what I needed to put myself together, to get back my strength so I could continue my studies successfully. They were hard to convince, but they gave in when I promised them I would study hard and pass the necessary exams to enroll for my third year at The Center in the fall. I got my first passport and packed one bag, carrying as little as possible in order to stay mobile. I exchanged the dinars my father gave me for 180 U.S. dollars. I estimated that it was enough for about five days in a hotel, plus round-trip, open train fare. I didn't want to risk asking for more. I didn't want to push my luck.

"Once the train left the station, I could breath again. It was a hot June afternoon. I was leaving behind pressure and unhappiness and looking forward to magic. It felt surreal to be on my own for the first time and leaving my homeland, which was gradually tearing itself apart. The train was full of small Bosnian, Macedonian, and Serbian black market merchants. There were some lost Western tourists and, as always, Gypsies prowling around like coyotes, waiting patiently for the perfect moment to rob them. The train was old, slow, and without air conditioning. The trip took a day and a half, by way of southwestern Bulgaria.

"When we arrived at the customs post, the conductors collected our passports for inspection. Passengers got off the train to stretch their legs and have a drink or a smoke. As I finished my first cigarette, I noticed a short customs officer staring at me. I tried to look nonchalant, but he continued to smile at me and signal me with his over-anxious eyes to follow him. Out of dumb curiosity, I did. He led me to the barracks and gestured for me to go inside. When I walked in, another officer was there.

"Abruptly, the short officer turned and slapped me. He slapped me again and I fell down, disoriented. I wasn't sure what was going on, but I heard them argue. Then the second officer lifted me up. The short one opened the door and I was tossed out.

"Cautiously, I trod back to the car, covering my mouth with a handkerchief as if I had just vomited. Most of the passengers were still waiting outside. Shivering in the middle of the summer, I couldn't explain then what had happened and I haven't been able to, since. I guess the officers mistook me for a criminal. It was a scary way to be welcomed to Turkey. I applied makeup to my face before it turned purple and collapsed into my seat. An hour later, the conductor returned my passport. He wasn't sure the picture on it was mine, not because I kept covering half my face, but because I appeared androgynous in it. I'd heard this was a good omen for Istanbul.

"After arriving at the city station, I took a taxi to the hotel in the Aksaray quarter that the travel agency had recommended. I paid for the night and then converted some dollars into Turkish liras. I left my passport and my ticket at the desk for safekeeping. The hotel was small and dirty. I had the cheapest room and it showed. I used the communal shower, changed, and went out to look around.

"Aksaray was full of Yugoslavians who ran businesses there. Most of them were Turkish descendants who had left the Balkans after the Ottoman Empire crumbled. Istanbul was huge. Its streets bustled with life, day and night. I had hoped that the Turks, like most other Mediterranean and Balkan folk, were fond of music, beautiful singers, movies, and good food, but I hadn't expected so much entertainment to be offered in one quarter. *Çay*, a tea, was consumed everywhere, always hot. I've heard that it keeps one from perspiring during the summer months. Since I was on a very tight budget, I bought a small portion of cheap *Aryan* yogurt and a *Simit*, a bread ring. They tasted much better than the ones we make here at home, even though we inherited the recipe from the Ottoman Turks.

"The drivers honked and whistled at any decent-looking tourist appearance, regardless of sex. It felt bizarre to experience it, but it was also thrilling and fun and it made me laugh. That was exactly what I needed. Eventually, I ended up at the pier. As in any big-city pier, men were cruising around. Most of them were young, flamboyant students, waiting to be picked up by older men who circled in their cars like sharks. I started chatting with one guy, but he was not friendly. I think he resented that the men were paying more attention to me than to him. He was glad to send me somewhere else, though, when I asked him where I could find a gay bar or club. He mentioned Taksim, and I immediately set out in search of the quarter. I walked in order to save money, asking for directions occasionally and using all my knowledge of Turkish, Macedonian, Serbo-Croatian, French, and Bulgarian. As the sunset colored the city's roofs, its streets became even more crowded. I reached an area full of cheap shops, hotels, restaurants, and taverns. I overheard many people speaking Yugoslavian, and I began running like a vampire from garlic and the cross. The last thing I needed was to meet my people. My aim was to escape them. Everywhere I went there was music, making it seem like I was attending a big festival or party. I noticed lots of men smiling, winking, whistling, and gesturing at me. A number of them even pinched my butt. I was puzzled."

Mila took a deep breath, shook her head, and said, "Most men spend half their lives thinking about sex and getting laid. It seems as if they're obsessed with it."

"True, but can you blame them? It's in their nature. They're hunters." I smiled, then continued. "Two guys in particular were very anxious to meet me. One of them looked hot, more Middle Eastern than Turkish. His friend looked like a weasel, and I wish I had sensed his slyness sooner. He was a skilled liar, and he and his sexy friend made a good tourist-hunting team. The weasel did most of the talking. They had odd names, difficult to remember. They invited me for tea. When I asked them how close we were to Taksim quarter, the weasel hurriedly replied that we were far from it. I was lost, so I let them guide me back to my hotel. The weasel offered to show me around town the next day. Honored, I agreed to meet them in front of the hotel. They were waiting for me when I left the next morning. I asked them to take me to Taksim. The weasel said we had to take a bus and asked me for money. I pulled my wallet out of the carrying bag I had hung around my neck and stuffed under my shirt. Two hours later, we ended up in a small town with a number of hotels and restaurants overlooking the sea. It looked like any middle class, Mediterranean resort. There was a small park across the bus station. When we entered it, I asked them if we were in Taksim. The weasel laughed. His buddy, also. The weasel stepped in front of me and pulled a shiny blade from his pocket. He pointed it at my stomach, then sliced open my carrying bag and took my wallet. He told me to follow his orders if I didn't want to end up in the nearby garbage dumpster, that was reeking with terrible stench.

"They took me to one of the hotels. The weasel paid for a room and gave the receptionist his and his friend's ID cards. I wished I had left at least half my money with my passport and ticket. As we climbed the steps, the receptionist gave me a pitying look that screamed that I was in trouble. When we got to the room, the good-looking one raped me. Afterward, they made me go with them to the beach. The sea was crystal clear, but, in pain, I couldn't enjoy a second of it. Neither of them had swimsuits. They looked like homeless people, in their shitty underwear. Later that afternoon, they took turns napping while I huddled in a corner, trying to calm my fear, pain, and hunger. When evening came, the weasel explained in broken Serbo-Croatian that we were going into town for dinner and to a disco after that. I felt even less safe after hearing him speak Yugoslav. I kept trying to figure out how to get rid of them as we left the hotel and walked down the long street leading to town.

"Most of the houses were family inns, with children screaming and babies crying on their terraces. The weasel led us to a restaurant. Belly dancers and singers were performing inside. I had seen enthusiastic audiences, but never those like these Turks. The Westerners were amazed. I was finally allowed to eat something. The weasel ordered a plate of kebab in gravy for all of us. The outdoor club we went to afterwards was tacky. Colorful lantern lights were hung all around it, reminding me of the way some houses in the U.S. are overly-decorated at Christmas to the point where they look like cheap, redneck motels. The place was crowded, mostly with teenagers and foreigners. The music was a mix of Turkish, Euro, and American pop. It was tempting to let my guard down, but I couldn't. I was formulating an escape plan while my captors got drunk. They started with beer and eventually switched to whiskey. After a while, I told the weasel that I needed to use the rest room. He asked the bartender where it was and whispered something to his buddy, then gestured for me to follow him.

"The second we entered the men's room, I began checking the stalls, pretending I was looking for a clean one. I was actually looking for a window or vent. The last stall had a window above the toilet. I ducked into it and began making straining noises, watching the weasel's reaction through the door's crack. He was singing in front of the mirror, fixing his hair. As I continued to grunt louder, men began to stare at him, then towards my stall. Looking uncomfortable, he called to me that he would wait outside. I told him it was going to take a while, groaning.

"When he had left, I hopped onto the toilet. I had to jump to try to reach the window frame. I failed twice, but got hold of it on the third try. The window was tiny, but since I had lost a lot of weight, I was able to pull myself up and squeeze through it. I dropped to the ground and crawled away as quickly as possible, while keeping a lookout for the two men. Once I was outside the club, I got up and ran as fast as I could away from the beach, to try to find the highway. Pain was slowing me down. Thank god it wasn't a long run. Soon I was walking along the highway's edge, hitchhiking, biting my nails, and cursing everything alive and dead whenever a car or a truck flew by me. I thought I was going to have a nervous breakdown, that those sons of bitches would be breathing down my neck any minute, when a truck stopped.

"'Istanbul?' the driver asked, as he opened the door.

"'*Evet*,' I said in Turkish and jumped in.

"When I turned, I saw the bastards running behind us, waving their arms in the darkness. As we left them behind, I started breathing normally again, comforted by the driver's crooning along with the music.

"His name was Hasan. He had that typically Turkish look: a thick mustache, thick eyebrows, and jet-black hair. He kept singing, occasionally exchanging glances with me, until we got to the city. He pulled over in front of a small restaurant. I tried to explain that I was robbed. He smiled, escorted me in, and told me to have anything I wanted. I let him order for both of us. He served me the salad and appetizers before serving himself. We were both hungry and finished the meal quickly. I explained that my belongings were at my hotel and that I planned to spend the night at the train station, then head back to Yugoslavia. Hasan smiled and offered to take me back to my hotel. He drove his truck to a parking lot and called a cab. He paid for a nice room with a bathroom, and after he showered, he immediately fell asleep. I shaved my facial fuzz, took a bath, and went to sleep on the other bed. His gentle hug woke me up, and we cuddled, as if we were old lovers, and fell back to sleep until afternoon. During lunch, he offered to take me to a place not far from the famous Aegean resort of Izmir where his brother owned an inn. He said that I could stay there and enjoy the sea, and that he would pick me up in three weeks, after he'd finished his business in Ankara. Of course, at that point, I didn't want to go back home. He seemed trustworthy, so I agreed. The whole trip, we sang along to loud Turkish music, with a rhythm similar to our folk music, another sign of the Ottoman Turks' influence after five centuries in the Balkans. I felt secure with Hasan. I also had fun. We rested at a couple of places along the coast, and I enjoyed their beauty and their mystical Ottoman ambiance.

"Hasan's brother was younger then he was. He was married to a pretty woman who seemed unhappy. He was an extremely greedy man. His inn was right on the beach and had a veranda-style restaurant-bar that served great food. The accommodations were horrible, however, like a cheap motel in the middle of nowhere. The rooms were tiny and they shared a communal outhouse. There were no showers, except the ones on the beach that the swimmers used. Hasan carried my bag to the room, and when he hugged me good-bye, something told me I would never see him again. I thanked him as we embraced. He smiled as he stuffed money in my hand. When his truck disappeared from sight, I opened my hand and saw a one hundred deutsche-mark bill.

"Hasan's brother was a perfect host for a few days, then suddenly his attitude changed. He began pressuring me to use my language skills and promote his place at a nearby complex full of Western tourists, in exchange for my free stay. I did my best and succeeded in convincing two Dutch couples to come over. They left after one night, disgusted with the inn's terrible conditions. The complex they'd come from had lots of international entertainment and food, more in accord with the guests' Western standard of living. Nevertheless, the Dutch enjoyed at least one thing: the singer and her belly dancing. She was a barely fifteen-year-old beauty, constantly escorted by her Mother to keep her from falling into prostitution.

"Eventually, Hasan's brother got pissed at me since I didn't succeed to bring any guests after the two Dutch couples. He moved me to the worst room. It looked like a dungeon without windows. He also stopped letting me eat there. On top of that, his workers stole half of my money. Luckily, I had broken the hundred deutsche mark bill. I hid fifty marks, along with my passport and ticket, in a jar behind the big wild rose bush by the outhouse. Two weeks passed, and all I did while waiting for Hasan was swim and visit the town at night. I couldn't enjoy much, hanging on to what little fortune I had and eating one bread ring and a cup of yogurt per day before bed. I begged the brother to give me Hasan's number. He gave me three numbers, all wrong. After the calls, I had a couple of coins left in my pocket, but not enough for my miserable dinners. One night, when I returned to the inn, I found my bag waiting for me in front of the room. Hasan's brother had thrown me out.

"I walked towards town, along the beach, until I found a dense thicket of shrubs growing in a circle. I checked the center and lay down. The lights of the town's port were blurry. I wrapped my towel around me, laid my head on my bag, and tried to sleep. The sand turned cold after midnight, but the sound of the waves, the smell of the air, and the star-ornamented inky sky soothed me, and I eventually dropped off. The seagulls woke me early in the dawn. My body ached, but a swim in the sea helped me recover. I thought of hitchhiking, but at the same time I was hesitant. Besides, I didn't know where the highway was, and loitering around like as a homeless tourist was risky. The locals already viewed me with suspicion. I wanted to sneak somewhere near the inn and wait another week for Hasan. I was sure I could handle my mental and physical exhaustion, as well as the hunger, but I absolutely couldn't afford to be thrown in a Turkish prison for vagrancy.

I went to the bus station to buy a ticket to Istanbul. It was seventy marks. I knew it was less, but I also knew it was a common practice in most places to rip off tourists. I went to the bazaar and sold my ring. I sold it for less than its value, but I couldn't take chances. I bought a bread ring and yogurt, and I decided to take an evening bus and sleep all night. I couldn't, though. I kept thinking of Hasan and his generous smile.

"I arrived in Istanbul late the next morning, starving. The city's yogurt and bread ring tasted much better. But I nibbled it slowly. It felt as if I had more food that way. At the station, I found that a train was scheduled to leave for Yugoslavia at 10 o'clock that night, so I decided to see more of the city that I had quickly fallen in love with but couldn't afford to stay in. I couldn't believe I still had the strength to walk that much with my bag on my shoulder, under the hot Turkish sun, and after all the abuse I had experienced. I realized then that the fear of my town, my home, and my society was the fuel that nourished my body and made me keep going and going."

I paused for a moment. "In spite of the fact that my train was leaving soon, my mind was unable to come to a decision. *Should I return home to the society that seemed to despise me? Or should I stay in a country where the only problem seemed to be common thieves?* There was no quick answer, and I wondered what Mother's Savior would have advised."

24

Happiness

Mila listened. She listened hard and she cried. I felt confident that I was going to find out who my biological father was and what actually happened at the time of my conception. Her expression seemed to hold promise on that score.

"I can understand your sociophobia," Mila said. "That's exactly what made me run from Macedonia after I lost you. I can feel it as if it happened yesterday. I felt both apathy and repugnance about going back home; I didn't want to live among those evil people, in that closed-minded society. I know what it's like to hate myself and everything associated with me. It's a feeling shared by many of those who give up a child, as well as those who search for their roots."

"Hmm," I murmured, and for a moment, I saw compassion in a glance that was both motherly and soothing. Despite my skepticism about whether Mila truly understood what I was saying, the promise in her glance made me want to tell her as much as possible.

"Another force gave me strength and motivated me to keep going. It was Istanbul," I said. I walked to the bookshelves, recalling that I had saved a big photo of Istanbul somewhere in the world atlas. I pulled it out and flipped through it. The photo was pressed between the pages for Europe and Asia, exactly where I had stored it a decade ago. I handed it to Mila and said, "Look. Isn't it beautiful?"

For a few minutes, she studied the panoramic image of the Bosphorus and its city, then she said, "Wow…gorgeous…impressive."

"I was desperate for a bath. I was filthy. The hot Turkish sun and hunger were burning my body. Still, my reflection in the shop window didn't look as terrible as it should have, because I felt very happy walking through the city."

I took the picture from her and put it in the atlas with care, back where it had been, as if it were my last possession. I placed the book back on the shelf and sat in my rocking chair. Lighting another cigarette, I continued my story.

"I ended up in an area that looked like many west-European cities. It was neat, with some modern tall buildings and hotels. It was Taksim Square. I had finally found it. I entered a park and sat in the shade to recharge. The skyscrapers of the Hilton and Sheraton looked outstanding from a distance. Another giant hotel faced the park. It had the name 'Etap Marmara' on top of it. In order not to get lost, I decided to use the hotels as landmarks.

"I was about to cross a wide busy street when I noticed a speedy Cadillac approaching. I backed off, fervently staring at a car that I had only seen in the movies. The man in it honked, and the car slowed down and pulled over. The driver backed up to where I stood at the pedestrian crossing. Some pedestrians cursed at him, as they had to walk around his big car. He rolled his window down and asked me in French, 'Do you need a ride.' Our eyes met, and while I was debating what to do, he asked me the same question in English. His penetrating look swept away my fear and hesitation. It was overwhelming. He got out of the car and opened the door. He was tall, at least 6'4", in his late thirties, and wearing a tailored shirt and jeans that fit his well-built frame perfectly. His light brown hair and stylish glasses made him look more Western than Turkish. He oozed sex appeal, even more so when his smile dimpled his cheeks. I smiled back. He took my bag from my hand and placed it on the back seat.

"Speechless, I got in his car as if I were hypnotized. People stared at us, like we were movie stars or something. His eyes shone with anticipation when I said, *Merhaba*, 'hello' in Turkish. I introduced myself and expected a handshake, but to my surprise, he kissed the top of my hand. *A handsome stranger kissing my hand in the middle of Istanbul?* I was stunned.

"After he tried to pronounce my name unsuccessfully, twice, he said, 'My name is Genghis. Like the cruel Mongol's Khan and conqueror. But I'm gentle.' He laughed, then continued. 'So, where are you staying?' he asked, offering me a cigarette.

"I took it lustily, having craved one for weeks, and then muttered sadly, 'Well, today is my last day in Turkey, before I go back to Yugoslavia.'

"'Yugoslavia. Great. What part?'

"'Macedonia. The southernmost part.'

"'I can see why you know Turkish. There are many of us in Macedonia. At first, I thought you were French. You look French.'

"'Hmm. Many people have told me that. I should check with my mother,' I said, making him laugh. I was seriously considering the possibility, thinking that a French woman might have given birth to me."

"No, you are not French," Mila interjected, smiling.

"It wouldn't have been a problem. I like the French. Of course, many conquerors plundered this land, and the chance that we carry Gaulish blood can't be ruled out absolutely," I said. "Anyway, Genghis drove out of the city. I had no idea where we were, but I didn't care. Not anymore. I completely forgot about the possibility of danger. I was too busy enjoying the comfort of my first ride in an American car and the clear, spontaneous sound of his voice. It was usually difficult for me to understand Turks when they spoke fast, because I had learned the Macedonian dialect of Turkish, which uses many Ottoman words and phrases. Nonetheless, I could understand everything he said.

"'I want you to stay longer,' he said, in a demanding tone.

"'Is that an order? What if I told you I can't?'

"He gave me an earnest glance. Simultaneously, he said, 'Stay!' and I said, 'Yes!' We both laughed. He was pleased, and I felt lucky not to be going back home.

"After he spoke briefly to someone on his car phone, he said, cheerfully, 'I want to show you something very special. You'll love it. Everyone does.' He sped up and took me to a place where the view of the Bosphorus was spectacular. We sat on a rocky clearing, staring at that mass of water surging between two continents. When Genghis moved closer, it was impossible not be captivated by his big, brown eyes. His sculpted lips began moving towards mine.

"'Wait,' I said, backing off.

"'What's wrong? Is there something wrong with me?' he asked, confused. He was one of those types of men who weren't used to rejection.

"'To the contrary! You're too intriguing to be a one-night stand,' I explained. I could feel my heart pounding. I also felt his when he slid towards me and his firm chest touched mine. He almost kissed me, but again I turned away.

"'And you're too enigmatic to be my quickie. Let's go eat something,' he said, forcing a smile so as not to show his disappointment. We returned to the car, and he hit the gas and turned up the music. His driving was reckless. He was a man who always had to win; he always had to be in control and make you submit to his orders. He wasn't aware of it, though. It was an unconscious thing with him, a trait that most Balkan men possess.

"My eyes probably glowed after he mentioned food. I had looked away so he wouldn't notice, but when we arrived at the upscale restaurant in the Divan Hotel, its cozy decor and colonial atmosphere awed me. I trembled in anticipation of finally having a real meal. He smiled, aware of it. He ordered the house specialty, kebab in yogurt, for both of us. A good omen, we had similar tastes. When I refused a second glass of wine, telling him that I didn't drink much alcohol, he fell silent. I didn't think I had hurt him, though. He reacted like any man who finds out that his partner is not going to be his drinking buddy. I thanked him for the delicious meal. Unfortunately, on our way out, I had to run to the toilet and throw it all up. My stomach, accustomed to being empty, rejected all that food. Of course, I didn't tell Genghis about it. I didn't want him to get the wrong idea, to think that I was sick or something. I didn't want to spoil the beginning of our relationship, when the infatuation has to be kept unblemished.

"Genghis drove around the city for a while. We then went to one of the posh villages of the Rumeli, the European shore of the Bosphorus strait. The area had numerous impressive mansions. His was like a villa in a mixed modern and traditional Ottoman style. It had a beautiful garden with a baroque fountain in the center and an outdoor pool with turquoise tiles. I wanted to jump in the minute I saw it. Again, I felt embarrassed to show my desperate desire for a bath. A stocky and bold man greeted us and parked the Cadillac. He was Genghis' servant, gardener, and chauffeur. His attitude was cold. He was one of those people who always seem to be angry. In contrast, the maid who waited at the entrance was warm and gracious. Genghis introduced us and escorted me into the foyer. The spacious interior was mostly contemporary, with the hint of a classical touch. When I saw the indoor pool with the adjoining Turkish bath, *Hammam,* and a Jacuzzi and gym, I couldn't wait any longer.

"'Genghis, would it be all right if I took a swim?' I asked.

"'You can have anything you need,' he said, smiling.

"I thanked him and quickly undressed. He watched me closely as he strolled to the mahogany bar to fix a drink. His eyes pored over every centimeter of my body, as if he were going to operate on me. I jumped into the pool, and I could tell he enjoyed watching me even more than I enjoyed the water. It felt good to be adored by Genghis. I felt honored and important because of my youth. When we ate dinner on the terrace overlooking the Sea of Marmara, it seemed as if he never took his twinkling eyes off me. We talked until dawn over champagne and chocolates in the library. We didn't talk much about ourselves, just things in general, mostly about Turkey and Yugoslavia. It was too soon to expose our inner thoughts to one another. We were still stunned by our chance meeting. We ended up sleeping in our armchairs, exhausted from the excitement of that day.

"The next morning, I called my parents first thing. Understandably, they were frantic because I hadn't called them since I'd left. They were glad I was alive, but they roared when I told them that I was going to stay in Turkey and that I had found a job as a bartender. Of course, they didn't believe me. By then, they knew I wasn't on a week's vacation with college friends. Mother was asking God if He knew what I was actually doing in Turkey. If I had told them the truth, they would've had apoplectic fits. They accused me of breaking my promise to study hard after vacation. The usual bullshit, over and over. I wasn't important. Neither was my happiness, nor my well being. I couldn't take their screaming any longer, so I hung up. It was a great moment, making it clear to them that they no longer had control over me.

"Genghis was working out. He invited me to join him, but I swam instead, then enjoyed the medieval aura of the Hammam and soaked in the Jacuzzi. After we dressed, he made several calls and told the servant to prepare his red sport Mercedes cabriolet. He collected luxury cars the way a child collects toys. We had breakfast in the Konyali Restaurant located in a magnificent palace, the museum of the Ottoman sultans, Topkapi Sarayi. Walking with Genghis, I felt like the Grand Vizier had invited me to meet his Sultan, after seeing the famous Imperial Treasury, the Harem where the women of the ruler lived, and the exciting Ottoman miniatures. I could still taste that passionate kiss Genghis had given me at the terrace of the Park Restaurant during lunch. I think people noticed. He didn't care. He took a fork and fed me with delicious *manti* raviolis, then he guided me through the small cobblestone street and leaned me against the portal of the Victorian building to kiss me again.

"He took me to Maslak, a part of Istanbul known for its ice cream. When no one was looking, I hurriedly kissed him. A broad smile crossed his face, full of the joy of an adolescent and with a contagious vibe that made me crave more of it. The view of Anadolu, the Asian shore, was revealed as we crossed the Bosphorus. We strolled throughout the streets and parks until sunset, and then went back to the European side. Genghis chose the lavish brasserie of the Çiragan Palace Hotel for dinner. It was a former sultan's home, and its guest list had included presidents and celebrities. The whole day was like a dream. Istanbul was an amazing place, and I had just begun to explore it with a guardian angel next to me."

Mila's face glowed. "It sounds like a dream. I wish I could have been there." She sighed.

I smiled. "The dream didn't stop there. The fun really began when we went to Club Valentino. The patrons were mostly male and mostly residents, with the exception of a few intoxicated tourists laughing in the corner. Clusters of tall, slim, long-legged, and fashionably dressed girls were dancing, looking as if they had just arrived from a Parisian fashion show. Genghis and I took the middle table. Loud men, who were joking, smoking, drinking, and flirting with the girls, surrounded us. Some of them winked at me. I reddened. Genghis grinned at me, proudly.

"Shortly after we made a toast, I asked him to dance. He refused. He was like most Turkish and Yugoslav men, who would only dance to certain all-male traditional songs with rugged rhythms. The idea of doing modern, Western dances conflicted with their macho images of themselves. Although I was dying to hit the dance floor, I stayed with him out of courtesy. I knew how much our men respected that kind of attitude.

"Gradually, I realized there was something peculiar about the girls: their Adam's apples. When I said something about it to Genghis, he shocked me further by stating that all of the girls were transvestites or transsexuals. The place began to empty after 3 o'clock in the morning, and the girls left with their boyfriends. As we left the club, I realized why the weasel and his dumb companion didn't want me to go to Taksim. It was definitely a place where I could easily meet someone and slip out of their filthy hands.

"I thought we were going home, but Genghis suggested we have a snack and see a belly dancing performance. The action never stopped in Istanbul, I realized, while watching the women's seductive dancing. I thought about the girls in Club Valentino, wondering what I would look like in drag. That night was a new experience for me. The second I met Genghis, life became as colorful and unpredictable as a surrealistic mural.

"'Is everything all right?' Genghis asked me.

"'Perfect, thanks. When I think, I look like I'm worrying.'

"'I'll never let you worry. I promise.' He took my hand and kissed my palm.

"We got back to his villa at dawn. We couldn't sleep. We whispered sweet words to each other, like infatuated souls do during their first time in bed together. Welcoming the light of the new day in Genghis' bedroom, I felt ecstatic. Making love with him was like traveling back to the days of the Ottoman conquest at the hands of the Grand Vizier. It felt like I was his obedient servant and secret lover, who escorted him to battle after battle as he led the Sultan's army on its conquests of the Balkans, all the way northwest to Vienna. It felt like I was reliving the Ottoman glory while flirting in his commander's tent and galloping on his horse back to his city and the Golden Horn. When running and chasing each other through the marble corridors of his palace overlooking the dreamy Bosphorus. While hugging in his velvet rooms and cuddling between his satin sheets. When drinking lustfully the coconut milk that he offered with his strong hands. While kissing his full-sculpted tasty lips wrapped in the silk of his balcony's door curtains and the smell of his rose garden.

"A couple of nights later, back in Valentino, Genghis insisted that I dance.

"'Will I have the pleasure some day of dancing with you?' I asked.

"'You will. We have many nights ahead. We've just met.' He sounded as if he were planning to marry me or make me his concubine. It felt wonderful to be wanted. It felt safe. I took to the floor and began to dance. From time to time, I would smile at Genghis, whose eyes attentively took in every move I made. When I returned to our table, he whispered, 'You look better than any of them.'

"I realized he was talking about the girls. Confused, but intrigued, I tried to picture myself in one of the girls' dresses. I mentally debated which one would look best on me; whose shoes and make up I should wear; whose wardrobe I would never touch. I wondered how differently I would act if I went among them like that.

"'Do you want to try it?' he asked me gravely, gesturing with his eyes at the girls.

"'I don't think I would be good at it. I never wore women's clothing before…except as a child…my mother's,' I blushed.

"'Oh, yeah, you'll look excellent,' he said confidently. I kept studying the girls swinging under the spotlight. 'Just by looking at you, I can tell how much you want to be among them,' he added, twitching his left eyebrow up.

"I said nothing and kept smiling, watching the girls who seemed so happy.

"'Tomorrow will change everything for you,' Genghis stated.

"I loved hearing that. That was what I wanted. To change everything. To forget my past. To get completely out my identity. To stop thinking about mothers, fathers, homes, societies, and countries. To become a new person, a happy Homo Sapiens. And Genghis was absolutely right. The following day changed everything for me.

"He took me to a beauty salon in his Porsche. He could scarcely contain his excitement as he drove there. His friend Nora, a transvestite, owned the salon and took clients by appointment only. She was a brunette, in her late thirties, with a perfect complexion, almost Oriental eyes, and a pleasant voice. Genghis introduced us. Nora guided me, with Genghis following, to a room that had a cosmetic bed and a machine in the center. She told me to undress and lay down, then began examining my bare body, going over different parts with her gentle hands, and singing along with the soft tunes coming from the wall speakers.

"'Soon you'll look like a million dollars, baby. Genghis always had good taste,' she said, winking at him. Her assistant, a real woman who looked like a housewife, nodded.

"Genghis grinned. A second assistant came from the back. He wore stylish designer's feathers, but didn't look nearly as good as Nora. He was a young chicken, wild and funny.

"Nora leaned over my face and said, 'Honey, it's gonna be quick and easy. Your facial hair is rare soft fuzz, so shaving will do it. Your legs, chest, underarms, and arms need a little depilation. You might consider hip pads, but it's not necessary. We'll fit you with a padded brassiere. We can bleach your hair, dye it, or get you a wig. That's up to you. You have pretty long hair that's easy to play with, so I'd recommend a wig. That way you can alternate from blond to brunette. After that, all you'll need is a dress and high heels, and you'll be set.'

"'I don't think I want fake hips.' I finally spoke. 'Everything else sounds fine.'

"'Okay, Miss Macedonia. By the way, that's a great name for you,' Nora said. 'I've been there. I drove the whole Adriatic coast. I visited Belgrade, Zagreb, Sarajevo, and Skopje. I had a great time. Yugoslavia is beautiful.'

"'Yes, it is,' I said, wondering what else she knew about me. Probably many things. Genghis and she were good friends, perhaps even lovers in the past.

"The assistants turned the machine on. Nora's face changed, as she concentrated on my transformation. First, I was shaved and my eyebrows were shaped. Next, she depilated every hair on my body. She gave me a complete facial, a manicure, and a pedicure, and she pierced my ears. To finish off, she rubbed down my entire body with exotic-smelling moisturizers and conditioners. Genghis intently watched the whole makeover, occasionally exchanging jokes with Nora. She was skilled. I felt very comfortable in her hands. When I stood up and looked at myself, it felt odd. I appeared much gentler and more androgynous then before.

"'Let Genghis shave the rest tonight. It's gonna look better with the tiny, new panties you'll be wearing from now on.' Nora gave me a suggestive glance and added, 'He likes to be shaved as well.'

"No doubt, I thought, as I recalled that Muslims shave themselves as a part of their Islamic tradition. I began flushing while Genghis stared at me, stunned. Nora pinched and shook his cheek, to snap him out of it.

"'Wait until we apply the make-up and apparel. You'll go crazy.' She winked at me, the way people do when they are satisfied with their achievement.

"She stepped into the back room and came out with an accessories bag. 'We are ready for shopping. Aren't we, Miss Macedonia?' She grinned at me, then at Genghis, who treated us to tea before driving us to a boutique located in the modern quarter of Maçka. My transformation was organized meticulously by Genghis and Nora.

"The owner of the place was a classy, older woman, a friend of Nora's. She helped us a great deal in choosing the right wardrobe. She was good at assisting drag queens and cross dressers with their fashion needs. We selected a white summer minidress, a couple of pairs of hot pants, casual trendy sandals, shirts, padded brassieres, and lingerie. For evening wear, we picked a black minidress and a small purse and black heels to go with it. The owner held the dresses in front of me, exclaiming, 'Wonderful, wonderful.' Two conservative-looking ladies stopped browsing and stared. The owner signaled for Nora and me to go to her office, so I could try the clothes on in private. Everything fit perfectly. The owner had judged my size correctly.

"Nora opened her accessories bag and sat me before the vanity mirror. She applied moisturizing foundation and creamy peach-beige makeup that matched my facial tone. She brushed my face and neck with aromatic light powder, curled my eyelashes, and went over them with mascara. She penciled and stroked my eyebrows, then applied carmine lipstick and coordinated nail polish on my fingernails and toenails.

"While waiting for the polish to dry, the owner observed that my face was made for makeup and that my eyebrows and lips could be easily emphasized.

"'Uh-huh,' Nora confirmed. She gelled my hair back and put the blond wig on me.

"Finally, the moment came for me to see my new self. I couldn't believe what I saw. It exceeded my expectations. I was about 6'2" in my heels. The minidress displayed the glory of my long straight legs and the makeup accentuated the girlish aspect of my already androgynous appearance.

"'I look damn good,' I muttered to myself, and sashayed out of the room with Nora to my right and the owner to my left. A chill passed through my body, as I realized I was entering an unknown realm. Suddenly, I felt frightened by the whole thing. Then I saw Genghis. He leapt from his armchair and his newspaper fell to the floor.

"'You look sensational,' he sighed, and the fear evaporated like ether from me. Customers stopped shopping and stared at me. The sales people looked amazed, as well. Genghis seemed like a contented child who had just won a game. He hugged and kissed me.

"'Let's have dinner together,' he proposed to everyone.

"'Thank you, baby,' Nora said. 'Some other night. Tonight, you two should be alone.' The owner smiled, then Nora added, 'It's gonna be a whole new experience for both of you...Especially for her.' She lifted her eyebrows twice at me.

"Genghis smiled, and I reddened again. We kissed the owner goodbye, then dropped Nora off at her salon. I thought we were going home, but Genghis said, 'You're not complete yet. You need jewelry.' Overwhelmed, I had completely forgotten how much Turkish men, as well as Yugoslavian, loved to buy jewelry for their lovers. It was a symbol of prestige. The more gold on their loved ones, the richer and cockier they felt. So I smiled at him, nodding."

Mila lifted her body slightly from the seat. "You must have looked gorgeous. I can picture you." Her eyes swiftly scanned my frame as she said that. "How did you feel?"

"I felt inexplicably, quaintly different. It was fun to listen to the noise of my heels and feel the fabric of my dress, along with the air caressing my legs through the stockings. Especially that first time, while I was walking in public through the dome-vaulted halls of The Grand Bazaar, the famous Kapali Çarsi. With each passing moment, I felt more comfortable playing the role that Genghis had contrived for me. He was delighted, observing my new body language closely. He squeezed my hand possessively and with pride when men's eyes would lustily take me in, from my toes to my head. They would turn, flirt, whistle, and wink at me in that jungle of gold, kilim, copper, leather, and water pipe stores. Why not take on this role? I thought. It's boring being a male all the time. This was amusing. I laughed, after seeing all those new reactions. I laughed even harder thinking about the people back home and how they would drop dead if they saw me like that. Actually, it would've taken them a while to recognize me. I looked quite convincing.

"The heart of the Grand Bazaar, called Iç Bedesten, was a myriad of goldsmith and jewelry stores. I saw more gold there than I'd ever seen in my life. We entered one store, and the manager greeted Genghis with a hug and a kiss. When he kissed my hand, his lips quivered, and he kept telling Genghis how great I looked.

"After an employee served us tea, Genghis said, 'Pick whatever you want, honey.' It was hard to choose from so many designs of gold combined with any precious stone you could imagine. An emerald set caught my eye.

"When I showed it to Genghis, he said, 'Sold. The emeralds are beautiful, but not nearly as dazzling as your eyes,' then kissed my hand. On the way out, he stopped in front of the case and purchased another contemporary set.

"'To wear during the day,' he explained, smiling and kissing my half-opened lips.

"Words cannot express how liberated I felt when Genghis held my hand before Para Palace, in the elegant suburb of Beyoglu quarter. He explained that the hotel opened in 1892 to welcome passengers from the Orient Express and that many famous people stayed there, including Greta Garbo and Marshal Tito. Amazed by the hotel's period décor, sumptuous ornamentation and engravings, I felt as if I were in another world. All I could do was smile as we ate a first-class meal, accompanied by the music of a live Orchestra.

"During dinner, curious and thinking that the timing was right, I asked him, 'So what do you do for a living?'

"'I'm involved in the auto industry,' he replied quickly. It was obvious he didn't want to go into details. He was right, I thought. Words were superfluous then. They would wreck the rich web of emotions that was forming between us. I felt stupid disturbing it. I said nothing more until we finished dinner. Our appraising glances at each other led to jokes and giggles as we walked out of the hotel, holding hands again.

"'Let me show you Istanbul,' Genghis proposed, and took me to the Panorama Restaurant on top of the Etap Marmara hotel. The city of two continents divided by the Bosphorus was at our feet as we ate dessert. A pianist played Chopin in the background.

"'Who did you have before you met me?' Genghis asked.

"I couldn't spoil that night by sharing my misery with such a kind person. I replied briefly, 'I only had suffering and trouble. I'm free of them now, because of one great lover who made me so happy, I can't even recognize myself.' I kissed my index and middle fingers, then touched the tip of his well-defined nose.

"'Thank you,' he said, extending his hand. He took me onto the floor, and we began to waltz. The ancient, mystical lights of Istanbul were glittered in the background as he kissed me. Again, it felt like we had gone back in time thousands of years, to somewhere in the veiled quarters of the Grand Vizier's palace.

"Every day felt like a holiday, as Genghis showed me his city of thousands of mosques. I would cry with amazement, staring at the elegant minarets against the sky. Being inside one of the most sumptuous temples in the world, Aya Sofya Cami'i, or Divine Wisdom, was an elevating experience. As I walked the grounds of the church-turned-mosque, I could sense the spiritual meeting of the two cultures, the Byzantine Christian and the Ottoman Islamic. Likewise, my Christian and Genghis' Moslem backgrounds were merging as he explained the history of his city and country and led me through the temple, holding my hand tight.

"Everything painful began to vanish. Laughter replaced sorrow. Happiness was all I felt while we played hide-and-seek in the reservoirs and aqueducts of Belgrade Forest, which reminded me so much of my county, Prespa. Enlightened was all I felt while we read poetry to each other at the Byzantine Land Walls and went horseback riding and running on the beaches of Princes' Islands. Romance was all I felt during sunsets, when we kissed quietly and spontaneously as each new star appeared, or when we dined in the splendid gardens among the fountains and the roses of the restaurants overlooking the Bosphorus strait. Lust was all I felt dancing until dawn, holding his erotic body next to mine in Club Maksim, among all those beautiful people and celebrities, or at Club 33 or Galata Tower, a discotheque overlooking the city. Drowsiness was all I felt after attending the shows at the casinos, then going back to his villa in the morning light, where his servant, like a eunuch, revived us with sherbet and tea. Ecstasy was all I felt belly dancing on Genghis' silk and satin bed, which reminded me of a tent in the middle of the Sahara desert. Heat was all I felt while cooled by Genghis' sculpted lips and his long tender touches. Thirst was all I felt ridden on Genghis' strong hands that seemed like columns of camels taking me behind the sandy dunes to his secret oasis. Shielded was all I felt, clenched in his strong arms and legs, while listening to his deep, clean, and confident voice. Spending day after day, night after night with Genghis was addictive, highly addictive. And I welcomed it. I yearned for it."

25

Change

I could sense passion in Mila. I couldn't quite grasp the nature of that passion and towards what it was directed, but the fact of it helped me to analyze her. I could see her beauty breaking many men's hearts and being featured in thousands of their wet fantasies at one time. She could still be a heartbreaker and a wet dream. Seductive people, no matter what their age, are always attractive. I wondered if she would ever win my heart as my mother. Only an idiot wouldn't want to have a beautiful and seductive mother.

She interrupted my thoughts. "I also would've been addicted to Genghis. Who wouldn't want to be with such an ideal lover?"

"Yeah," I sighed. "Genghis was the type who could convert a faithful housewife or a closeted man. He could even turn a nun into a slut, easily. By the way people acted around him, I could tell he was important. I never learned his whole story—only that he was loaded with money. He was evasive. Didn't ask me much about my life, so I didn't ask him. He wanted to keep things quiet. That didn't bother me, though. With him, I had all I wanted. His charisma and virility were infectious. Most important, Genghis was intelligent. He was cosmopolitan. He knew several languages and loved history and travel. The video collection of his trips around the world was impressive. Luckily, I had the chance to know that side of him.

"After exploring Istanbul, we traveled along the Aegean coast. We visited Pergamum with its imposing ruins from the days of Alexander the Great, and the famous Cities of Troy and Ephesus. We stayed in the popular Marmaris resort and bade farewell to fiery sunsets from its medieval fortress. We went further south to the city of Antalya, not far from Cyprus. It was awesome. When Genghis took me shopping, salespeople would grow weary of packing all our purchases. I accumulated an expensive collection of clothes and jewelry. Every time I came out of the dressing room in a new dress, Genghis grew more impressed by my natural ability to adapt to my new image. My walk became elegant and seductive, as I easily became accustomed to my clothing and high heels. Actually, I had always kind of walked on my toes. I felt more comfortable walking that way, particularly as a child, when I sang and danced for hours in front of the mirror in my lonely room. Only a very astute eye could detect that I was a man after I had mastered the role of a woman. It was great acting. It should have been hard for me, for anyone who had never felt like a woman. But in my case, the comfort of escaping my identity overwhelmed any hardship."

"Genghis must have loved to show you off," Mila said.

"A lot." I nodded. "It was the beginning of autumn, during my third month in Turkey, when Genghis told me that his best friend, Osman, was back from Germany and had invited us to his party. He said Osman threw the best parties of all his friends. He asked me to give a lot of thought to what I would wear that night. He wanted me to look my best. He was like any man with a trophy at his side, so I didn't want to disappoint him.

"I did an exhaustive beauty treatment. I changed my hairstyle from blonde to platinum. I had a new, straight wig that fell to my shoulder blades in a leisurely way, giving me a younger look than my wavy wig. I selected a skintight minidress of silver crushed silk with a haltered top, low-cut back, and a slit up the right thigh. It was from Versace, and the Chanel purse and Manolo Blanik matching heels looked stunning with it. While debating what jewelry to wear with it, Genghis surprised me with the most expensive gift I had ever received. It was a platinum set that included a necklace, ring, bracelet, and hoop earrings. I didn't wear the necklace. It was too much with a silver dress. Genghis wasn't insulted. He was confident in my ability to create a tasteful look.

"He looked striking in his dark Armani suit, Bally shoes, and a Versace gold tie that contrasted with his dark eyes. He was ruggedly elegant as he opened the door of his Lamborghini for me. We drove to an area full of dazzling waterside mansions. The gate security examined our invitation, and we entered the splendid grounds of Osman's estate.

"Only in Hollywood movies had I seen so many luxury cars in one place at the same time. The mansion was huge. It was built in an eclectic contemporary and Baroque Ottoman style. The valet took the car keys, and two handsome door attendants welcomed us into the big marble vestibule. Fancy hors d'oeuvres and drinks were offered by servants whose uniforms matched the neo-classical interior. Each corner of the room had a piece of sculpture in it, and its walls were decorated with beautiful paintings.

"The party featured a variety of entertainment in different parts of the mansion. There was a live band playing traditional music, a disc jockey playing a mix of pop, rock, and dance tracks, and a number of dancers and singers performing. The crowd was as glamorous as the ambiance, a mixture of straights, gays, transvestites, and foreigners, both young and old. Genghis said artists and celebrities were occasional guests at Osman's parties.

"We were about to raise a toast when a third person came up behind me and joined us. It was our host. Osman was Genghis' contemporary, a preppie, business type, with dark hair combed to the side and a thick mustache that intensified his typical Turkish appearance. Genghis introduced me as Miss Macedonia.

"Osman kissed my hand and exclaimed, 'Ancient and exotic Macedonia. The land of one of the most powerful emperors of all time, Alexander. The one I adore and with whom I am proud to share a special trait: the desire to screw beautiful guys,' he laughed.

"The guests who overheard him chortled. I was impressed by his boldness. All wealthy people should have such nerve and be as open about their sexuality. I smiled at him.

"'You're one of the best companions Genghis has brought to my parties, Miss Macedonia,' Osman complimented me, pronouncing my name as if I were a countess in exile from the former Kingdom of Yugoslavia.

"'Thank you,' I said, blushing. 'But now you have me wondering how many more companions Genghis has brought here before me?'

"'Well. Let me think…Best not to get into it,' Osman said, laughing. 'Please make yourselves comfortable and enjoy the party. I'll see you in a while.' He hugged us, then melted into the crowd to welcome his guests.

"I smirked at Genghis, which was stupid and immature of me. Just from looking at him, it was clear that he could have anyone he wanted. He twitched his left eyebrow and pulled something out of his pocket. A neatly engraved platinum cigarette holder glittered in his palm. He placed my burning cigarette in it and kissed my cheek.

"'Now, my baby is complete,' he said. I said nothing.

"I let him lead me to his friends, who were waving at us. It was Nora with her quiet boyfriend, Doctor Ali, and a stockbroker, Suleiman, with his elegant and sickly possessive wife. Oh, my goodness, she couldn't stand me. She eyed me jealously throughout the night.

"'Excuse me, gentlemen. Time to fix our makeup,' Nora announced, taking my hand. Before the toilet mirror, she sounded like a madam when she said, 'Men are checking you out from head to toe. You look like a bitch that would never be kept in the kitchen. I like it. It intimidates them, but they can't help craving you. If you had come here alone, they would've been all over you in a second.'

"'Thanks to you,' I said, then added, 'I hope Genghis doesn't regret spending all that money, if all these men want me.'

"'Oh, no. Absolutely not. Don't worry about him. He's loaded. A little jealous, but he's mad about you. Just be careful not to make a mistake when guys start coming on to you,' Nora advised, while powdering her face.

"Walking back to our group, I paid close attention and noticed that men were undressing me with wolf-like eyes. Women never looked at men that way, but had equally dangerous fox-like looks. I saw the difference that was the basis for an old stereotype: that men are dogs, always ready for action, and women are bitches, always ready for lifetime satisfaction. The deejay began heating up the atmosphere with a blend of Turkish, European, and American pop. Nora and her boyfriend, and Suleiman and his wife, began to dance. Genghis and I joined them.

"'You drive me crazy,' Genghis whispered, kissing my ear. He moved in perfect time with the swing of my shoulders and hips. Whenever Genghis' acquaintances commented or signaled that he'd made a fine choice, he would squeeze my hand. He did that frequently when men complimented or made a pass at me. Suddenly, a cute guy around my age jumped into our dancing circle, and Genghis' body became affixed to mine. When the guy began to hang around me, Genghis pulled me out of the hall, saying that he needed fresh air.

"In the topiary garden, he said, 'If that prick shows up near you again, I'll break his neck!'

"'You're jealous? That's silly. He's a young, horny chicken. Let him have fun,' I said, smiling. 'I've never liked immature guys. They're dull. No way could he ever be your competition. Few men can compare with you, my love.'

"Genghis' face lit up. He plucked a rose and gave it to me. As our lips met I thought, 'I'm lucky that I'm attracted to older men. With a young jerk, I wouldn't have the security, the knowledge, and the politeness that mature men offer. Not to mention the huge gifts.' I guess, in some way, I was looking for a father figure. Many people, if not most, are attracted to those like their parents. They want to find someone who will repair the damages their parents have done to them. Sounds pathetic, yet it's a natural thing. I was justifying my actions as if I were committing a crime, because all my life I was told that getting involved with an older person was wrong and unnatural and that only gold diggers did that."

Mila, shaking her head, broke in, "No. It's not a crime. It's natural to do it. I married an older man. I mean, I thought he was older. When you're in the blossom of your youth, everyone over thirty seems old."

"I never saw it that way," I said. "And I never went with them because of the money. Even now, I can't picture myself with chickens, no matter how hot they are. Older people have wisdom, and I can never get enough of that. Besides, maybe I'm still looking for a daddy. Actually, you know I'm looking for a father." I hesitated, wondering if I'd approached the subject too suddenly, too directly.

Silence. Mila's posture straightened. Her left leg began trembling. She embraced my old toy.

"Who doesn't look for the father we never had. We all do...So what happened at the party?" she asked changing the subject anxiously, and lit a cigarette.

Well, I thought, she's not ready to tell me about my father. But she will before she leaves!

"There were buffets of international cuisine arranged in the east wing of the mansion," I said, continuing my story. "The food was exquisite. Sauntering through one of the hallways, I happened to see myself in a mirror.

"'Mirror, mirror...' I whispered, but didn't need to finish the phrase. I looked awesome.

"I smiled at my own vanity. No wonder people were appraising me with their eyes as if they were tailors sizing me up. No wonder Genghis' curious acquaintances practically ran to meet me and would start to gossip the moment we turned our backs. Even to myself, I was a total surprise. I really looked fabulous. I had more confidence in myself than ever. I didn't need to worry that others wouldn't want me and I would end up alone like before, when my parents bragged how adorable I was, but still I had no friends. Then Genghis, the one who taught me to adore myself without doubt, was next to me, grasping my hand. I stood on my toes and kissed him. He smiled and kissed me back, then guided me to the grand room where a traditional Turkish band was playing. Three exotic belly dancers performed on the center stage. One of them was a transsexual. After the dancers, a young man sang modern Turkish folk songs to taped music. Osman was near the stage, talking to a group of guests. As soon as he noticed us, he came over and asked me, 'Are you enjoying the party, Miss Macedonia?'

"'Fully. Merci,' I said in French, as most Istambulis would often do.

"'I've heard you like dancing and singing. A lot,' he said.

"'Who doesn't?' I replied, jesting.

"'Let Osman's guests see you how good you are,' Genghis suggested.

"'Are you crazy? I'm not a professional performer!'

"'Most entertainers sing to a tape, as you can see.' Osman smiled.

"'You wouldn't understand the lyrics and or know the music anyway,' I said, blushing.

"'Wrong. We get lots of music from Yugoslavia. Especially Bosnian, Macedonian, and Serbian, which has lots of Turkish influence. I love your biggest star, Lepa Brena. I know you love her, too,' Osman said.

"'I'm amazed you know that,' I said, adding facetiously, 'Genghis probably told you what color underwear I'm wearing tonight?'

"'He's like my brother. We grew up together.' Osman tapped Genghis' collar.

"As I stood between them and listened to them joke with each other, I felt their true friendship. I envied it, since I'd never had one.

"'Try it. I'll get your tapes from the car,' Genghis said enthusiastically.

"I shook my head. 'Come on, Genghis! Don't be ridiculous!'

"'Please do it for us,' Genghis urged. 'You'll make them go mad here.'

"It was obvious that they had pre-arranged the whole thing. My fright was off-set by my desire to make Genghis happy. I thought of how much it excited him when he had me sing, dance, and strip before we made love, or when he showed me off and teased other men.

"When I nodded my assent, Genghis and Osman got impatient like children visiting a candy shop. Genghis ran to the car and brought out two of my tapes: one of Lepa Brena and another by Madonna.

"Osman said, 'We have the same taste. I mean in music. Ha, ha,' and escorted me to the deejay's cabin. I told him to set up Brena's song first, one called 'Sheiky,' a cute expression for the 'Sheik,' then Madonna's 'Burning Up.'

"Two girls finished performing, and Osman asked me if I was ready. I took a deep breath and nodded. He held my hand and we climbed onto the stage. Saluting the guests, he announced me as 'a surprise from Macedonia.' People applauded. I handed my purse to Osman, then took the microphone from his hand. I realized I was still had my cigarette holder in my hand, so I quickly stuck it in my bra. Standing before that expectant crowd, I felt as if I were in Madison Square Garden. Genghis gave me the 'thumbs-up.' With a flock of butterflies in my stomach, I signaled to the deejay. The exotic Yugo-Turkish-Arabic tune started, and I began to lip-synch a song about a black-eyed, wealthy sheik who fell in love at the first sight of me; who asked me to pay homage to him, to give him my face and body and accelerate his heart rhythm, and who offered his treasure without asking about the cost.

"I finished the first verse, still tense. The crowd began dancing and clapping. I loosened up and gradually began moving my body to the beat. The refrain followed: 'Hey Sheiky, Sheiky, I swear to your Allah, to get me won't be anything chic, since I'll bring you over to the suitor's stick.' The swing of my hips, shoulders, and hands intensified as the second verse began about the sheik going mad for me and sacrificing his powerful hoard and shaking his loaded pockets to solve my all problems, swearing to his brothers that he'll give away all his black gold and Bedouins to make his wish come true, to possess me.

"Genghis and Osman jumped on the stage and squatted to either side of me. They began clapping and spreading their arms wide, while I gyrated between them. I performed *Chochek*, our version of Turkish belly dancing that was inspired by the Ottomans. During the second refrain, I made the audience scream, lip-synching: 'The Sheik doesn't know my wishes, nor does he know how things work here. Even if he owns all of Kuwait, with me, he'll end up without it.' Then the final verse, as a chorus, was the Sheik's response: 'I swear to my brother, I don't have that much black gold. Your wishes are bigger than my crazy heart for you.'

"The song ended, and applause blasted through the hall. More guests from the other halls came. Genghis and Osman kissed each of my hands, then left the stage as Madonna's 'Burning Up' began. I ran to the edge of the stage and grabbed a chair. Straddling the chair, I began riding it. Thanks to the slit in my dress, my legs were able to move up and down with ease. Sweat began pouring from me. In a mirror, I could see my back muscles tightening and the bare skin glistening enticingly. The crowd became ecstatic. I was delighted to look professional, not outrageous and grotesque like many drag queens. I didn't feel like either a woman or a man. I was a pure exhibitionist, trained to do this at the parties my parents attended, where I was forced to recite poems, play the heavy accordion, know the names of all the presidents in the world, and take my clothes off after government officials and their wives placed bets on what gender I was. Who am I? I asked myself, moving my body to the beat. I'm a fusion of four influences: two from my adopters and two from my unknown creators. I'm the product of two mothers and two fathers.

"As the song ended, people clapped loudly, wanting more of me. It felt exactly like it did when I performed at those government parties, when I would blush, yet feel like a little star. The flashback was fun, but confusing. It felt like I had thousands of aspects to my personality, and I would never be able to discover them all in one lifetime. We're such complicated creatures, and our lives are so short. Sometimes, we shorten our lives even more by not enjoying them, while trying to understand and fix our messes, the left overs from our childhood. Questions about myself plagued me that night. But I tried not to over-analyze myself, and enjoy my life.

"'Great. The songs suit you perfectly. You should consider doing that professionally,' Genghis said, as he took my hand and escorted me from the stage to the bar. 'We have many popular entertainers who are gay, drag queens, and even transsexuals. Turks respect talent, no matter where it comes from.'

"'Maybe I'll try it one day.' I smiled, thinking of Bulent Ersoy, one of the most popular Turkish singers. He had a powerful voice and a sex change that turned him into a beautiful woman. He/she was known all over the Balkans and beyond."

"I would've loved to see you," Mila said eagerly. "Do you have any pictures?"

"I had, but they disappeared. My parents probably found where I hid them and burned them. I never asked. Can you imagine me asking them? 'Mother, Father, where are those pictures of me as a hot, stunning drag queen?' They would've had heart attacks."

Mila laughed, shaking her head. She seemed young, like a teenaged girl.

"It was a happy time. I have wonderful memories of those days. When I'm down, I think about them and cheer up…Well, to continue, the happy times rolled on with Genghis. I almost forgot about home, except when I would call my parents once in a while to let them know I was alive. I stuck to my bartender story, whether they liked it or not. I enjoyed the total control I had over my situation.

"On days that Genghis had business, I would read, write poems, or paint in the rose garden or on the terrace overlooking the Bosphorus. In between, I would take relaxing walks around the area. I'd have fun, watching movies, working in the garden, or playing chess with the maid. She had a great sense of humor and made excellent cookies. Every Monday I'd usually go shopping and get my beauty treatment at Nora's. Every Sunday night, Genghis would leave a pile of money on my boudoir table. When I gave him the balance, he only smiled and shook his head. After a while, I accumulated quite a sum. He didn't care. His main concern was how many men approached me.

"I would tease him, complaining that it was too bad I couldn't do anything. I was always watched closely by his moody servant, who wouldn't let me exchange a single glimpse or smile with anyone. Genghis, as an insecure, jealous chauvinist, acted like all Balkan men and was convinced it was all right for men to fool around but never for women. October passed, and my parents were beside themselves that I remained in Turkey. One quiet and otherwise ordinary night, Genghis and I were having Ottoman-style boiled beef at the Orient House when he said, 'I want you to marry me.'

"'What? Marry you? But I'm not a woman,' I said, stunned.

"'I can turn you into one. Easy. I'll pay for your sex change. I know a great doctor. Then I can marry you with no problem.'

"'What the hell are you talking about! I don't want to be a woman. Aren't you satisfied with me?'

"He was surprised. It was the first time I'd raised my voice to him.

"'Ever since I saw you, I can't fuck anyone else,' he said, intently. 'You have no clue how many times I jerk off thinking of you. I want to marry you legally. I love you. I want to take you to Morocco and have the wedding at my villa in Casablanca.'

"'No, no, no. I don't want to be a woman. This is just a game. Thanks for the proposal, Genghis, but you really don't get it.'

"I threw my fork, knife, and napkin on the table and walked outside. Istanbul's lights were blurry. I felt the familiar touch of Genghis, embracing me from behind.

"'I didn't mean to upset you or make you sad. I just want to keep you with me, forever. I love you.'

"'I love you, too,' I said, as I spun around in his arms and hugged him back.

"'I have never seen you cry. Even disturbed, your beautiful eyes sparkle like polished emeralds after the rain. I love to watch them. I want to see them from dawn to dusk,' he whispered. He kissed my forehead, then the tip of my nose, then my eyes, and he escorted me back to the restaurant.

"That night, I faked making love with him. I couldn't sleep. I was analyzing my situation. I loved the proposal, but I hated the idea. Almost every day afterwards, Genghis mentioned the sex change and tried to convince me to turn myself into a 'woman' and marry him. He promised absolute loyalty and protection. He said that the biggest benefit for me was that it would be put an end to my troubled life in Macedonia, and I could begin a new, carefree, exciting, and glamorous one. He seemed serious. I was so uncertain. I couldn't function normally after a while. That didn't last long, though.

"Two weeks later, on one of those picture-perfect mornings, as I strolled around the neighborhood, a blue Maserati cut me off as I crossed a small bridge. The car pulled to the side of the road, and a dazzling-looking woman got out. Her long, silky black hair moved alluringly as she walked towards me. Her perfect porcelain skin was a striking contrast to her dark glasses, and when she took them off, her big, dark eyes glowed with sadness.

"'My name is Leyla. I'm Genghis' wife,' she said, gently extending her hand.

"'What?' I said, although I'd heard her well enough.

"'Yes. I'm Genghis' wife and we have two children. Right now, he's with one of them at the dentist. Later, he has to do some shopping for them, so he'll be home late. I finally decided to meet you and tell you what's going on. I couldn't call you. The maid would recognize my voice. Let's go to a safe place and talk. You never know who might see us.'

"We got in her car and drove off. I said nothing. She was speeding and seemed nervous. She stopped at a place that looked like an abandoned park. It scared me. It reminded me of the forest near my town, where I would go to hide from people during my lonely days.

"'I can't believe Genghis was lying to me all this time,' I said.

"She nodded. 'He probably told you he does business when he's away from home. In fact, he doesn't need to work. He is very wealthy. We broke up when he began cheating with my best girlfriend two years ago. Since then, we have separated. Their relationship didn't last long. He caught her sleeping with his friends. Then Genghis got involved with a beautiful young Frenchman. He convinced him to have a sex change operation, promising him marriage and a lavish lifestyle. Shortly after the operation, Genghis accused 'her' of being unfaithful and ended it. So I'm here to tell you the truth before you do something you may regret later.'

"'Thank you. You're very kind. I never would've imagined this. I've noticed people tended to gossip about me, and I doubted that it was only because of my looks. They were probably sorry for you and ridiculing me as some provincial Balkan whore in drag.' I lit a cigarette.

"'Who cares what they thought? My friends told me that you're good looking. Honestly, you look striking as a woman.' She smiled and lit a cigarette, also.

"'Thank you. We're fools, but we're both fine. I can't believe he'd want someone else after having you. Well, it's obvious now that Genghis wants variety, especially a he/she combination."

"'I can't blame him for it. I understand. The thing that hurts me most is that he never told me his wishes.' Leyla said, dragging hard on the cigarette.

"'Did he ever ask you for a divorce?'

"'Yes.' Her eyes filled with tears.

"I took her hand and said sharply, 'Oh please. The asshole doesn't deserve a single tear from us. Look at you! Look at me! Any man would love to have us. Come on, girl! Cheer up!'

"Leyla laughed, but I'll bet she wouldn't have if she'd known how hurt I was and the strength it took for me to comfort her.

"'I wish I could be strong like you, Miss Macedonia. I care for Genghis. He's good to the children. He still completely supports me.' Her face turned serious.

"'Well, think twice about why I'm so strong,' I said, glancing towards my crotch. 'Maybe I should open a school for dumped women!' I laughed at my silly joke.

"She laughed even harder, but her face became sober when she asked me, 'What are you going to do?'

"'Leave him. What else? I've stayed here too long anyway. I don't want a sex change, and I'm not afraid that Genghis can force me to do it. I just don't want to wake up next to a person who is a complete stranger now. I don't trust him. It's over.'

"'Maybe he really loves you. Maybe you would be happy together. I don't want to be the cause of your break-up, believe me. I want Genghis to be happy. I also don't want your feelings towards him to change because of me. All I wanted was to tell you the truth, so you could decide for yourself.'

"'Thanks again,' I said. 'I believe you. Leyla, I can usually recognize phonies even staring down at people from an airplane. But with Genghis I failed…Well, enough man grieving. Let's have fun and do some shopping.'

"'And damage,' Leyla added with a nefarious expression, as she opened her purse, took out Genghis' platinum credit card, and waved it.

"'With pleasure,' I said, laughing. 'You're getting better girlfriend.'

"We drove to Taksim Square, then took a *dolmush*, a communal taxi, to Teshfikiye, one of the chic suburbs jammed with Westernized shops and boutiques. We had a blast loading the car with imported luxury goods and flirting with men at the bar of the Haci Baba restaurant, near the gorgeous French consulate. Before parting, we exchanged numbers. As we hugged and kissed good-bye, a passing man commented that he'd love to join us. We both giggled and called him a dog. As I turned to wave to Leyla, I could see she was crying. It wasn't easy for her to put up with Genghis or to tell me all those things. She still loved him. I burst into tears.

"When I got back to Genghis' villa, I forced a grin as I stepped inside. The maid informed me that Genghis had called and wanted me to be ready to have dinner at one of the floating restaurants on the Bosphorus. That night, as we dined, I held in my tears and planned my trip back home. Genghis noticed something wasn't right. When he asked me, I told him I had a headache. A week later, I scheduled my flight to Belgrade. I couldn't go back home right away, but I couldn't imagine myself either staying in Turkey or being with someone else. I loved him.

"Our last day was one of the most romantic in my life. I insisted he take me back to Dolmabahçe Palace, the grandest of the imperial Ottoman residences. The building was a white marble beauty, constructed in baroque classical style by sultan Abdül Mecit. It seemed as if it was dancing with the Bosphorus. Once again, I felt like I'd gone back in time. I was captivated by the palace's extravagant Indies' adornments, the murals by Russian and Italian artists, and the rococo Baccarat crystal chandeliers. All that beauty dispelled my blues and elevated my spirit. I took in every bit of it, gripping Genghis' hand firmly as we exchanged glances with passion and lust as we used to. It was a sweet denial.

"The night was as wonderful as the day. He put Johann Strauss' Blue Danube on his stereo and we waltzed through the corridors of his villa as if we were at the Viennese imperial ball. Then, he lifted me in his arms and carried me into the bedroom. He laid me gently in the middle of the royal blue silk and satin bed and lit candles placed on every flat surface in the room. It looked glorious and mystical. The many reflections of the candle flames on our bodies were like brilliant tongues, enhancing our lovemaking in the seductive, royal blue darkness.

"'You have an aristocratic bearing,' Genghis said, 'in your movements and your features. Has anyone ever told you this?'

"'Only two people who meant it. My mother and an artist, a sculptor.' I looked out the window, past the lights reflecting on the Bosphorus, towards Macedonia.

"'I love you. Truly.' Genghis whispered.

"At that moment, bitter reality transcended my dream state, and all I felt was terribly hurt.

"'What is true love?' I asked the darkness.

"'True love is when the most beautiful and tempting creation stands before me and I refuse to touch it. I just leave, thinking only of one who is better, who is more important than any excuse for delusion, deception, and betrayal. You, my love,' Genghis answered.

"He was the darkness, glittering with royal blue sweat. I wrestled with my craving for Genghis and my wanting to spurn him. My body floated in ecstasy between the light and the darkness, while I concealed doleful thoughts of never seeing Genghis again. The funeral of our relationship took place in that bedroom of royal blue candles, silk, and satin. I might have had a future with Genghis, I thought. Whenever someone or something approaches perfection, someone or something else will come along and destroy it. In real life, perfection cannot exist. I had to go.

"The morning I left, I ordered the taxi to pick me up from the street, out of sight of the house. I tucked my jewelry, money, and passport in a fitness bag and left the mansion in my jogging suit, so as not to provoke suspicion. The maid was supervising the cleaning service in the upper quarter, and the servant was doing something in the garage. Neither of them noticed anything unusual.

"The flight was that afternoon. I picked up my ticket at the agency and went to bid farewell to Istanbul at one of my favorite places: Sultan Ahmed Cami'I, the Blue Mosque. As I strolled through the grand and elegant architectural marvel, memories haunted me. Once more, my romantic feelings towards Genghis were revived as I passed the Mosque's spacious courtyard. Maybe he was serious and loved me and was afraid he'd lose me if he told the truth. I would never know for sure. But he *had* lied to me, and the thought of changing my sex for someone I didn't know was unbearable, even had I wanted to be a female. In addition, I felt guilt staying with him after meeting his wife. Even though he didn't love her anymore, it felt strange to be part of such a situation. I was too young to handle it.

"When the Blue Mosque's magnificent series of domes and its slender minarets were out of sight, I felt as if I had just arrived in Istanbul, as if I were starting over and I was going to meet Genghis again. When I stopped the taxi on the street where everything had begun, I realized that the happiness was over and I'd probably never experience such joy again. It was tough to leave, to forget, to be without Genghis, even tougher to stay calm at the airport, as I waited for my flight. In the lavatory I dumped my wig in the trash, wiped the make-up from my face, and, again, I was who I was. It felt bizarre staring at my former self. The flight was short, but it seemed long, because I couldn't wait to land even though, the thought of going back to my old identity was scary. The transition was not easy. Not at all."

26

Belgrade

Raising her eyebrows, Mila said, "Wow. What an experience."

"Unforgettable," I said, yawning. I thought: Would Mila have let her *will* shape her decisions as I had? If she had a strong will, she would never have let me go. I guess I inherited my strong will from the other side, the unknown one.

"We should sleep. It's almost dawn," she said.

"It would be a healthy sleep, after refreshing my mind with the beautiful memories of Istanbul and Turkey." I yawned again and stood up.

"For me, too, dreaming of being in your place with Genghis." She smiled.

"You wish, ah?" I asked her, jesting.

"I do. May I?" She stood up.

I hugged her. The rosy Macedonian dawn tinted her sleepy face. As I kissed her good night, she hugged me tight and began to cry. Her tears sprang from combined pain, guilt, and optimism that one day she would win my heart as my mother. I pulled away from her hug and she followed me down the hall. Before entering the bedroom, she whispered, smiling, "Sweet dreams of Istanbul."

"Sweet dreams of Genghis," I whispered back, laughing. It felt great to see her face animated and relaxed. We both needed some gaiety for a change.

After a few hours' sleep, I took care of Mother's regular maintenance. She was very quiet. She asked me for additional methadone drops, then curled up in bed after nibbling a tiny slice of French toast.

Mila was waiting up in my room. "Good morning. How's your mother?" she asked.

"Depressed and in pain."

"You should stay with her."

"She sleeps. Drugged. The cancer is merciless." I felt so frustrated. I wanted to throw the tray with her breakfast and coffee to the floor. Instead, I sat and vigorously moved to-and-fro in my rocker.

"Did you dream about Istanbul?" Mila changed the subject to divert me from my hopelessness.

"No. How about you? Did you dream about Genghis?" I asked.

"Unfortunately not. I dreamt about taking a long trip with you, somewhere far. I didn't recognize the place." She took a bite of her bagel.

"I dreamt of Belgrade and boating on the Danube to the Black Sea. I woke up as I was reaching nowhere in particular," I said frustrated.

"Back to your roots, to the place where everything began for you and me." She sipped her coffee and lit a cigarette. "Tell me what happened after you left Turkey?"

I also had some coffee and lit a cigarette before I resumed my story, "Once in Belgrade, I put my jewelry and money into a safe deposit box. I bought some clothes and checked in at the Hotel Moscow, a block from Knez Mihaila Street, a principal thoroughfare. I realized right away that the hotel's famous confectionery and coffee bar was a main gay hangout. The city had no official gay club, but two of them were known to be gay friendly: Academia, a rock and new-wave place, and the Majestic, a trendy club. It was easy to tell the gays from the straights. The gays danced a lot in comparison to the straights, who paraded around trying to look as macho as possible. Meanwhile, the girls danced with each other, seducing and showing off. There were many handsome men around. Most of them sat in a typical Balkan manner, with their legs spread, exposing their crotches. They drank, smoked, flirted, and ran their fingers through their hair a lot. Many of them were magnificent on the surface, but none stirred feelings in me the way Genghis had. Apart from looking great, Genghis was mature. Nothing and no one could compare to him.

"November passed, and winter approached. I spent a lot of time visiting historical sites and museums. For the first time, I enjoyed my loneliness. One day, I was getting cigarettes from a vending machine, and as I pressed the button, the box got stuck. The guy behind me kicked the machine and the box fell into the dispenser. He handed it to me and we began chatting. We ended up having a drink at the bar.

"Mrki was his name. He was a seventeen-year-old, hot, Montenegrin hustler. He worked at a secret bordello in the neighboring town of Zemun, to support his wife and children in Southern Serbia. He was a hard worker, always anxious to make money. Unfortunately, the owner was cheating him. Mrki had to work extra on the side. His clients were mostly government officials and company directors, and occasionally, when luck was on his side, foreigners who paid well. I never realized until I met him that this underground world existed in a country that was so strictly against prostitution and drugs.

"Mrki took me to private parties held by his clients in the most exclusive quarter of Belgrade, Dedinje, where for the first time I met real descendants of the old Yugoslav aristocracy. They still radiated their status, old money, high education, and class, despite the fact that the communist government had confiscated their property after World War II and their titles were swept away. In those pro-Western circles, no one called anyone 'Comrade.' Messieurs, mesdames, counts, and countesses, that was all I heard. People were distinguished and sophisticated, speaking French and English to their Western guests. They accepted homosexuality with no problem. It was amazing to see how our old society was still percolating under the soil of our so-called 'classless system,' socialism.

"New Year's of 1988 arrived, and I celebrated in the former Yugoslav Mecca of tourism, Dubrovnik, after Mrki continually told me how much fun it was to spend the holidays there. Its fortress was impressively decorated and jam-packed with guests ready to party. I paid for everything, and I didn't mind a bit. Mrki had a tough life and he was my friend. Our friendship didn't last long, however. He met a loaded German tourist and stayed with him. I returned to the capital right after New Year's Day. Belgrade in winter looked romantic, with its Kalemegdan Fortress that seemed as if it was waltzing with the Blue Danube River. But Belgrade wasn't Istanbul. Genghis wasn't there. On top of that, I realized that meeting new people couldn't repair the parental damages that made me trust them too much and tolerate the hurt and disappointment that they caused me so easily. I realized that, with my constant escapes, I couldn't address the source of my misery, my parents. I needed to impress upon them that I wasn't their possession, but a human being. Finally, I realized that I had to face my fear and fight against it. I said good-bye to the statue of the Messenger of Victory, rising up before the city, and flew back to Macedonia."

Mila tears sparkled on her cheeks. "Your poor parents must've been dying to see you."

"They almost fainted when I showed up unannounced. They hugged me for hours, thanking me over and over for my return. They looked ill. The neighbors told me they had not left the house since I was gone. The locals' rumors that I abandoned them after finding my biological parents had thrown them into a deep depression. Almost everyone tried to gain my confidence and find out if all that crap was true. It was ridiculous.

"Mother had four letters for me from Genghis. She told me someone had called a number of times, asking for me in different languages. I burned the letters. I couldn't build a future on something that was over. I had to bury my past and keep going. I was certain of that.

"That evening, I went to pick up a special cake Mother had ordered for my arrival. People stared at me, as I expected they would. My depilated face looked quite different than before, and they acted as if they'd never seen anything like it. Thank goodness it was winter, and no one could see my hairless body, or the locals would've put up billboards of me around town and my parents would both have had strokes.

"The town hadn't changed. It never changed. A couple with a small child giggled and stared at me as I approached. I eyed the man provocatively and licked my lips. I enjoyed watching the fear that put in his wife's expression. She pulled her child towards her, as if I were a kidnapper.

"I winked at the man and whispered like Marilyn Monroe, 'Why didn't you show up last night at our spot, baby?'

"Oh God, the woman freaked out. The man was speechless. The child clung to the woman's dress. She began yelling at her husband. I couldn't resist egging them on even more.

"'Junior,' I said to the child, 'you'll be at my door one day. You'll see. You're too young now, but I'll wait for you.'

"The mother almost fainted. The father acted like a rooster with its head cut off. The child started crying. I strolled off before a crowd could gather around the distraught family. I felt like I could fly. Cruel? Yes. However, nothing compares with putting stupid people in their place. I needed it.

"Everything was as it used to be for *Koleda*, the day before our Orthodox Christmas. Children ran from door to door, collecting money and chestnuts. Throughout the holy night, they gathered around bonfires, loudly bragging and counting their little profits. The Christmas Eve dinner consisted of homemade leavened bread with a coin hidden inside. Mother strictly adhered to the tradition of rotating the shallow bread pot three times, and as always, she did it in a way that would let me find the coin in a flash.

"On January seventh, Christmas Day, Father made fun of the holiday and religion, as he always had in the past. Mother ran to church early that morning to light candles and thank Jesus for bringing me back home. Now, when I look back, I realize how much more sensible our humble Christmas was compared to the one in America, with the paganish character of Santa Claus and the buying-selling frenzy that has nothing to do with celebrating the birth of Jesus. The major holy holiday in America is a contradictory mix of Christian fundamentals and greed. All it does is line the pockets of businessmen, not to mention the already wealthy churches.

"Father would invariably interrogate the religious freaks. 'Why don't you build shelters and hospitals to help the unfortunate instead of fancy churches, if you're so just? You're contradicting yourselves. It's all lies and bullshit!'

"He was absolutely right. Religion is a purely human-made entertainment, a form of therapy, and, worst of all, a business machine. I saw that more clearly after going to America and finding thousands of different churches, where they held fancy ceremonies and collected huge amounts of money, even danced and sang as if they were holding concerts rather than a holy spiritual gathering. It was so different from our humble ways: praying and dropping some change in the wooden box of our modest, ancient churches. It was as illogical as the faith itself. I was shocked.

"It was pathetic but funny to see my parents desperately trying to maintain the fiction that everything was normal. They knew I wasn't a bartender in Turkey, yet they acted as if I had been one and bragged to everyone about what a workaholic I was, earning my first paycheck. They were infuriated that I was so far behind in my studies, but they hid it and were pleased when I asked to transfer to law school that February. They even found a connection I could use to enroll in the new school. She was Mother's high-school friend, a secretary there. The transfer, which would normally take a month, was processed within a day through her. My parents also found me a room to rent. It was a basement studio in a house owned by an old, almost deaf, woman with a mean, black Angora cat as her only companion. The room was dark and extremely cold because it was next to the garage and the storage room. It was so small that my bed plus a small table and two chairs were the only furniture I could fit in it. The landlady was terribly cheap and would only allow me to use her shower once or twice a month. I was grateful for the sink in the tiny lavatory attached to my room. It was very difficult, but it was still much better than being stuck in my hometown. With the money and jewelry I got from Genghis, I could've rented a better place. Instead, I decided to save my little fortune, which after Belgrade consisted mostly of jewelry, for rainy days and my eventual escape to the West.

"The law college was huge, public, and diverse. Nothing like The Center. It was located in the Saints Cyril and Methodius University, thirty minutes away from my place by bicycle. I began my second year after my credits were transferred and attended the boring classes only to be nice to my parents. I ate in the student cafeteria. My parents' allowance was just enough for food, necessary clothes, books, and rent. I had to use my savings for fun and extra fashions. My parents thought that if I had money, I would pay men for sex. That's how most Macedonians perceive male homosexuality. I guess that's because men are usually more willing to pay for sex than women.

"I panicked when I spent the cash and I sold the emerald set. To preserve my savings, I decided to work at the Student Cooperative. I always craved indepen dence. That was one of my very American traits, and it made me proud, even if no one else in our socialist society gave a damn about it. Usually, only students with connections could get jobs in the Student Cooperative, and the irony was that most of them didn't need the money. It was pure depravity. I used Father's reputation and got a job in a bank. A month later, my career was over. Someone with better connections replaced me. The Cooperative never called me again. I didn't push. Working in the Cooperative was considered low class, and my parents would've been ashamed if they had found out. I'd given them enough trouble. I decided not to disturb them anymore and studied hard, mostly to restore their lost hopes in me.

"My hopes were already lost in the University, which was just as corrupt as our decaying political system. Exchange students, mainly from the Middle East, Greece, and Africa, were being given diplomas without speaking a word of any Yugoslavian language by bribing our sinister professors with their valuable foreign currencies. Domestic students also paid professors off, usually with produce or providing labor on their properties, even with sexual favors. The poor, the honorable, and the ugly ones had to rely solely on discipline and hard study. As the economic crisis worsened, more students dropped out because they were unable to afford room and board, even though their education was free. Things were changing dramatically for worse."

Mila face looked grim, even a little fearful. I figured she was mentally reliving the time when the economic crisis spread like cholera around Yugoslavia. People panicked. It was the beginning of the end. But few realized it, unfortunately.

"Mother insisted I visit them for Easter and celebrate Jesus' resurrection," I continued. "She was convinced that I was back to normal, thanks to He who helped me on his birthday.

"Easter Saturday, after dinner, as we cracked open the Easter eggs Mother had dyed scarlet red, I said, 'I want to tell you something very important.'

"Both of them looked at me as if I were about to admit I was a serial killer. They could tell I was serious and they were terrified of what I might say or do.

My father sat straight up on the couch. Mother looked like she had stopped breathing.

"'I want a man instead of a woman,' I said.

"'No, it can't be true!' Mother wailed. 'You lie! You're making it up! You've had many girls. It can't be true!'

"She got up and began to walk around the room, howling and hugging me from time to time as if I were going to die. My father was numbed, from Mother's madness and my boldness. He knew exactly what was happening, and I'll bet he regretted telling me once about those cute German prisoners he captured and fucked during World War II because of lack of women.

"Mother couldn't wait until midnight to celebrate Jesus' resurrection with the locals. She called Bisera and told her she had to go to church immediately.

"'Oh, I hope Jesus will listen and fulfill my wish tonight. I will beg Him to help you, to cure you!' she said, directing her remarks to the ceiling.

"My father interjected loudly, 'Beg who? The icons? The woods? And kiss them! Will you throw money in the dirty, piggish priests' pockets, so those fuckin' fat farts can spend it on vacations? Insane woman! It's paganism! It's a ritual! It's organized crime! The church only steals your money! It has nothing to do with Jesus!'

"'Oh, leave me alone, you heretic!' Mother clamored back.

"'Just get out my face and go circle those wooden, crucified dolls of Jesus around the damned church! Go and be fooled by those damned priests, who don't even know the psalms and sing like donkeys while they collect your money in the name of Jesus! Go entertain yourself by crushing and exchanging dyed eggs! Go to your fucking therapy with your pathetic and hopeless friends!' Father choked from screaming.

"'Why are you ruining this holiday?' Mother asked in despair. 'It's just four hours before the time that the Holy Son was resurrected. Please, stop it.'

"'Resurrected, wake up from death, my ass!' Father shouted. 'You stupid woman. He's been recycled, as all of us will be! He can't help you!'

"'This is a sin. I'll hope He'll forgive us,' Mother whispered glancing at me and Father doubtfully, then she glanced at the ceiling and hugged me tightly.

"'Well, Mother, you always taught me that Jesus sacrificed himself to save us from injustice, to protect us from evil, and to tell us the truth. So I chose this Easter to tell you the truth, so you would no longer be in denial.' I broke away from her quivering, yet strong embrace, and left the room.

"For days, neither of them would look me in the eye. Eventually, Mother went back into denial. She insisted that I was making it up and that I should get help before the devil possessed me completely and it was too late.

"Sick and tired of her constant ranting and nagging, I took the first opportunity that came along to wake her up. Sebastian, a virile, Spanish-looking Gypsy, was our gardener's cousin from the capital. The first time he came to help his uncle, I was instantly attracted to him. However, I kept my distance, waiting for the right moment.

"One evening, my parents went to visit my aunt and I came on to him, lying that they wouldn't be back for a long while. When they returned, Father walked into my room to find me sitting on Sebastian's lap, kissing him. Father ran out and came back with his Walther pistol. Mother, my intended victim, stood frozen behind him.

"'You motherfucker! I'll kill you!' my father screamed, shooting above Sebastian's head. Sebastian bolted past my parents and ran down the stairs.

"'Oh, Lord, have mercy! Gypsies, the lowest class of people! God knows who else you've been involved with.' Mother once again spoke to the ceiling. 'I hope not with those disgusting Arabs, Turks, and Albanians, who probably drugged you and made you do it. Don't you know that they carry terrible diseases and you might get seriously ill?' Mother still thought of me as her perfect possession, accusing everyone but me.

"I was speechless during her diatribe, but happy that she finally understood, and that her denial was over. Finally, both of them began to see reality and realize that I was different, that I was upset with them, and that my extended runaways were a reaction to that. After that, they tried to handle things as calmly as possible, each one correcting the other's words if they could possibly offend me. They struggled to keep the peace and not provoke me to leave them again, their greatest fear.

"Of course, the gardener was fired right away. I felt bad about him losing the job, but on the other hand, I felt happy that my domineering parents would no longer yell at him while he worked hard for us. Sebastian didn't give up on me. I began sneaking him into the house and, later, into my room in Skopje. Gypsies make difficult friends for ordinary people. They are discriminated against more than any other people in Europe, have the lowest standard of living, and their identity is constantly questioned. Some think they came from India, others from Egypt as nomads. Sebastian considered himself an Egyptian. I've always wondered if I have Gypsy blood, since I have such a nomadic spirit and unclear identity.

"Sebastian and I got along well. We became very close as we shared our bad experiences. Sebastian had lots of them. Abused by his father, he left home as a child. Everyone thought he was dead until he showed up twenty years later in a white Mercedes with briefcases full of money. He lost that quickly, because he was a compulsive gambler, spendthrift, and alcoholic. Sebastian was one of a number of Gypsy children recruited by the Yugoslavian mafia to steal throughout Western Europe, especially in neighboring Italy. It was a huge business. Children who were white enough were sold for adoption and the good-looking ones into prostitution. Constantly running from the police, who were trying to deport them, many of them tried to break away from the dirty and exploitive hands of the Mafia. Unfortunately, most of them were caught and never seen again. Sebastian was lucky. He slipped away from both the police and the mob and survived as a gigolo in Rome.

"Sebastian's home was in the Shutka ghetto, at the north end of Skopje. It consisted mostly of hovels, but here and there you saw large homes built by those fortunate enough to immigrate west, mostly to Germany. The streets smelled from the town's garbage and sewers, and were crowded with boys seeking a day's work. Many were children born out of wedlock, who didn't have more than an elementary school education. The men often worked as loaders or garbage men. The women generally stayed home or were maids. It was unusual for Gypsies to have Macedonian lovers, unless they were good-looking, and even then they were usually prostituting for small change.

"Despite their hard lives, Gypsies loved entertainment and they were the best at creating it. Every night in the ghetto was a party. I loved to dance and sing among them by the bonfires until dawn. It was uplifting to see their shiny, colorful garments, their cheap jewelry glittering against their chocolate complexions, their happy faces, and their fascinating, exotic dances that simply celebrated life. I envied them. I still do. Our greedy, uptight society is such a contrast to their poor but happy one. Unfortunately, my happiness ended a month later when I broke up with Sebastian. He had begun to steal from me. I guess it was because of the unhealed wounds from his past.

I paused, looked towards the window, and uttered, "One way or another, we all carry unhealed wounds from our past to our graves."

27

Aunts

Mila was breathing heavily. She tucked one leg underneath her and pulled back strands of hair that had fallen over her face, refastening them with her barrette. She moved the ashtray closer to the edge of the table. I'd become familiar with that move, and I pulled out a pack of Marlboros and offered her one. I lit her cigarette and her fingertips were sweaty as she steadied my hand with hers. I had noticed they were always sweaty when she longed to touch me.

"Unhealed wounds from our past that we carry to our graves," she said. "They're still bleeding in me, but I don't care. All I want is for yours to stop bleeding."

"They stopped, after I found you and started telling you the truth about my life. I'm sure the wounds will never completely heal, though. The scars will always be there to remind us." I sipped my Coke.

"That's our harsh reality," Mila murmured. Her facial muscles twitched as she ran her hand over the stomach where I once grew, and whose loss had caused her to bleed forever.

It was hard to look directly at Mila's rueful expression and to watch her shaking hand wipe tears off her face. They never stopped. How many tears can a human produce? I wondered, as I left my chair and walked to the window.

"Maybe I succeeded in letting my parents know who I was, but I was still trapped in the social cage that was so much against my nature," I said, continuing my story. "There was no way I could follow the so-called normal track, to study, socialize, and have a lover, like anyone else, when society would not let me be myself. In order to survive the repression, I needed to find kindred spirits. Of course, there were no openly gay places in Macedonia, but there were common gay hangouts in its towns, like the train stations and the parks. There's a joke among local gays: if a village consists of three houses, gays are living in one of them. The point is, we are all over, whether you like it or not. So I began to visit the Aunts' hangouts. Yugoslav gays call each other Aunts."

"Aunts?" Mila repeated, raising her eyebrows. Her mouth stayed half-open for a moment, then she laughed and added, "That's really funny."

It was a common reaction. I had seen it over and over from most straight people who hadn't the slightest idea about our secret world.

"Yes, Aunts," I confirmed. "In Skopje, the main cruising area was in the center of the city at a place called the Terminal. It was a small abandoned park behind the peasant's bus station on the north bank of the Vardar River. I'll never forget the first night I went there and met Dimitar. He was over thirty, and like most of the Aunts, he looked younger. He had a pale face with a long nose and wore a sharp Versace leather jacket and pants that were tightly belted around his thin waist. His walk was feminine, and he spoke faster then any woman I've ever heard. He was a government worker and a member of the Communist party. His nickname was "Maggie Thatcher."

As we walked through the park, I saw lots of silhouettes moving among the bushes. We eventually reached a clearing, where a rowdy group of people were gathered.

"'Gosh, look who's here. Our congresswoman!' someone shouted. 'She promised she'd change the bashing law or else we would send a big Albanian to beat the hell out of her ass.' Other shrill voices piped up.

"'I'm ready, darlin'.' Maggie Thatcher said. 'Hush now. You don't want the cops to hear us and black-and-blue our asses with their long, fat nightsticks.'

"'Uh-huh! Ah! We dooo...' The Aunts cried out, some moaning.

"'Girls! Aunts! Quiet!' Maggie Thatcher ordered. 'I finally met Alexis.' He smiled at my stunned expression. 'We know everything about you. You love to date rich men. The name suits you, doesn't it?'

"Blushing, I began to laugh, thinking of Joan Collins and *Dynasty*. Maggie Thatcher turned to the group and said, rhetorically, 'Isn't she gorgeous?'

"'Let's take her to our office and look at her under the light.' The suggestion came from an overweight man who looked like a typical drugstore-cashier lady. He grabbed my arm and began dragging me across the park. The Aunts' noisy entourage followed. We all went inside the public men's room, where they took a good look at me.

"'Not bad, not bad,' the fat man said. 'She looks fine.'

"'Oh, you ghastly nestlings. You jealous little bitches.' Maggie Thatcher smirked at couple of young Aunts who were shaking their heads, then she turned to me and said, 'Alexis, I would proudly start my introduction of our Aunts' association with our legendary queen called Prima Donna.' He bowed to the overweight man, the oldest in the group and a former famous ballet dancer. 'Next,

I'm pleased to present The Countess.' Maggie Thatcher gestured broadly towards a slim man in a sleek outfit and jewelry. He was a successful businessman. 'Here's our vicious Princessa Lucrezia Borgia.' He looked towards an evil-eyed and well-kept middle-aged pharmacist. 'This is charming Yvonne de Kozle.' Yvonne referred to the famous actress Yvonne de Carlo, and Kozle was the section of the city where he owned a bar. 'Meet Braid Brows,' Maggie Thatcher continued. He was a lawyer, named for a character in an old Macedonian folk song. 'This is our clodhopper, maid Auntie Dobrila.' He inclined his head towards a bulky man with a bad complexion, who was obsessively knitting a doily like a typical Macedonian peasant wife. 'Here's Lily de Madjaro.' The poorly dressed guy was named after the blue-collar area in which he lived, Madjari. 'Look at our ambitious Evita. Doesn't she look revolutionary?' Maggie Thatcher grinned at a Hispanic-looking Croatian-Gypsy; a medical student whose Macedonian language was a mess. 'And, finally, let me acquaint you with Keti The Broom, the youngest moppet and the most outrageous Aunt. She wanders the streets, day and night, performing mostly outdoor fellatio and other receiving activities. Sweeping the streets and pleasuring horny men, from juniors to seniors, Muslim to Christian, straight to confused, are Keti's specialties.' Everyone laughed. The barely seventeen-year-old Aunt didn't seem put out. In fact, he looked rather proud of Maggie Thatcher's description, batting his long eyelashes, stroking his long hair, pursing his full, pink lips, and shaking his bubble-butt.

"'So, Alexis, have you found anyone since you buried your husband? Or are you still a widow?' Princessa Lucrezia Borgia asked me sarcastically, glancing at the others as if he were competing for something.

"'She's still young,' The Countess said.

"'Oh, sure. She'll trap somebody soon. And maybe bury him quicker than her latest, the pure sculptor,' Princessa Lucrezia Borgia jeered at me. 'But make sure you get in the will before the funeral, honey.'

"I didn't say a word. I reddened like a lobster, my eyes jumping from one Aunt's face to another. I wasn't used to the Aunts' outrageous attitude.

"'Leave Alexis alone. You spiteful sluts!' Maggie Thatcher shouted, pulling me aside. 'Let me show you our garden, darlin'. Watch out for the turds, dear.'

"Outside, ghostlike shadows were moving all around the park. They were mostly older men hunting for younger ones.

"'You see the good-looking one over there.' Maggie Thatcher motioned to a guy leaning against a wall, smoking. 'He's a gigolo. Albanian. Notice the white socks and black loafers. That's their dress code. Like their uniform. They're usually good in bed, but dangerous. There are many hot-looking robbers and bashers around who are experts in tricking the Aunts into action, then attacking them and stealing their money. Be very alert!'

The men reminded me of a horde of hungry wolves, searching for a kill. Later, I found out that law offices bordered the park, and thought it bizarre that the Aunts would gather there. Everything was fine until around midnight, when people panicked. Some ran out of the bushes with their pants down to their knees.

"'Holy Jesus, Mohammed, and all the known prophets! Run, Alexis! Follow me!' Maggie Thatcher ordered. 'We've got bad visitors. The police!'

"'As we galloped through the park, I heard a cacophony of high and low screams and curses. I glanced back to see the cops clubbing the Aunts. We ran from the Terminal and crossed the wide street in front of the Macedonian Peoples' Theater. Once we had disappeared in the shadows of the huge concrete complex, Maggie Thatcher stopped running.

"'We're safe now. Walk normally!' he said, panting. 'It happens a lot. What you saw is nothing. Usually it's much worse.'

"He stopped, suddenly looking suspicious. 'But who am I explaining this to? To a police sister? We know you fooled around at The Center and caused lots of headaches for the faculty. We know that you transferred to law school, but you might still be working for the police. Don't stare at me as if I were a Martian. The Aunts know more than any other social group, of any kind. We're a network, a chain. We get information from each other easily. It's a man's world we thrive in. Men's hunger for sex is our power source to quickly link and get connected.'

"'I had no idea that the police did these purges.' I confessed in astonishment. 'I don't belong to them. I never did. I swear.'

"'Who do you belong to then? To my father's cock? Give me a break.'

"'Trust me. I hate The Center, the police, and the inspectors. I always did. I was forced by my family to be part of them. It's a horrible institution. Completely corrupt.'

"'Okay, okay. Let me tell you about your ex-friends in blue when they do a sweep in the Aunts' cruising areas.' Maggie Thatcher's voice filled with rage. 'They usually go for the youngest. They are happiest when they catch them in the act. Recently, two high-school-age Aunts were taken by a group of cops to the police station, where they were raped and beaten brutally. On top of that, the officers shamed them before their families and neighbors. The Aunts couldn't stay in school nor could they get jobs. Disowned by their families, they had no choice but to leave Macedonia. And that's not the only story. Everyone's against us...Forget it! No one can do anything about it anyway,' Maggie Thatcher muttered, pessimistically.

Mila shuddered. "That's so cruel. So inhumane." She sighed.

"Nothing new. Bashing happens all over. Even in America," I said, then continued. "Suddenly, Maggie Thatcher broke into a smile. 'Let's go to the Turkish Bazaar. That's another place where the Aunts have fun. Sex is the best escape from misery, isn't it?' he asked, then added, 'At least temporarily.'

"The Bazaar's ambiance brought back memories of Turkey. Its hundreds of small shops overflowed onto the narrow, cobblestone streets. They were predominantly run by Albanians. The street we were on was dark, and it led us to a Turkish teahouse crowded with nothing but men. Women were not allowed to join Muslim men in such a setting. They had to stay home and take care of the house. The place was noisy and smoky. The men were drinking, joking, and gambling with cards or backgammon. Some of the Albanians wore traditional skullcaps. Two groups of Aunts occupying the furthest corner tables were giggling and flirting with the men by sucking the straws in their drinks as hard as possible.

"Maggie Thatcher ordered tea for both of us. As soon as he finished his, he gestured for me to follow him. Two men made jokes about his sashaying as we climbed the stairs to the men's room on the second floor. Maggie Thatcher entered one stall and signaled for me to enter the one across from his. I did it quickly, making sure the door was locked. I had no idea what we were doing, but I put the toilet cover down and took a seat.

"The show had already started. The partitions between the stalls were made of wooden slats, cracked and full of holes, and I could easily see through them. In the stalls to either side of mine, Aunts were servicing men in succession, one after another. As the traffic of men built up, I noticed two men entering one stall and a young Aunt begin servicing them both at once. It was completely absurd. Those men, who would never be seen in public with an Aunt, had no problem with coming to see one in a men's room, even though it was obvious to everyone what was going on. When Maggie Thatcher left his stall, I followed him, bumping into a man who smiled at me suggestively under his thick mustache.

"Downstairs, when I offered to pay for the tea, the waiter told us that someone already had. Maggie Thatcher laughed. 'I think I deserve at least a cup of tea for all the fuckin' work I've done in this place.' As we left, I stumbled on a loose pavement stone as we walked out, and he screamed, 'Watch your heels, girlfriend!'

"My stomach hurt from laughing, and I couldn't take another step. Passersby stared at us. Their faces were humorless.

"'Dull asses. They don't get it. Many straights just don't have a sense of humor. They're so uptight and bored. Such a tragedy. I'm so glad I'm an Aunt,' Maggie Thatcher declared, swinging his hips and sticking his chest out pompously.

"But he soon became serious and said, 'All these teahouses and coffee bars are full of horny Albanians and Turks. All you have to do is wait in the stall for men to come and stand before you. Then you just pull their pants down and the show begins. If you turn around, they bang you. It goes very quickly. Usually without kissing. Kissing makes them gay; that's how they think. You never find out who they are. Most of them are good-looking and clean, especially down there, and often are shaved around the crotch as Muslims. Sometimes they beat us, when they are in a funk or angry. But it doesn't happen as often as with the cops out in the Aunts' fields. Some lucky Aunts find relationships here. But it's rare.'

"'Do you have to go through that?' I asked, pained by his admission.

"'What else can we do? We have no freedom in the prison called Macedonia. The law prohibits being gay. We have no safe place to socialize and no right to a normal life whatsoever. The Albanians and Turks, as Muslims, customarily have no sex before marriage, so we are a supplemental convenience for them. They're satisfied and we're satisfied. It's a sad trade-off, but better than none.' Maggie Thatcher exhaled.

"For days, I thought about Maggie Thatcher's difficult life. I didn't want to become like him. I didn't have much choice, but I had to survive in a different way. Some lucky Aunts were able to find jobs and move away to Slovenia, Croatia, where things weren't as tough on homosexuals. Belgrade, as the capital and the biggest city, had the best gay life in Yugoslavia. I had to escape. I didn't want to become a sidewalk slut or a provincial whore. When I tried to picture my future, there was none. I was terrified. I had to leave Macedonia.

"Meanwhile, I tried hard to stay away from the Aunts, but I didn't succeed. I became an Aunt like many others who had nowhere to turn, who needed a friend, a family. I got sucked into it, and I even started hosting orgies in my small room. Everything I could catch, or that the Aunts could pick up in their patrols on the river Vardar quay, or under The Turkish Stone Bridge, or around Daut Pasha Hammam Art Gallery, or in the clubs, the bars, the restaurants, the parks, the streets, or of course the Terminal, came to my place. Muslims and Christians, young and old, handsome and ugly, professionals and trash, priests and peasants, even the handicapped were accepted. I was proud of not discriminating, and I felt I was so special because of that.

"The circle got wider and wider as the men brought friends, even relatives. Some of them were involved in the Mafia, especially the Albanians from Kosovo, who drove me around in sports cars I'd only seen in action movies. I didn't care. I enjoyed being a pioneer 'gay madam' and turning my room into a 'bordello.' The Aunts started calling it the first free, gay house of love in Macedonia. They seemed to greatly appreciate my efforts to protect them. They no longer had to go out and expose themselves to danger day after day, when they could use my room anytime they wanted. I had hordes of willing, curious, horny, and all kinds of unused men waiting to be hooked up and exploited by the Aunts.

"'You're writing yourself into the archives,' Maggie Thatcher told me once.

"'I'm helping my community, and I'm glad that I'm fairly busy,' I said. 'Maybe I should install a punch clock for the horny kittens lining up at my door.'

"'Who else talks about sex and men more than we do? No one. If we were women, we wouldn't have been this way. Maybe only simple, bored housewives.'

"'Definitely not me and you, baby,' I replied, shaking my head.

"'Well, we're men. Gay or straight, men have been hunters since the beginning of time. The biggest sluts, don't you think?' Maggie Thatcher asked.

"'Absolutely. When a man is horny, he thinks with his lower head instead of his upper, and only about getting more sexual pleasure in that moment. When a woman is horny, she thinks with both heads, and it's about getting into a deep relationship, about commitment and the future, and how to suck as much pleasure as possible out of it. Men are sluts, but women are whores.'

I paused and grinned at Mila. "I'm sorry, mother, but that's true.' I said, nodding my head like a Hindu Guru.

I don't think Mila agreed with my statement, but my calling her "mother" made up for it. She teary eyes looked grateful, and as she bent forward to take a cigarette, I noticed her eyes changed color the way mine would sometimes. It was another trait we had in common, and it made me feel even more nervous and guilty when I thought of Mother downstairs. I continued my story, if only to suppress my emotions.

"No matter how decadent my life may have been, I was helping people, and not only the Aunts, but any people and in any way I could. I've always had an appetite for doing that." I said, proudly. "I remember meeting Pavle, a struggling poet, at a poetry competition that I had entered anonymously. His writing was incredible. Quickly, our fondness for poetry bonded us. We began visiting each other. He was a very poor villager from Eastern Macedonia. His father was an alcoholic who constantly abused him, his mother, and his sister. His sister couldn't take the torture anymore and disappeared one day. He believed she had ended up in the Middle East, working as a sex slave. I had to do something, and through one of my lovers, a company director in the capital, I helped Pavle and his mother to get jobs and move there.

"Pavle and I tried to get published at a couple of publishing houses. They all rejected us, saying that his poetry was 'too pathetic and gloomy,' and mine 'too Western and unpatriotic.' They also said I overused Serbo-Croatian and other foreign words and expressions and had abandoned our beautiful Macedonian language. Later, I succeeded in getting published in Serbia, Bosnia and Herzegovina, and had one poem published in Macedonia, in the student paper.

"Pavle quit writing. He got sucked into the married life and began calling me only when he needed financial aid. Actually, almost all my 'friends' hung around me because I had money. Damaged, without the ability to create and manage friendships, I was spending my money recklessly and unselfishly to help them. Naive and desperate, I could not see clearly that I was paying for friendship and that people were using me. When the money and the jewelry were gone, I was left alone again. My self-destruction was leading me towards insanity, and it seemed to parallel the destruction of our socialism, 'the perfect system' that was no longer functioning.

"Inflation was rising rapidly. People's money was being wasted on the giant government administration, while the politicians and the bureaucrats in their long conferences and meetings were telling fairy tales and making promises to people without a future. Hatred and nationalism became evident among the majority Christians and the minority Muslims. The fundamentalists and the nationalists worked hard, aided by the economic crisis, to destroy the Federation. It was sad to see the Balkan unity that Tito had worked so hard to establish crumble in the midst of a struggling Europe desperate for its own union. The West was watching, but contrary to its highly promoted humanitarian and democratic unionism, they were not doing much to stop it. They secretly wanted Yugoslavia to die.

"I was lucky not to be in denial like so many of my countrymen. Confident that the End and the War were both coming, I began an intensive search for an escape. I kept hoping to reach a 'Promised Land' one day, even though I doubted such a place existed. To escape anywhere in Europe, especially from the turbulent Balkans, was hard. Our country's passport wasn't nearly as welcome as when Yugoslavia was stable. It wasn't a surprise to me. The West Europeans always considered us savages. I heard that going to America, my old dream, was easier, but without someone to invite you, it was an illusion.

"Despite the harsh reality, I kept my hopes up and put all my energy into finding a possible connection. I concentrated on foreigners, naturally. In my first attempt, I bumped into two Iranians who were searching for a vulnerable and desperate victim like me. Yugoslavian passports were like 'holy documents' compared to theirs when it came to traveling to the West. It wasn't hard for them to convince me to give mine to them after they promised me a visa to Germany. That was the last time I saw them.

"A month later, during lunch in the student cafeteria, I met Ahmed, an exchange student, and clung to him like a leech. When his fellow countrymen found out about our relationship, they lured me to his apartment on the pretense that Ahmed had been in a car accident. They beat the hell out of Ahmed and me there, accusing me of possessing Ahmed and degrading him as a Muslim. They broke his bones in front of me, shouting at the top of their lungs that he had shamed his people in the holy war, jihad, against the Jews and the Christians, by letting himself be corrupted by a worthless piece of Crusader's shit like me.

"After the beating I had no guts to contact Ahmed again. I waited for him to contact me...I remember Ahmed told me once that he was Jordanian; his friend said he was an Arab; another one said he was Palestinian. They all lied. They said he left for Croatia. I hope he ended up in Germany. That was his dream.

"Ahmed never contacted me again, but he clearly wrote my name with his finger on a dusty bus window the day he left, one of his friends told me later. That completely broke my heart. We could've been so happy somewhere, in better circumstances. I'm sure of it. But life's a bitch, as they say in America. Some people we love pass through our lives like shadows and never return. Some assholes get stuck in our lives like bacteria and we can never get rid of them. Is that luck or destiny? Or is it Karma from our past lives? Does our sadness or happiness depend on how many sins or kind things we've done to others and to this earth? Life is not fair, and in trying to comprehend it, I've found the principles of Karma to be the most logical basis for the way I view the world."

I paused, collecting my thoughts. "I don't believe in an afterlife...or reincarnation," I continued. "But I feel that Karma exists in the physical world, also. There is cause, and there is effect. And when the universe is working properly, the inevitable consequences occur, whether for good, or for bad, as the person warrants."

28

Psycho

Mila could tell from the tone of my voice that I was longing for something that was gone. Her eyes moved from my face to the ceiling, then to her lap, back to my face, and again to the ceiling. Her look manifested a longing for something that was gone, also.

"You're absolutely correct, my dear. Life is not fair to all of us. I wish I had been somewhere else, or in better circumstances, when I was raped and conceived you. Imagine how different life would've been for you and me. It's my bad destiny, though. My punishment has been to have no luck. If I could only know the reason, what I did wrong..." Mila sighed, staring at my fluorescent star on the ceiling and wiped her tears.

"Life for some of us is an angel," I said, "and for others a vampire that sucks the blood out of our veins, leaving us with dry sadness and hardship. No one can figure out why some of us have it easy and others don't. No one is able to explain this order, law if you will, that we refer to as nature or universe or destiny or luck or God. In the end, all of it is just bullshit. And I hope it ceases when we begin rotting three meters under the dirt. I'll be so disappointed if it doesn't. And here we keep going like tricked children with a toy in our hands called hope, playing this tempting game called life. Some of us make it, some of us don't, and we have no clue why such awful discrimination exists. Many times I have wished there were a different, more perfect version of Homo sapiens that I could join. Entrapped in this game, I keep playing as well as possible, but I question myself: why bother, when nothing lasts forever, no matter what we do or leave as our legacy? I don't know. You don't know. Will we ever know?...So I just keep playing and testing my luck and exploring the unknown. This game is all about making it to the next day."

Mila nodded, and her tears sparkled like stars. I sipped my Coke, lit a cigarette, and enjoyed consuming my two favorite American products in silence for a while. I walked to the window and my voice shook when I spoke again.

"I didn't give up. I was determined to be a good player. But I almost lost my life searching for that stranger who would offer me my connection to the West. It happened late one night, as I strolled through the Center Mall on my way back from the Terminal. The mall's 24-hour drugstore was a midnight stop where students could grab a snack during a long night's studying; where the Aunts would quench their thirst, after coming back from hunting; where couples had ice cream after romantic strolls by the river quay; and where losers would keep getting loaded after all the bars were closed.

"Among those wandering around was a macho, clean-cut, non-Macedonian-looking man in his late thirties. He wore imported fitted jeans, a biker's leather jacket, and combat boots. He was holding a bottle of beer. As I passed him, out of the blue, he said in Serbo-Croatian, 'I've lost my dog. Can you help me find it please?'

"'What kind of dog is it?' I asked. His intense expression grabbed me in a flash. The masculine smell of tobacco and alcohol on his breath was soothing. His neatly trimmed sexy beard evoked fantasies of my lips brushing along the hairless line of the scar he bore on his left cheek, just below the eye.

"'Black German Shepherd,' he replied, looking around quickly. He began walking towards the parking lot. I followed him, searching between cars. Five minutes later, he walked to the curb and said, 'Fuck it,' hailing a taxi.

"'Good night,' I said, as the cab pulled up. As I turned to leave, he said, 'Come with me for a drink?'

"'What about your dog?' I asked, delighted to hear his invitation.

"'Fuck the dog. Let's hang out.' He winked and grinned, taking a swig of beer.

"'Okay,' I said, thinking it would be better than another boring night, and got in the cab with him. He offered me a cigarette, then one to the driver as he gave him the address in the Airodrom quarter. When we arrived at his building, he pulled out a handful of money, paid the driver, and led me to an apartment on the second floor. It was spacious, furnished with expensive contemporary furniture. He offered me a seat. I sat at one end of the cushioned turquoise sofa.

"'What's your name?' I asked.

"'Yugoslav.' He grinned and walked to the bar, where he picked up a bottle of Ballantyne. He poured some for both of us, handed me a glass, and said, 'Cheers!' swallowing his brandy in one gulp.

"'Cheers,' I repeated and sipped from mine.

"'Come on, baby. Drink it all! Don't be a pussy!' he shouted.

"'I don't drink much,' I replied, cautiously. 'Indeed, I don't drink at all. Sorry.' I sipped the drink again and again, feeling embarrassed.

"'Good boy. You have to be good company. That's why you're here.' He took off his jacket. His well-developed chest seemed as if it would burst through his tight black sleeveless T-shirt. A black eagle holding a cross and a burning torch in each claw was tattooed on his big right upper arm. His jeans were glued to his sculpted legs. His salt-and-pepper military hair cut, his full, jet-black eyebrows above cold blue eyes, and his aquiline nose made his facial cast tougher than my father's. He double-locked the door, threw the keys on the table, took a cigar from his humidor, and as he lit it, he jested, 'We know why we are here. Don't we?'

"'To be good company for each other,' I responded, hurriedly, taking a cigarette from my pocket and placing it between my trembling lips.

"'Great fuckin' company!' He nodded. 'Strip me!'

"I stubbed out the just-lit cigarette. First, I took his T-shirt off, then I pulled his jeans down. His body was contoured with muscles. There was not a gram of fat on it. He was not only muscular; he was a real hunk. I pulled his underwear down. There was another tattoo, a black panther with a death skull in his jaw, on his solid groin. I discovered a third tattoo on his left ankle when I untied his combat boots. It was a snake wrapped around a struggling female figure.

"'Strip yourself!' he commanded, refilling his glass and mine.

"He was either a police officer or a criminal. Hesitantly, I began to unbutton my shirt. Suddenly, he grabbed it with both hands and violently ripped it open. The sound of buttons scattering all over the parquet was intimidating.

"'Hurry up!' he shouted, and when he turned to pour more brandy, I saw a fourth tattoo on his upper-left back. It was a sword cutting something I couldn't recognize immediately. As I focused more on it, I could see it was a human body, on fire and being sliced in two. It was drawn above a huge scar, which made the image extra morbid. I felt bloodless then, and slowly I backed off. When he turned and jumped on me, I thought he would hit. He didn't. Instead, he began playing with me like a toy. He grasped me so hard it left bruises. I felt stinging pain on my butt when he spanked me. Then he turned me around and slapped my face.

"'You're a spoiled son of a communist, aren't you!' he screamed and slapped me again, harder.

"I flew to the floor. 'No, I'm not. My father is.' I said, defensively.

"'Fuckin' liar! You commie bastard! "Brotherhood and Unity!" That's what all you fuckin' Bolsheviks believe in. Sucking those Muslim cocks that are destroying our country! Those smelly pigs that want special Muslim states all over the Balkan lands! You fuckin' traitors! Fuckin' assholes!' He spit on me as he yelled.

'I'll make sure you never forget the Christian cock again! The real one! The right one! You piece of shit! You're a hungry cocksucker! Turn around, you son of a commie prick! Bend your hungry ass over now!...Look at that! Your fuckin' Moslem faggots even shaved your fuckin' ass to be like them!' He began smacking my butt, my back, and my sides.

"My whole body began to burn in pain. He started pushing his flaccid penis persistently, his humping, knocking my head into the wall. I covered it with my hands to protect it. I realized I had a real psycho-Nazi-motherfucker on my hands.

"'I'll teach you to go back and respect your Christianity! Your roots! Your people! Your tradition! Your uncut brothers! You fuckin' Marxist traitor!' He got up, went to a cabinet, and pulled out a gleaming chef's knife. Then he lifted me from the floor and punched me, throwing me upright onto the love seat. Blood oozed from my nose and mouth. Before I knew it, he had grabbed my hair with his left hand and was pushing my head down over the back of the sofa, stretching my neck to its limit. The blood flow slowed, but my sweat and tears poured, mixing with the blood below my breathless, half-opened mouth. When he placed the knife's point between my eyes, I could feel more blood ooze from me, run down my chin and drip on my chest and stomach. I turned to stone. I was frightened that the slightest move would provoke him to do worse. I pictured him stabbing my head with his shining blade and splitting it in half like a melon. His lips brushed my left ear. He bit my earlobe.

"'Turn your pretty ass around, baby,' he whispered, gently.

"Gingerly and with great effort, I obeyed, my eyes fixed on the blade pointed at my skull. He reached into a drawer with his free hand, and I could hear a metallic sound. Damn, another cutter, I thought. Probably getting ready to chop me to shreds. I stopped breathing when he grabbed one of my wrists and folded my arm behind me.

"'Cross them!' he ordered. I joined my wrists swiftly, gulping for air as the cold metal cuffs clamped them firmly. I had never felt so vulnerable, weak, useless, and abandoned.

"'I'll teach you family tradition and values! No more fuckin' communist agenda of "Brotherhood and Unity"!' he roared, running the blade along my cheeks, down to my neck.

"'Please, don't do it, comrade,' I begged in a whisper.

"'I'm not your fuckin' comrade! I'm your sir!' He pressed the blade against my Adam's apple.

"'Please sir,' I corrected myself, realizing how stupid I was to forget that he hated everything associated with communism. My half-open eyes were looking at death's blank wall. He stroked the knife against my neck, then brought it further up, scraping my right cheek, until it reached its previous position, between my eyes. The second the sharp blade's tip pierced my skin, an endless darkness appeared, and my mother's and father's faces came out of it, so close that I could kiss them. I squeezed my eyes shut tightly, expecting his knife to plunge through my head and end it all. I didn't feel the heaviness of his body, not a gram of it, when I said to myself 'It's over,' and my warm blood streamed down the left side of my nose, seeping into my mouth. His ghastly chortle of pleasure exploded, opening my numbed eyes. He lifted me off the love seat and threw me to the floor, on my knees.

"'Clean me up! You son of a Bolshevik fuck!' He waved his bloodstained knife about.

"I began to totter like a bird with cut wings on the floor. The blood pouring from the cut between my eyes spattered around as I moved. Eventually, I managed to find my shirt somewhere behind me with my cuffed hands.

"'Stupid Marxist cocksucker,' he said, laughing. I dropped my shirt, realizing despite my cloudy mind that I couldn't use it. I squatted before him with my head down, and everything in it was gray and pounding like a church bell on Sunday from the hopelessness and humiliation I felt.

"'Clean me up with your tongue, dummy!' he screamed, kicking my shirt away. My body went cold again. I began searching for my bloodstains on his skin. I began to clean them off carefully with my quivering tongue, wary of his unpredictable mood swings. I'd rather be dead then feel his knife scraping my back, I thought, and began licking the salty traces of blood from him faster. He took the bottle of Ballantyne and pulling my head up by my hair, began pouring it in my mouth. I usually never wanted to drink and be out of control, but at that moment I found the booze eased my pain and horror. He put the bottle on the table, picked up his knife, and after waving it a couple of times before my eyes, he placed it on my lips and yelled, 'Now clean this!'

"I was too scared to stick my tongue out at first. He pulled my hair harder, hollering, 'Clean it, I said!' I stuck out my numbed tongue and placed it on the shiny metal. Once. Twice. I licked it carefully, not touching its sharp edges. My blood tasted much better there than on his salty skin. I could feel my pupils widen when he flipped the knife over and yelled, 'More! Quicker! Better!' My mouth went dry. I could feel my trembling Adam's apple, but nothing else.

Again, the darkness came, even though my eyes were wide open, but my parents' faces didn't reach me because he abruptly knocked me to the floor.

"I closed my eyes and felt his strong, massive body jump on me. When he began rubbing it against mine, it felt like sandpaper. My hands were squashed behind my back. My knees began shaking as he placed them above his broad shoulders. The dense line of hair that rose from his stomach to his pumped chest and spread over it like a pair of wings brushed against me. He picked me up in his arms and changed position. My cuffed hands and my back bounced against the wall. All I felt was pain, but I made pleasurable noises as if I felt orgasmic.

"I was willing to do anything to make him think his limp tool was useful. I was willing to do anything not to provoke his sadistic behavior. I wished I could reach the knife lying on the floor and slice his throat when he began to slurp alcohol mixed with my blood from my face, shoulders, chest, and stomach. Handcuffed, I could only be a subservient toy in his morbid pleasure game. Even without the cuffs, I couldn't have matched his strength. So I held in my anger and obeyed his wishes. Then he said, 'Go and wash yourself, you commie bastard!' and pushed me away, pointing down a narrow hallway."

As I told this story, Mila sobbed loudly. "How could you, handcuffed like that? What a sick idiot."

"I almost asked him the same thing. I slowly rose, stiff and sore, still feeling his punches and the friction of his heavy, rough body rubbing against mine. I murmured, 'Can I go home? I have classes early tomorrow.'

"'The teacher is pregnant! The classes are canceled!' His face reddened as he screamed, and then he spat on me. 'Wash yourself, I said!'

"I didn't know where the hell he came up with that one, but I realized that any more comments could set him off. I shut up and tramped like a turtle down the hall. I kept thinking that he would stab me in the back any second. It was definitely the longest walk of my life.

"When I finally reached the fancy bathroom, I saw the horrible results of what he had put me through in the mirror. I felt like an old punching bag that smelled like him, like sewage. Of course, I didn't have the courage to use the bathtub or the shower; I wasn't on vacation. So I turned around to use the sink. I couldn't reach it at first, so I got on my tiptoes. I tried once, twice. On the third try, I somehow managed to turn the faucet handle. I stuck my head under the cold flow of water, and when I glanced back at the mirror, my nose and mouth were still bleeding. My blood spattered the white sink. I couldn't wipe it off. I couldn't clean it off my face either. I splashed my head once more, turned the water off, and walked slowly back to the living room.

"I sat on the chair next to him managing to control my shaking knees. He smirked at me, and then he grabbed my handcuffs and propelled me down the same hallway. He opened the door at the end of it and grinned as if we were entering a honeymoon suite.

"'Let's sleep in my bedroom!' he said, joyfully and invitingly. He pushed me inside.

"I stood in limbo, in total darkness, until he lit a kerosene lamp on top of a small, shabby dresser. The spooky room looked like a dungeon. In the middle was an old metal bed, made before World War II. The window had been bricked up, except for a small opening, and the radiator had been yanked out of the wall. He had me lay down with him on the bed's tiny mattress, which barely covered its iron springs, and pulled me towards him. Not only my blood, but also my veins froze as he pressed me against his solid chest. His heartbeat gradually slowed as he started to snore.

"The room was so different from the rest of the apartment. I'd never seen such a scary room. I've never examined a single, almost vacant room, in such detail as I did that night.

"Eventually, a weak light from the bricked-in window told me that dawn had come. The first sunlight encouraged me to think of an escape. The dumb fantasy of a nude, hopeless fool, I realized, as I gazed at his sleeping face. I was shaking uncontrollably, like a Parkinson's patient. When his fiendish, burning eyes opened, I got up my nerve and whispered, 'I have to go back to college, sir.'

"'For Christ's sake! I told you the teacher is pregnant and the classes are canceled!' He pulled me to him so hard it knocked the wind out of me. His rough palm caressed my bruised back, and I almost made the mistake of moving away from him. Luckily, I checked the impulse and, instead, slid closer to him, grinding my teeth together while the memories of last night flew through my mind. I repeated to myself that I had to curb my anger and not cause his vile temper to flare up if I wanted to get out of there alive.

"He began kissing my bruised face gently, as if he were applying an ointment. He touched my body cautiously, as if not to cause any pain. What the hell was going on? Romance? Or was this the beginning of another episode of terror? Confused, I almost burst into tears. I felt trapped in his world of multiple identities. I forced myself to kiss him back. The chilliness of the room dissipated as I lay in his arms. He radiated heat and passion. I couldn't believe he was making love to me as if I were the most delicate thing in the world. His joyful eyes seemed to glimmer with divine light.

"When the sun had completely risen, he got up and went to the bathroom. Listening to the running water, I shivered again, wondering what was next. I moved to the corner of the bed. There was a long silence, then the noise of his footsteps getting closer. When he reached the door, he stopped and leaned against its frame.

"'I hope you learned your lesson, pretty boy. You can leave now,' he said.

"Warily, I trailed after him to the living room. He took my handcuffs off and spread out on the sofa, watching me like a hawk would its kill as I put my clothes back on. He began whistling carelessly and jumped up as I finished dressing. He unlocked the door, and as I started to leave, he grabbed my arm. I felt the shit freezing in my ass.

"'You are Christian. Not a fuckin' commie! Remember! Respect your fate! Your roots! Your people! Your uncut brothers! Never let those fuckin' Muslims turn you into their docile pig! Never let them ruin your country and build their states here! Never let them wipe out your Christian history, tradition, and heritage! The teacher is dead, and her baby, also. There are no more traitors' classes! I am your teacher from this day on. Forever! And never forget that. I am the best one!'

"I almost bowed as I nodded. The last glance at his demonic, swollen, red-veined eyes froze me once again, and I nearly broke my neck from rolling down the steps after he pushed me out. I stayed still for a few minutes, and then crawled back up the stairs. There was no name on his door! He could have been any fundamentalist motherfucker, poisoned by hatred. I hurried out of the building.

"Two boys playing in front ran away the moment they saw me. The taxi driver's hands shook on the wheel as he drove me home. I looked like the living dead, with my blue, bruised, swollen face. But no one was more frightened of me than myself, when I thought about my motive for going with him. It wasn't only my desperate desire to find a connection so I could leave home. It wasn't his masculinity. It was something beyond that. It was the danger. Before meeting him, it seemed so irrational to be attracted to it, yet that night it pulled me like a magnet towards him. People say things happen for a reason. I think they are correct. Otherwise, would I have ever learned so directly how sickening hatred, fundamentalism, and nationalism can be? If I hadn't been brought to the edge of my existence that night, and my skin, body, and mind hadn't been burned in terror, I don't know if I ever would have learned how evil humans can be.

"The moment I left the cab and stumbled down the street towards my studio, my existence seemed unreal. Was I alive? I closed my eyes, and the yellow points, the reminders that I was alive, appeared before me as they always did when I was in trouble. They sparkled in the dark like stars. Should I consider them signs of my unfortunate life or my hope? Who knew? When I opened my eyes, the light came and the yellow points disappeared, along with my inner universe. Reality killed them. I loved my mysterious yellow stars. They always came when I needed them most, when I had to fight against the light, the reality. I noticed a car speeding towards me. I couldn't move, waiting for my yellow points. I felt metal brushing my thigh. A centimeter made all the difference. Something was protecting me, for sure.

"As soon as I entered my room and flopped onto my bed, visions of the people I knew and adored for their qualities, or abhorred for their stupidities, ran by me like a fast-forward motion picture. The yellow points appeared in the darkness, and I began counting them uncontrollably. Kept counting. Slowly at first: one, two, three. Then I strove to keep up as they sped towards me like meteors, faster and faster. Like counting the revolutions of a machine that was accelerating of its own accord. And I was moving through the yellow points at an unbelievable speed. Sometimes it would last several hours. When the journey was over, I felt like I was recovering from a fever. It scared me as a child, but later, I got kind of used to it.

"My life seemed like an endless field enshrouded in yellow fog, and my purpose was to trudge through it, lost and exhausted. I even considered going back to Turkey and calling Genghis. But I knew I had to fight on, as a good player in this game called life. What was, was gone; what would be, would happen. My all-time favorite motto. There was no point of return. I couldn't change the past or present by walking backwards. I could only analyze my past and step confidently towards my future, which seemed at that moment as if it were a place of fragile, glassy streets on which I had to walk extra carefully."

29

America

Mother was sleeping when I went to check on her. The familiar smell of her body dressings was there. It was a mix of her rose perfume, the colostomy bag, the painkillers, and her deteriorating flesh. The smell of cancer and the way it affected her body, causing her facial muscles, lips, and hands to quiver in short bursts, never felt more upsetting. I ran back upstairs.

"Everything alright?" Mila asked, anxiously.

"I guess. She's sleeping," I muttered, and sat back on the rocking chair.

"So how did you escape to America?" Mila asked, eagerly.

"In the midst of my troubles, when my self-destruction was reaching its peak, making me fly like a bat towards the sun, then sending me into the blank field of fog that felt like insanity, my luck finally changed. That summer of 1989, my neighbor, Jasmine, visited from America with her grandmother. It was her first time back since she'd left as a little girl. Mother, as a proper neighbor, took me to welcome her.

"As we walked to her old house, I tried to recall the little girl playing shyly with me in our garden while her blue-collar parents would sweat on our property. She was still shy, an artist and a nonconformist who was just reaching adulthood. She strongly resembled Angelica Huston, but an underground version of her. Locals began to gossip about her strange appearance as soon as she arrived. She remembered me as a little prince who possessed an immaculate collection of toys in his beautiful house, a fortunate child, who led such a distant life from the other kids in the neighborhood. She told me that even in America, people from my county who had visited her family told them about how weird and unacceptable I had become. For some reason, she had pictured me growing up as a nut, wearing nerdy glasses, and being completely into school. She was very happy she was wrong and that my thoughts and appearance were as rebellious as hers. Her first comment to me was, 'You belong in New York. Definitely!'

"Sporting all-black new-wave clothes, makeup, and attitudes, Jasmine and I looked removed from Mother Earth, as if we'd come from hell, in the eyes of our small-town and pinheaded provincial folk. We bonded instantly, and we painted the locals' eyes with a new picture of ourselves. No one talked about us being weird any longer, perceiving our strong friendship as romance. We felt fortunate to be able to reunite and help each other in a system that was so against our ways. More than anything, we were delighted to become true friends.

"My parents were against me leaving the country, therefore, Jasmine secretly married me. To our surprise, when our families found out, they were ready to explode from happiness. They felt relieved, and we joked about how easily straights could be tricked. My parents loved Jasmine like a daughter. My mother enjoyed dressing her up to look glamorous and chic and going out with her. They got along well. They sent us on vacation to different places around Yugoslavia and we had fun, especially Jasmine, who was fascinated with the old Balkan people, culture, and architecture.

"That autumn, Jasmine went back to New Jersey, and she sent me the invitation I needed to visit the U.S. My parents began freaking out. They became closer to me than ever. Hour after hour, they tried to convince me that they would accept anything I wanted, if I only stayed home. It was amazing to witness their transformation, the way they desperately tried to change my destiny, even though, in the back of their minds, they knew I was going.

"Traveling through Kosovo to the American embassy in Belgrade was like entering a different country during a civil war. The police and special forces from all six states were everywhere, trying to stop the violence caused by the Albanian nationalists, irredentists, and fundamentalists, especially in the capital of Pristina. My bus was inspected from its tires to its roof twice, including our luggage, clothes, and ID's. It was happening. It was scary. But after all that effort, the Americans refused to issue me a visa. One month later, Jasmine sent me another guaranty letter for Canada through relatives, and I got the visa. The Canadians were more generous.

"New Year's of 1990, the last one with my parents, was the worst one. They lamented over me as if I were dying. The day before my flight, they organized a farewell party and invited relatives and neighbors. I'll never forget my parents' bedroom that January dawn, when I was leaving. Their bodies were shrunken in pain and hopelessness under a heavy white comforter with a blue triangle in the middle. They were reluctantly waiting for me. My father's soldierly frame looked like a boy's. I thought I was dreaming when I pulled the blanket from his face and saw tears washing down his cheeks. His expression was full of pain, love, and need, a sort of naïve, childlike expression.

"'Oh, my gold,' he said. 'What are we going to do without you? Oh, woeful us!'

"I leaned over him and hugged his old body, and he turned away after we kissed. He buried his face into his pillow to mute his moaning. I went to Mother on the other side of the bed, and she hugged me with all her strength.

"'Please call us. Write to us. Don't forget us! Look out for yourself! Don't do anything wrong. Be careful! America is tough! Please, my gold. Please!' She sobbed, kissing my face and hands.

"'Don't worry, Mother, I won't forget you. Any problem, you just pick up the phone and I'll be here. I promise. Please no more crying. We agreed. Didn't we?' I held everything in my heart. All my emotions and pain were camouflaged with fake calm. They wailed over their loss as they escorted me slowly to the main entrance. Mother had placed a copper pitcher full of water on the threshold. She told me to kick it with my right foot, because doing it with my left would bring curses into my life. The flowing water symbolized the easy flow of fortune and luck that my life in the New World would bring.

"The taxi was waiting in front of the house. The driver came in to pick up my luggage, and Mother and Father wrapped their hands around me, like chains around a treasure chest, kissing my face and stroking my hair with their trembling fingers. I struggled to get out of their embraces, and as I waved to them before entering the cab, the sound of the breeze through our beautiful pine trees suddenly filled me with guilt. Damn, it was so difficult. But I had to leave that love, that hell, and those people. I had to leave that Elysium-like province called Prespa.

"Every Friday, I called my parents. When Yugoslavia broke up a year later, Father and Mother finally blessed my departure to the U.S. Neighbors told me they bragged to everyone about how wise I was to predict everything and leave, while most of my generation was barely surviving without a clear future in the war-torn country. When I suggested visiting them, they would convince me that the time was not right yet, fearing that I could get stuck without American citizenship in an unstable territory such as ours. But things quieted down, and in the summer of 1994, I visited Macedonia and stayed for six months.

"It was the best time I'd ever had with my parents. They were healthy then, and we had developed excellent communication. They completely accepted who I was and acted as if they respected my actions now, and whatever I had done in the past. They were proud of me, and they welcomed with open arms my American boyfriend, Fred, who visited me for a couple of weeks.

"Father loved him. He found in Fred what he never had with me, a son who drinks. They loved to sit in the garden and sip the Jack Daniel's that Fred brought him as a present, or cool down with Macedonian beer that Fred loved, while Father talked about World War II and showed him his gun and medallion collections. It was amazing how much they enjoyed each other's company, not understanding a word that the other said, one speaking in English, the other in Macedonian.

"Mother would cook local specialties for Fred, often giggling with him, affectionately hugging him, or pinching his cheeks while constantly serving him food. Fred gained a lot of weight, but he didn't mind. He enjoyed Balkan hospitality and the easy social interaction, something he had rarely experienced across the Atlantic, and definitely not among the mostly cold and always busy Anglo-Saxon Americans. He was overwhelmed and impressed. I kept my promise to my parents. I came back when Mother needed me the most, after Father suddenly died. She didn't seem to be feeling right, so I convinced her to get a checkup, and she was diagnosed with cancer. It was then that I finally convinced Rambo to help me find you."

Mila said, "I hate Rambo for what he did to you, but on the other hand, I have to like him. He connected us." Her eyes gleamed. "I'm so glad you foresaw the end of our country and left."

Then her eyes dimmed and she said, "It was awful to watch Yugoslavia dying. The separation of Slovenia, Croatia, and Macedonia in 1991. The civil war escalating and the break up of Bosnia and Herzegovina in April of 1992. All of the Balkans on fire again. It was scary and confusing. Orthodox Serbs, Catholic Croats, and Bosnian Muslims who had lived, worked, danced, eaten, and married together just days before were killing each other. Brothers killing brothers. Same people, same blood, South Slavs, Yugo Slavs, destroying each other. It didn't make any sense.

"Death and poverty were everywhere. Refugees were fleeing their homes. Ethnic cleansing led to the creation of concentration camps and mass graves. The beautiful places, even historical landmarks, were being wantonly destroyed. I was very ashamed that my people were raping and torturing women, children, the old, the disabled, and the sick. I would never have imagined that Yugoslavs could be capable of such things. Bombing hospitals and nursing homes. Sick things. What kind of 'soldiers' were these who wouldn't fight one another honorably, who targeted the innocent and the helpless? Where was our Yugoslav dignity? Where did all that hatred come from? I tried to find a reason for the killing, tried to understand it, even though I knew there is no excuse for killing. The bloody war between the Bosnian Serbs and Muslims intensified and the Croats got more deeply involved.

"One night, my sons and I were watching TV, when a soldiers' patrol came in and literally dragged your two half brothers out." Mila began crying. "The Army conscripted them. My devastated husband started fighting them, and they beat the hell out of him. The soldiers pushed your half brothers into a truck. I began running after the truck, screaming to my sons, 'Watch yourselves! Watch yourselves, please!' As a former Orthodox Christian, and a converted Catholic after my marriage, I was always a good Christian. That night, I stopped praying to God. I lost faith in Him. 'Why are You jeopardizing the lives of my sons?' I asked. 'Didn't I suffer enough by having to give up my first child? Do I have to lose them all? How can you allow such a thing? Who is the king, You or the Devil? What kind of Protector doesn't give a damn about His believers? God, go to Hell!' I was howling in the middle of the road, as your half brothers' terrified faces disappeared from view. I fainted." Mila stopped talking. She began to sob loudly, breathing heavily, and gasping for air.

I handed her a napkin. "I guess sometimes God falls asleep on the job. I don't blame Him for being lazy and depressed after He made us such poor and miserable creatures. He blessed us with zeal for the material world and enabled us to destroy so much for a piece of land and money. I'm glad you realize that God will never come close to doing what we expect of Him. He's never done his job properly. Sometimes I picture God playing chess or cards with the Devil and losing all the games. Look how He created this earth and us, my dear. Just look around.

"Anyway, it's we who are to blame. Everything about him is a myth. We're the creators of our beliefs. We're the source of good and evil. Our big mistake was creating Him and all these evil religions, so we can be divided and hate each other to death as enemies. Whether Muslim, Buddhist, Christian, Jewish, or whatever, we stress the 'other'-ness of others when true differences between us don't exist. We are all humans. We're a grown-up race. We should see that religions are superfluous. In the past, religions made some sense: to give young nations identities and a reason to fight for survival. Now, we need a new identity. We need global unity. We need a new order and a new progressive faith of peace and love. It's time to put the holy books where they belong, on the shelves of museums. It's already happening. MTV and the Internet will make all the conservative, greedy old farts decompose faster. The new liberated world will be established. You'll see," I declared, emphatically.

Mila smiled briefly, despite her tears. "I still long for our beautiful Yugoslavia. I still miss our only savior, Marshal Tito. Now some people are trying to make Tito look bad. They're spitting on his grave and downplaying his fight against the Nazis. They put down what this genius achieved for forty years, even as Europe is still trying to figure out how to become united. Even so, I saw Tito's portrait hanging in many former Yugoslavs' homes. Many people still long for that land. Do you?"

"I grew up as a Yugoslav and I'll die that way. Since you've told me that Macedonian, Croat, and Serbian blood flows in my veins, I feel more than ever like a real Yugoslav," I said.

"While war was burning the Balkans, I questioned the entire world's morals," Mila said. "The superpowers, Europe and America, with their well-promoted democracy and high values, were watching but not moving a finger. Why were they letting us go through the hell of World War II again? I wondered who was more evil, us for engaging in a crazy war or them for shamelessly watching from the sidelines? Sometimes, I wished that the war would go to them, so they could see clearly that they were sinners as well."

"We don't have oil," I said, as Mila sipped her Coke. "For the superpowers, war and killing are part of doing business. At the dawn of the twenty-first century, morals equal money. Some people are making big bucks out of wars, growing super-rich from the misery of others. War is big business. Sadly, that's all it's about, my dear. The West had no interests to protect in Yugoslavia, thus, no reason to save it from dying. Its socialism promised them a tiny profit. Its existence bothered them. They needed to break it in order to conquer this Balkan land.

"However, the West couldn't, can't, and never will save us. What kind of credibility do they have? They've never saved anyone. Have they? They invaded, colonized, enslaved, and murdered numbers of civilizations and nations. They carry vile genes. I would never trust them. Every attempt they make to 'help' other, less powerful countries, has a huge price to be paid underneath it. The big fish eat the small ones. The big powers pick on the small countries that don't follow their ideology. Their secret services start civil wars inside of them to destroy them. Then the big powers as 'humane forces' offer to help rebuild them, give them credits and loans, make them work and pay debts, and simply make them dependent. In other words, the big powers turn the small countries into modern colonies of slaves. That's what happened to Yugoslavia and the Balkan nations and what will happen to similar countries around the world. That's how modern imperialism works. It's simple. Divide and conquer, then make a profit. That's the motto of the big powers. Disgusting, sad, ugly, and inhuman, isn't it?" I paused to take a drag on my cigarette and continued.

"I was working in a department store. One day, the manager and some coworkers started pulling labels that read 'Made in Bosnia' off the merchandise. When I asked why they were doing that, they replied, abruptly, 'We're at war with Bosnia. They're our enemies.' I couldn't believe it. The U.S. at war with Bosnia? Ignorance, propaganda, stupidity, and misdirected patriotism are destroying America and the rest of the world. Busy people rapt with greed in their race for profit, who don't want to learn basic geography and history. Individuals who don't want to know what the hell is going on around them. With leaders who want them to be dumb, so they can control them. The fruits of modern society. Disaster."

"There were paid soldiers in the war. Foreigners paid to kill. Mujahideens in Bosnia and Kosovo protecting Islam. My sons told me that," Mila remarked.

"Of course, the poorest and the most brainwashed ones. Governments don't give a fuck if soldiers die, as long as business is done. To die for your country is an honor, that is every government's motto. And while the politicians are vacationing on tropical islands with their families, the soldiers' lives are destroyed forever on the battlefields. And when those brainwashed boys die, you hear only great things about the dead heroes, and their governments hold fancy funerals. Then the soldiers' families are left to cry and wonder why they let their children get paid to kill and be killed. It's too late for regret, though. The damage is done. Absurdly stupid, isn't it?" I took a sip from my Coke. My mouth had gone dry from all that talk of injustice.

Then, in a sadder tone, I said, "One evening, as I was going home from work, in New York City's Penn Station I saw a homeless, Vietnam veteran who was ranting and making 'up your ass' gestures with his hand each time he mentioned the government. He was angry because he had been discarded without any benefits or support. War, death, and paid soldiers. What will it take for the world to appreciate peace? Hasn't there been enough suffering, enough war, already? I watched the poor guy who had fought for his country and thought of the young soldiers I knew in the Army. I spent the rest of the day wondering if they were still alive."

"Like me going mad, hour after hour, fearing that the soldiers would bring the bodies of my children home in a bag," Mila said. "Then your older half brother called from Italy. He managed to desert there. But the younger one was stuck as a new recruit, and I had to do something before I went completely crazy. It took me a while to find connections and bribe the right people to pull him out. I ended up going directly to the Croatian army headquarters to pick him up. After the war, he was a different person."

Mila sighed, looking pensive. "He used to be happy and cheerful. He's been very quiet since, and his outgoing personality and sense of humor are gone. He's sensitive like you. He experienced the concentration camps, the hell in the heart of our beautiful Yugoslavia. He confessed to me that a number of times he saw fathers being forced to rape and shoot their wives and children, or sons made to kill their parents and siblings, who were all lined up at the edges of mass graves. Fortunately, he didn't become one of those individuals who became cold inside after killing others. He was able to stay human in a real sense."

Mila stopped talking. Jumping from the armchair, she ran over to where I sat and hugged me. "Now, after hearing what you've been through, I only wish I could have been there to understand you, to support you, and to help you. Trust me, I would've protected you. I would've been the best mother," she shouted, confidently.

I stood up, disengaging myself from her embrace, and walked to the window. Staring at the bright afternoon sky, ornamented with sleepy clouds, I spoke, "It was a cold winter morning, a few days after Mother had the operation. I was about to enter the main gate of the hospital when I saw a woman begging, with her child in front of her. She had covered her little boy with a stinky, old blanket like a mother bird would shield her offspring from a predator with her wings. I thought of you then. Intrigued, I asked her, 'How much for the child? I want to adopt him.'

"'You cannot have him, even if you offered me a gold mine,' she replied firmly, though her jaws that were shivering from the cold.

"'But he's freezing, dirty, and hungry. I can provide him with a warm home, food, and education.'

"'Go away! Only over my dead body!' she yelled, and her already-red eyes brightened like an ember after a wind blows it back to life. The woman tried to hide her boy. The boy clutched at her, and she began weaving back and forth, in a panic. I dropped the money I had on me in front of the poor woman and left."

I turned and stared into Mila's disturbed eyes and said sharply, "You had given up on me a long time ago. How can I believe your wish? Why should I, when you are still hiding him from me?"

Mila looked as if she would collapse. Her extended arms, prepared to hug me, dropped to her sides, and she walked from the room like a captured soldier being taken away for execution. She locked herself in her bedroom.

I had been damn hard on her. Who cares? I thought. Let her suffer for her actions. I can't make this reunion happy, anyway. We are damaged. We are hurt. She has people who will be nice to her: her friends and family. Or pretend friendships: her coworkers. *I* am the reality. The brutal truth. And she has to face it.

I went downstairs, midway in the house between the living room of my dying mother and Mila's upstairs bedroom, and heard the cries of "my mother of a virgin birth" brought on by my words of revenge. I wanted her to share the pain I bore, as I waited for her to tell me the last secret: who *he* was, my rapist of a father. I was still very angry at my destiny and whatever had created it. And I still held Mila responsible for it.

30

Parting

After having lunch with Mother, Mila wasn't waiting in my room when I went upstairs with hers. I left the tray on the desk and gently knocked on her bedroom door. No response. A few minutes later, I knocked again. She opened the door, but wouldn't look at me. She passed me silently and walked into my room. I could tell she was angry. The fact that this was our last day together probably made her try to suppress it. She refused to eat or even drink her usual glass of water or soft drink. My humiliation of her last night had erased her appetite completely.

"I want to meet your mother," she said determinedly, crouching in her regular spot, the armchair.

"I don't think it's a good idea," I said, putting the dirty glasses and plates on the tray.

"Please. It's my greatest wish," she begged.

"I'll see what I can do," I muttered doubtfully, and before leaving the room, I turned to her and said, "I'll walk Mother outside, so you can see her better."

I took Mother into the garden, stopping as many times as possible to show her the infected roses as we walked the manicured paths. Mila was peeking at us from behind the sheers on my room's window, and I got panicky when the wind blew and exposed her face. Luckily, Mother's attention was so focused on the well being of her favorite plants, she didn't notice. She almost seemed healthy as she instructed me on how to protect her roses, her "best friends," as she called them.

"Mother, a number of times a woman has called looking for me. She didn't leave a name. I think it's her…If I ever meet her, can I introduce you to her?" I asked.

Mother's face grew even more pallid. The corners of her trembling mouth turned down, and her pupils widened in her afflicted and concerned eyes. She took her hand from mine and mumbled with effort, "Yes…You can."

Mother's ever-lasting desire to be recognized as my one and only mother was attacked again. She hated it when I mentioned my biological mother, and she was even less inclined to discuss her. The woman who had borne me was her rival. Mother constantly feared that I would meet my biological mother some day. But what really threatened Mother was the possibility that her rival would replace her in my heart

I felt ashamed for stressing Mother, while planning to make up to Mila for that afternoon when I had put her down and, for the first time, she had walked from my room hurt and angry. I was disgusted with myself, thinking that if I tried harder and fulfilled Mila's wish, she would tell me who my biological father was. There was no way I could achieve my egoistic goals and avoid hurting both of my mothers. I was running with the hare and hunting with the hounds. My stubborn nature wouldn't allow me to give up easily though, and I came up with an idea. After we came in from the garden, I positioned Mother on her side so she faced the wall, and as soon as she fell sleep, I ran upstairs.

Mila stood up as soon as I came in.

"I'm sorry, but I don't think it is a good idea for you to meet Mother. That's the last thing she needs right now." I said firmly.

Mila's face paled in disappointment. She lowered her head and clenched her hands.

"However, I have another idea," I said.

Taking her by the hand, I led her out of the room to the stairway. I instructed her to walk on the far right side of the steps, where the wood for some reason never squeaked. When we reached the first floor, I guided her into the kitchen, directly off the living room, and left her there. She peeked at me from behind the sliding door like a curious child as I tiptoed cautiously into the living room towards Mother. She was in a deep sleep, so I signaled Mila to proceed. She came over, slowly and gingerly. When she reached the bed, she leaned over Mother's body and both of us stared at her gaunt, drained face. Her dry lips and eyelids quivered sporadically from that damned cancer.

Suddenly, Mila embraced me hard, burying her face in my neck. I did the same. We cried on each other's shoulders, holding each other firmly, trying to stop our shaking. My sadness was a vicious octopus wrapping me in its tentacles and squeezing my breath away. I could sense Mila's guilt, stinging her heart like a scorpion. But our monsters were harmless compared to the cancer, which slithered through Mother in the manner of a snake and slowly poisoned every part of her. I removed Mila's hands, which felt like a vise gripping my neck, and glanced towards the door. Before moving, Mila leaned over Mother's face and gently kissed her hand, lying on the pillow above her head. After we left the room, she whispered, "The cancer makes her look much older. Poor woman."

I said nothing, realizing that the stairs were no longer dividing the worlds of my two mothers, that the three of us were somehow united. It felt perfect, even though Mila and I couldn't look into each other's faces, because she was engulfed in guilt and I in regret over hurting Mother after I mentioned introducing Mila to her. After about a half hour of staring at the floor, crying on and off, and thinking back on everything that had happened for the last four days, I started hoping again that Mila might tell me what I eagerly wanted to know. I couldn't wait for the last secret between us to be revealed.

"So what do you do in America?" Mila asked, although she knew what I really wanted to talk about.

"Painting, while getting disgusted with people who treat art as if it were simply a commodity, like soap or potatoes. Or hearing them say that my painting doesn't match their curtains. Writing poetry and prose, while being infuriated that I have to meet the restrictive common moral code and taste and show my work to many who don't give a damn about art, but pretend that they're fervidly in love with it. In other words, I'm just trying not to suffocate in this mostly unliberated and phony world theater, where everyone is trying to act like someone else, and honesty and truth are pushed into a communal abyss. And somehow, as you see, I'm still breathing after escaping to an unknown country with only sixty bucks in my pocket, and not knowing a word of English. Of course, my parents didn't give me money; they were too angry that I was leaving. They said who ever took me should take care of me, figuring that I would come back after experiencing difficulties and being broke. But they were wrong, and I proved to everyone that I'm a survivor. Most of the thanks go to two individuals who gained my trust: Jasmine, who offered me the compassion and kindness of America, and Fred, who offered me the promise and assurance of America."

"I thought I was fighting to reach America, but that wasn't the case. I kept fighting, and I still do for my freedom, dignity, independence, and identity. I'm still struggling to know the ultimate truth. Can't you tell me?!" I yelled, staring into her lifeless face.

Mila stared back at me. Five minutes passed. It's her turn now to tell me who he is, I thought. I tried to satisfy her, and I took a big risk. Mother would've dropped dead if she knew what I was doing behind her dying body. But Mila kept silent. No answer. I got up and walked out, slamming the door behind me. Going down the stairs, I slipped and fell, making a terrible racket and almost breaking my neck. I heard the door to my room opening, and Mother's doomed voice coming from the living room, "Bazhe, are you okay?" Then, like an echo, Mila's sharp whisper followed, "Are you okay?"

"Yes, Mother," I shouted towards the living room. I looked up at Mila's face, then got up and ran outside to have a cigarette.

I didn't go upstairs for the rest of the day, to let Mila know I was serious. I cleaned the floor when Bisera took Mother for her regular walk. Each day, the walk got shorter due to Mother's weakening condition. After dinner, I helped Mother shower, assisted with her colostomy bag, and gave her the medicine. I didn't bring Mila dinner. She didn't want to eat anyway. She had cookies and a drink that were left from the morning. I was in the middle of watching a burlesque show, when Mother asked, "You haven't gone upstairs to read. The whole afternoon and evening you've been here. How come?"

"I'm taking a break. I don't want to overdo it. Moderation with everything is a golden rule, isn't it, Mother?"

"Yes, yes," she said, nodding, but she knew something was cooking. Poor Mother, she would probably die if she knew I was hiding her "rival" under own her roof. Feeling remorseful, I hugged and kissed her. I told her fairy tales about how much fun we were going to have when she came to America. I told her we would visit all the exciting places and shop until we dropped in all the department stores and boutiques. She cheered up then. Visions of the American dream worked very well on depressed cancer patients. I learned that during her radiation treatment, when I would tell stories of America to her roommates. Even as they struggled with pain, smiles would spread on their faces and they would forget their agony, at least temporarily.

I stayed downstairs way after Mother fell asleep, until the TV program was over at 2 o'clock in the morning. When I climbed upstairs, I noticed the light was still on in my room. Mila was waiting for me. It was our last night, and no doubt she was dying to spend it with me. I hesitated for a while, then decided not to say goodnight, to make my point stronger. Raged and exhausted, I curled up in my bed and fell asleep immediately.

The first morning light was brightening my window, when my mother's screams woke me up. She was calling my name. "The colostomy," I mumbled to myself and jumped from the bed like a soldier hearing an alarm. Mila was poking her head out the door of my room, looking frightened. She had probably hugged my toys and flipped through my photo albums all night, because she looked fatigued. I ran downstairs. Mother was at the bottom of the steps, grasping the handrail. Her nightdress was stained brown around her abdomen. I noticed fecal matter oozing through the material.

"I'm sorry to wake you up. I tried to clean myself," she moaned, shaking her head with disappointment.

"Everything is all right, Mother. Let me help you." I took her arm gently and walked her back to the living room. The runners in the hallway from the living room to the bathroom were spotted with excrement, as were parts of the living room kilim where she walked. The things she had touched were also marked. She would've made less mess if she had stayed in bed, but I could never order her to lie there and just wait for me in her own waste. Mother had been an extremely neat woman before the cancer, and even if she had been sloppy, I never would have suggested it.

Mother gave me that familiar, hopeless, look she got when an accident happened. I laid her on her back and, from under her bed I pulled out the emergency kit I kept in a shoebox. I put on gloves and pulled her nightdress up cautiously. I picked pieces of excrement off of it, as well as her thighs and underwear. Stains were all over the sheets. While I did this, Mother didn't stare up at the ceiling anymore. I was glad that she had become completely comfortable with me. It was hard to clean her in the beginning. She wasn't cooperative due to her embarrassment. I thought about those days as I pulled the colostomy bag off the rest of the way and tossed it in a plastic bag. I closed the bag tightly, carried it outside, and disposed of it in the garbage can.

I cleaned off the waste around the colostomy base and disinfected the area with homemade brandy. The base was sturdy, so there was no need to replace it. Carefully, I cut an opening for the new bag and attached it to the base evenly. I filled a basin with lukewarm water and, using gauze and toilet paper from the shoebox I cleaned all the stains off of her. I wiped off the phlegm-like discharge that had collected around her sewn rectum and disinfected her rectal and vaginal areas with the brandy. I assisted her in getting up from bed, and I undressed her for her shower.

In the shower, I soaped and rinsed her twice. Then I had her sit on the toilet, and I soaped her once more and let her rinse herself. I did that regularly. Letting her do things for herself was my way of keeping her confidence up, of showing her that she was doing fine. While she did that, I changed her bedsheets and took clean clothing from her drawer, placing the clothing on a chair. Mother was still rinsing herself with the handheld showerhead when I got back to the bathroom, and she stopped when she saw the look in my eyes. She had been getting water in the area of the colostomy, which tended to weaken the adhesive part of the base, but she couldn't resist the joy of doing it. Hygiene had always been her prerogative as a true civilian lady.

I wrapped the bathrobe around Mother's body, then walked her back to the living room and sat her on the edge of the bed. I dried her off completely with a towel and rubbed her entire body with her favorite plum brandy, followed by lotion. I dressed her slowly and neatly, combed her hair, applied cream and some make-up on her face, and sprayed her with her beloved rose perfume. I put the dirty clothes and sheets in the washing machine, cleaned and re-supplied my emergency shoebox, and made her mint tea. She didn't want to have breakfast, but she took her medicine and, as usual, closed her eyes shortly afterward.

I washed her dirty slip-ons and hung them up to dry. I had my coffee and cigarette, my breakfast, and a shower, then I went back to cleaning. I filled a bucket with water, added my favorite Xtra Pine cleaner, and using a brush and rags, I scrubbed the stains in the living room, the hallway, and the bathroom. I meticulously disinfected and dried off every object Mother had touched, and I did a final cleaning with Windex. When the laundry was done, I hung the clothes out back on a wire to dry. I knew that my nosy neighbors were watching me. When I hung out a lot of sheets and clothes, they knew Mother had an accident.

People pitied Mother and glorified me as the reformed son that you so rarely find. The number of people who admired my devotion grew. Originally, the locals and my family thought that my leaving for America showed that it wasn't worthwhile to adopt; that an adoptee could never be as connected to a family as a child of the same blood; and that my leaving was a shameful "thank you" to my parents who had done everything to raise me like a prince. They didn't expect I would move back from America and take care of Mother. It was too far, too much to give up, too much for an adoptee. They didn't know that there was no career, no country, no relationship, and no disability that would have stopped me from helping my mother. I believe that, for any child, their mother is the holiest creature. People found it ironic that the black sheep of the entire province would be ready to perform the ultimate act of filial dedication.

Then, my love towards Mother changed them. It made them gossip about me with delight and admiration, especially the ones who were disappointed with their sons and daughters. My bad reputation was transformed. Overnight, I became the son every parent wanted. My devotion encouraged couples to adopt that were once hesitant to do so. It was peculiar to go from being a queer and an outsider to being celebrated as an angel. People really are shallow and full of baloney. They don't use a quarter of their brains when they judge others. They just do it without reason. I was still the same. I hadn't reformed. What was wrong with people?

I thought about that as I dusted and vacuumed downstairs. The doorbell rang. It was our neighbor, Frosa, bringing lunch.

"Again?" she said, when she saw Mother asleep. "Woe, woman. Woe on you."

"Shhh! Don't wake her up for lunch. She had a tough night."

"I won't, I won't," Frosa mumbled, walking into the kitchen on her toes. On her way out, she said, "Your mother's biggest wish, to go to America with you, doesn't seem possible. She won't make it like this."

"Thanks for the meal, Frosa. Bye." After she left, I locked the door and began cursing her. I was dying to slap that negative bitch. Instead, I tried to forget her words and opened the windows to ventilate the floor. I sprayed each room with orchard nectar freshener. I was so involved in cleaning, I almost forgot about Mila. I always tried to keep the downstairs immaculately clean and disinfected. It was my way of fighting Mother's cancer, my revenge. I would often imagine the cancer as an evil human or a demon, and I would curse at it as if it were sitting before me. Initially, I thought I was going crazy, but later I figured out that picturing the cancer as a creature helped me to deal with it and vent my anger. I arranged lunch for Mila on the tray and took it upstairs.

Mila surprised me. She was sitting halfway up the stairs. "I spied on you. I'm sorry. I saw the two of you walking in hell. If you allow me, I'll stay here and take care of your mother. It would be in humble gratitude for all she did for both of us, and my way of making things up to you. You can go back to the U.S. and live your life as any young person should. I would love to do it. I'm ready."

"No," I said firmly, and placed the tray on the step. "What was, is gone; what will be, will happen. Continue your life as if nothing happened. There is no need for more complications here or in your family. Let's make it as simple as possible."

"I'm sorry that my presence has made it harder for you these days. But please reconsider my offer. Be rational. I can help you a great deal," she said, nudging my upper arm.

"Listen! I invited you. You don't need to feel sorry at all. You have only tomorrow left before going back to Croatia, and your parents are waiting eagerly to see you. I don't think I can stay upstairs with you much more, anyway. I can't leave Mother alone today. She is very down."

"Well, there's not much I can tell you about. My life is so conventional compared to yours. I'm going to live for our next meeting, so you can tell me more about your exciting life."

She had something to say. The anger in my eyes spoke louder then any possible words and told her that I was not buying it. I was losing hope, and in some respects, I was glad that the colostomy accident had occurred and created tension, so she would leave sooner than that evening.

"Staying a few hours more or less won't make a difference," she said. "It's better that I go soon. Also, as much as I want to be near you, I know that your mother must consider every single second with you to be precious. I want to let you know something, though. I doubt that your half brothers would do nearly as much as for me as you've done for your mother. I doubt that there are many children out there who would sacrifice a day of their young lives and risk everything to take care of their parents as your have. You are a noble son, and I am very proud that I bore you."

"Thank you," I said, faltering. I leaned against the stair rail, wondering if I could truly say I was proud that she had borne me.

"Call a taxi, please. I'll be ready in fifteen minutes," she said warmly. Her perfume filled the air with a pleasant aroma. She got up and climbed the stairs to her bedroom.

I picked up the tray, walked to my room, and called the taxi. I couldn't sit in the rocking chair for long, staring at the empty armchair. It felt strange not seeing her crouched there, listening and crying. I began circling the desk, confused. I thought I wanted her to leave as soon as possible. Did I?

Mila came in, looking stunning again in her red suit, carrying the black leather suitcase in her right hand. She placed it on the floor, opened her black shoulder bag, and took a burgundy box from it. She handed it to me, forcing a smile despite her obvious sadness, and said, "This is for you. I hope you'll like it."

"Thank you," I said, taking it. I opened the box and pulled out an attractive hand-woven gold chain. "It's very pretty...I've got the perfect pendant for it," I said. I took a card from my wallet and handed it to her. "My address and telephone in America."

"Thank you. I'll write. You have my address, don't you?"

"Of course," I said. "Excuse me. I'll be right back." I left the room and went to my bedroom. I felt obligated to give her something in return. I took a key hidden in the chandelier and pulled out a metal bank that was stuffed between piles of blankets in the cabinet. I unlocked the bank, took out the pearl jewelry box that contained a contemporary gold set, the last present I had bought my mother at Neiman Marcus, and went back to my room.

"Mother only wore it once when I showed it to her. I don't think she will again. I want you to have it," I said, as I handed it to Mila.

"No, I can't take it. It's for your mother." She shook her head.

"It's okay," I said, placing the jewelry box on her hand.

"Are you sure?" she asked me, as if I were committing a crime. Even so, she could barely suppress her happiness, which made her glow more than the pearls on the jewelry box.

"Yes, I am." I said sharply.

"Thank you, very much," she whispered through her tears. She lifted the lid and looked inside. "Gorgeous collection," she said, and began taking her jewelry off. She replaced them with the new set and walked over to the mirror in the corner of the room.

"They look charming on you," I complimented her.

"I'm greatly honored to have this beautiful gift that was for your mother. Many thanks," she said, then walked towards me. She stopped a few centimeters in front of me, and she stared into my eyes intently for a couple of minutes. Then she hugged me, crying louder.

What the hell was I doing? Crowning her my mother? My subconscious seemed to be drunk. I hated it. My mind was cloudy, making me do things that I would never usually do sober. At that moment, while she was preparing to say something, I was convinced more than ever that she would reveal the identity of my biological father. That's why I was trying to make her feel as if I were crowning her my mother, I realized, my heart beating hard in anticipation.

"Before I leave, I wondered if I could have a picture of you...And one as a baby, please," she requested cordially.

I was so disappointed, I wanted to scream, but I controlled myself and said, "Yes, of course. Choose any you want from the albums."

She had already decided which ones she wanted to take. I could tell that by the way she quickly flipped through the photo albums and pulled three pictures out. She stored them carefully in her purse and said, "Thanks a lot."

The stairway would soon no longer be the divider between my two mothers' worlds. Walking down felt lighter and easier now, even with her suitcase in my hand. Mila's shadow was melting time to time into mine, and as we walked out, the sun faded it out. My shadow didn't disappear. It was still moving close to her, and hoping that she would tell me who he was. We went out by the rear door, crossed through the orchard, and came out on the back street. There were no curious neighbors around, but I couldn't have cared less anymore. I realized she wasn't going to tell me anything, and all I wanted was for our visit to be over and my disappointment to end with it. I was ready to go back and concentrate on Mother's world, a world that, unfortunately, would soon end.

When the taxi came, Mila began crying more loudly, and she embraced me one last time. I hugged her back, and as I kissed her, I whispered, "Who is my father? How can I find him?"

"I have no idea. I really don't know. Trust me," she said. But she didn't look into my eyes, and that was a sign she was lying.

"Okay," I said, parting from her hug. I opened the taxi's trunk and put her suitcase inside. Then I opened the back door for her. "Say hello to your brother."

"Thanks." Mila got in the taxi, weeping harder.

The taxi backed up to the main road. She waved, and I could still see her tears sparkling like precious stones on her cheeks. I waved back, but I didn't wait for the car to disappear completely from my sight, as I would usually do during farewells. Instead, I ran back inside, feeling betrayed, angry, and manipulated. That all stopped when I sat beside Mother's bed and gently placed my hands on her body. I didn't want to wake her up. I just wanted to feel her love, a love that I respected more than ever at that moment.

I hated the emptiness of my room. The armchair resembled an abandoned bird's nest with its crumpled cover. I cleaned and straightened up the entire upper floor, except the armchair. I needed to keep some trace of Mila alive for a while.

I let the answering machine take messages until the following night, Mila's last one in Macedonia. There were several from her. I trudged around my room, like a wounded tiger trailed by a hunter, as I listened to her voice.

She said, "This reminds me of the days when I was hiding my secret, being pregnant with you. My parents constantly ask me about our five days together. They keep staring at your pictures and trying not to show their guilt. It hurts. It's embarrassing to talk to my brother and sister, who look at my parents and me as if we were aliens since we confessed our sin to them. They all want to meet you. I hope you'll call me back, because I can't eat and sleep for thinking about you, your mother, and our reunion. Believe me, I didn't want you to grow up like a fern out of the rocks, in such strange circumstances as an adoptee! I tried to keep you, but…"

The machine beeped. I pressed the stop button. I couldn't take it anymore. Mila's words stabbed my heart like spears, particularly since she was still hiding a significant secret from me. Nevertheless, so as not to look like an uncivilized asshole, I called her back before bedtime.

"I wish you a good trip tomorrow," I said, trying to limit the conversation to pleasantries.

"It's you! Oh, God, I thought you wouldn't call me," she said, sounding like a little girl who'd just gotten a beautiful doll from her parents. She had probably been waiting by the telephone since she'd returned to her parents' home, waiting for my call.

"Being with my parents doesn't mean anything to me, even though I haven't visited them for a long time." Her voice became slow and sober. "I don't want to go back to Dalmatia. I don't think about my husband and your half brothers. You are all I'm consumed with. I'd rather stay here in Macedonia and help you."

I imagined myself walking up and down the stairs again between the two worlds of my mothers, and Mila once again interfering with my mission. Who needed more of that purgatory, I thought.

"Call me when you get home," I said, making it sound like an order. With that, I killed the last trace of her by straightening up the armchair cover.

"Okay," she said, sobbing.

"Good night," I said, and hastily hung up.

What if she decides to stay in Macedonia? What if she comes by the house? I couldn't sleep, thinking that Mila could do such crazy things in her current state of mind. I was finally able to relax when she called me from Croatia the next morning. The most longed-for event in my life was definitely over, but it didn't give me the closure I had hoped for. I still didn't know who the biological father was.

For some reason I remembered a cliché I had heard from movies in America: "There are some things man was not meant to know…"

31

Nurse

It was June of 1997, and a year had passed since Mother was diagnosed with colon cancer. As the cancer metastasized, her body deteriorated further. It became increasingly difficult to care for her, and there was less and less we could do. No more renting a car and going out to dine. I had to force her to eat. As her legs got weaker and her limp worsened she stopped going for walks with Bisera. She refused to use a cane. She considered it an embarrassment. Instead, she supported herself with a rake as we strolled near the house. We usually walked around the backyard, to avoid the curious looks of passersby on the main street.

Now and then, before sunset, she would make me walk with her in the rose garden, so she could see and talk to her best friends. I kept telling Mother she would get better and be able to walk normally soon. But by autumn, she stopped leaving the house. She could only walk as far as the bathroom by then. It was heartbreaking to watch her trudging around. She used the furniture to support herself and literally hung on our arms when Bisera or I would walk her back and forth in the hallway. She would stop at the open front door to watch the sun set or see a rainbow decorate her beloved garden, praying that someday she would regain her strength. She denied her condition and felt hopeful, except when the pain intensified. I often had to call an ambulance, so she could get morphine injections from the nurses.

Now and then, Mother seemed to lose awareness of her surroundings, as well. Her eyes would go unfocused. I began monitoring every pill and shot of morphine, every plate of food, everything she drank, how many hours she slept, and what she did when she was awake, to try to figure out what was causing that. The cancer was doing it, though I would find myself crying helplessly, afraid that I had not given her enough attention or water or tea or food.

In addition to blaming myself, my body began to ache occasionally. Mother's cancer was making me sick now. I tried hard not to let myself get run down. Mother's lips began to dry out frequently, and she requested her pink handkerchief and glass of water, so she could moisten them from time to time. I became more scared, but not enough to quit my stubborn war against her cancer.

On a gloomy September evening, Fred called me from New Jersey. The INS had informed him that I should expect to take my citizenship test in December. When I told Mother, she said, "You must take the exam! You failed to take it once because of me. I won't let you do that again." She watched as lightning flashed over our garden. "You could get stuck here. You know that better than anyone. You've proven to me that you are good at predicting our country's destiny."

"Well, Kosovo is next. Then Macedonia." I murmured. My eyes tingled as I said it.

"I believe you. Before that happens, you'd better get your U.S. citizenship. Nothing can be one hundred percent guaranteed here, but it would definitely help you in case of war."

"How could I leave you though?"

"In an airplane," she smiled, a bit of her old humor shining through. "We'll find someone to take care of me."

"Who? You know these people. They have such a complex about being caregivers and nurses. It's going to be hard finding someone, Mother. Trust me!"

"Hard or not, you must get your citizenship...Even if I have to rot here alone, you must do it!" Once again, she was thinking only of me.

"If I don't find a replacement, I won't go!" I declared firmly.

"First of all, no one can replace you, my gold. Secondly, you'll go back whether or not you find help! Haven't you had enough of me? Of the smell of my colostomy and my decaying body? You need a break anyway!"

"Oh, stop that! Don't talk like that, Mother! You know I can't leave you alone. You're afraid to be alone."

"It seems that you are afraid of America. Is anything wrong back there? Are you happy in America?"

"Well, Mother, I'm going to be completely honest with you about America, particularly what we call the Tri-state area. As you know, I began dreaming about America a long time ago. But the dream and the reality, as always, are totally different. In the first place, don't think that life in America is like any of Hollywood's 'feel good' movies, where everyone is rich, glamorous, and happy. Not all American stories end happily. There is both abject poverty and enormous wealth. There is a great deal of crime and a lot of tension between various groups. Many Americans are brainwashed to believe that their system and country are perfect, the best. America is definitely better than many countries, but no country is the best.

"Lately, there have been so many fascists over there that hate gays, blacks, Jews, Hispanics, Asians, and minorities in general. There is a lot of hypocrisy in the American legal and moral systems. There is a lot of religious Puritanism that is outwardly so righteous, but so decadent on the inside. Their mentality is completely different from ours. In America, people have money, but I don't think they enjoy life half as much as we do in the Balkans with much less. Each day is like a holiday here. Over there, you have to work hard for that damned dollar. Americans are always praying for Friday to come, so they can have the weekend off. People here have much more time to experience life. As a result, they're much more relaxed and friendly. People over there are colder, more uptight, and more alienated. They definitely deserve more vacations. Americans are hard-working people. Americans live to work, and we work to live. Sadly, most of them don't realize it, and that affects their well-being and happiness. Except for the minorities, their parties are like funerals compared to ours. Most of the time, all they talk about is business and money. I miss our parties, with their group dancing, jokes, anecdotes, and smiling people all around you. I miss our humble little cafés, having company over anytime I want, and gossiping with the neighbors. Over there, neighbors can live next door to each other their whole lives and never exchange a single word.

"In the Balkans, every major event produces deep emotion. Any gain or loss, any happiness or sadness, is greeted with strong brandy and tears. Births, weddings, divorces, deaths, all of these occasions are handled in a routine, business-like manner in America. I'll always miss that combination of Western European, Mediterranean, and Eastern influences, the way the Christian world meets the Muslim world, that makes the Balkans such a unique and overwhelming place culturally. America restricts the importation of different cultural influences. It is a very self-centered place. The profit motive is behind it, of course. They'd rather export their mass-produced products.

"We have to remember, though, that America will always be one of the newest colonies. You can't expect Americans, who are nouveaux riches compared to Europeans, to be wise and take an academic approach to their cultural growth. They're too obsessed with the dollar and material things. America is not flowing with milk and honey, and success doesn't fall from the sky. But there are more opportunities for survival in America than anywhere else on this planet. And as one of the youngest and richest countries, it has the greatest potential to become a truly democratic, humane, and free place. I'm sure about that, and that's what makes America so special. I long for the Yugoslavia we knew, but now it's dead. I'll feel the nostalgia and the pain for it until I die. But I have to live and keep trying to find true freedom, peace, and love, because we all aspire for them. I'll fight for them everyday, while I long for my lost country and help build and reform the new one we call America."

Mother was staring at me, her mouth half-open. She was waiting to hear more about America, but I stood up and said, "Pardon me, Mother." I ran upstairs to my bedroom and pulled my poetry notebook out from under my pillow. I ran back to her and sat in the middle of the room. Opening the notebook, I flipped to the page I was looking for and announced, "Here is a poem I wrote about America. It's entitled:

"New Country.
I am here. New air, food, faces, bodies, more ideals, ambition, and sadness.
Behind my back, everything I left comes to mind.
My country is dead, X Yugoslavia.
In all these looks, I am trying to be part of them. I am trying to find the path, to grab my part that is only mine, and nobody else's.

I am commuting on the subway from NJ to NYC. The homeless are sinking,
The businesses are rising, and the American daydream is before me.
I am stepping peacefully, at first naively, without much noise,
across this country alive with contrasts, risks, and lots of hopes, America."

"Nice," Mother said. "You still recite magically, like when you were a child."

"Thank you." I kissed her. I didn't feel the rage that I once had while remembering the times when I was forced by her and Father to recite at their parties. I *did* remember the humiliation, as if it happened yesterday. I remembered when everyone would giggle after I swallowed a letter or two, or bit my fingernails, and the way Father would freeze me with his angry expressions. I hugged Mother again. I kissed her and forgave her for her mistakes. And she looked as though she knew it.

Immediately, I began searching for an aide. I tried word of mouth, classified advertising, and the local radio stations. September and October passed, and I received no calls. I visited several hospitals and social centers, in search of unemployed people. When I would offer them the job, they would say, "Who wants to wipe up an old lady's stinky shit?" I couldn't believe they refused my offer. I was willing to pay double what a regular nurse would make, and provide free food and clothing from the U.S., just to change Mother's colostomy bag, give her painkillers, and stay with her for no more than an eight-hour, rotating shift per day. Again, I faced our stubborn and discriminatory outlook towards certain jobs and professions. I was disgusted. I often hoped the economic crisis would escalate to the point where those morons would suffer so much they would finally learn their lesson.

Mila called me a lot, but I would only answer twice a month. She usually brought up the same things, over and over: her family, my mother, how much she missed me. I tried to keep our conversations as short as possible. I didn't want to talk to her if she wasn't going to tell me about the father. I didn't believe her story about not knowing him. Anyway, chatting with her was not a pleasure while I struggled to find someone to care for Mother before I had to take my citizenship test.

Fortunately, good karma or kismet, as we have called it since the Ottoman era, awarded me with luck. One bright Gypsy summer morning, a peasant woman knocked on our door and said she had a Bulgarian nurse who wanted to work for us. Anxious, I invited her over right away. Mother wasn't even upset that I didn't have her sitting in a chair before our guest came over, to make her seem healthier. Mother hated for people to see her in bed, but by then everyone knew she had cancer.

After we all got acquainted over cookies and Turkish coffee, the country-woman said that she was very excited about being in the former governor's house. She shared some local news and events, speaking in a thick, provincial dialect. Mother seemed to enjoy the gossip more than ever after being isolated from the social life for so long.

"I'll be honest," the countrywoman said with a serious, but not very convincing, expression. "My main reason for helping you is to take revenge on my aunt, who is a real bitch. She has done many evil things to me and my family. She has been terminally ill for almost three years. Too long, isn't it? I pray every hour for her to finally go to hell. A Bulgarian nurse came to our village to take care of her a year ago. She can't stand being in my aunt's house any longer. For the last couple of months, the bitch has threatened not to pay her monthly allowance if she doesn't help in the apple orchids on her own time. On top of that, my alcoholic uncle has tried to molest her a number of times.

"When I told the nurse that a civilian family was looking for an aide, she told me to come and set up an appointment so you could meet her. She needs money. Poor lady." The countrywoman shook her head. "She is a very good nurse. Feel free to ask any of the villagers. They'll tell you how skilled a worker she is. She is

a good cook and a good maid, as well. Even in villages way up by the Greek border, people have heard about her. Many want to hire her. She takes our blood
pressure and gives injections when we get sick. She is a wizard. You can't even feel
the pinch of her needle."

The peasant woman extolled this nurse's virtues as if she were Mother Teresa.
Neither Mother nor I trusted her completely, but having no choice, we arranged
the meeting.

Nurse Rodna was Mother's contemporary and a widow. She had retired as a
licensed head nurse after working for leading oncologists in the hospitals of Bulgaria's capital, Sofia. She had a daughter, also an adoptee. The daughter had two
children by an alcoholic boyfriend, who badly abused them all. The Bulgarian
economy, as those in other former communist countries, was collapsing after the
transition to capitalism. Rodna came to Macedonia, which was doing better than
other countries for some reason, to earn money and help her daughter and her
grandchildren educate themselves. I had great respect for her devotion as a
mother, which was so much like that of my own mother. I hired her and stayed a
few more weeks to observe her performance.

She wasn't as good a cook as our neighbor, Frosa, and she wasn't a very good
housekeeper either, but as a medical worker, she knew her job very well. In addition, she knew how to be friendly and quickly became very close with Mother.
Frosa was greatly disappointed not to be able to steal from us anymore as our
shopper and cook. She visited Mother less and less. The house no longer smelled
of Mother's money; it just stank of her body. I had expected that from Frosa. A
person's true colors always come through when you are in trouble, don't they?

On a dreary December afternoon, I scheduled a flight back to the U.S. As I
carried my bag downstairs, I noticed Mother had applied makeup and combed
her hair, in an attempt to look as healthy as possible. Bisera and Frosa made me a
special farewell lunch. It was one of my favorite vegetarian meals. It had *Taratur*,
a plain yogurt mixed with garlic, cucumbers, walnuts and mint, and *Sarma*,
boiled rice wrapped in young grape leaves. Rodna, Bisera, and Frosa constantly
joked, trying to create a happy atmosphere. Mother played along by forcing herself to eat and laugh, pretending as if I were going to Disneyland or something. I
faked my mood as well, grinning like a lunatic, even though their jokes weren't
funny.

"Keep laughing," Mother said to me at one point. "I love when you smile. I'll
miss that glimpse of light in this tomb. I would've been dead by now without
your smile."

The laughter and the jokes stopped. I didn't give the silence a chance to conquer us. I jumped from my chair, announcing that I had peed in my pants. The women laughed again. I ran to the bathroom, as I had many times before, sat on the toilet, and burst into tears. I waited until I had calmed down again, then I put on my happy mask, flushed the toilet, and went back out. It was an exhausting act, but I managed to keep it up.

The act crumbled, however, when the taxi arrived to take me to the airport. Mother and I cried and held each other in a long embrace.

"Safe trip, my gold," she said, kissing me. "I'm so happy you're going back to the U.S. Concentrate on the citizenship test and don't worry about me."

"Thank you, Mother." I kissed her yellow-fawn face, which smelled of lilac-scented French cream. I wondered if we were sharing our last hug, if she would live to see me again, and I could tell she thought the same. It was reflected in her eyes when we exchanged one last look before I left.

I studied my subjects intensely: American history, law, and government. Every morning, I rushed to check my mailbox, hoping to get the dates of my citizenship exam. The holidays passed, and I still didn't have the dates. When I called the INS, an officer told me that she had no idea what had happened, that the testing schedule was an internal matter, and that I would probably get a date in February. I didn't, and again I had to face the hell of dealing with the INS bureaucratic machine, spending hours on the phone to get a clue about what was happening, being switched from officer to officer, being yelled at and disconnected repeatedly. I was reliving my experiences with them years earlier, when I applied for my green card and the INS treated me as if I were a foreign invader.

When I told Mother what was happening, she tried to sound as happy as possible, bragging about how well Nurse Rodna attended to her and how much better she was doing. She insisted I stay in New Jersey. The nurse confirmed Mother's statement, swearing that I should not worry a bit as long as Mother was in her hands.

Every Friday, I called home. It was a comfortable old routine. The nurse would answer, and she would bring the cordless phone to Mother, so I could talk to her first, then she would talk with me. The conversations were similar. Most of the time, Mother would insist that I stay in the U.S., convincing me that things were in perfect order.

At the end of March, Nurse Rodna complained for the first time. "Bazhe, this is becoming very hard for me," she said. "Your mother's appetite has increased. Her colostomy bags fill up faster than ever, and she has many accidents. Sometimes I have to change her more than three times a day. Besides cleaning her feces, the mucous is dripping intensively from her sewn rectum, which the cancer enlarged so it looks like a giant mushroom. I'm constantly wiping it. The whole house stinks so badly that I would probably suffocate if I didn't run outside for a breath of fresh air now and then. I can't ventilate the room. It's a cruel winter here, and her weakened body can't handle the slightest cold. Even though the room is very warm, she often complains of the cold, and I have to turn the heat up and wrap her with an extra blanket. Then I have to leave because I can't breathe from the boiling temperature. It's a pain in the neck. But that's not the main problem, Bazhe."

"The pain has increased along with her appetite, and her pension is not enough for food and medication. Prices are going up every day. Even though I'm a compulsive saver, I have to use money from my allowance at the end of each month, and then compensate myself when the new pension arrives. You must increase my salary! Otherwise, I have to quit. I can't take it any longer!"

"Why did you wait until now to tell me this?" I said, suppressing my anger. "Fucking bitch," I muttered to myself, wishing I could be there and slice her throat.

"Well, I know how important getting your citizenship is to you and your mother. I didn't want her to worry. She is obsessed with it."

"Never mind. I'll cancel it and come back to replace you immediately."

"Oh, no, no, no. Pass the test. I'll try to stay until then, but only if you increase my salary and pay me extra for the time I've been here. Don't rush to send it to me now. When you come back home. Okay? I wouldn't dream of inconveniencing you."

"Are you sure you can stay? I cannot leave Mother alone."

"I'll manage it. But you have to promise me that you'll give me the increase and pay me the extra money."

"I promise. No problem. I can send you the money right now if you want."

"No, no! We'll handle that when you come back."

"Are you sure?"

"Positive."

"As you wish. But you also have to give me your word that you'll take good care of my mother."

"You have my word…We've made a deal then? I'll let you go, so you won't spend a lot on this call. See, I'm constantly trying to economize for the sake of your house, out of respect for you and your mother's well being. You'll never find a nurse like me."

"Thank you. You are absolutely right."

"So long then until Friday. Please don't talk to your mother about this. Okay?"

"Of course I won't. Are you out of your mind? Bye, bye."

As I hung up, I said sarcastically, "She economizes for the sake of our home, out of respect for me and Mother's well being. Ha! My ass! What a classic cunt."

I ran to the basement, where I kept my bike, and rode to the bank. Balkan people considered Bulgarians to be among the biggest and boldest liars and thieves in the region. Maybe it was a stereotype, but after our conversation, I had no doubt that Nurse Rodna was cooking up some disgusting plan behind my back. Her Bulgarian had never sounded so ugly and phony. At the bank, my hands trembled as I wrote her name on a thousand-dollar money order. I was damn scared. Terrified. Events were moving beyond my ability to control them.

32

Citizen

The beautiful spring days passed. My insecurity about the situation back home followed me like a ghost as I waited anxiously for the INS to schedule my citizenship test. It was difficult to study, now that Nurse Rodna had revealed her true, rapacious nature to me. I no longer doubted that she was stealing Mother's pension and maybe even things from the house. I was pretty sure that her threat to leave Mother was a bluff, part of a plan to drain more money from me. Still, the mere possibility that she could abandon Mother before I returned was killing me. Finally, in April, the INS letter of appointment arrived. I passed my citizenship exam a week later, and immediately booked the first available flight to Macedonia.

As soon as I stepped inside the house, I could tell that Mother's condition was worse. The stench in the hallway was stronger than ever. I was afraid to open the living room door. I took a deep breath and slowly turned the handle. Bisera, Frosa, Uncle Bogdan, and Rodna were there, and they rose from their seats as I came in. I dropped my bag and ran to Mother's bed. Her frame had shrunk further. I held her and kissed her face.

"You're here, my gold," Mother whispered, patting my hair. Her forced smile was deformed by the cancer into an unattractive grimace. "Don't look at me," she ordered in a frail voice. "I'm ugly now...Very ugly...I stink. Aren't you disgusted? Don't kiss me. You might get some disease from me."

Everyone lowered their heads, trying to hide their tears from her. I gulped hard to stop mine, and before it was too late, I smiled back and said, "What are you talking about? You look the same. You're my mother, the one person I love more than anyone in this world."

"Me too, my gold. Me too," she murmured, coughing.

I picked up a piece of wet gauze that had fallen from her fingers to the couch and gently placed it on her dry lips. Then I turned away quickly, so she wouldn't see my eyes tear up. I greeted everyone with a kiss and hug, including the nurse,

287

even though I really wanted to throw her through the window. I controlled myself, for Mother's sake, recalling how much she hated it when I shouted, especially in front of other people. It reminded her of Father, and she'd had enough of that. She wanted me to solve problems in a civil and peaceful way.

Bisera served me coffee and cake, which she baked to welcome me home. Uncle Bogdan asked me about my trip and about America. Everyone except Mother joined the conversation, expressing their media-based views of the Promised Land, the myth that they all wished to see one day. Rodna remarked that the only reason she wanted to go to America was to find a rich old man to take care of, preferably one that was terminally ill, so she could inherit his money and build herself a castle in Bulgaria.

Everyone was straining to prolong the laughter, to cheer me up as I gazed at Mother. Her eyes alternated between the ceiling, the window, and me. It was heartbreaking to watch her. I excused myself and went to the bathroom. Again, I employed my old tactic. I sat on the toilet and cried for a while, then flushed, washed my face, put on some makeup to hide the colors of my agony, and forced a grin as I went back.

Mother was the absolute prisoner of the cancer now, I thought. She stared without expression out the window at the shadows of the sunset, at the branches of a plum tree tapping at the glass, and at the stray cats that climbed those branches to satisfy their curiosity with a look in to our living room. Her jowls moved, then the wet piece of gauze between her lips, but she was chewing nothing.

The moment her eyes closed, Bisera whispered to me, "She takes only injections of morphine now."

"She won't stay alive for long. She doesn't move from her bed anymore," Frosa added, shaking her head.

"I have to change her position every day so she won't develop bedsores from laying on one side too long," Rodna broke in.

"She's developed an immense desire to live, especially since your father died. She wanted to visit you in America, badly. But the faster she goes, the better. She's suffered enough. Be strong now. Okay?" My uncle patted my shoulder.

"Let's go, so he can be alone with his mother," Bisera said. She got up and gestured Frosa and Uncle Bogdan to leave with her. They left the table and followed Bisera out silently, as if they were her obedient servants. As I muttered goodbye to them, I noticed Uncle Bogdan exchanging a clandestine glance with Nurse Rodna as she went to escort them. The old womanizer had a crush on her. Apart from his loneliness as a widower, that was the only reason he was visiting our house often.

I sat there and stared at Mother, who had changed drastically while I was away. What a liar she is, I thought. An even bigger liar than I am. I remembered her convincing words over the phone about how much better she was doing. She probably couldn't eat solid food anymore. Mother's skin seemed to hang on her bones and had a fawn cast that in some places resembled bruises, particularly under her eyes. She was turning into a skeleton. I hated the way she lay in bed. Her deathlike posture and the wet piece of gauze between her lips were intimidating. She looked as if she were preparing to expire any minute. I hated the climate of death that her hopeless body created. A few minutes passed, and I realized another change.

"Mother, Mother," I said, shaking her. She opened her barren, glazed eyes instantly. Her hand rose towards my face, but didn't reach it. It reminded me of Adam's hand extending towards God's on the ceiling of the Sistine Chapel in Rome.

"Sorry to wake you up, Mother." I grabbed her hand, then I asked urgently, "Where are your earrings, rings, your chain and bracelet, your watch?"

"I gave them to Rodna. She wanted them. She was good to me."

"What!" I turned towards the door. I felt like running out and killing her. "Rodna! Rodna!" I yelled, feeling like I was about to explode.

The door opened instantly. I knew she must have had her ear glued to it, trying to hear our conversation.

"Is anything wrong?" she asked casually, as if she weren't completely aware of what was going on. Her nervous face betrayed her false state of confusion.

"Give me Mother's jewelry! How dare you take it! Who gave you permission?"

"Your mother. She did. Didn't you, Kostadina?" she replied defensively.

Mother nodded. Her frightened eyes begged me not to continue arguing. I ignored her and shouted, "Without my permission, you're not allowed to take anything from this house! I am the boss here!"

Mother's pale face turned a deep grayish-brown. At that moment, I realized how much I sounded like my father, and how much she despised it. I didn't care, though. I raged at Rodna as she poked around reluctantly in her dresser drawer. She took the jewelry from a handbag and abruptly placed it on the table.

"Cunt," I murmured, and placed the rings, the bracelet, the chain, and the watch back on Mother. As I tried to put her earrings back on, I noticed the hooks were cut off.

"What's this?" I yelled at Rodna.

"I had to use pliers. The hooks were so difficult to open. As if they were welded." She spoke without remorse.

My entire body began to shake. I could just see Nurse Rodna, poised like a scorpion with the pliers above Mother's helpless face, cutting off the earrings, treating her as if she were already dead. I took a deep breath and somehow managed to bend the hooks and make the earrings stay on Mother's earlobes. Then I turned on Rodna, bellowing like a wounded lion in battle with a hunter.

"You humiliated Mother! You made my life hell the day you threatened to leave her if I didn't give you a raise and extra money for the time you had been here! You were lying when you said that Mother's pension wasn't enough for food and medicine! I know why Mother was lying about how good you've been to her; so I wouldn't come back and miss my citizenship test. But I'm sure you didn't stay here for the same reason. To help me do my business in America and out of respect for Mother, you said. You don't give a damn for us! You don't even have respect for yourself. You stayed here to grab as much as possible. And I was willing to pay you as much as you wanted. In dollars. But not after what you did. Not after looting her jewelry and pulling her earrings off with pliers! What a savage act! Disgusting! Shame on you!"

"Please don't fight my gold. Don't." Mother mumbled, trying to get up.

"Mother, keep out of this please. I'm not retarded," I said. "Nor will I let anyone treat you like you are, Mother. No way!"

"I'll show you all my expenses. Here they are." Rodna pulled a notebook from the drawer and opened it on the table. She began reading how much she had spent, week by week, since I had left.

"Listen, lady, stop handing me that nonsense! There's no way that Mother's pension couldn't cover the expenses. When my mother was healthy, we didn't spend more than two-thirds of her pension. It's still one of the biggest in the country. After she became ill, we spent even less. And you're telling me her has appetite increased? Since you arrived, she can't even eat half a plate of food per day. Do you think that I buy your crap? Eh? Come on!" I paused to take a breath. "I gave you a great salary. Free food. I even sent presents for your family. I thought I was fair, but I guess it wasn't enough for you. You asked for more, and I immediately sent you an extra thousand dollars. That's about five months of decent pay around here. In the meantime, you've taken even more from Mother's pension. Do you think I'm a moron or something? I trusted you! But not anymore!"

"I've had enough. I'm leaving now. This is what I get after caring for your mother?" Rodna began weeping and ran into the kitchen. She took one of Mother's sedatives, then left the room, slamming the door.

"Go to hell, bitch!" I yelled after her.

"Son," Mother spoke up quietly. She looked slightly puzzled, as if trying to process everything I had just said. "I know you are right, my gold. It's obvious she lies. Rodna came here to make money. Don't create scandals. Locals will ridicule us. You know how difficult it was to find someone to help. She deserves some credit. We have enough money. Pay her as much as she wants and let her stay. Give her the jewelry. Money doesn't mean anything, my gold. Can't you see? It can't help me. Nothing can help me. I would trade everything I have to get my health back. To hell with the money and the jewelry." Mother spoke thoughtfully and soberly.

"No way. She's stolen enough. I won't let her fool us anymore. I'm here. We don't need her. I'll take care of you as I always have. I'll bring you back on your feet."

"Bazhe, you are a very good liar. Almost two years have passed, and you have turned every day into April Fools Day, in order to comfort me. I know what I have." Mother still couldn't say the word "cancer." She nodded and arched an eyebrow knowingly as she said, "I'll never visit you in America. You've helped me stay in denial for a long time. Rodna told me everything, my gold. I'm dying. Soon I'll be gone. And you need help. It will be hard for you to move me around alone. Rodna can barely manage it by herself. She's had to call Bisera for help. Let her stay, please. She knows how to inject me better than any nurse I've ever had. When the cancer attacks, I need her badly. Now it hurts worse than ever."

Raging, I left the room and ran upstairs. Rodna was packing her belongings. "How dare you tell Mother about her cancer without consulting with me?" I said.

"The truth always hurts. I told her in order to ease her suffering, and so that she could start her journey to Elysium. She knew it anyway. She didn't want to admit it. She is probably in pain now, suppressing it so she won't disturb you on your first day back home." Rodna stopped packing and sat on the edge of the sofa. "I also told her that you found your biological mother and that she stayed in this house for a week last year. But I convinced her that what you did was normal, that looking for your identity was a natural yearning for any adoptee. My daughter did the same. I even helped her. By the way, the whole town knows about it. I spoke to Mila when she called a couple of times from Croatia to find out about your mother. Nothing in this world stays secret, my dear."

Rodna paused, then asked me for a cigarette. I took a pack and a lighter from my pocket and handed them to her. She pulled out a cigarette, lit it, and gave them back to me. I waited silently while she took a couple of puffs.

"The locals are always talking about your gayness," she said. "They're always asking me, sarcastically, what you do in America. You have so many enemies who don't want to see anybody from this house succeed, who are glad that your mother is suffering. But I stood behind you. I told them to their faces that it's none of their business and that they are primitive, ignorant, and stupid creatures. I also explained to your mother that your sexuality is normal. Some of the best doctors in the hospitals where I worked were gay, and we were best friends. All that matters in life is to be happy, whether you love a man or a woman. I told your mother that a hundred times. What do you think we've been doing all this time together? We revealed many secrets to each other. Many more than you have ever shared with her. We are two women, of the same generation, and we are both adoptive parents, as well."

I didn't know what to feel, how to react, or what to say to Rodna. Should I hate her or adore her? I knew she wasn't being fake, now. For Mother's sake, I let her stay, even after I found out that she had done several other miserable things in my absence.

Neighbors told me that she had banned visitors from the house so that she could have total control over it. She had taken money from Mother's pension and kept it at Frosa's house, and she had bribed Frosa not to tell anyone about it. Bisera confessed that she had caught Rodna yelling at Mother a number of times; now and then, Rodna refused to serve Mother meals and drinks. She claimed that too much food and drink were bad for her, but she actually did it to avoid having to change Mother's colostomy bag, clean the discharge from her rectal area, and help her urinate. Bisera explained that Mother was afraid of her, but that she endured the humiliation so I could continue to take care of business in the U.S.

Then I found out that, back in February, Rodna's daughter stayed at the house for a week with friends from Bulgaria and plundered most of Mother's expensive wardrobe, as well as some china, small electronics, and appliances I had brought her from the U.S. When I asked Mother about it, once again she lied about allowing her to take the stuff, so as not to cause friction between us.

I'd heard that people often give away their possessions when they sense it's time to die. Mother was preparing for the last journey.

33

Death

Mother was getting further and further away from me. I wanted the believers to be right. I wanted to think she was starting her journey to heaven. Mother's ears and nose were thinning rapidly and becoming pointy. The locals said it was a sign that she would die soon. Mother's body continued to shrink, as if she were already preparing to turn into dust and be recycled back to nature.

That May, on my birthday, Mother surprised me with a present. It was a beautiful gold ring with a scarlet garnet that matched other jewelry she had bought me. Bisera had bought it from the local goldsmith. That was just a month before Mother died.

I've learned that people have the incredible ability to sense when their time is over. The day before Mother died, she refused her morphine injection. She took only the liquid painkiller, so she could stay awake. When Rodna went shopping, she had me sit next to her. It was horrifying to look at her. Her movements were lethargic. Occasionally, she would take a deep breath, to steel herself against the pain and keep from crying out. She was breathing harder than usual that morning and holding the air in longer. I suggested changing her position, to ease her struggle, but she shook her head and slowly reached for me.

Taking my hand into her cold palm, she said: "Give the almond-shaped antique ring to Bisera. The contemporary one goes to Frosa. And give this set, as I promised, to Rodna. The rest, you take with you...You can do whatever you want with the house, but don't be in a rush to sell it. Remember, we are in the middle of Europe." She paused to cough, and then she tried to speak as clearly and calmly as possible. "Put costume jewelry on me. The mortician and gravediggers will pillage the gold from a corpse in these miserable and uncertain times. Tell the women to dress me neatly, but don't let them makeup my face. You do that. You are good at it. Make sure to spray the strongest perfume on me, so my body won't smell bad. You know, I never attended funerals, so I don't think many people will attend mine. But you still have to make me look nice."

I hugged her, unable to speak. I could feel the pestilent chill of her palm as she stroked my face and hair in a soothing manner. Then she said sharply: "It's good that you have found her. At least you'll have someone to look after you when I die."

"What?" I asked, pretending that I didn't understand.

"Shh!" She caressed my lips with her trembling fingers.

The final hours of her life, I thought, and she was still trying to protect me. She would even recognize the woman who she feared and hated most, all for the sake of my well-being. I curled up next to her, the way I did as a child after Father yelled at us. I listened to the weak beats of her heart and stroked her face. I kissed her, again and again.

"Stay with Fred," she said. "He's a nice man. He loves you."

When she said that, I wrapped my arms around her and hugged her tight. At that moment, I felt as if the room were changing into the Elysian Fields. Mother was flying above me like an angel. I sensed that she completely accepted me, and I began dancing with her, as we once did, to music from the first stereo she bought for me.

"Enjoy life, wherever you go, whatever you do, and as much as you can. Life is short, very short. Live life, don't let life live you!" Mother stated emphatically. "Every minute of happiness is priceless. Try hard not to waste any of them. And don't care about material things. They stay behind you. Try to enrich your spirit with joy, love, and peace. That's all that counts. That's all you take with you. The happy memories you've had. Nothing more, nothing less."

"Yes, Mother," I said, crying as I gazed into her shimmering eyes, then at the wet piece of gauze that she slowly placed back between her dry lips. I continued to hold her until Rodna showed up. Mother took her morphine injection then, and shortly afterward, she drifted to sleep. All day, I sat beside Mother and thought of her love. It was greater than I had ever known. To this day, I don't think I can really appreciate how boundless my mother's love and devotion were.

The next day, June 25, Mother didn't wake up until evening. I was sitting next to her and she was staring at the ceiling, when she whispered, "Bazhe."

I leaned over her. "Water," she said.

I jumped up and retrieved a spoon. Filling the spoon with water from her glass, I extended it towards her arid lips.

"Soak a piece of gauze instead," Rodna said.

"Stay away," I told her firmly. Wet gauze wasn't enough for her. I always gave Mother water, in addition to replacing the wet gauze on her lips. I had no problem with cleaning my mother's bedpan every hour if I had to. I wasn't Mother's employee, and that made the difference. You can't buy love and affection, I thought, as I watched Mother drink slowly and laboriously from the spoon. I gave her more.

She closed her eyes, and a few minutes later, she began mumbling something. The only part I could understand was Father's name. Her eyes opened and started moving in little jerks until they met mine. Death is not a single episode. It's a series of events. Only those who are intimate with you can sense those events. I sensed them in the gleam of Mother's eyes, in the motion of her head and hands, in the sound of her last breaths. She was looking directly into my eyes. Does she recognize me? I wondered. I don't think so. I hugged her and pulled her closer to me. I sensed her heartbeat, and it resounded like a chime from the Elysian Fields. Oh, I would have given anything to make that chime keep sounding. She heaved a great breath, blew it out, then lay completely still. It was exactly 7 P.M. I continued to hold her in my arms. Her eyes kept staring straight into mine, and I kept looking at them. Selfishly, I embraced her. Tighter. I began kissing her face until Rodna's hand touched my shoulder.

"Your mother is dead," she said.

"Are you sure? Maybe she is not?" I said desperately, placing my ear to her chest. I held my hand above her mouth, to see if she was still breathing. I began crying. I felt regret, relief, and rage.

"No, son. She is dead," Rodna said somberly. She was crying. With a sweep of her hand, she closed my mother's eyes. "We became very close. We shared many secrets together. Believe me, I'll miss Kostadina."

"She loved you, too. She wouldn't let you stay if she didn't."

"I know," Rodna said, nodding and wiping her tears. She left the room so I could be alone with Mother.

Everything had died around me. Even my thoughts ceased with Mother's movements. I moistened some gauze and placed it on her lips. Her skin was warm. I gently shook her face, hoping she would ask me for water or medicine. I lay next to her, hugging her and kissing her, waiting for a miracle. I heard Rodna's steps coming and jumped up. As she came in, she suggested that I call the neighbors and relatives after we took care of the colostomy equipment. I began cleaning Mother's stoma as neatly as ever. I kept thinking she would wake up. It felt good to take care of her again, so I took my time. But when Nurse Rodna gave me Band-Aids instead of a new colostomy bag to close the stoma, I sobered up. I realized that Mother was dead and that this was the last colostomy maintenance I would perform. I wished there could be others.

I never felt more of a need to talk with Mother than when I found several photographs of me in America hidden under her pillow. I could picture Mother showing them to our neighbors and guests, bragging about my looks. She was always so proud of my looks. Framed photos of me hung on the walls all around her. I was stunned when I saw a couple of unusual pictures of me stuck in the pile. They were taken right after I got to America. I was into the New York club scene at the time, and I looked so androgynous, people probably thought I'd had a sex change. I was almost nude in those pictures, wrapped in tiny leather outfits that I'd designed myself and wearing lots of costume jewelry. I was too peculiar and harsh for the provincial minds of the townspeople to deal with. I imagined Mother, bragging about "my perfection," and not giving a damn about their opinions.

Death possesses the aptitude to clobber the extant reality at us before we turn into dust. Death endows us with pure soberness to admit to ourselves the facts of life that surround us, and the places we exist. Death forced Mother to realize the frequently unacceptable, misapprehended, and farfetched possibility shared among the plebeians, that I could be both, her son and daughter at the same time. I could see that clearly. I cried, as I looked through the photos. Then I hugged Mother's cooling body. I wished that she could wake up and that I could apologize for all the things I'd done that made her and Father the maddest. I wanted to thank her for their compromises, for suppressing their conservative views out of love for me, and for respecting my allegiance towards them. Suddenly, I had so many questions to ask Mother. But it was too late.

I telephoned the neighbors and relatives. Shortly afterward, a number of people arrived. Most of them were Mother's girlfriends, who immediately began preparing the house for the wake. Bisera, Frosa, and Rodna bathed Mother's body. I was told to go upstairs and bring down the box with the outfit Mother had picked out a long time ago, which was kept in the top left compartment of Mother's bedroom cabinet. I couldn't stop my tears when I found out that she had chosen one I had bought for her at Lord & Taylor's on Fifth Avenue.

The women began to dress Mother, and Frosa and I went to choose the coffin. I purchased the best-looking one. Back home, while waiting for the coffin to be delivered, I gave the almond-shaped antique ring to Bisera, the contemporary one to Frosa, and the golden set Mother had worn to Rodna. Before Frosa had a chance to put the ring in her pocket, Rodna grabbed it from her hand and exchanged it for the one I gave her. She complained that the one I gave her didn't fit. Frosa, like the rest of the women, wasn't shocked. Our nurse's greed was well known around the province.

The women began applying Mother's makeup, but I stopped them. I did it myself, after carefully choosing her favorite colors. I selected costume jewelry that matched her outfit and decorated her ears, neck, and hands. I sprayed her favorite Damask rose perfume all over her body, as she had requested. When the coffin arrived, we displayed Mother on the second floor. Her deep blue dress and her polished brown purse and shoes went beautifully with the roses that Bisera had cut from our garden. She had arranged them in perfect symmetry around Mother's body. Everyone agreed that Mother looked good. I felt immense pride. Mother had won the final battle with cancer by going out looking classy and stylish. I wished that she could see it for herself.

Bisera and Frosa brought food and drinks for the guests. A few hours later, after the proceedings were finished, I registered her death at the police station. I printed and posted flyers, hired the church clerk to announce her death by ringing the bell in the main church's belfry, and paid the priest to sing at the wake and burial. Mother was religious, so I obeyed her wishes, even though she doubted God's existence and even cursed the Holy Family when the pain was unbearable during the final stages of her suffering.

People visited our house in groups of two or three with candles, boxes of cookies or chocolates, and small flower bouquets. They usually stood or sat next to Mother's coffin and mournfully chatted about her for about fifteen minutes. Some nibbled the cold cuts or sipped the drinks, which Mother's girlfriends served continuously. Not many men showed up. Our men customarily didn't attend wakes, only funerals, unless they were close family members or friends of the deceased.

It seemed as if Mother weren't really dead, as if she were just sleeping as usual. I kept watching her, surrounded by her closest friends all throughout the night until the next morning. The women were saying good things about the deceased, as usual, and the few men were drinking in a separate room. The burial was scheduled for 1 P.M. Quite a large group of people had showed up to pay tribute to Mother. I wished she could have seen it, since she'd been so worried about a sparse attendance.

When the moment arrived for Mother to leave the house, a couple of the strongest men picked her coffin up and carried it downstairs. Halfway down, I stopped suddenly. It felt worse than ever to walk down those stairs. Bursting into tears, I finally realized that she was not coming back. Until then, I kept hoping in denial that she was still alive, sleeping. Then Bisera gently shook my shoulder, whispering, "Walk. It's over Bazhe."

I descended slowly, watching Mother's face as she was carried between lines of her rose bushes. She was leaving her best friends and her beloved garden. I closed my eyes and let Bisera lead me. Mother's coffin was placed in the hearse, and our young cousin began the procession, holding the tall candle, the *lambadia*, that would go on her grave. Two columns of children followed him, and each pair of them carried the wreaths brought by relatives and friends. The hearse pulled off slowly, and the priest walked behind it, singing and swinging an incense urn. Mother's closest relatives and friends, the remaining attendants, and I, followed.

Even the priest's awful rendition of the psalms, which had always made me laugh and imitate him, didn't alleviate my grief. I couldn't stop crying all the way from the house to the church, throughout the liturgy, and at the graveyard. A distant relative patted my back and told me I should stop weeping, that I was a grown man. I almost punched her in her horse-mouth, but I calmed down when another relative told me that I looked like my mother more than ever, and that part of her would live in me forever. Finally, my tears evaporated when I hugged and kissed Mother for the last time before they closed the coffin lid.

The grave workers lowered her coffin into the family grave and placed it above my father's coffin, which had not completely deteriorated yet. It was an odd sight, and the mystery of death never felt closer. I wanted to leave that place as soon as possible. I hated being there. I placed my rose ikebana neatly by the tombstone, and people followed suit, arranging their wreaths and flowers around the grave. Then, the closest relatives and friends, along with the priest, returned to our house to have lunch in honor of Mother's soul.

It was over. I would never see Mother's face again. The hell with my biological parents. Now that Mother's gone, I'm an orphan again.

34

Grieving

It was difficult to listen to the guests' mournful remembrances of Mother. I couldn't wait to be alone. If it were up to me, I wouldn't have any gatherings. I had to follow tradition, though, and do everything I was supposed to do. Besides, it was my mother's wish. The priest was the first one to finish eating. After he made sure that there was no more brandy left in his glass, he stood up to leave. Nurse Rodna and I escorted him out. On the way back, she said, "I'll pack my bags. I'm leaving tomorrow. I'll sleep at your uncle's house tonight. He needs help. He asked me if I could clean his house before I go. Extra money won't hurt me. You don't mind, do you?"

"Oh, no. It's fine. I'm glad you're helping him. He's a lonely widower. He needs company." I began to pray that Uncle Bogdan would get laid that night. As an old womanizer, he needed it desperately. The neighbors and the relatives gradually left the house. Rodna packed her belongings and went to Uncle Bogdan's place. Bisera was the last one to leave. She was about to open the door, when she swung around and proposed, "I'll stay over if you're not comfortable alone."

"I'll be fine. Thank you, Auntie Bisera." I said assuredly and kissed her.

"Don't clean tonight! You can do it tomorrow. Don't forget to keep the light in Mother's room on! It must stay lit during all forty days of mourning. Also, you cannot leave the house! Tonight, you have to do these things. Don't ignore these rules. Otherwise, you'll bring Mother back with an upset spirit. It's better to let her rest in peace. This is a warning!" Bisera said sternly, kissing me back. As always, she left on a cordial note. I watched her walk through the garden, and I could see she was weeping. Her walk seemed clumsy. I could tell she already missed her best friend.

Of course, I didn't believe Bisera's fairy tales, and all the local voodoo nonsense that had become a part of our Orthodox Christian faith. I couldn't wait to break the rules and experiment with superstition. I cleaned, and I made sure that the light in the living room where Mother died was off. For a couple of hours, I even left the house and walked to one of my favorite sanctuaries, the river at the edge of town. After I did everything I could to bring my upset Mother back, I went to my room, lit a bunch of candles, and sat next to the window, staring at the star-ornamented Macedonian sky.

The night felt atypically long and bizarre, as I waited for Mother's arrival. Out of habit, a number of times, I ran downstairs, but no more than halfway. I was afraid. Not of meeting my dead, upset Mother, but of the emptiness I would encounter. And it seemed as if Mother were still downstairs. The smell of her lingered, even after all the ventilation, the air deodorants, and the potpourri the women used to eliminate it. The wilting, dreadful stench of the cancer that consumed Mother actually felt soothing to me. I became scared of missing her more because of it. I ran to my bed and buried myself under the blanket to escape the smell. Later, when I threw the covers off and inhaled the air with the odor still in it, the fear had vanished. I envisioned her sleeping downstairs. She was looking out the window, watching the garden and waiting for me. My tears stopped momentarily as I held onto this image, but began pouring again when I realized it was just a fantasy. I dove under the covers again. The darkness under the blanket was frightening, like Mother's death, but I stayed there all night. The knowledge that Mother wouldn't come back was much more frightening.

Early the next morning, Nurse Rodna showed up at the door, smiling. I guessed that Uncle Bogdan had paid her well for her "cleaning service." I couldn't wait for her to leave. I took her to the bus station and gave her the extra money that I had promised her. She invited me to visit her in Southern Bulgaria. She offered me ten percent if I could find her a sick, but wealthy American to marry or take care of, so she could inherit his estate. Up until the moment we parted, she spoke of nothing but earning money, preferably in cash. It was such a relief when her bus disappeared from sight.

On the whole, I didn't want to see anyone. Mother's death was enough to deal with. The terrible memories of her suffering were still overwhelming. Things got easier when I began selling the furniture and making other changes to the décor. I barely spoke to anyone. I let the answering machine take messages. I hated hearing people's condolences, which sounded identical, more or less, and only reminded me of what had happened.

A week after the funeral, I called Mila to tell her about my mother's death. She said that Mother was safe from the cancer and happy that it was over. I wasn't happy. I would have taken on all the troubles of caring for her, even watching her suffer, just to have her back. I had never felt that way before. I knew Mother wanted to live. She had so much lust for life after Father died, after being liberated. I couldn't stand Mila's attempts to console me. I kept the conversation going, out of courtesy, enduring the torture of her perspective on Mother's death. After we hung up, I cursed myself for having called her.

Mila called again and again. She kept leaving messages, but I couldn't talk to her. I felt as if I were betraying Mother, as if I had given up on her. I felt this way even though she had wanted me to contact the woman she despised most and, in the end, recognized as the only one who would look after me when she was gone. I would rather have talked to Mother, and almost every day, I visited her grave. I would chat with her for hours, staring at her name in golden letters below Father's.

I used to see a woman there who was always sobbing. She had lost a child in a car accident. One day, I saw her kneeling beside the tombstone, her face literally buried in the dirt of her child's freshly dug grave. She wept continually. I wondered if Mother's death felt the same to me as her child's death felt to her? I wondered if my loss was bigger then hers? The reflection of the sun's rays off the golden letters of Mother's name glared brightly, and I hugged her grave. It was warm, and I felt like a child again, next to Mother's body on a long, cold winter night.

On the fortieth day of mourning, I organized a fancy memorial. It was done the way Mother would have wanted it, at one of the best restaurants in town. Now and then, a guest would mention Mother, but mostly they discussed their disappointment in the new system. They ridiculed our new Macedonian state and its independence, which had made our country more corrupt and more dependent on the West than ever. They longed for the stability of the former Yugoslavia and bemoaned the side effects of the new free-market economy: the faster pace, the collective greed, the escalating divorce rate, drug trafficking, the black market, sex exploitation, and the rise of radical Albanian nationalism and Muslim fundamentalism. They complained about inflation, the high price of burial plots, and the way the poor ended up in communal dumpsters without decent funerals and headstones.

They were shocked about the latest trend among the young capitalists, going to a psychiatrist. To older Balkan people, shrinks were only appropriate for idiots or the mad. They laughed about our Western immigrants' ways of showing off, then acting cheap, constantly looking for bargains, and always short of time. They hated our bureaucracy, joking that the service windows in government buildings were built low to make you bow to the bureaucrats. They were pessimistic, but I wasn't shocked. There was no future in Macedonia, unless you worked for the corrupt Macedonian government, Albanian Islamic terrorists and nationalists, hypocritical Western aid services, or the Macedonian mafia.

At home, I kept thinking of Mother. I remembered the childhood plays and dances I did for her and her enchanting and contagious smile. Then I would think about her body, lying in bed, weakened from cancer. I wouldn't mind taking care of her again, I thought. I wouldn't mind hearing Mother's slow and weak speech, which I interrupted so many times. I wouldn't mind seeing her again, despite the pain that it would cause me. Then I realized that I wouldn't want to relive that, and I ran outside to work on Mother's roses, to rid myself of the harsh memories with my old therapist, the soil, our garden.

Nonetheless, it was hard to live in the house and not think of Mother. The memories flew like angels, sometimes poked like devils, around the house. However, I endured and I finished all my chores on the property before leaving. I packed boxes of clothes, china, blankets, and many other goods from the house, and took them to the Red Cross. The secretary told me that I was one of the biggest donators in the history of our county, that even religious people had never given so much. I wanted to tell her that you don't need a Bible to be humane, but out of respect for the noble job she did, I simply smiled in response. I took the "thank you" certificate from her hand, thinking about how ironic it was that I, the reformed ex-demon, was now considered a darling.

When most of the furniture was gone, it seemed as if Mother and I had never lived there. Still, there were things that I couldn't change, and they made me cry and long for her. I honored Mother's dying wish not to sell the house and arranged for my parents' last gardener from Albania to take care of it. In exchange, I let him stay there for free. Finally, at the end of August, I flew back to the U.S. I didn't tell anyone. I didn't want anyone to see me off. I only said farewell to Auntie Bisera, Frosa, a couple of other neighbors, and Mother's closest friends.

Two months after returning to New Jersey, I surprised Mila with a phone call. "Hello, it's me. I'm in America now."

"I'm so happy you called me. I've been so worried that something might have happened to you."

"Sorry. I couldn't talk to anyone, except Mother's ghost."

"I understand. All I want is to hear your voice from time to time and to know that you are all right. Everything seems like a dream now. Your birth. Your adoption. My meeting with you…It feels like all these things never even happened." I could hear her start to cry.

I couldn't speak. I rushed to hang up before I burst into tears. "Aha!…Hum!…I really have to go…I'll call you later."

"Okay," she replied. "Call me."

I slammed the receiver down, thinking about how real my birth, my adoption, and my meeting with her were to me. I hated what she said. It hurt badly.

35

Orphan

I continued to think about Mother's last words: to live life and not let life live me. I tried hard not to think about material things. I worked hard not to waste a minute of my happiness and continually to enrich my soul with love and peace. I focused only on the beautiful moments I shared with Mother and other people and avoided anything that would remind me of Mother's cancer or the situation in the Balkans.

But it was difficult not to think of home when on March 24th 1999, NATO, led by the U.S., began bombing Serbia. Big Brother fed the media headlines, twenty-four hours a day, about how righteous the bombing was. After the Western mission failed, Kosovo turned into a bigger incubator for Albanian nationalism, Muslim fundamentalism, and terrorism. It was difficult not to think of home when I heard about Albanian fundamentalists destroying ancient churches throughout Kosovo, the center of Orthodox Christian culture in the Balkans, and throwing Christians out in the name of Allah. When the Albanian nationalists, extremists, and irredentists took their ethnic cleansing to my beautiful Macedonia, where they destroyed more churches and threatened its integrity with their poisonous fundamentalist views and their plan to create a pure Islamic place that would eventually link to Greater Albania. When I found out that the Albanians used Taliban mujahideen of Osama bin Laden, trained in Albanian camps, that were directly financed through banks in Kosovo by Al Qaeda. When witnessing the West and NATO still supporting the Islamic fundamentalists, when their evil intentions were so obvious. It was difficult not to think of home when, on September 11, 2001, thousands of my innocent fellow Americans died in New York, Washington, and Pennsylvania, due to Islamic fundamentalism.

Years have passed, and Mila hasn't called me or written. I called her, hoping to learn more, but she had nothing for me, really. Her words about my birth, my adoption, and our meeting being a dream, as if they had never happened, still burn in my heart. How could someone who got to know me so well, who had the privilege of getting closer than anyone else to my true self, say that it was like a dream or that those things never happened? Why do I grow angry anytime I recall our last conversation?

I ask myself this as I watch the smoke from my cigarette drift over the armchair, reminding me of the one back home where Mila sat. She once said that there was nothing much she could say about herself, that her life was conventional compared to mine. Conventional? Oh Yes! Sure! With many conventional secrets.

Mila let me grow up with people who surrounded me with books, who made me read literature and philosophy while most children my age couldn't even sing "Eenie, meenie, miney, moe." They were able to play patty-cake, but I was forbidden to do that, except with myself.

Mila let me grow up with people who made me feel like a stranger at school dances, at soccer games, at the prom. I searched for her desperately, made our meeting a reality, and still moved much faster towards her than she did towards me. I told her everything except my father's sin in the garden. But that had nothing to do with Mila, nor with Mother, who had enough trouble with Father, and she would never have understood it anyway.

My parents had more secrets than I had, and they left without confessing them to me. Like Mila Bibulich, the woman who bore me and gave me much less than I gave her. She has secrets. Even if I'd had the "perfect parents," I would never have built a completely honest relationship with them anyway. Who does? So why am I upset when I think about being the product of a rape between two strangers? How do I find the truth? Deceivers make us, and we die deceived. Such is the logic of our existence. People are the biggest damned liars. I wonder when this planet will stop tolerating our senseless, sleazy games.

My fingers pull the weeds, as I dig the soil in my garden. I'm trying to make it a replica of the one I had back in old Yugoslavia. It's the product of my nostalgia for the good old days with Mother and Father, the only ones I will remember from now on. The negative energy leaves me, along with my sweat. I wipe my forehead, and as I brush my tousled hair with my dirty hand, I can feel two bald scars on top of my head. A doctor told me once that they could have been caused by my biological mother trying to induce an abortion.

I was created as an accident. I pull out a fresh cigarette and light it with the old one. "Didn't we all come into this world as accidents?" I console myself aloud, stamping the butt out on the ground. The feeling of the roses' root tendons and the soil is uplifting. The garden has a supernatural power. I feel its energy

through the earth under my nails. The garden is my therapist. It has always puri-
fied my mind, my soul, and my body of negative and painful memories.

Today is a sunny day, and I run through my garden to celebrate it. I smell the
roses, and I can't help thinking of Mother, her permission for me to reunite with
Mila, her compromise with her rival, all for my sake. Mother would have been
devastated if she had heard Mila's last conversation with me. But Mila Bibulich
wasn't my mother. I always knew that. She couldn't be and never would be. People are absolutely correct when they say you have only one Mother—not the one
who bore you, but the one who raised you. I touch the fragile rose petals, and I
cherish that "something," my destiny or whatever it was, that brought me
together with Mother. I have no regrets whatsoever about being raised by the
woman who always and unconditionally was on my side, even though she was
constantly bombarded by terrible rumors about me, even though she never completely understood who I was. I'll never forget her telling people, no-holds-
barred, that anyone who uttered a single word against me would be banned from
her life as an enemy. She was my Mother in the ultimate sense, and I was her ultimate perfection.

I embrace the rose buds and blooms and inhale their enchanting fragrances.
They seem magical as a whole. Analysis sometimes complicates things and events;
it is not always best to reduce them down to their parts. Some things and events
should be allowed to stay whole or be made whole. It's not logical, but it's easier
to deal with them that way. Eventually, all things and events end, and we should
let them go back to nature and think about them again later. We comprehend
these fragments of our lives better after we let them mature. For instance, Mother
and I loved one another. Our love was a whole thing, despite the details of her
disappointments in me or mine in her. Our love was greater than any influence
or teaching that affected us. Am I the person Mother wanted me to be? Is she the
person I wanted her to be? It doesn't matter anymore. After all, Mother and I
found peace and accepted one another for who we really were. And that is the
bottom line. We accepted one another as whole individuals.

And there Mother is. I can see her. Ornamenting my new garden. Dancing
with the roses. Dressed with class, as elegantly as always, with a delicately spun
silk shawl loosely covering her shoulders, its shimmering tassels swaying lavishly
with her slightest movement. And I thought my father's death was more important than my coming to America. I thought that everything changed after his
authority was gone, after I was liberated, and I became the only master of the
house. I was wrong. Dead wrong.

The true change in my life happened when Mother died. I became an orphan again, and the emptiness has never left me since. I was hurt, critically and forever. But at the same time, I was reborn. I awakened to see the essence of life much more clearly, and I began to overcome my damages.

###

ALSO by B. K. Bazhe

ART (paintings)

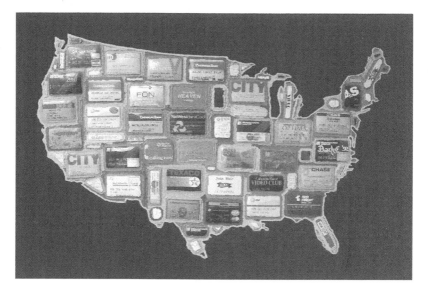

America by B. K. Bazhe,
(oil on canvas – mixed media)

Morristown Flower by B. K. Bazhe,
(oil on canvas)

Mother by B. K. Bazhe,
(oil on canvas - mixed media)

Balkan Steps by B. K. Bazhe,
(oil on canvas)

Identity by B. K. Bazhe,
(oil on canvas - mixed media)

Beautiful Fear by B. K. Bazhe,
(oil on canvas)

The Baby by B. K. Bazhe,
(oil on canvas)

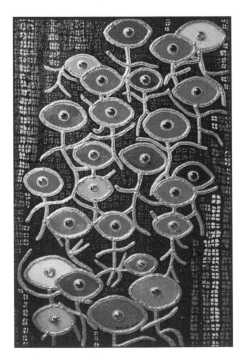

Dance by B. K. Bazhe,
(oil on canvas - mixed media)

The King Is Not Virgin by B. K. Bazhe,
(oil on wood - mix media)

Blue Eye-Web by B. K. Bazhe,
(oil on canvas - mixed media)

Prayer by B. K. Bazhe,
(oil on wood - mixed media)

Roses by B. K. Bazhe,
(oil on wood panel)

I-Witness by B. K. Bazhe,
(oil on canvas)

Self-Portrait Pose by B. K. Bazhe,
(oil on canvas - mixed media)

World by B. K. Bazhe,
(oil on canvas)

For more information regarding special discounts,
or for bulk Art purchases, please contact
B. K. Bazhe at: **1-862-345-6170**
or <u>bazhe@bazhe.com</u>

To See More of B. K. Bazhe's Art:

Visit **B. K. Bazhe's Website** at:
<u>www.BAZHE.com</u>

Watch **B. K. Bazhe's YouTube Videos** at:
<u>www.YouTube.com/bazhe</u>

Paintings are Available as Posters at:
<u>www.Amazon.com</u>

Or **Google, Internet Search**
Key Words are:
BK Bazhe

IDENTITIES (poetry) **by B. K. Bazhe**

IDENTITIES is about analyzing human manipulations through poetry. The poems deal with greed and ignorance, destruction and war, politics and phoniness, love and hatred, sex and ecstasy, loneliness and loss, and visionary musings of hope.

White Horses and I

White horses are coming, and You are Arriving in hasty gallop.
In the stable reigns desolation, and in my room the same.
The lawn with dense pallid Loneliness and I are all that is left.
Because you didn't stop—you just passed by, and ran away.

New Country

I'm here now, new air, food, faces, bodies, more ideals, ambitions and sad-
nesses. All that was left behind sneaks back into my memory. My country,
former Yugoslavia, is one dead stifled specter, but the ancient beauty of the
Balkans is still suspended before my eyes—like a painting.

In the midst of all these new and strange sights and human looks, I'm
struggling to be a part of it all. I'm trying to find the path, so I can take a
part that is only mine and nobody else's. I'm commuting on the train, from
the Garden State to New York City, and American reality spreads before
me—like a daydream.

The homeless are sinking, businesses are rising, and the bullshit is walking
while the money is talking. I'm stepping peacefully, naively at first,
and without much noise, across this country, alive with contrasts, risks,
and much hope—America.

Sleepwalker

Even the shadow of my shaking pencil on top of my open diary
understands how much your phone number means to me.
Above the 700 others that I have collected during these last four years
when, roaming around the gutter-pipes, I could descry
only the dark edges of love.

I'm sitting in my home hugging the cat in my lap, and you're inside of me,
above anyone else before, you're reigning my body totally.
Before I go out to hunt, before the moody moonset shellacs my soul
with lust and desire for a new attempt to fill in your absence,
only for I to forget you.

Quietening

Quietly I look on while you're replacing me with the water lily. You're quietening the springs that are quietly healing all around us. I'm as happy as this wrung crystal hour, now turning into a vinous and quietening one.

Be quiet, the fingers are greasy and the passages to our souls are quietly opened for exploration. Be quiet, and kiss amidst the sounds of that mountain little fawn—our only, nonjudgmental an innocent, witness.

Through the eyelashes, in the skin pores, our pains are, in masterly quiet, torn away from us. Play five hours, modestly, and you'll see that there's nothing else besides that something so dreamy, sweaty and quiet.

Our strings, our tendons, are poised very greedily to chase the universe into the quiet spot. Go on, our fervid breaths from our aroused throats are elixirs for this wild earthly game that quietens us completely.

Pause, two endings, quiet and indecent, and our lips, like razors in our hairs, and our sharp teeth that are gnashing into this whole quiet turmoil.

Ask quietly: Why are they flowing away? Why are they burning? Why are they crying? Those quiet springs of our love. The two tears on our palms. Not separated, yet lifelessly quietened for forever.

The Mask

We wander everywhere: at the bars, and on the streets.
We analyze the souls of others, and judge their actions.
We make assumptions about the destinies of strangers.
Some are rosy, some gray, some after born go away.

We fake it all over the place with no shame or grace.
And, as we do so, we always wear something else.
We keep it behind our eyes, and these visible faces.

And, it always comes out as we smile with no reason.
When we make those poisonous grins of hypocrisy.
Why do we repeat time after time this treason?

Alarm

A mouse came out of his hole and took a tiny bite—and, then, the people caught him and tortured him. Why? He was a gentle mouse and he had a cute maroon coat. But people thought that his coat contrasted oddly with the other attributed of his genus. Under their feet people crushed the mouse, eagerly.

I came out of my hole and took a little bite—and they caught me and tortured me. Why? Because I was natural—in the way one is when alive rather than dead. Or, maybe, because my coat was maroon, in contrast to the other attributes of my genus. Under their tongues people crushed me, eagerly.

Magnitude

The stars in my eyes tonight are for your eyes.
Yes, for no one else except you in this moment.
In this moment, dizzy, crazy, mad, heavenly mad.

Regression

John's father Richard was a very successful businessman, but he was homophobic and blackophobic. He was a failure of a father because, at 14 years of age, John had runaway from home with his lover and moved into the ghetto.

John's father Richard organized a dragnet—fortunately, not a successful one. Then, someone who looked like Richard killed John and his Afro-American lover at the subway.

John's father Richard was a successful businessman but a big failure of a father, of a man, of a human.

Vampire

With red cat eyes I am wondering in your room,
so which music am I listening now?
With shy and honest eager you are coming closer to me,
so whose breath am I feeling now?

Above the black satin and silk, I am ready to pounce
into a coconut milk like inviting skin.
I'm setting free my green lasers, to see better,
to touch better, and to bite properly.

Divine skin I'm smelling, the familiar and lusty scent,
and the biggest teaser of all.
I'm taking an infernal bath in your tasty sweaty drops
that have a brilliant red glow like a finest wine.

I'm enlivening as I'm puncturing my hungry teeth,
for who knows how many times again in you.
Oh you, my beautiful, found, and only loyal old friend,
the source of my life.

The Eyes

If I could see for a second through your eyes when you're speaking to me, and to all of us, saying that we matter to you. If I could see for a second through the mothers' eyes when they're sending their sons to fight on the battlefields for stupid reasons.

If I could see for a second with the eyes of the thousands and millions of barefooted, the starving children, the homeless, the ill, the handicapped, and those who are discriminated against. I don't know if it makes sense to exist after the veils of the truth are removed in this cold, selfish, merciless, short, mad, and absurd mortals' world we live in.

So, should I be blind and keep breathing as ignorant bastard like so many of us? Or should I support the radical changes we all need it badly? I'm disgusted by the ignorant, selfish, greedy SOBs who rule the world with evil. I'm angry at them. Aren't you?

Me, a Demon Most Merciful

Into the eyes of all and sundry I'm sleeping,
very tenderly and kindly I'm touching,
the most secret and sacred points I'm discovering,
Me, a demon most merciful.

I'm drawing the heavy and dark red curtains,
layers of Lokis' spun yarn of secrets,
and through my fingers the dreams are gleaming,
in shame they are tangling.

Outside, Me, a demon most merciful
over the dense and disturbing mortals' fields,
with radiant thoughts I'm passing,
and like a black angel I'm breaking away.

Where is Freedom, Dove?

How many years are left, hey dove? How many loves are left inside you?
How many freedoms are left, hey dove? How many joys are left inside you?

Our wings are bleeding, do you feel it dove? There are no freedoms for you and me.
It's dangerous now for everyone to embark on free flight.

Like you and me, like us: the writers, the artists, the poets,
—I mean, we, known to mortals as the other humans.

Prince

To be in a dreamy boat made of paper
—Is there anything more beautiful
than to sail in an ocean of clouds?

To write, to sing, and to paint on it
—Is there anything more beautiful
than to be a crowned prince of art?

And to not give the slightest damn
—If the people understand it.

For more information regarding special discounts, signed copies, or for bulk purchases of **Identities** (poetry), please contact
B. K. Bazhe at: **1-862-345-6170**
or **bazhe@bazhe.com**

To See More of B. K. Bazhe's Poetry:

Visit **B. K. Bazhe's Website** at:
www.BAZHE.com

Watch **B. K. Bazhe's YouTube Videos** at:
www.YouTube.com/bazhe

Identities (poetry) is Available
Wherever Fine Books are Sold, or at:
www.Amazon.com

Or **Google, Internet Search**
Key Words are:
BK Bazhe

VIDEOS (multimedia) by B. K. Bazhe

Watch **B. K. Bazhe's YouTube Videos** at:
www.YouTube.com/bazhe

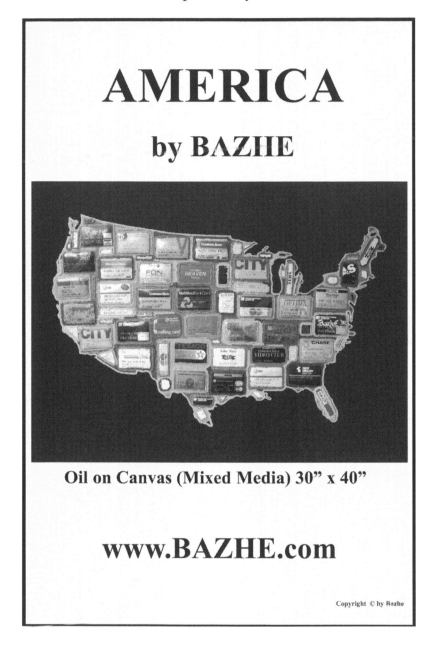

PHOTOGRAPHY (pictures) by B. K. Bazhe

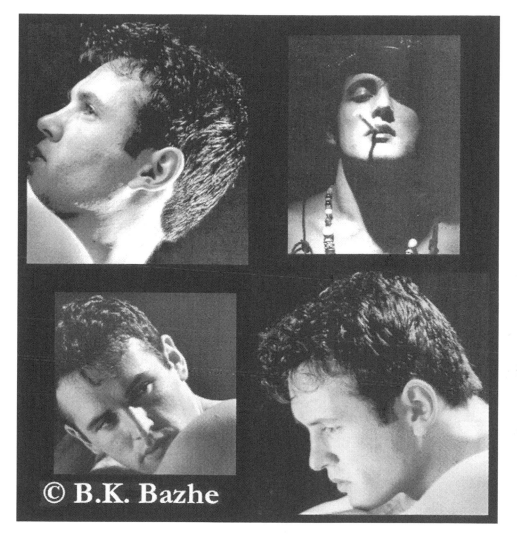

© B.K. Bazhe

NOTES:

B. K. Bazhe is a writer, poet, artist, traveler, and videographer.
He is the author of Damages (creative nonfiction)
— Winner in the Writers Digest Awards, and Identities (poetry).

He has published in the USA, and Europe: Serbia, Bosnia, Macedonia, and Bulgaria. His videos are published on YouTube, and many other sites across the Internet.

In America, his prose and poems have appeared in: Poetic Voices Magazine, Winter's Gems Anthology, Bay Windows, Opus Literary Review, River Run, and Reader.

His art has been exhibited in Europe, and in the USA in: New Jersey, Ohio, and New York City.

For More Information:
Reviews, Excerpts, Interviews,
Videos, News, Events,
Art, and Poetry,

Visit B. K. Bazhe's Website at:
www.BAZHE.com

Watch B. K. Bazhe's YouTube Videos at:
www.YouTube.com/bazhe

Purchase B. K. Bazhe's Work at:
www.Amazon.com

Or **Google, Internet Search**
Key Words are:
BK Bazhe

DEAR READER,

THANK YOU &
BEST WISHES.

B. K. BAZHE

DAMAGES by B. K. Bazhe

ISBN-13: 978-1469938332
ISBN-10: 1469938332

Library of Congress
Control Number:
2012901695

Made in the USA
Charleston, SC
10 June 2014